Richard Clogg is Emeritus Fellow of St Antony's College, Oxford. He previously taught at the University of Edinburgh, where he had been an undergraduate, and at the University of London, where latterly he was Professor of Modern Balkan History. He has published widely on the modern history and politics of Greece. His publications include *A Concise History of Greece* (translated into 13 languages, including all the languages of the Balkans); *A Short History of Modern Greece; Parties and Elections in Greece; Politics and the Academy: Arnold Toynbee and the Koraes Chair; Anatolica: Studies in the Greek East in the Eighteenth and Nineteenth Centuries* and *Anglo-Greek Attitudes: Studies in History*. He has been awarded the Gold Cross of the Legion of Honour by the Hellenic Republic.

Greek to Me

A Memoir of Academic Life

Richard Clogg

I.B. TAURIS
LONDON · NEW YORK

Published in 2018 by
I.B.Tauris & Co. Ltd
Reprinted in 2018
London • New York
www.ibtauris.com

Copyright © 2018 Richard Clogg

The right of Richard Clogg to be identified as the author of this work has been asserted by the author in accordance with the Copyright, Designs and Patents Act 1988.

All rights reserved. Except for brief quotations in a review, this book, or any part thereof, may not be reproduced, stored in or introduced into a retrieval system, or transmitted, in any form or by any means, electronic, mechanical, photocopying, recording or otherwise, without the prior written permission of the publisher.

Every attempt has been made to gain permission for the use of the images in this book. Any omissions will be rectified in future editions.

References to websites were correct at the time of writing.

ISBN: 978 1 78453 988 7
eISBN: 978 1 78672 262 1
ePDF: 978 1 78673 262 0

A full CIP record for this book is available from the British Library
A full CIP record is available from the Library of Congress

Library of Congress Catalog Card Number: available

Typeset in India by Integra Software Services Pvt. Ltd.
Printed and bound by CPI Group (UK) Ltd, Croydon, CR0 4YY

Therefore I see that there is nothing better than that a man should rejoyce in his affaires, because that is his portion.

> *Ecclesiastes* III v. 22

    O, how ridiculous
Appears the Senate's brainless diligence,
Who think they can, with present power, extinguish
The memory of all succeeding times!

> Ben Jonson, *Sejanus: His Fall*

And even I can remember
A day when the historians left blanks in their writings,
I mean, for things they didn't know
But that time seems to be passing.

> Ezra Pound, *Canto XIII*

Contents

	List of plates	ix
	Acknowledgements	xi
	Introduction	1
1	*Industria*. First steps in Greece: Edinburgh, Athens, London	11
2	The Colonels and the stage army	57
3	*Sancte et sapienter*. King's College and the School of Slavonic and East European Studies	103
4	Knitting a sock for my head: on washing dirty academic linen in public	175
5	The sock knitted	229
6	Greeks bearing chairs: chairs bearing Greeks	251
7	*Plus est en vous*. St Antony's College	287
	Epilogue	339
	Notes	347
	Index	349

List of plates

All images are from the author's own collection.

1. The author's introduction to *I kath'imas Anatoli* (The Greek East).
2. A partially uncovered wall painting in the Church of Hagia Sophia, Trebizond.
3. Andreas Papandreou shaking hands with the author, 1967.
4. Constructing socialism in Albania, 1975.
5. Singing the praises of Enver Hoxha, 1975.
6. Remembering the past: the BBC and the Greek Resistance, 1978.
7. 'The People united will never be defeated', 1983.
8. Nathan in 1989.
9. Books for Romania, 1990.
10. France Pavlowitch, Dick Crampton and the author in Romania, 1990.
11. 'A Night on the Bare Mountain': Mary Jo and Rachel in the mountains above Krasnaya Polyana, 1992.
12. Rachel and Nathan in the mountains above Krasnaya Polyana, 1992.
13. The author with Odysseus Dimitriadis, 1993.
14. The author discussing Caucasian affairs with John le Carré, 1996.

LIST OF PLATES

15. The author sharing a joke with Margaret Thatcher, 1998.
16. On Mount Athos, 1998.
17. Gough Whitlam and the author, 1999.
18. Mary Jo and the author, St Antony's, Oxford, 2002.
19. Rachel Clogg and the author, St Antony's, Oxford, 2002.
20. Archbishop Gregorios of Thyateira blessing the tombstone of the Ecumenical Patriarch Meletios II, 2013.
21. Byron and his dog, Lion, at Missolonghi, 1824.
22. Patriarch Athinagoras in the ruins of the Panagia Veligradiou Orthodox church in Istanbul, 1955.
23. Coming to terms with the past: Istanbul, 2000.
24. A Greek–American wedding in Salt Lake City, Utah, in 1921.
25. Ethnic politics in Australia: Bob Hawke in Melbourne, 1988.

Acknowledgements

In writing this memoir I have greatly benefited from the comments of Mary Jo Clogg, Lars Baerentzen, Nick Bouras, Dimitris Livanios, Peter Mackridge and John Iatrides. The standard disclaimer, that none of the foregoing bears responsibility for what I have written, applies with more than usual force.

Introduction

In the mid-1980s I was working on a book whose subject I found engrossing but which, when published, was to cause me uncovenanted difficulties. My researches took me one afternoon to Senate House, the quasi-Stalinist monolith which casts a depressing shadow over Bloomsbury and which houses the archive of the University of London. It is an ill-fated building. While it was being built in the 1930s, the then vice-chancellor, while on a tour of inspection, was crushed by a builder's trolley which toppled down an unfinished lift shaft, and he died soon afterwards. I first heard this macabre story at a lecture on the architecture of the university, given in 1986 to mark the 150th anniversary of its foundation. The story provoked a somewhat embarrassed titter in an audience largely made up of academics. The vice-chancellor in question was no doubt a modest and learned man of unquestioned integrity and exemplary fairness, ever ready to defend the academy against the barbarians at the gates. But some in the audience may have fleetingly and altogether unworthily wished a similar fate on time-serving and gong-hunting vice-chancellors of their acquaintance, for the lecture took place at a time when Margaret Thatcher's 'reforms' were wreaking havoc on the British university system and few vice-chancellors had put up more than a token resistance. It was entirely in character that Senate House, which had been requisitioned during World War II by the Ministry of Information, should have been used by George Orwell as the model for the Ministry of Truth in his dystopian novel *Nineteen Eighty-Four*. The motto of the Ministry (of Truth, be it said, and not Information), appropriately enough, was 'Ignorance is Strength'.

My purpose in visiting Senate House had been to consult the minutes, dating from the early 1920s, of meetings of the university's Board of Studies in History, of which I was at that time a member. These boards, of which there were over 60 in what has been described as the 'Byzantinely complex university' of London, dealt with such routine matters as syllabi and the appointment of examiners. It had never crossed my mind that I would have any difficulty in seeing the Board's records after more than 60 years. But, when I explained to the archivist what papers I wanted to consult, she appeared mildly disconcerted and told me that the Board's minutes were closed to researchers for 100 years, and I was politely sent on my way. A letter, broadly along the lines of 'physician, heal thyself', for professional historians should surely be the last people to place pointless restrictions on access to records, to the then chairman of the Board secured a special dispensation for me to consult these yellowing, 60-year-old papers. They proved quite as innocuous and boring as they sound and, alas, they yielded no dark secrets.

Historians are great ones for demanding access to other people's records, however sensitive. They have been known to complain even of the relatively generous 30-year rule that applies to British official papers. It was odd, therefore, that, as a collectivity, the historians of the University of London, one of the largest concentrations of professional historians in the country, should have attached precisely the kind of restrictions on their own records that the government stipulated for access to the hyper-sensitive papers of Scotland Yard's Special Branch or to papers relating to the affairs of the royal family. To be fair, I imagine that very few of my then colleagues would have been aware of these draconian rules. After all, who, myself apart, would have had much interest in looking at such humdrum papers and thus be alerted to the ban?

The restriction on access may have been odd, but it was certainly not uncharacteristic. For academic institutions, in Britain at least, are unusually reticent in allowing access to their records, perhaps for fear that they may throw unwelcome light on the not negligible number of skeletons that lurk in their respective cupboards. It is a curious fact that we historians seldom investigate our own, at times murky, doings with the persistence and rigour which we apply to the affairs of others. The American magazine *Lingua Franca* did, for a decade or so, provide a vehicle for exposing some of the seamier sides of life in the academy, but in 2001 it ceased publication in appropriately mysterious circumstances. One of its great services was to publish details of Alan Sokal's splendid send-up of postmodernism, in his own words 'a pastiche of left-wing cant, fawning references, grandiose quotations, and outright nonsense'. But, in general, while the olive groves of Academe may from time to time attract the attention of novelists, they are seldom seen as an appropriate subject for academic inquiry.

My wish to consult the minutes in question had to do with a long-forgotten controversy in the affairs of King's College of the University of London, the institution by which I was at that time employed. This was the furious, and latterly very public, row that erupted in the early 1920s between, on the one hand, the young Arnold Toynbee, the first holder of the Koraes Chair of Modern Greek and Byzantine History, Language and Literature, and, on the other, the wealthy Anglo-Greeks who, towards the end of World War I, had put up the lion's share of the money for its endowment, their supporters within the college and university, together with the Greek government, which had also made a financial contribution to the new department. The imbroglio, at the root of which lay Toynbee's sympathy with the Turkish nationalist cause during the bitter Greek–Turkish conflict of 1919-22, resulted in what he himself termed his 'involuntary resignation' from the chair in 1924, amid much recrimination and considerable public controversy. The row scarcely did Toynbee much harm, for he went on to become one of the twentieth century's best-known historians, not only in Britain but in the world at large. In the late 1940s, 'Historian Toynbee' even made the cover of *Time* magazine in his role of global historical guru. With characteristic hyperbole he was declared to have 'found history Ptolemaic and left it Copernican'. On his death, in 1975, *Der Spiegel* hailed him as the most renowned historian of the day.

The Koraes chair is the mother and father of the nowadays not uncommon phenomenon in the English-speaking world of the 'ethnic' chair, that is to say a chair intended, overtly or covertly, to legitimise and promote the national aspirations of the donors, whether governmental or individual, who have put up the money for it. Not without reason, its history has been described as bloodstained. Moreover, as we shall see, ever since Toynbee's precipitate departure from King's, the Koraes chair has been viewed with a degree of suspicion by some in the Greek community in Britain, who continue to see themselves as having a kind of proprietorial interest in it.

Unravelling the various strands of this strange and tangled, but to my mind engrossing, tale of academic and political intrigue proved a fascinating exercise, akin in some ways to penning a detective story. When I gave a copy of the resulting book to Ralf Dahrendorf on arriving at my final and most agreeable academic perch, St Antony's College, Oxford, of which he was then the warden, he thanked me for what he termed my 'thriller'. I was indeed fortunate in being able to uncover a mass of material which enabled me to write a detailed, some might say over-detailed, anatomy of one of the great academic *causes célèbres* of early twentieth-century Britain, albeit one that had been largely forgotten at the time my study appeared. One reviewer wrote that it must be one of 'the fullest accounts in print of the making of any British university appointment'. He might have added 'and of the unmaking'. University appointments, as anyone in academic life is aware, not infrequently occasion controversy, but the machinations to which they can give rise may be gossiped over, but, regrettably, seldom get written about.

Once my study had appeared in print, initially in 1985 as a very long article, and subsequently in 1986 as a correspondingly short book, what should perhaps have been obvious from the outset was gradually borne in on me. This is that writing frankly about a rather large skeleton in the cupboard of the institution by which you are employed may not be the smartest of career moves, particularly if the story involves wealthy benefactors and appears at a time when the impoverished college is planning to go once again, cap in hand, for money from well-to-do Greeks. Indeed, the writing of *Politics and the Academy: Arnold Toynbee and the Koraes Chair* was not unconnected with my parting company with King's College a few years later in circumstances that, like those surrounding Toynbee's departure from the college, were far from amicable. At the time, I contemplated writing an account of how writing a book about Toynbee's involuntary departure from the college was a factor, albeit a small one, in my own exit. But the more I thought about it the more it struck me that this was but one, albeit by far the most unpleasant, of a number of unusual episodes in an academic career that has focused very largely on the study of the modern history and politics of Greece, a bed of nails if ever there was one.

It seemed to me that there might be some interest, or even purpose, in placing on record some of these 'untoward events', not least because the sometimes murky goings-on behind the scenes, the *paraskinia* as the Greeks would say, of academic life seldom see the light of day. There are, of course, some notable exceptions, but historians in writing about their own affairs often seem to lose sight of Ranke's famous dictum that history should be written, in so far as is possible, 'wie es eigentlich gewesen', as it really was. The saying that 'academic politics are so vicious because the stakes are so low' (apparently coined not, as is sometimes claimed, by Henry Kissinger but by Jesse Unruh, a California state politician) is uncomfortably near the mark, while F.M. Cornford, the Cambridge don, in his famous guide for the aspiring academic politician, *Microcosmographia Academica*, first published in 1908, cautioned that to involve oneself in the politics of the academy was to enter a 'world of unreason'.

Nonetheless, tales of academic intrigue and skulduggery can be entertaining, even if seldom uplifting. A fascinating academic memoir, addressing the interface between history and politics, is Noble Frankland's *History at War: The Campaigns of an Historian* (1998). This relates, *inter alia*, the tussles that he had as the official historian, together with Charles Webster, of the strategic air offensive during World War II, with some of the wartime RAF panjandrums who had been strong proponents of the area-bombing of German cities rather than the targeting of transport bottlenecks and oil production. Another instructive tale of academic intrigue is Elie Kedourie's account of his failure to be awarded a DPhil degree after studying at the newly founded St Antony's College, where I was to end my academic career. He had the misfortune to fall foul of one of his examiners, another panjandrum, Sir Hamilton Gibb, the Laudian Professor of Arabic at Oxford, who insisted that Kedourie make significant changes to his thesis. Kedourie thought these to be unjustified and declined to do so. On the basis of the referred and unamended thesis, which was soon published as a book, he was appointed to a lectureship at the London School of Economics and his career went from strength to strength. In the introduction to a subsequent edition of the study which had incurred Gibb's wrath, *England and the Middle East: The Destruction of the Ottoman Empire 1914–1921* (1987), Kedourie recounted this salutary story and demonstrated the perhaps self-evident fact that even the most eminent of DPhil examiners are not infallible.

More recently, in the snappily entitled *History Lesson: A Race Odyssey* (2008), Mary Lefkowitz has chronicled her battles at Wellesley College with a colleague, Anthony Martin, who was teaching in the Africana Studies programme that the ancient Greeks had appropriated their philosophy from the Egyptians and passed it off as their own. What is particularly interesting about her book is that she was taking on a member of her own faculty. Another epic clash in the academy is chronicled in Norman Finkelstein's *Beyond Chutzpah: On the Misuse of Anti-Semitism and the Abuse of History* (2nd edition, 2008). This is a devastating critique of Alan Dershowitz's *The Case for Israel* (2003), and prompted the Harvard professor's intervention in Finkelstein's tenure review, which, scandalously, went against him.

Maria Jesus González' *Raymond Carr: The Curiosity of the Fox* (2013) throws penetrating light both on the academic career of the second warden of St Antony's, on the factors that contribute to the college being such an extraordinary institution and on the curious ways of Oxford in general. It has much to say about Carr's wardenship between 1968 and 1987, three years before I arrived at the college, and his not altogether successful efforts to raise funds and to counter the public perception of the college as an annexe of MI6. Towards the end of his wardenship he seems to have tired of those fellows who were 'demanding prima donnas'. Oddly, when the eccentric Lyudmila Zhivkova, the daughter of the Bulgarian communist party boss, Todor Zhivkov, was appointed, in unsatisfactory circumstances, to a scholarship at the college bankrolled by Robert Maxwell, Carr found her a 'delightful young lady'.

Academic memoirs, while at times instructive and sometimes entertaining, can also be shocking. An intriguing exemplar of such a book is the classicist Kenneth Dover's *Marginal Comment* (1994). A sometime president of the British Academy, Dover wrote, *inter alia*, of his time as president of Corpus Christi College, Oxford, when he had felt 'no qualms about causing the death of a Fellow [the historian, Trevor Aston] from whose non-existence the College would benefit'. 'My problem,' he wrote, 'was one which I feel compelled to define with brutal candour: how to kill him without getting into trouble'. Victor Davis Hanson and John Heath allude to these 'ghoulish revelations' in their extraordinary and highly readable philippic about the 'tiny, incestuous and decaying world of Classics', *Who Killed Homer? The Demise of Classical Education and the Recovery of Greek Wisdom* (2001). They have an almost equally astonishing revelation to make. This is that Professor Judith Hallett, a professor of classics at the University of Maryland and a prominent member of the guild of American classicists, the American Philological Association, reported the authors to the FBI as possible suspects in the hunt for Unabomber, the 'anarcho-primitivist' terrorist who turned out to be a sometime university mathematician, Theodore Kaczynski. The tip-off was apparently made on the ground that the authors' pungently expressed views on the present state of the classics in the US were akin to those of a deranged killer. See how these classicists love one another. Incidentally, Professor Hallett is the co-editor of what she terms 'the first collection of theoretically informed "autographic" writing in the field of classical studies'. I suppose that I might equally claim that this memoir is one of the first 'autographic' writings in the field of modern Greek studies, although it is wholly without a theoretical foundation.

My memoir contains no ghoulish revelations or scarcely credible allegations of this kind. It does, however, contain material that does not often see the light of day on the making of academic appointments in a particular, somewhat recondite field. 'Byzantine' has in recent decades entered the English language as a synonym for devious or tortuous. A recent example appeared in the *New Yorker* shortly after the inauguration of Donald J. Trump as president of the United States: 'in a White House characterized by chaos and conflict – a Byzantine court led by a reality-television star, family members, and a circle of ideologues and loyalists'. Whether the 'byzantine' machinations that in this sense tend to accompany, appropriately some might say, appointments in the field of Byzantine and modern Greek studies are to be found in other fields of academic endeavour is for others to reveal, although I fully expect they do. Certainly, academic institutions on both sides of the Atlantic seek to cloak their activities in a mantle of secrecy. When, in the late 1990s, Professor Charles Nesson of Harvard Law School got one of his classes to try to penetrate the wall of secrecy surrounding the university's decision to deny tenure to the political scientist Peter Berkowitz, Nesson declared that Harvard 'had been built on secrecy [...] the idea of confidentiality runs through the university and is ingrained in us'.

Needless to say, the shenanigans and intrigues I recount throw light on a side of academic life that seldom rates a mention in the authorised histories of academic institutions. These tend to be bland at best and monumentally boring at worst. One of the contributors to a recent history of the University of Southampton had his piece emasculated at the behest of the university's external relations department to such an extent that it resembled 'a limited company's annual report'. A characteristic example of the inadequacy of such institutional histories is the collective volume *SOAS Since the Sixties* (2003). This examines the recent history of School of Oriental and African Studies of the University of London, an institution similar to, although significantly larger than, the School of Slavonic and East European Studies, where I taught in the 1970s. SOAS and SSEES at that time shared similar problems, not least an authoritarian management style.

SOAS Since the Sixties is fulsome in its praise of Cyril Philips, the director of SOAS between 1957 and 1976. Philips was undoubtedly a skilled academic entrepreneur and an adroit academic politician, but the book gives few indications of the autocratic fashion in which the School's affairs were conducted by Philips and a junta of heads of department, who for the most part paid little heed to the views of their subordinates.

The contribution on the social sciences recounts how the once happy and cooperative atmosphere in SOAS's Department of Economic and Political Studies lapsed into bitterness, ill feeling and a breakdown in communication. This sorry, but, alas, by no means unusual, state of affairs was occasioned by the sacking of a Marxist economist, Dr Biplab Dasgupta, for supposed 'lack of commitment' to his department. This became something of a *cause célèbre*, and the occasion, so the author tells us, of 'grave disquiet' both in the School and nationally. But, despite whetting the reader's appetite by saying that there had been no concrete grounds for the non-renewal of his appointment; that there had been no due process; and that Dasgupta had been peremptorily treated, the author insists that his chapter is not the place to give details of a controversy which clearly split the school from top to bottom, much in the way that the Toynbee affair polarised King's College in the early 1920s. But if a history of SOAS in recent times is not the place for a detailed account of the Dasgupta affair, one has to ask what would be the appropriate one.

While we learn something of Malcolm Caldwell, the lecturer in the economic history of South-East and East Asia, and of his Marxist critique of imperialism and underdevelopment from Indonesia to China, we are told nothing of the murder in 1978, in circumstances which remain to this day obscure, of Caldwell, the unabashed apologist for the Khmer Rouge regime in Cambodia, while staying in a government guest house in Phnom Penh at the invitation of the genocidal Pol Pot. Further and better particulars of scandals in the life of the School are contained, not in the volume published by SOAS itself, but in a 1973 pamphlet, *Oriental Despotism*, written by a dissident member of the staff, Ralph Russell, a scholar of Urdu at the School.

SOAS Since the Sixties is nonetheless correct in its characterisation of the club-like atmosphere that prevailed in SOAS as late as the 1960s. When my wife, Mary Jo, in the late 1960s, was working on a bibliography of pre-Islamic Persia under the direction of J.D. Pearson, the School's librarian and the progenitor of the *Index Islamicus*, she found herself made unwelcome in the common room by the attitude of some of the academics, of the kind who would come up to SOAS one day a week to teach some obscure Oriental or African language before retreating to their homes in Dorset or some such agreeable location. At least these curmudgeonly souls put in a weekly appearance. The Professor of Chinese in the 1930s, Sir Reginald Johnston, is said to have showed up at SOAS only once a year, obliging the School to advertise for someone to do his teaching. Rumour has it that Johnston was one of the applicants.

The *History of the School of Slavonic and East European Studies 1915–1990* (1991),[1] SOAS's sister institution, by I.W. Roberts, likewise gives only a partial insight into the history of the institution at which I taught in the 1970s. Roberts' treatment, for instance, of the purging in the late 1940s, seemingly at the behest of the Foreign Office, of Andrew Rothstein, an avowed communist who lectured on Soviet institutions and subsequently ran the Marx Memorial Library in Clerkenwell, is inadequate. But I shall have more to say about the School and its history when I write of my own experiences as a member of what was at the time a troubled institution.

Characteristically, the Toynbee fracas, which so divided King's College in the early 1920s, barely rates a mention in F.J.C. Hearnshaw's centennial history of the college (1929). It is not mentioned at all in Gordon Huelin's sesquicentennial volume (1978) or in Christine Kenyon-Jones' history published for the College's 175th anniversary (2003), by which time *Politics and the Academy* had long been published. But then Kenyon-Jones makes no mention of the then principal of the College, Ronald Burrows, who was responsible for the establishment of Toynbee's chair and was one of the pioneer proponents in Britain of what would nowadays be termed area studies. I should be surprised if what I have to say about King's College in this book were to find

INTRODUCTION

its way into the College's bicentennial history, but it is unlikely that I shall be around to check.

Some years ago, M.R.D. Foot, the great expert on the Special Operations Executive (SOE), and I were two of a small band of (in my case extremely dilatory) historians working on official histories of SOE, he on SOE in the Low Countries and I on SOE in Greece. His military demeanour (he had served in the Special Air Service Brigade during the war) led me to look upon him as the Senior British Officer (SBO). We both had rooms in the Old Admiralty Building in Whitehall, and one day, in true SBO style, he summoned me to his presence and said that he had heard that I was intending to write an account of the fracas at King's that had resulted in my departure from the college. He told me that were I to do this then I should lose a lot of friends. I was somewhat nonplussed by this no doubt well-intentioned advice but managed to refrain from saying that the matter was none of his business. Whether his prediction will prove correct remains to be seen, but at my age I have a decreasing number of friends to lose.

Historians, of all people, should be aware of the pitfalls involved in trying to write history 'as it truly was', as Ranke would have us do. They should know, in particular, how firsthand observers can form differing impressions, sometimes radically so, of the same event. I used to quote to my students a Greek example of this phenomenon as a salutary warning that even eye-witness accounts composed very soon after the event by individuals with no particular axe to grind should be treated with a degree of circumspection. By the autumn of 1944, Winston Churchill, as his personal doctor, Lord Moran, attests, was suffering from exhaustion, both physical and mental, not at all surprising in a man of his age, subject as he was to such unrelenting pressures. This manifested itself in a mounting obsession with thwarting a communist takeover of Greece of the kind that was beginning to take place throughout the Balkans.

Churchill's fears reached a peak in December 1944 as British troops in newly liberated Athens fought with communist guerrillas, with whom they had until recently been allied. This was by all accounts one of the lowest points in his wartime premiership. Churchill sought to use his immense prestige as a wartime leader to try to bring an end to the conflict and, on Christmas Eve 1944, ordered his personal plane to be readied for the potentially hazardous flight to Athens. At first, his entourage did not take his plans seriously, and his daughter, Mary, has recalled seeing her mother, Clementine, crying for the first time during the war at the prospect of a ruined family Christmas. But Churchill was insistent, and the party, which included Anthony Eden, the foreign secretary, left for Athens to attend what Jock Colville, the prime minister's assistant private secretary, with some justification considered to be the strangest meeting, held by lamplight and with the protagonists still clad in their overcoats, ever attended by a British prime minister and foreign secretary. On the return flight to London, a day or two later, it dawned on Colville that, besides himself, Moran and Pierson Dixon, Eden's principal private secretary, had also written accounts of Churchill's dramatic dash to Athens. They read to each other the relevant passages from their diaries: 'all were true, but each was written from a different angle'. 'Indeed,' Colville recorded, 'had the names of the participants been omitted, we might have been reading descriptions of three distinct events.'

This memoir is based on the voluminous documentary record which I have retained over the past half-century. I must apologise if I am unable to follow Kenneth Dover's example and incorporate matters that may appear ridiculous, embarrassing, contemptible or disgusting, or, at least, not often. I am well aware that some of those who may read this narrative will have different perspectives on some of the events described and I hope that they may air these.

1

Industria. First steps in Greece: Edinburgh, Athens, London

'I saw rain falling and the rainbow drawn
On Lammermuir. Hearkening I heard again
In my precipitous city beaten bells
Winnow the keen sea wind […]'
—Robert Louis Stevenson, *Weir of Hermiston*

One morning in May 1958, aged 18 and having just left school, I arrived, tired and dishevelled, after a three-day train journey from London, at Gevgelija/Eidomeni, the border crossing between Yugoslavia and Greece. A fiercely mustachioed Greek immigration official gave me a reproachful look as he stamped my passport. He also muttered something I could not understand. But it was apparently intended to be, no doubt with some justification, offensive about Cyprus, where the EOKA struggle for the *enosis* of the island with what was then the kingdom of Greece was at its height. This was a somewhat inauspicious introduction to the Greek world with which I was to have a close connection for over 50 years. But thereafter, during a month-long visit, I heard not an angry word about Cyprus.

I had just left Fettes College in Edinburgh with a travelling bursary, aiming to be the first holder to set foot in Asia, a modest enough ambition in this age of global gap year peregrinations. I was hoping to achieve this by travelling on from Greece to Istanbul, and then taking a ferry across to the Asiatic shore of the Bosphorus. Hitherto my connection with Greeks, still less with Greece, had been practically nil. I suppose the first Greek on whom I knowingly set eyes was Georges Guétary, born Lambros Vorloou in Alexandria, in a performance in London of the musical *Bless the Bride* in 1948. I can also remember being teased by my father and older brother, John, about not knowing the difference between gorillas and guerrillas after watching a cinema newsreel which had an item about the civil war in Greece, probably in 1948-9. I had started on Greek at my prep school, Ascham House in Gosforth, a suburb of Newcastle, but did not continue when I moved on in 1953 to Fettes, a school with a fine tradition in the classics. This was clearly in some ways a disadvantage, given my later interest in the Greek world, but, on the other hand, in my experience few of those who have studied the ancient language, which has changed remarkably little over the past 3,000 years, are able to view the land and the people save through the distorting mirror of antiquity. Years later I saw the person who taught me what little ancient Greek I knew at Ascham House, Miss Gardiner, or someone who looked remarkably like her, in the National Gallery of Scotland. She had become one of the seemingly endless supply of little grey-haired old ladies that inhabit Edinburgh. I have always regretted not going up to speak to her.

I also set eyes on Greek shipowners when I attended launches at the Sunderland yard of Sir James Laing and Sons, owned by the father of a boyhood friend, James Marr, but do not recall ever having spoken to any of them or their richly bejewelled and befurred spouses. When I went sailing on the Marr yacht, *Shiris*, the taciturn retired shipwright who helped crew this magnificent craft, and whom I knew only as Fred, occasionally spoke of his time posted near Lake Doiran on the Greek–Bulgarian border with the so-called 'Gardeners of Salonica' during the World War I.

A good part of my adolescence was spent in cinemas, much of it watching war films, and I had duly admired the heroics of Dirk Bogarde's portrayal of Patrick Leigh Fermor in the April 1944 kidnapping of General Karl Kreipe in German-occupied Crete in the 1957 film *Ill Met by Moonlight*. This has caught the popular imagination and knowledge of the kidnapping tends to be the sum of most people's knowledge in Britain of wartime resistance activity in Greece. It was to be some years before I became aware of the implications of what in essence was a schoolboy prank, albeit one carried out with great daring and panache. Leigh Fermor's comrade-in-arms, Stanley (Billy) Moss, was only 21 at the time. He was subsequently the author of the classic account of what M.R.D. Foot, who knew as much as anyone about the Special Operations Executive, has described, correctly in my view, as a 'tremendous jape'. But it was an escapade which the military authorities should have moved smartly to interdict, as some had vigorously urged at the time, an action which might have averted the mass German reprisals on the island following an operation that served no obvious military purpose. Bickham Sweet-Escott records in *Baker Street Irregular*, undoubtedly the best introduction to the tangled history of SOE, that Kreipe was so unpopular with his fellow officers that they celebrated his abduction with champagne. He once told me that he himself came near to being court martialled for insubordination in opposing the plan. A BBC documentary about Leigh Fermor, shown in 2008, not surprisingly had much to say about this 'Byronic' kidnapping but made no mention of the reprisals against Cretan villagers that had ensued. It also included a clip from a 'This is your life'-type programme shown in 1972 on YENED, the military broadcasting system in Greece (which no longer exists), during the deeply unpopular Colonels' regime. This showed a reunion with the general with whom, in the course of spiriting him out of Crete, Leigh Fermor had famously swapped passages from Horace's Soracte ode. Following his death in 2011 a Patrick Leigh Fermor society has been established and it is now possible to take an organised hike following in the steps of Leigh Fermor and Moss, accompanied by Cretan resistance fighters, as they escorted Kreipe to the south coast of Crete from where they were evacuated by launch to Egypt.

At Fettes, I had studied history, French and English in the sixth form. It has become almost a cliché to claim to have disliked one's boarding school education. But I was not unhappy at the school, although I was unfortunate in that my time should have coincided with a period when the cult of rugby reigned supreme under a philistine, rugger- and hunting-mad headmaster, Donald Crichton-Miller. As the history of the school euphemistically and tactfully observes, teaching was 'not his absolute *forte*'. During my time the first 15 had an almost unbroken run of victories: it was unbeaten in Scotland between 1950 and 1956. At times we were required to play the game seven days a week. I quite enjoyed rugby but was never much good at it, and it gave me comfort to read many years later in the memoirs of Alexander Glen, as a young man an arctic explorer and a wartime stalwart of SOE in Yugoslavia and Albania, that the memory of the east wind howling over the Fettes playing fields in November made Spitzbergen and the mountains of Yugoslavia feel like the Ritz. Not for nothing did Robert Louis Stevenson describe the Edinburgh climate as a 'downright meteorological purgatory'. Like Glen, I did not suffer unduly under a regime that in the 1950s was still spartan, with cold showers and harsh discipline enforced by the prefects, although, alas, beer was no longer served to the older boys as it had been in Glen's time. But if alcohol was no longer available, the shared studies were still heated by coal fires, the coal being stored in huge quantities in a basement which resembled a small coal mine. There were no fireguards or fire doors but, surprisingly, no wider conflagrations.

Despite the tyrannous cult of rugby, the philistines did not hold universal sway and there was plenty of scope to follow one's own interests, while, as

I got older, there were opportunities to enjoy the cultural life of the Scottish capital, although under the restrictive regime which prevailed at the school during the 1950s there was little contact with the city or its residents. Scottish nationalism was very much a fringe movement in the 1950s, and indeed, as late as 1955, the Conservatives, who were strongly unionist in sentiment, won a majority of the vote in elections to the Westminster parliament. I first became aware of the strength of Scottish nationalism in the 1990s when I sought to change some Scottish pound notes. The otherwise mild, middle-aged lady cashier in the Bank of Scotland on the Mound in Edinburgh was unamused by my wish to change these notes into 'English' money and thus escape the hassle that often attends attempts to use Scottish banknotes in England. Fortunately, I was protected from her wrath by the anti-bank-robber defences atop the counter. Although during the years I lived north of the border nationalism was not a significant force in Scottish politics, I was always conscious of being English in Scotland, despite the fact that my home was not far south of the border. Perhaps this helped in some small way to shape my subsequent abiding interest in religious and ethnic minorities in the Ottoman Empire.

Typical perhaps of the prevailing atmosphere at the school was the attempt by the second master, an antiquated fogey called Freddy Macdonald, to remove the composer Michael Tippett from the School Register because he had been a 'conchie', a conscientious objector, during World War II. Tippett had declined, at the age of 13, to join the Officers Training Corps when at the school. No wonder that the Tippett Foundation website makes no mention of his time at Fettes. I was in the same house as John de Chastelain who, as a general, a former chief of the Canadian Defence Staff and a sometime Canadian ambassador to the United States, was appointed under the terms of the 1998 Good Friday agreement to check on the de-commissioning of the weapons of para-military groups in Ulster. I imagine that because of his name and the Canadian accent that he had acquired since leaving school most people thought of him as a Quebecois and professional Canadian peace-maker brought in from the New World to redress the balance of the old, standing above the sectarian strife which was rife in Northern Ireland and, indeed, in the west of Scotland. Fettes was scarcely a sectarian school but the numbers of Catholic or Jewish boys were minuscule, although, oddly enough, one old boy had gone on to become a cardinal. De Chastelain has never tried to conceal his British roots, and, indeed, has spoken at a school speech day since becoming involved in the so-called 'peace process'. He was senior to me so I did not have much to do with him but I do recall one, possibly apocryphal, story. Each house had a house tie and ours was bright red. De Chastelain, intending to visit his father, Gardyne de Chastelain, a veteran of SOE's Romanian operations then living in New York, needed an American visa. The young de Chastelain, so the story went, was given quite a grilling about why he was wearing a 'communist' tie by the US consul-general in Edinburgh. The early 1950s, after all, were the height of the McCarthy era.

I had long left the school before its best-known alumnus, Tony Blair, was there. There are a number of strange stories in circulation about his school days, some of them put about by Blair himself and some manifestly without foundation. In the summer of 2004, some 50 years after first entering the school, I tried, no doubt in vain, to stifle at birth one of the more absurd myths about Blair's time at Fettes, a dozen or so years after my own. In an article for the *London Review of Books*, David Runciman, a Cambridge political scientist, sought to throw light on Blair's attitude to risk and its implications for his disastrous entanglement in Iraq. According to Runciman, when the (13-year-old) Blair, 'then still a Tory', arrived at the school in 1966, he would (note the *would*) have imbibed the attitude of the British political establishment to risk by folk memories of an event that had occurred at the height of the Suez crisis ten years previously. This was the burning in effigy on bonfire night, 5 November 1956, not of Guy Fawkes but of Hugh Gaitskell, who, as leader of the Labour Party, had strongly opposed Eden's Egyptian entanglement. Runciman claimed that the humiliations of Suez would have been particularly keenly felt at Fettes because the foreign secretary at the time, Selwyn Lloyd, was an old boy of the school. (Indeed, I remember Selwyn Lloyd speaking at the annual speech day in 1955.) Runciman painted a picture, worthy of Lindsay Anderson's depiction of a public school running riot in *If...*, of the school being turned out to witness the ritual immolation of Gaitskell so as to impress on the boys the meaning of treachery.

It made a good story but, alas, the reality was altogether more banal. I was in my upper sixth year, and at the time reasonably politically conscious, but have no recollection of such a bizarre episode, nor have a number of my contemporaries whom I have consulted. We would surely have remembered had there been any such macabre scene involving the whole school or any significant portion of it. There was no campaign encouraged from on high of unquestioning support for Eden and Selwyn Lloyd and of execration of the 'Wykehamist' (as if this had anything to do with it) Gaitskell. Indeed, I remember taking part in a debate in which, no doubt from a position of almost total ignorance, I opposed the Suez intervention.

What seems to have happened is this. A master called Charles Whittle, an ex-navy Lt-Commander, who was in the habit of stalking round the school grounds shooting magpies, and who struck me as a posturing buffoon and was described by a fellow master as 'a difficult and irascible character', did apparently burn an effigy of Gaitskell on a fire (bonfire night as such was never celebrated in the five years I was at the school) in front of a small group of the most junior boys. One of these, Richard Thorpe, subsequently a distinguished biographer of Tory grandees, mentioned the episode in his life of Anthony Eden. This was presumably the source of Runciman's story. To extrapolate from this ridiculous and (in every sense of the word) childish incident that it so traumatised the school that memories of it continued to reverberate ten years later, giving the young Blair his initiation into the world of *Realpolitik* and impressing upon him the lesson that imperialist adventures should not be conducted save in conjunction with the Americans, was simply absurd.

Alas, however, letters of correction, such as I wrote to the *London Review of Books*, seldom enter the historical record and this particular hare will doubtless be repeated in future books on the Blair premiership. It will no doubt join other myths about Blair's time at Fettes. The most egregious of these is that, so fearful was he of having to return to the 'ultra-establishment' (Runciman's expression) nightmare that was the school in the 1960s, he smuggled himself on board a plane bound from Newcastle for the West Indies. The fact there were at that time no flights from Newcastle to the Caribbean was not allowed to stand in the way of a good, and at the time politically convenient, not to say politically correct, story. This particular tale was put about by Blair himself not long before he became prime minister. Although he is clearly given to Walter Mitty-like fantasies, sometimes giving the appearance of living in a dream world far removed from reality, in fairness it has to be acknowledged that Blair had nothing to do with the genesis of the burning of Gaitskell in effigy canard. This did not stop Paul Routledge from citing it as another example of Blair's mythologising in the *New Statesman*. In trying to nail this particular story on the head I was told that a master at the school, who was there in my own day, has written a 20-page exposé of Blair's schooldays which he has deposited with his solicitor. On his death, one copy is apparently to go to Fettes, and one to Churchill College, Cambridge. One of Blair's problems is his ignorance of history. At Oxford, he read law, a subject which in some ways can shrink rather than expand horizons. In the US, law can, quite rightly, only be studied at the postgraduate level. Had he been aware that Saddam Hussein, like Saladin, came from Tikrit, Blair might have thought twice before joining in the invasion of Iraq.

Sometime towards the end of my time at the school, a master, Bob Roberts, gave an entertaining account of a trip he had recently made to Greece, an undertaking which, in the days before mass tourism became the norm, had an intriguingly adventurous sound to it. On leaving the school in 1958,

INDUSTRIA. FIRST STEPS IN GREECE

I applied for the Lawrie travelling bursary, emphasising my aspiration to be the first holder to set foot in Asia, and was awarded £40 to enable me to visit Greece and Turkey. Francis King's edited volume, *Introducing Greece*, was published at about this time and it was one of the first of the very large number of books which I subsequently amassed about the country. He wrote in his introduction that were Greece less remote there would be no more perfect destination for the British tourist. After all, in 1958, the year of my first visit, barely a quarter of a million tourists from all countries visited Greece. By the beginning of the new millennium this figure had increased almost fiftyfold to 11 million. By 2015 it had increased a hundredfold to 26 million.

In the summer of 1958, Greece had not yet been overrun by noise, litter, concrete and drunken British clubbers, let alone been routinely devastated by forest fires. Fewer than ten years previously, George Mikes had witnessed the innumerable beggars in the streets of the capital as it was emerging from the horrors of an exceptionally brutal German, Italian and Bulgarian occupation and from the savage civil war that ensued, once graphically described by Joyce Loch as a conflict 'of the poor against the deadly poor'. These beggars, so Mikes wrote, included the young mothers who 'used to gape through the restaurant windows, infant on arm, and look right into your mouth as you ate your steak'. Greece, indeed, in the late 1950s stood poised on the cusp of the extraordinary rate of economic and social change of the past 50 years, with few equals in Europe, and a development which I have been privileged to observe over the years. The upward trajectory of the Greek economy, however, came to an abrupt halt in 2009 when the country was revealed to be on the verge of bankruptcy and had to be bailed out by its European Union partners who imposed, with devastating consequences, a fierce programme of austerity.

On that first visit I did the round of the usual, mainly classical, tourist sites. But I did stay in one of the Meteora monasteries, precipitously perched atop pillars of rock near Trikala. I also secured a permit to visit Mount Athos, but unfortunately was not able to get to the Holy Mountain, although I did make two subsequent visits. My brief stay in the Meteora did, however, give me a tantalising glimpse of the post-classical Greek world. What particularly sticks in my mind from this first visit to Greece was the extraordinary hospitality of the people, some of whom even went so far as to put me up in their homes with no thought of accepting payment. Television had yet to reach Greece, although I remember seeing a football match on Italian television in a shop window in Corfu, to the excitement of those watching.

Following my Greek travels I took a boat from Piraeus to Istanbul and duly made the crossing to the Asiatic shore. I remember seeing the damage in some of the Greek churches in the city caused during the *Septemvriana*, the fearful anti-Greek rioting that had occurred three years earlier on 6/7 September 1955. The rioting was directly linked to events in Cyprus where EOKA had launched a violent campaign for the *enosis*, or union, of the island, with its substantial Turkish minority, to Greece. The *Septemvriana*, the September events as they are known in Greece, marked the beginning of a sad process which effectively doomed the once large Greek minority in Turkey to virtual extinction. Of all this, however, I was ignorant.

The beauty of Greece had been breathtaking and its inhabitants extraordinarily friendly and hospitable, and I decided that I wanted to learn more about the country and, in particular, its recent history, about which I knew nothing. I had some opportunity to do this as an undergraduate at the University of Edinburgh, which I entered in the same year, 1958. During my first summer vacation in 1959 I travelled again to Greece and Turkey, this time in the company of David Reid Thomas. Reid Thomas was somewhat older than me and had done his national service in the Cameron Highlanders. He subsequently became a priest in the Scottish Episcopal Church and died shortly after being appointed rector of St John's in Princes Street, Edinburgh. Although he was sadly young when he died, while hill-walking on Arran, it is difficult to imagine a better way of meeting one's maker than that.

In 1959, with David I visited some of the sights, including Crete, that I had missed on my first trip, and also penetrated much further into Asia Minor than on my first visit the previous year, reaching not only Ephesus but Trebizond on the shores of the Black Sea, not far from the border with the Soviet Union. I have few memories of my visit to this last city save an appalling 24-hour bus trip on poor roads from Ankara. Suffering acutely from gut rot, I was wedged into an extremely uncomfortable seat at the back of the bus so arranged that every time I nodded off I banged my head on the seat in front. I also recall the villainous-looking character sitting next to me who from time to time proudly showed me his loaded pistol. Among the sites we visited in the city before taking the coastal steamer to Istanbul was the Church of Hagia Sophia or Divine Wisdom, the Church of the Comnene Emperors of Trebizond, and one of the best preserved examples of thirteenth-century Byzantine architecture to have survived. It had been converted into a mosque after the fall of the Empire of Trebizond to the Ottoman Turks in 1461. Now the Russell Trust was sponsoring an expedition to uncover the wall paintings that had originally decorated the church, a building that I was to get to know much better the following year, 1960.

That summer, a friend, Alan Flashtig, also reading history but specialising in the history of art, asked whether I might be interested in joining him during the long vacation in working on the Hagia Sophia wall paintings which I had briefly glimpsed the previous year. This sounded an interesting way of spending part of the summer and was certainly more enticing than the possible alternative. This was to act as a 'Baron Officer' at the Binns, near Linlithgow, the ancestral pile of the Dalyell family and known in particular as the home of the notorious General 'Black Tam' Dalyell, scourge of the seventeenth-century Covenanters. The role of Baron Officer appeared to involve acting as a live-in guide to the property, at the time somewhat run down. Although under National Trust for Scotland ownership, the family retained the right to live there. Mike Davenport, a university friend reading economics, and I had been out to the Binns to be interviewed. After looking over the property we were given lunch by the chatelaine. This was a rather bizarre and stilted affair. All I remember of it now is the dogs being allowed to lick the plates clean, and being served hard-boiled eggs still in their shells. As I was contemplating what the most elegant way of shelling them might be, our rather eccentric hostess picked one up and smashed it on the edge of the fine, highly polished antique table at which we were eating. We duly followed suit. As I recall, we were offered the job, but declined what I suspect would have proved a rather trying assignment. The eleventh baronet was the former Labour MP, Tam Dalyell. Dalyell built up a formidable reputation over the years as a radical Labour MP and the very antithesis of a time-server. However, a few years ago, as we shall see, his radicalism deserted him and he uncharacteristically sided with the establishment in a curious controversy at the University of Edinburgh when he was serving as Rector. I refer to this dispiriting episode in the epilogue.

Alan took me to see David Talbot Rice, the Watson Gordon Professor of Fine Arts, who oversaw the Hagia Sophia project on behalf of the Russell Trust. He readily agreed to my accompanying Alan, despite the fact that I had up to then manifested no particular interest in Byzantine art. Talbot Rice was a gentleman scholar of the old school, and was apparently known to neighbours of his country house in Gloucestershire as a breeder of polled Hereford cattle rather than as a scholar. As an undergraduate he had been a drinking companion of Evelyn Waugh and a prominent member of the Hypocrites' Club, described by his widow, Tamara, as 'a fashionable, perhaps snobbish drinking and eating club'. In his beautiful rooms in Tom Quad at Christ Church he was famed for his 'exceedingly entertaining and delicious luncheon parties'. Waugh in his autobiography spoke of him as leading a life of 'carefree pleasure' while being 'secretly studious'. One of Waugh's biographers describes a pub crawl involving Waugh, Richard Plunket Green and Talbot Rice which ended in 'quarrels and broken glass', which scarcely sounds like the avuncular Talbot Rice whom I knew in the 1960s. His secret studiousness took the form of working for a doctorate at the École des Hautes Études in Paris under

Professor Gabriel Millet, one of the pioneers in the study of Byzantine art in France, just as Talbot Rice was to become one of the pioneer British historians in the same, at the time recondite, field. This research was reflected in the book he wrote with Millet, *Byzantine Painting at Trebizond* (1936).

Talbot Rice had earlier written, with Robert Byron, *The Birth of Western Painting*, published in 1930. After a brief stint at the Courtauld Institute, he had been appointed, at the age of 31, to the Watson Gordon Professorship of Fine Art, the first such chair to be established at a British university and held this until his death in 1972, a total of 38 years, dividing his time between Edinburgh and his native Gloucestershire. His pro-predecessor, Gerard Baldwin Brown, had actually been appointed for life, likewise at the similarly early age of 31, and held the chair until shortly before his death at the age of 83. Until after World War II, Talbot Rice was required to reside in Edinburgh for only two of the three terms of the academic year, leaving the summer free for archaeology or exploration. During the war he had been in the Special Operations Executive working on Greek and related affairs, although he never spoke to me of his wartime experiences, nor, at that time, did I have the interest in this field that I was subsequently to develop.

Talbot Rice, enjoining me not to treat the Turkish workmen as 'canaille', gave me a large (in size if not in value) cheque for £25, drawn on the Ottoman Bank, whose London branch wisely declined my attempt to open an account on my return to the UK. Thus equipped, Alan and I set out for Trebizond. After another wearying rail journey, we arrived at Erzincan, in Eastern Anatolia, the nearest railhead, from where we took the bus over the fabulously beautiful Pontic Alps to Trebizond. The city had recently been put on the map by Rose Macaulay, whose novel *The Towers of Trebizond*, published a few years previously, had become an instant bestseller. The novel ends with Macaulay putting into the mouth of the character Laurie, who appears to have been based on the author herself, a paean to the city: 'still the towers of Trebizond, the fabled city, shimmer on a far horizon, gated and walled and held in a luminous enchantment'. Macaulay had actually visited Trebizond in the early 1950s, but my own visit a few years later to this rather run-down and somewhat grim town did not exactly summon up visions of 'luminous enchantment'. Still, the name had a romantic resonance as the last outpost of the Byzantine Empire to fall to the Ottoman Turks in 1461, some eight years after the fall of Constantinople itself.

The pocket Empire of Trebizond had come into existence shortly before the sack of Constantinople by the Franks, the culmination of the Fourth Crusade of 1204. For some 257 years, the 'petty Greek princes' of the Comnene dynasty had escaped, as H.F.B. Lynch wrote at the end of the nineteenth century, the 'storms of Mussulman conquest' behind the wall of mountains that protected the coast from the interior. George Finlay, the great historian of medieval and modern Greece, harboured few romantic illusions about the Trapezuntine Empire. In the mid-nineteenth century he observed that 'we inquire in vain for any benefit that it conferred on the human race. It seems a mere eddy in the torrent of events that connects the past with the future.' 'The tumultuous agitation of the stream,' the dour Scot opined, 'did not purify a single drop of the waters of life [...] The greatest social defect that pervaded the population was the intense selfishness which is evident in every page of its history.' Quite why he should have felt this way is not clear.

What makes the coast in the region of Trebizond so striking is that the East Pontic Alps include a number of the highest mountains anywhere in the world that are visible from the sea, some of them rising to well over 3,000 m. Certainly, in the mid-nineteenth century, Finlay, while dismissive of the Trapezuntine Empire, was struck by the beauty of its setting:

> there are few spots on the earth richer in picturesque beauty, or abounding in more luxuriant vegetation, than the south-eastern shores of the inhospitable Euxine. The magnificent country that extends from the mouth of the Halys to the snowy range of Caucasus is formed of a singular union of rich plains, verdant hills, bold rocks, wooded mountains, primaeval forests, and rapid streams.

Half a century later, Lynch expressed the hope that the church of Hagia Sophia, in which we were to work during that summer of 1960, might one day be restored to Christian worship or at least be preserved as 'a relic to instruct an enlightened age' by disclosing 'in some of their ancient brightness the solemn faces and gorgeous robes of the Grand Comneni as they looked down upon the congregation of monks and pilgrims six centuries ago'. Lynch's two volumes were published in 1898, only five years before Talbot Rice was born, and his description of the wall paintings which Talbot Rice was subsequently to be responsible for uncovering reflect the uphill task that he faced in fostering an interest in Byzantine art in Britain. The impression, Lynch wrote, that we should take away from the church should be 'one of sadness, perhaps of pain'. For the art represented within was 'an art in shackles, an expiring phase of life'. The 'peculiar wooden quality of these expressionless faces' demonstrated that

> strict conventions had taken the place of realities alike in life and in art; and how sad after the unsurpassed beauty of Hellenic vigour are the gaudy get-up and childish love of baubles which mark the declining years of the Greek world!

Underneath 'the inexorable whitewash' lay 'the vivid evidence of that departed age'. This was 'repugnant alike to the spirit and to the mission of Mohamedanism', and, so Lynch considered, this 'rich collection of Christian images' must, from the outset, have 'courted effacement'.

The effacement of Hagia Sophia had occurred following its conversion from a church into a mosque after the fall of Trebizond in 1461, when the wall paintings had been covered in 1573 with plaster and whitewash. One can all too readily imagine the anguish of the Trapezuntine Greeks, 400 years previously, when their much cherished church had been turned into a mosque and the magnificent wall paintings covered from sight, seemingly forever. It would be our task to remove, often using dental picks, the overlay of plaster and the 'inexorable whitewash'. It was a project that, for me at least, had sounded more enticing in prospect than proved to be the case in reality. Even when the plaster was laboriously removed the underlying wall paintings were often badly pocked with holes hacked to make the covering plaster adhere.

Perched atop rickety wooden scaffolding, in the humid summer heat of Trebizond, I must say that I found the work boring, and rapidly abandoned any thoughts that I had entertained of becoming an archaeologist. The work required an infinite degree of patience that I soon discovered I simply did not have. Of course it was very exciting to uncover tiny areas of painting on which no human eye had gazed for the best part of four centuries, though in my case the excitement soon wore off. But the company of David Winfield, who oversaw the work in the church, and of his partner, June, and that of the three other student assistants was good. Besides Alan, who went on to became an art historian in Australia, there were two undergraduates from Oxford, Tom Richardson, who subsequently became a diplomat, and Bill Hale, who later became professor of Turkish politics at the School of Oriental and African Studies. Two years earlier, another of the student assistants had been Robert Thomson, who subsequently became professor of Armenian language and literature at Harvard and later at Oxford. Thus three of the small group of students (there were six in all) involved in the expedition subsequently developed academic interests in the fields of Armenian, Turkish and Greek studies respectively, presumably influenced in part at least by their sojourn in Trebizond, which for centuries had been home to all three communities. This was certainly the case with me. Perhaps the three of us should have collaborated on a book about Turkish, Armenian and Greek Trebizond.

During the time I was in Trebizond, Bill Hale stood on a nail protruding from the shaky scaffolding. He was whisked off to hospital for a tetanus injection, which somehow caused complications. I remember visiting him in hospital with a bag of grapes. On opening his bedside locker I was alarmed when several cockroaches tumbled out. One day, on my unsteady perch and busy scraping away, I was surprised to see a young Turkish soldier enter the church/mosque and cross himself. He turned out to be a Turkish Armenian doing his military service.

After the archaeological work was completed in 1962 a new mosque was built, and in the early 1960s Hagia Sophia was designated a museum. It is difficult to imagine in the current political and religious climate in Turkey that permission would be given by the authorities to uncover Christian images in a mosque or for a mosque to be secularised. From the outset of the Russell Trust expedition there had been disquiet on the part of the religious authorities in Trebizond at the prospect of Hagia Sophia ceasing to be a mosque. The müfti of the city, who had been agitating for the frescoes to be covered up with boarding and for the building to revert to use as a mosque, was deposed as a consequence of the military coup of 27 May 1960 which led to the execution of the prime minister, Adnan Menderes. There were subsequently intermittent calls for a return of the building to Muslim worship, notably in the mid-1990s by Necmettin Erbakan's Welfare Party. In 2011, the church of Hagia Sophia in İznik (Nicaea) was returned to Muslim worship. The meeting place of the Seventh Ecumenical Council in AD 787, it had been converted to a mosque in 1331, seriously damaged during the Greek–Turkish war of the early 1920s, and had been subsequently restored and had initially functioned as a museum.

In the following year, 2012, there were ever more insistent calls for Hagia Sophia in Trebizond to be de-secularised. This time they were successful. Following a legal case launched by the General Directorate of Pious Foundations (Vakıflar Genel Müdürlüğü), which argued that the church had been 'illegally occupied' by the Ministry of Culture and Tourism, in the summer of 2013 the museum reverted to its earlier status on the ground that once a building had been used as a mosque it could not be used for any other purpose. The frescoes were screened off by a false ceiling and the *opus sectile* floor was covered by carpeting. Whether visitors wishing to see the frescoes which we had so laboriously uncovered could still do so was not clear. This decision was greeted with alarm not only by Turkish secularists but by café owners and souvenir sellers in the neighbourhood of Hagia Sophia, which was the prime tourist attraction in Trebizond.

Those Turks who were alarmed at the rise of Islamism in Turkey feared, with reason, that what was happening to Hagia Sophia in Trebizond in 2013 would prove to be merely a foretaste of what might happen, sooner or later, to Hagia Sophia in Istanbul. A committee of the Turkish parliament was already looking at the possibility that the Emperor Justinian's great sixth-century edifice might be restored to Muslim worship. In 1934, on the same day that parliament bestowed the title of Atatürk, the 'father' of the Turks, on Mustafa Kemal, it had been turned into a museum, after serving for centuries as the principal mosque of the Ottoman capital. Although the return of Hagia Sophia to Muslim worship might be of concern to Christians, it should be remembered that during the British, French and Italian occupation of Constantinople after World War I there was a vigorous campaign in Britain, led by the Saint Sophia Redemption Committee, to end what was termed the disgrace of leaving the church 'under the shadow of the Crescent'. The British High Commissioner in Constantinople, the crusty Admiral Sir John de Robeck, might complain of 'the thunder of the Canons of Canterbury [...] the outcry of Near Eastern cranks, and [...] the ingenious enthusiasm of Dr Burrows [the principal of King's College, London]', but the campaign enjoyed influential backing, including that of two future foreign secretaries. One of the committee's secretaries, Canon J.A. Douglas, wrote that 'without treachery to England's history [...] that [British] fleet cannot sail away and leave the great Greek city of Constantinople a Turkish city [...] its Mother Church a mosque.' During Ramadan in 2016, shortly before the attempted military coup in Turkey, huge crowds called, in early morning prayers offered outside the church, for the reversion of Hagia Sophia to a mosque and for the first time since its conversion to a museum in 1934 prayers were chanted within the Emperor Justinian's great building.

The tedium of the archaeological work in Hagia Sophia, as it struck me at least, was relieved by the excursions which we made at weekends into the fabulously beautiful hinterland of Trebizond, where the Pontic Alps fall precipitously to the Black Sea. These were led by David Winfield in the expedition Land Rover. One such *ekdromi*, in the literal sense of being off the beaten track, was to the spectacularly situated monastic ruin of Panaghia Soumela, dedicated to the Virgin Mary and known in Turkish as the Mereyemana Manastırı. Clinging precipitously to the mountainside 1,000 ft above the Panayia Suyu, the river of the Virgin, it was the best known of the monasteries of Matzouka, founded originally in Byzantine times, the others being Vazelon (dedicated to John the Baptist) and Peristera (dedicated to St George). Finlay has left a graphic description of Soumela in its mid-nineteenth-century prime: 'the galleries and cells clinging like swallows' nests to the precipice, the sound of the convent bell continually announcing the arrival of parties of pilgrims and the nasal chant of the continual masses was grand, solemn and picturesque'. Such, indeed, was the fame of Soumela as a centre of pilgrimage that in the eighteenth century a pilgrim guide was published in *karamanlidika*, that is to say in Turkish printed in Greek characters, for the large numbers of Turkish-speaking Orthodox Christians of Asia Minor. This naturally focuses on the famous miracle-working icon of the Virgin, supposedly painted by Saint Luke, that was the monastery's proudest possession and an object of great reverence. The story has it that after the Greeks were expelled from Pontos in the early 1920s, along with those in the rest of Asia Minor, a monk returned to retrieve the icon where it had been secretly buried. It continues to be revered at the monastery of New Soumela, near Veroia in northern Greece, built in the 1930s by Pontic Greek refugees.

After the monastery was abandoned in 1923 it rapidly fell into ruin. This is how we found it in the summer of 1960, although the chapel, painted inside and out with early eighteenth-century frescoes, survived, albeit heavily scarred with graffiti and other signs of vandalism. At that time the ruin was not easy of access and was scarcely visited at all, and on the day of our *ekdromi* we had the place entirely to ourselves. Not until the early 1970s was a custodian appointed to protect it from further vandalism. Nowadays, since the authorities have taken on the task of conserving the ruin, it is visited by tens of thousands of visitors a year. The overwhelming majority of these are Muslims, for whom, faithful to the traditions of religious syncretism in Asia Minor, it is also a place of pilgrimage. When I visited Soumela, in the summer of 2010, for the first time in 50 years, there was great excitement at the prospect of the Ecumenical Patriarch, Bartholomaios I, being permitted to celebrate the liturgy at the monastery on the Feast of the Dormition (Assumption) on 15 August. This was attended by large numbers of Pontic Greek pilgrims from Greece, the Russian Federation and elsewhere. Such liturgies have been celebrated in succeeding years.

After the hot and dusty work in Hagia Sophia it was a pleasure to walk down to the nearby beach and swim in the murky waters of the Black Sea. This is something that would not be possible now, as Hagia Sophia has been cut off from the sea by a motorway that runs along the coast. From time to time, we would eat in the Yeşilyurt restaurant in the *meydan*, where 'fried testicles' were, as I remember, a permanent feature of the menu. On Sundays, although not ourselves Catholics, Winfield and I used to attend mass in the Capuchin chapel in the city, Santa Maria Trapezuntis, virtually Trebizond's only link with its Levantine past. There was never more than a handful in the congregation. Afterwards we would chat, sipping banana liqueur, with the Italian friar and the lay brother on their balcony. Often the talk would turn to the problems they were having with the authorities in trying to evict squatters from the Latin burial ground in the town, which required repeated visits to Erzerum to try to resolve. Tragically, in 2006, one of the Italian priest's successors, Antonio Santoro, was gunned down while praying in his church, in an attack seemingly linked to the wave of anti-Western demonstrations following the publication of cartoons satirising the Prophet Muhammad in a Danish newspaper. In 2010, Mary Jo and I attended a service in the church. The congregation was tiny, worshippers staying away because just a few days previously a Catholic bishop, the apostolic vicar for Anatolia, had been murdered by his driver in İskenderun in southern Turkey. The priest was not present as he was attending the bishop's funeral. Mary Jo was pleased to be asked to read the Epistle and Gospel in the bilingual service.

In the course of the excursions with David Winfield or in walks around the rather uninviting city of Trebizond itself, I was surprised to encounter evidence of a recent Greek presence and of Orthodox churches, half-ruined, or turned into warehouses or barns, that had clearly been restored or even built in the nineteenth century, long after the fall of the medieval Empire. There were also fine neo-classical mansions and school buildings, dating from the nineteenth or early twentieth centuries. Particularly striking was the building that had housed the famous Greek *Phrontistirion*, or Academy, of Trebizond, with its Ionic columns, designed by the architect Alexandros Kakoulidis in 1902 for a school that had been founded in 1682. Another noteworthy building was the sumptuous summer mansion built in 1903 for the Kapayannidis banking family on a hill overlooking the city and which, after the expulsion of the Greeks, was presented to Mustafa Kemal (Atatürk). On a smaller scale there was the attractive neo-classical building that is now home to the Trabzon Journalists Club.

Tamara Talbot Rice records that, while travelling with her husband in the hinterland of Trebizond in 1929, they came across many deserted villages, in one of which they found a table still laid for a meal by the departing Greeks. We made no such dramatic discoveries. Nonetheless, it was gradually borne in on me that, well within living memory, large numbers of Greeks had been settled in Trebizond and in Pontos generally, something of which I had been entirely unaware before that summer of 1960. The Greek population of the region had been uprooted and transplanted to Greece, along with the rest of the Greeks of Asia Minor, under the terms of the Treaty of Lausanne of 1923, only 37 years previously. In fact, writing this in the year 2016, it is longer since my sojourn in Trebizond in 1960 than between 1960 and 1923, when the Greeks had been forced out of a region which they had inhabited since antiquity.

I returned to Edinburgh University determined, firstly, not to become an archaeologist, and, secondly, to find out more about this recent Greek presence in the region, whose ghostly traces lingered on in the architecture of Pontos. It is undoubtedly due to that distant Trapezuntine summer that I have always been as much interested in the history of the large numbers of

Greeks who lived outwith the boundaries of the Greek state as in the history of those who are settled within the country's present-day borders, which in other circumstances might have assumed a very different shape. Ignorant as I was of the history of the Greeks of Pontos, I had still less of an inkling of other fascinating aspects of the region's history. Trebizond and its hinterland had, for instance, been home to a large Crypto-Christian population. This had its origins in those Greeks who had converted *en masse* to Islam in the seventeenth century when they had come under pressure from their Muslim overlords. But they had clandestinely maintained Christian practices (and names) and had revealed themselves as Christians at the time of the Tanzimat reforms in the mid-nineteenth century, which, theoretically at least, proclaimed the equality of Muslim and Christian, in the Ottoman Empire.

There were also in the region Greek-speaking Muslims, living in the Of valley and other villages in the region of Trebizond. These were the descendants of Greeks who had likewise converted *en masse* to Islam in the seventeenth century, but who, into the twenty-first century, retained their Pontic Greek speech. At the time I was in Trebizond, Pontic Greek would have been more widely spoken by these Oflu Greeks than is now the case, for the language is effectively dying out among the younger generation. Nonetheless, it was fascinating to hear Pontic Greek, all but unintelligible to me, being spoken in 2010 in Tonya by Turks and three Pontic Greek speakers from Greece and the US, whom we had met with in Trebizond. Then there were the Hemşinli Armenians of the region, the Armenian-speaking descendants of converts to Islam. But of all these fascinating historical and linguistic curiosities I had no idea.

Although I decided against aiming for a career in archaeology, I nonetheless took Talbot Rice's special subject on early Christian and Byzantine art. I also signed up for a course in Turkish with John Walsh at the William Muir Institute, but after a while this proved too high-powered and time-consuming for my needs. Like many of those teaching Turkish in Britain at the time, Walsh had been a student of Paul Wittek, the Vienna-born refugee who taught at the School of Oriental and African Studies. This coloured Walsh's teaching style and resulted in classes two or three hours long which proved impossible to fit in with my obligations as an honours history student.

My growing interest in the art of the Byzantine era had a particularly fortunate outcome for me personally, because, on what Scots would call a dreich February evening in 1961, I attended a lecture on the rock-cut churches of Cappadocia organised by the Middle Eastern Society in the William Muir Institute in Buccleuch Place. The only other undergraduate present was Mary Jo Augustine, so we naturally ended up chatting to each other. Mary Jo was in her junior year at the University of Oregon and was spending this at the University of Edinburgh. This was before poverty-stricken British universities sought to boost their income with high fee paying overseas students. Edinburgh certainly did not make much out of Mary Jo or her two friends who had joined her in venturing abroad to study as they were not on one of the pricey Junior Year Abroad programmes for American students. They paid a mere £35 in fees for their year at the university.

In travelling from her home state of Oregon to Edinburgh she, and her two college friends from the University of Oregon, journeyed by the cheapest way. This involved a three-day train journey from Portland to New York, followed by a seven-day sea voyage from New York to Liverpool in a rather elderly Cunard liner, the *Britannic*. A few years later the inexpensive way to undertake such a journey would have been by plane. As it was, Mary Jo was lucky enough to experience a mode of travel that was soon to disappear. One thing that bemused her and her college friends on the trip was the pattern of almost continuous eating on the Cunard liner as it ploughed its way across the Atlantic.

In those halcyon days of the British university system, the First Ordinary class in Islamic History was laid on for Mary Jo's sole benefit, for she was the only student to register for it. The line up of teachers was a distinguished one, consisting of Walsh and William Montgomery Watt, who, besides being professor of Arabic and a great authority on the life of Mohammed, was a priest in the Scottish Episcopal Church. Three times a week, in the late afternoon, Mary Jo was solemnly lectured to. One afternoon, Montgomery Watt, donned as usual in a gown for his lecture, briefly dozed off. I had always tended to regard Mary Jo's tale of the professor rather than the student nodding off in a lecture with a certain degree of scepticism.[1] A few years ago, however, we learned that Montgomery Watt suffered from apnoea. What had happened was not that he was asleep but that he had stopped breathing for a short time. Apnoea is clearly not a life-threatening condition, for Montgomery Watt lived to be 97, dying only in 2006. It was characteristic that when Mary Jo came to take her examination in the introductory course on Islamic history at the end of the year, the invigilator should have given her a copy of the Qur'an, which had been provided by Walsh. This was in Arabic, which she had not studied.

During her time in Edinburgh, Mary Jo developed a taste (which I did not entirely share) for bagpipe music. One afternoon we made for the sound of a military pipe and drum band and caught up with it just as it was about to go down into the Grassmarket. I noticed that the officer in charge was Major R.A. ('Cocker') Guild, who was a master at Fettes. I managed to catch

Cocker's eye and gave him a wave. To our astonishment, he broke ranks and came over for a short chat. My standing with Mary Jo increased noticeably.

That summer Mary Jo and I travelled extensively in Greece and Yugoslavia, with the aid of a grant from the Carnegie Trust for the Universities of Scotland. We visited a number of sites of Byzantine interest which had figured in my course with Talbot Rice. These included Nea Moni on Chios, the monastery of Osios Loukas on the way to Delphi, and Mistra. By this time I had become an enthusiastic photographer. Although by no means an expert and with only a modest camera, I managed, more by accident than design, to take some good photographs of the eleventh-century mosaics at Osios Loukas. The late afternoon sun reflected off the floor of the narthex to provide perfect natural illumination and I secured some excellent images. When I returned to Edinburgh I showed the slides to Talbot Rice. He asked if he could use two of the transparencies in his next book, *Art of the Byzantine Era*, which was published in 1963 and has been continuously in print ever since. The first was the crucifixion in the narthex. The second was of the Virgin and Child in the semi-dome of the apse, together with the depiction of Pentecost in the dome itself. Gentleman that he was, Talbot Rice not only published the transparencies but arranged a reproduction fee with the publisher, Thames and Hudson. Three guineas in those days was a not negligible sum. It was likewise characteristic that, when I briefly taught at the University in 1968–9, he should have invited Mary Jo and me to the lunch for André Grabar, the Byzantine art historian at the Collège de France, when he was given an honorary degree.

After visiting a number of Byzantine churches in Yugoslav Macedonia and Kosovo, we attended the Twelfth International Congress of Byzantine Studies in Ohrid. We naturally took the boat down to the church of Sveti Naum at the southern extremity of Lake Ohrid. To the east of the church was a rather crowded beach. To the west there appeared to be no one and so, as Balkan neophytes, we duly headed west, undeterred by some strands of rusty barbed wire over which we scrambled. A few steps further on an armed sentry made it unequivocally clear that we should climb back, as we had inadvertently strayed into the no man's land between Yugoslavia and Albania. On a happier note, we were swimming in the lake one day when someone, hearing us speak English, swam over to us. This was John Fine, who was subsequently to establish a formidable reputation as an historian of the medieval Balkans. From Ohrid we made our way back to Britain. While hitchhiking up through Italy a lorry driver made off with our cameras and, by that time, numerous rolls of exposed film. But after a dramatic high speed car chase (in a very small car) driven by a helpful Italian we managed to retrieve the stolen property in short order as the lorry driver had fortunately stopped to stow away his ill-gotten goods.

The next summer, I travelled to Oregon to marry Mary Jo. On arriving in New York before heading out west by Greyhound bus ($99 for 99 days of unlimited travel), I had been surprised and, as someone with an enthusiasm for westerns, somewhat flattered to have been asked by the immigration inspector if I were a sheepman. 'No', I replied, asking what had led him to think that I was. It turned out that he was from Klamath Falls, the nearest town to Lakeview, where Mary Jo had attended high school. Shepherding was the only reason he could think of why anyone would be heading for this remote community in the high desert of eastern Oregon.

At that time, in addition to a marriage licence, a certificate was required from the Oregon State Board of Eugenics, the first such body to be established in the US, which, beginning in 1917, presided over the compulsory sterilisation of teenage delinquents, homosexuals, the feeble-minded and insane, criminals, 'moral degenerates' and 'sexual perverts', some 2,500 in total. Besides having a blood test, one of the questions I was asked by the man who issued the certificate was whether there was any history of madness in my family. In my experience there is madness in all families, without exception, but I duly perjured myself and received what was in effect not so much a permission to marry as to breed. It is salutary to remember this grim heritage (the law was not repealed until 1983) given Oregon's current reputation for progressive legislation. For example, it was the first and is currently one of only very few US states to countenance voluntary euthanasia. After we were married I spent what should have been our honeymoon working the night shift in the Oregon Fruit Growers Association cannery in Eugene, the home to the University of Oregon, one of the most beautifully situated campuses in the United States. As a temporary employee, I was able to fend off efforts to enrol me in the Teamsters Union in the bad old days of Jimmy Hoffa.

By a happy coincidence, some 35 years later our daughter, Rachel, developed a strong interest in the cultural history of Abkhazia, writing an Oxford DPhil thesis on Fazil Iskander, the author, *inter alia*, of Sandro of Chegem, and one of the best-known writers in Russia. Of Abkhazian descent, Iskander had, like the indefatigable Ottoman traveller, Evliya Çelebi, an Abkhazian mother. Abkhazia lies just a short boat journey across the Black Sea from Trebizond and, like Pontos, is an extraordinarily beautiful region lying between the sea and a high range of mountains. It is also home to the monastic complex of Novy Afon, or New Athos, that had been built in Tsarist times. No doubt the Oregon Board of Eugenics would have been able to detect a genetic predisposition on the part of my branch of the Clogg family to study the eastern reaches of the Euxeinus Pontos, the euphemistically named 'Hospitable Sea' of the ancients. Our son, Nathan, on the other hand, developed interests in IT and frequently rescued his mother and me from word processing and other computing problems, in the process saving us a small fortune. Incidentally, the curious American usage of 'Caucasian' for 'white' has its origins in the same eugenic fantasies that led to the establishment of state boards of eugenics. Russians, by contrast, are in the habit of calling the inhabitants of the Caucasus 'blacks'.

On graduating, I originally intended to study for a PhD at Rutgers University in Byzantine history under Professor Peter Charanis and I was offered a teaching assistantship in the history department there. We duly set sail in an ancient Dutch tub, the *Groote Beer*, with our cat, for a ten-day voyage across the Atlantic. We boarded the ship not in Southampton harbour but from a tender in the Solent, it presumably being too expensive to pay harbour dues. But my proposed studies at Rutgers did not work out. I had not realised that, under the American system, I would still be in for a large amount of course work, of which I had had enough in Edinburgh, and what little I saw of Charanis did not encourage me to stay. Pending my return to the UK, I worked in a university laboratory determining the gender of flies, not an easy task, and to what end I do not now recall. This rather tedious work was relieved from time to time when Jim, my African-American boss, took me in the departmental van to a rather grisly slaughter house in Paterson in New Jersey to get fresh supplies of blood on which the flies feasted. Meanwhile, Mary Jo worked in the Rutgers Library.

On my return I taught, with no obvious qualifications, for a disastrous term as a prep school master, while Mary Jo stayed in America for a few more months. The school concerned was Ketteringham Hall, near Wymondham in Norfolk. Along with another master, Nick Cavanagh, I managed to get myself fired but, for some reason, I did not have physically to leave the school premises. One of the things that had annoyed the headmaster was our managing on sports day, in a scene worthy of Evelyn Waugh's *Decline and Fall*, to fly the Union Jack upside-down. I do not think either of us knew that there was a right way up, a degree of ignorance which nowadays would no doubt lead to the refusal of an application for British citizenship. Nonetheless, I, together with my fellow member of the awkward squad, had to eat the rather good school food, much of it grown in the large kitchen garden, at a separate table in the dining hall. A few days later a solicitor, whose fee was the princely sum of three guineas, secured our reinstatement and we staggered on until the end of term. Grim though the school was, and inadequate though the qualifications of some of the staff, myself included, were, the physical environment was most attractive. Ketteringham Hall was, and remains, a fine building in fine surroundings. I later read with more than usual interest Owen Chadwick's *Victorian Miniature*, first published in 1960. This was the engrossing tale of the Trollopian clash in the mid-nineteenth century between the austere vicar of Ketteringham, the Reverend William Wayte Andrews, and the more worldly squire of Ketteringham, Sir John Boileau. The tension between the two was exacerbated by the fact that the church was literally a stone's throw from the hall. True to form, a century later the headmaster in our time was feuding with the vicar, and the church, close enough to serve as the school chapel, was never used by the school.

Following this curious experience, I was lucky enough to be awarded a Major State Studentship which, when put together with a smaller scholarship awarded by the University of Edinburgh, enabled us to live in relatively greater comfort in London and Athens over the next few years than we could when I acquired a full-time academic job. Mary Jo meanwhile got a job running the Shaw Library at the London School of Economics. The Shaw Library was the LSE's effort to provide a cultural life for its students, and one of the duties of the job was to organise recitals, given for the most part by promising young music students. A welcome perk was that Mary Jo was regularly given free tickets for recitals at the Wigmore Hall. At the same time she was able to study part time for the Diploma in Librarianship at University College.

The subject of my proposed thesis, which, alas, for a variety of reasons I was never to finish, was the Greeks of Asia Minor in the eighteenth and nineteenth centuries. This was a subject directly inspired by my experiences in Trebizond. I developed a particular interest in the *karamanlides* (Turkish *karamanlılar*), the Turkish-speaking Greeks of Asia Minor, many of whom were monoglot Turkish-speakers, and for whom an extensive literature was published in Turkish printed with Greek characters in the eighteenth, nineteenth and early twentieth centuries. When Mustafa Kemal decreed in 1929 that the Turks should adopt a modified 29-letter Latin alphabet (devised by an Armenian) in place of the Arabic, books in *karamanlidika* formed a ready-made source of texts already transcribed into Greek characters and could thus be more readily transcribed into the Latin alphabet. For a few years after the exchange of populations between Greece and Turkey in the 1920s, printing in *karamanlidika* continued in Greece for the benefit of the sizeable number of Greeks who were transplanted to Greece in the early 1920s but had no knowledge of the language. Once, when browsing in a bookshop in Salonica, I picked up a copy of what may well be the last publication ever to be printed in *karamanlidika*. This was a small pamphlet, published in Salonica in 1929 and entitled *Aziz Alexiosun ve cümle Azizlerin ve Mahşer Divanının Nakliyetleri ve Cana faydalı Nasıhatlar Iakov on iki Evlatları ile* (St Alexios and all the Saints and the Last Judgement; traditions and advices useful to the soul; Jacob and his 12 sons). This is one of my treasured possessions, not because it has any particular monetary value, but because, while one may sometimes be in a position to possess a copy of the first book printed in a given language, it is rare indeed to be able to say that one possesses a copy of what is probably the last book printed in a language or a form of a language. I found a rich cache of Bibles and religious texts in *karamanlidika* in the library of the British and Foreign Bible Society, together with much material on the printing of biblical texts in Turkish in Greek characters in the Society's annual reports and in the archive.

The library and archive was housed at that time in the Victorian splendour of Bible House in Victoria Street in the City. The Society vacated Bible House many years ago when the library and archive were moved to Cambridge University Library. Sadly, Bible House has now ended up in the hands of the Scientologists. On the basis of the Bible House archive, which I was one of the first outsiders to consult, I published a number of pedantic articles on the publication and distribution of Bible texts in 'Greco-Turkish', as the form of the language was known to the Bible Society. I also made a record of the inscriptions in *karamanlidika* (the easier ones I subsequently published with the help of some of my graduate students) to be found in the courtyard of the church of the Zoodokhos Pigi (life-receiving source), situated just outside the Byzantine land walls of Istanbul near the Silivri Kapı. This entailed not only photographing them but recording the inscriptions by hand. This was painstaking and, in the winter, rather chilly work and Mary Jo and I were grateful for the invitations to the hut of the gravediggers in the nearby Muslim cemetery for a glass of tea.

In these articles I was careful to avoid taking any position on the ethnic origins of the *karamanlides*, whether they were, as Greek scholars insist, Turkicised Greeks, or, as their Turkish counterparts maintain, Hellenised Turks. In one of these articles I wrote that the question of the origin of the *karamanlı* Christians was a matter of controversy and was likely to remain so:

> Greek scholars incline to the view that the *karamanlides* were of Greek descent and adopted Turkish as their vernacular, either by force or as a result of their isolation from the Greek-speaking Orthodox Christians of the coastal regions.

Turkish scholars, on the other hand, look on them as 'the descendants of Turks who had migrated to Byzantine territories before the conquest or had served as mercenaries in the Byzantine armies and who had adopted the religion but not the language of their new rulers'. That seemed to me at the time, some 50 years ago, and indeed seems to me now, a relatively unobjectionable statement, not of opinion, but of fact.

Nonetheless, shortly after the publication of my study an anonymous article appeared in *Prosphygikos Kosmos* (*Refugee World*). This was a newspaper that was still published in Greece in the 1960s for the refugees from Anatolia and their descendants. The article detected a sinister parallel between my supposed view of the origins of the *karamanlides* and those of the Yugoslav Communist Party newspaper, *Borba*, which was of the firm opinion that they were of Turkish origin. At first sight it was not easy to see why the Yugoslavs should have felt the need to take a position over the issue. But the ethnic origin of these Turkish-speaking Christians was of concern to the Yugoslavs as a consequence of territorial claims to 'Aegean' Macedonia, that extensive area of northern Greece, Salonica included, that Macedonian nationalists claimed belonged by right to Yugoslav Macedonia. The more the Greek presence in the region could be played down, the stronger the Macedonian territorial claim might appear, hence the insistence that the *karamanlides* were of Turkish ethnic origin. Many of the Turkish-speakers caught up in the population exchange of the 1920s had been settled in Greek Macedonia. Some were settled in Slav-speaking regions and acquired in their new homeland a knowledge not of Greek but of the dialect of their Slavophone neighbours. This was not the last time that issues of Macedonian ethnicity were to impinge on my work.

Another undertaking to which I devoted many pleasant hours in the North Library of the old British Museum Library was the reconstruction of the extraordinary collection of pre-revolutionary Greek printed books built up by the eccentric Frederick North, the fifth Earl of Guilford, for his beloved Ionian Academy in Corfu, in the years after the notionally independent state of the Ionian Islands came under British protection in 1815. Guilford was given to dressing in what he deemed to be ancient Greek attire and had secretly converted to Orthodox Christianity. He spent lavishly. Andreas Papadopoulos Vretos, appointed librarian by Guilford, estimated the number of books in the library printed in Greek for a specifically Greek readership at about 600, a sizeable proportion of all the books aimed at such an audience in that period. Guilford intended this collection and other books from his vast personal library to stay on Corfu and go to the Ionian Academy, the first university to be established on Greek soil, on his death in 1827. But greedy relatives, seemingly bent on recouping the considerable fortune spent by Guilford in furthering Greek education in the Ionian Islands, contested his will.

As a consequence, the modern Greek books, one of the richest collections anywhere, were shipped to London. Papadopoulos Vretos cites an anecdote told him by one George Papanikolas to illustrate the cupidity of Guilford's relatives. Papanikolas had been brought to England by Guilford to study navigation and, after his death, had sought the wherewithal to return to Greece from Guilford's cousin and heir, the Reverend Lord Francis North. North is reported to have dismissed this not unreasonable request in the following terms: 'If my cousin was mad enough to spend his money on you Greeks, I am not. Go in peace, for you Greeks have "eaten" enough of the money of Count Frederick Guilford.' The Greek books were sold in London in 1835 and were described in the sale catalogue as 'the most Extensive Assemblage of Modern Greek Books ever submitted to Public Sale'. No one had possessed more opportunities of 'forming the best Collection of Modern Greek books, and no one ever availed himself of his opportunities with more zeal, ardour or liberality than the late Earl of Guilford'. This 'matchless library', consisting of 627 volumes, was bought by the British Museum for £137 11s.

The survival of the original accession slips from the 1830s made it easier to reconstruct the library and a proper catalogue of the collection has recently been prepared by Chris Michaelides, who is in charge of modern Greek books at the British Library. I have always remained an agnostic on the issue of the return of the 'Elgin' marbles, adopting a vicar of Bray-like position that, were I Greek, I should want to see them returned to Athens but, as I am not, I am happy to have them easily accessible in London. I was always fearful, however, that Melina Mercouri, the larger-than-life actress, PASOK's minister of culture in the 1980s and a passionate advocate of the return of the Elgin marbles, would find out about the Guilford books, which were removed from Greece in circumstances more scandalous than Elgin's acquisition of the Parthenon marbles, and seek their return as well.

The archives of the various missionary societies proved a valuable, and up to that time scarcely exploited, source for the history of the Greeks in modern times. I was particularly pleased to learn a few years ago that Athanasios of Smyrna, of whose life and painful death in Smyrna in 1819 I had written in *The Eastern Churches Review*, has been incorporated in the canon of Orthodox 'neo-martyrs', that is to say of martyrs for the faith in modern times. At much the same time I also wrote, with a quite unnecessary degree of pedantry, a long article in part relating to the attempt made in 1788 to secure a post in Oxford for Adamantios Korais, subsequently to emerge as the intellectual mentor of the Greek national movement in the late eighteenth and early nineteenth centuries which culminated in the outbreak of the war for independence in 1821.

Korais' French patron, the classical scholar D'Ansse de Villoison, wrote in 1788 to the Reverend Thomas Burgess, a fellow of Corpus Christi College, and subsequently, as Bishop of St David's, the founder of St David's, Lampeter, to ask whether a position might be found for a young Greek who was a classical scholar of quite exceptional brilliance. No post was forthcoming for him. It was hardly to be expected that the indolent and port-sodden backwater that was Oxford in the eighteenth century, so well described by Edward Gibbon in his memoirs, would open its doors to a foreigner, however learned. And so, in that same year, 1788, Korais moved not to Oxford but to Paris where he was to live until his death in 1833. He thus experienced at firsthand the turbulent years of the French Revolution and the revolutionary and Napoleonic wars, an experience that was to have a profound influence on him, although he was scarcely a political radical.

It is tempting to speculate how Korais' career and thinking might have evolved had the dons at Oxford been more open-minded and had Koraes spent his career sequestered among the dreaming, albeit somnolent, spires of Oxford rather than in the turmoil of revolutionary and Napoleonic Paris. Might his interests have been entirely devoted to classical scholarship rather than in trying to instil a sense of national identity into his fellow countrymen under the Turkish yoke, an awareness that the Greeks were the heirs to an intellectual inheritance that was universally revered in the wider European and North American world? It is sometimes forgotten that Koraes was among the *koryphaioi*, the most outstanding, of the classical philologists in the Europe of his day. Richard Porson, the great Cambridge scholar, had nothing but contempt for most of his contemporaries but had the highest respect for Korais' abilities as a textual critic. However, if room could not be found for Korais in Oxford, it is pleasant nonetheless to record that what appears to be his first publication in the field of classical studies, the *Observationes in Hippocratem*, was published by Burgess in Oxford in 1792.

I spent the academic years 1964/5 and 1965/6 ploughing these and other more or less obscure furrows in London where I worked under the (somewhat notional, but then that was my own fault) supervision of Cyril Mango, the Koraes Professor at King's College, London. Mango had an extraordinary knowledge of all aspects of Byzantine civilisation and was a highly productive scholar. He was very knowledgeable, too, about post-Byzantine Greek culture. He was born in Istanbul to a Greek father, ultimately of Chiot origin, and a Russian mother. In the registers compiled by the Turkish authorities in the implementation of the notorious 1942 Varlık Vergisi (capital tax), aimed principally at fleecing non-Muslim minorities, A.A. Mango, Cyril's father, is described as a Chiot Christian and British subject. The Constantinopolitan Greek author, Aikaterini Laskaridou (Arria Claudia), has left a picture of the polyglot and polymathic '*mikroskopikos gentleman*', Cyril, still a schoolboy, putting aside his toy soldiers and acting instead as mentor and guide to visiting Byzantinists.

To fund research trips I took to acting as a courier for Wings Air Tours to Greece and Turkey. The deal was that I would accompany their tours for a fortnight and would have a further fortnight in Greece which I could devote to my own research. I found this work congenial despite the fact that it entailed wrestling with hotels and travel agencies at a time when tourism in Greece, and still more so in Turkey, was more or less in its infancy. Wings' parties were for the most part excellent company, and frequently a great deal more knowledgeable than I was about the ancient sites that we visited. At the time, however, both Greece and Turkey had a strict rule that only local guides should be hired, which enabled me to cover up my ignorance. Wings' clients were also generous dispensers of tips, which were usually more or less enough to keep me for my fortnight of research. Perhaps they realised that, far from going along with the (albeit petty) scams which a few of Wings' local agents sought to perpetrate (particularly on the island of Corfu as I recall) and from which I would myself have marginally profited, I vigorously resisted these. But many of Wings' clients shared what was, from my point of view, a disastrous interest, indeed almost obsession, with the botany of the Mediterranean. I could never answer the questions that were continually asked about wild flowers, being almost completely ignorant of the flora of the British isles, let alone those of Greece. Another drawback was that there seemed to be an inflexible rule that every party of 40 or so would contain one or two troublemakers, who were unprepared for the then hazards of Levantine travel, which the rest of the group put up with cheerfully enough.

These hazards could be considerable. On one tour I was due to meet the group in Corfu as they arrived by plane from London. But Corfu airport at that time was a primitive affair, which airline pilots regularly threatened to boycott as too hazardous. On the night in question a terrific storm brewed up. This blew out some of the oil flares that at that time were used to light up the runway, despite the valiant efforts of the man whose job it was to run up and down re-lighting the lamps as they blew out. This was in the autumn of 1966! Not surprisingly, the pilot on this occasion decided to give Corfu a miss and to fly on to Athens. I was able to fly to Athens only the next morning to encounter a situation of utter chaos, with the party scattered around different hotels up and down the coast in the vicinity of the airport.

On another occasion, the tour included Bursa, having made the short flight from Istanbul in a clapped out Türk Hava Yolları Dakota, in which few of the seats were equipped with seat belts. We were staying at the rather stylish Çelik Palas hotel, which had its own *hamam*, or Turkish bath, fed by hot springs. Although the hotel was relatively luxurious, the food that was served to our party was very ordinary, whereas that fed to Turkish guests looked really rather good. So after dinner I spoke to the manager in the hope that our remaining meals might improve. He was busy entertaining the police chief and other members of the local equivalent of the 'good ol' boys' in the bar. I duly put my complaint to him. 'I quite understand,' he replied, 'I have a European wife too.' Needless to say, there was no significant improvement in the food. On yet another occasion, being, as a good courier, the last to board, I was bumped up to first class on a British European Airways flight from Athens to Istanbul. The only other passenger in first class was a Queen's Messenger, in charge of the diplomatic bags, who seemed a little the worse for wear after the flight out from London. I, too, made the most of my upgrade and imbibed a rather large amount of champagne on a flight lasting barely an hour. Fortunately the alcohol did not have time to take effect before I had safely checked everyone in to the Pera Palace hotel in Istanbul, a hotel of great character and historical interest that had clearly seen better days. It has recently been restored to its former splendour.

On one of these tours, having a free afternoon, I made a trip to Halki (Heybeli), one of the Princes' Islands at the entrance to the Bosphorus, to visit the Greek Theological College, or Greek Monk School (Rum Ruhban Okulu) as it was known in Turkish. This was to be closed by the Turkish authorities in the early 1970s and has since been the focus of regular complaints by those protesting at restraints on religious freedom for minorities in Turkey. There I met with the Ecumenical Patriarch, Athinagoras, a very tall man who hugged me so tightly that I was left gasping for breath. On another of my trips to Istanbul I attended a liturgy sung at the Turkish Orthodox Patriarchate (Türk Ortodoks Patrikhanesi) in Galata. This was headed by the self-styled Turkish Orthodox Patriarch, Papa Eftim (known successively as Karahisaridis, Hisaroğlu and Erenerol, each version of his name more 'Turkish' than its precursor). By then an old man, at the time of the Greek–Turkish war in the early 1920s Eftim had caused something of a stir by establishing a Turkish Orthodox Church which declared allegiance to the Turkish nationalists under Mustafa Kemal, subsequently Atatürk, and sought to rally the Turkish-speaking Greeks to the Turkish cause in the hope, forlorn as it turned out, that they would be exempted from the exchange of populations and thus be able to remain in their ancestral homes in Asia Minor. Papa Eftim had little success in winning adherents to his breakaway church but the Turkish authorities tolerated, and at times encouraged, him as a means of putting pressure on the Ecumenical Patriarchate in the Phanar. He was able to seize two or three Orthodox churches in Galata, with official connivance. When I attended a service at the 'Turkish Orthodox Patriarchate' in the mid-1960s there was virtually no one in the congregation. Eftim had two sons, and when he died in 1968, one of these, Turgut, succeeded his father as 'Patriarch'. Turgut was in turn succeeded by his younger brother, Selçuk. Just as the Romanians used to joke that communism in Romania was not a case of socialism in one country but rather of socialism in one family, so Papa Eftim's breakaway church was very much a family affair.

What happened after the death of Selçuk is not clear, although Eftim had a wife, an unusual appendage for an Orthodox hierarch, and a granddaughter, who pops up from time to time at nationalist demonstrations. She was alleged to have been implicated in the mysterious Ergenekon affair, as the purported plotters of a coup supposedly met in the Panagia Kafatiani, one of the 'Turkish Orthodox' churches in Galata. One Sunday morning in 2001, I headed for the Turkish Orthodox Patriarchate to see what, if anything, survived of the movement which at the time of its foundation had occasioned great interest. Indeed, an American journalist, Clair Price, in the early 1920s made the hopelessly erroneous prediction that 'Papa Eftim Efendi' might yet develop into 'a phase of the new Turkey more important for Christendom than Kemal [Atatürk] himself'.

There is, or at least was, a law in Turkey permitting only the Ecumenical Patriarch (and presumably also Eftim, his sons and heirs), together with the Armenian Patriarch among the Christian clergy, to sport a full beard. When I emerged from the diminutive underground railway that links the bottom of İstiklâl Caddesi with Karaköy I was intrigued to find a young priest with such a flowing beard heading in the direction of the Eftim's 'Patriarchate'. I naturally assumed he was making for the same destination but two or three hundred yards short of Eftim's relatively lavish compound he disappeared into a building which turned out to house on an upper floor a chapel for the Russian community in Istanbul. In the Eftim Patriarchate, however, there was no sign of life and the doors remained firmly locked at what should have been the time of the liturgy.

On yet another Wings trip, I had to shepherd my group from Ayvalık in Turkey to the island of Mytilini in Greece, a short journey by caique. This was a rather more complicated undertaking in the mid-1960s, when there was little traffic between the Greek islands and the Turkish mainland than it would be today. Our departure was delayed and we arrived in the harbour of Mytilini well after nightfall. The Turkish fisherman taking our party had no navigation lights on his boat and the harbour master proceeded to give him a hard time. I interceded on the fisherman's behalf and he was allowed to return to Ayvalık the next morning without penalty. A year or two later, Mary Jo and I returned under our own steam to Ayvalık, which before the exchange of populations had been an almost entirely Greek community. Strolling along the harbour front we were recognised by my fisherman friend who was most insistent that we stay with him. We had a most enjoyable visit, but our host took me aside one day to observe that, although good looking, Mary Jo, who had suffered from dysentery in the course of the nine months that we were spending in Greece, needed to be fattened up.

In the course of our exploration of the delightful surroundings of Ayvalık we took a boat out to the islands that the Greeks call Moschonisia and were surprised to hear the young boatmen talking in Greek. They would have been the grandchildren of Greek-speaking Muslims from Greece, particularly from Crete, who were exchanged for the Greeks of Asia Minor, many of them Turkish-speaking, in the early 1920s. They continued, and continue, to speak Greek in a number of communities in western Asia Minor. Pleasant although our stay in Ayvalık was, I think it was probably there that I contracted scarlet fever, although this did not manifest itself until a few days later on the island of Halki/Heybeli near Istanbul. I was really quite ill and was somewhat alarmed when the Greek widow with whom we were staying got out an icon which had apparently not sufficed to save her husband when he was dying a few years previously. We summoned a doctor who misdiagnosed the problem but whose dose of penicillin seemingly did the trick. It was in the immediate aftermath of the Six Day War and, before giving me the jab, the doctor asked me whose side I was on. Although feeling distinctly under par I fortunately had the presence of mind to say Israel as he was poised with his syringe. I gave the right answer in the circumstances, for he was Jewish. It was only some time later when we had returned to the UK that a doctor uncle noticed that my skin was peeling and retrospectively diagnosed scarlet fever.

During one of my early visits to Athens to conduct research I called on A.A. Pallis, who had been raised in Liverpool, home in the second half of the nineteenth and early twentieth century to a prosperous Greek community. The wealth of this community is strikingly illustrated by the imposing but now somewhat decayed church, built in the neo-Byzantine style, of St Nicholas, the patron saint of seafarers. Pallis was the Eton-educated son of Alexander Pallis, the Liverpudlian demoticist, whose translation (printed in Liverpool) of the Gospels into demotic, or spoken, Greek at the beginning of the last century had prompted rioting, and some deaths, in Athens by theology students and others who looked on the translation as blasphemous. Translations into the modern language of the New Testament may be authorised only by the Church of Greece and the Great Church of Christ (the Ecumenical Patriarchate) in Constantinople. There is still an article in the most recent Greek constitution (1976) stating that the Septuagint text of the

Old Testament shall be unaltered. The younger Pallis had had a distinguished career and had been the Greek High Commissioner in Constantinople after World War I, in which capacity he had been closely involved in the Exchange of Populations between Greece and Turkey. His autobiography, *Xenitemenoi Ellines* (Greeks living abroad) (1954), affords a fascinating insight into the way in which some of the more prosperous Greeks, many of them originating from the island of Chios, the *englezochiotes* as they were known, living in nineteenth and early twentieth-century Britain had become rapidly assimilated, as a result of their public school education, into the English upper-middle classes.[2] I wanted in particular to talk about Pallis' work with the Greek refugees but he seemed to prefer to talk about the way in which the 'blacks' were ruining the England that he remembered from his youth.

We spent the academic year 1966/7 in Greece at the British School at Athens, which at times has designated itself as the British School of Archaeology. This was a year that was to see an uncovenanted shift in my academic interests from somewhat arcane aspects of the modern history of the Greeks to contemporary politics. Mary Jo was half-way through her librarianship course at University College and we were able to negotiate a financially advantageous deal whereby she worked in the School's library in return for free board and lodging for the two of us. Mary Jo was the first trained librarian, or at least half-trained, for she had yet to complete her course, to have been employed by the School. Sadly, her presence was perceived as a threat to the culture of wilful amateurishness in library matters that prevailed at the time. By a curious coincidence, some 40 years later the deputy librarian of the American School of Classical Studies, which is situated next door to the British School, came from a very small and isolated town in northern California, which is the nearest community to the equally isolated and small town in which Mary Jo grew up in southern-eastern Oregon. Both communities are situated on the western edge of the Great Basin Desert, the largest in the United States.

I cannot say that we shared the sentiments of the future diplomat, Pierson Dixon, who wrote that, on graduating from Cambridge, he had arrived in Athens and driven to the School where he was to spend the academic year 1927/8 and had 'immediately hated' the 'clean bare corridors and atmosphere heavy with academicism'. During his time in Athens, Dixon met his future wife, the half-Greek Ismene, the daughter of S.C. Atchley, Oriental Secretary at the British Legation. This gave him, during his Foreign Office career, a perhaps rather more sympathetic view of Greek aspirations and a less negative view of Greek politicians than that held by some of his colleagues.

Compton Mackenzie has drawn an evocative picture of the School as he found it in 1915:

> the photographs upon the walls of temples, theatres and mountains: the faded groups of student archaeologists in old-fashioned straw hats, who in bygone years had sojourned here for a while and hence sallied forth to excavate some classic site; the library of Hellenic scholarship and research; the long table in the deserted dining room; the subtle air of learning which permeated the whole place with a faint dusty perfume.

His description will strike a nostalgic chord with those familiar with the establishment in the later twentieth century. It was one that certainly held good when Mary Jo and I first spent time at the School during the academic year 1966/7 some 50 years after Mackenzie's encounter with it, and, indeed, his picture in substantial measure held good when I was Visiting Fellow at the School for three months in early 2002. Mackenzie headed British intelligence in Athens during World War I and actually lived for a time in the hostel of the School, possessing the only spare key to the School's grounds. The Assistant Director, F.W. Hasluck, and his wife, Margaret Hardie, a former Student, whose marriage had seriously upset the old guard of the School, worked for the euphemistically named Passport Control Office, the traditional cover for the recently founded Secret Intelligence Service (MI6), and maintained at the School its meticulously organised card index of suspicious characters.

Mackenzie gives the impression of being unable to resist embroidering his tales of derring-do in the interest of a good story, and his stories really are extremely entertaining. He tells how A.J.B. Wace, the School's director, who was likewise engaged in intelligence work on behalf of MI6, invited him to lunch every day in the director's house. Mackenzie records that there were 'few things that I remember with such pleasure as that Mess, which provided every day an opportunity to slip back out of the war into a civilized existence'. In 1986, I was invited to give a lecture on the School and its relation to the modern history of Greece at a conference held in Athens to mark the centenary of its foundation. I mentioned that Wace had worked for British intelligence in both world wars. This was no secret and would have been apparent to anyone who had worked on the relevant papers in the Public Record Office or who had read Mackenzie's published account of his Athenian heroics. But Wace's daughter, Lisa French, herself later to became director of the School, subsequently told me that, when she heard what I had to say in my lecture about her father's wartime connections with British intelligence, her first thought had been that I had scuppered her chances of following in his footsteps, given the widespread, if unjustified, credence that exists in Greece in the sinister machinations of an omniscient and omnicompetent British 'Intelligence Service'. I had assumed that Wace's wartime activities were common knowledge. As it transpired, my remarks did not prevent his daughter becoming director, as she did in 1989.

Among Mackenzie's numerous, and not infrequently far-fetched, anecdotes is one which deserves retelling. It concerns a Captain Potts of the Royal Naval Volunteer Reserve, a 'great genial Punch of a man' of immense physical strength who once, when crossing an Athenian street, had with one arm pushed a horse back on its haunches to stop a hackney carriage from running into him. Potts visited Mackenzie one evening at the School, where he was laid up with one of his periodic bouts of gout. On leaving he had unwisely refused Mackenzie's offer of a candle to light his way downstairs. But Potts's electric torch failed him and he was left in pitch darkness. Primed to expect the worst in the dubious world of intrigue in which Mackenzie moved, he was alarmed to see the outline of a lurking form against the glimmer of light coming in through the front door.

'"Look here", said Potts, "if you don't say who you are, it will be the worse for you..." The sinister form neither spoke nor moved.' So Potts, as Mackenzie relates,

> determined not to take any risk of getting a knife under his ribs and thinking that it behoved him to take precautions on behalf of me lying upstairs with a game leg, drew back a mighty fist to a massive shoulder, and then drove it with all his force below the jaw of the taciturn assassin. That the jaw of the assassin, which was of Parian marble, did not completely smash Potts' knuckles, was due to its owner being a bust on a pedestal, and so less stable than a life-size statue. Still, even as it was, the assassin made a pretty mess of Potts's hand.

This was, of course, the Roman portrait bust that graced, and continues to grace, the entrance hall of the School. There is a slight chip in the sinister form's beard. Could this have been the result of its encounter with Potts's fist?

Many will be familiar with Mackenzie's extraordinary stories of intrigue and skulduggery in Athens and elsewhere during World War I in the service of British intelligence, the notorious 'Intelligence Service'. From time to time I myself have been credited with working for it, notably by Lady Amalia Fleming, the Greek-born widow of the discoverer of penicillin and a stalwart of the resistance to the Colonels. She was convinced that I had been charged with infiltrating the anti-Colonels' movement in the UK during the late 1960s and early 1970s. But how does one prove a negative? Mackenzie's tales are certainly hugely entertaining, but many, by their nature, are incapable of independent verification. There is one anecdote, however, which, had I the time, I might be able to try to verify. When some frozen, and presumably rotting, meat carcasses had been thrown overboard from a troopship near Athens, Mackenzie claimed that a Royalist, anti-Venizelist newspaper had declared these to be headless victims of the 'British Secret Police'. Presumably a search of the newspapers of the time would reveal whether or not this particular anecdote is true.

It is not immediately apparent that Mackenzie's tireless intrigues were ultimately of much value to the cause of the Entente Powers, Britain and France. They may, indeed, have been counter-productive as is suggested by the story, not necessarily apocryphal, recorded in the unpublished memoir of a former director of the British School, J.M. Cook, about one of Mackenzie's arch-rivals, Baron Schenck. In Mackenzie's words, Schenck resembled 'a kind of gigantic spider [...] spinning webs of marvellous intricacy' as he directed propaganda from the German Archaeological Institute in Athens at a time when Greece was still a neutral country. When, after Greece had entered the war on the side of the Entente Powers, Schenck was obliged to leave Athens, his parting words to a group of well-wishers who had come to see him off were apparently: 'I leave the cause of the Central Powers in the best possible hands – those of my dear friend Mr. Compton Mackenzie.' There was also a major feud between Mackenzie and the American minister in Athens, the strait-laced Garrett Droppers, who reported to Robert Lansing, the US secretary of state, that Mackenzie had organised not an intelligence agency but rather a band of 'worthless scoundrels who use their power for infamy'. He was to be seen

> almost every night at some place of entertainment surrounded by his mistresses [note the plural] and often in a state of exhilaration [by which he presumably meant intoxication], or at one of the well-known theatres of Athens with his harlots, occupying what was known as the British Legation box.

Small wonder that when the Special Operations Executive was taking its first hesitant steps in Greece in 1940 in preparing for post-occupation mayhem it begged London not to send out another would-be Compton Mackenzie.

Compton Mackenzie wrote four books on his intelligence activities in Greece during World War I, for much of which Greece was neutral. For publishing one of these, *Greek Memories*, he was charged in 1932 with breaching the draconian provisions of the Official Secrets Act. Valentine Vivian, SIS's head of counter-intelligence, complained of 'flagrant transgressions' which would set a 'pernicious example' to others in the service who might be tempted to follow in Mackenzie's footsteps. The book was withdrawn and issued in an amended form. The original, unexpurgated edition became a collector's item and very expensive. However, an American publisher issued a reprint a few years ago of the unexpurgated version with the offending passages helpfully highlighted. On perusing these it is difficult to believe that Mackenzie was letting much out of the bag in the book's initial recension, but then intelligence services tend to be hypersensitive in matters of security. The trial and the £100 fine that was imposed on the author inevitably served only to enhance the reputation (and finances) of Mackenzie, who wreaked his revenge on the authorities by penning a novel, *Water on the Brain* (1933), in which he mercilessly satirised his erstwhile masters in British intelligence.

Mackenzie, novelist, teller of tall tales, wartime *praktoras*, or intelligence agent, and, by his own account, someone once considered for the directorship of M16, towards the end of his life became the grand old man of Scottish letters. At school in Edinburgh in the 1950s I did once meet the great man, by then well into his seventies, but, unfortunately, my interest in the Greek world had not at that time developed and I thus missed the chance of hearing Mackenzie's reminiscences of his Athenian intrigues and escapades at firsthand. All I remember of that distant encounter was that he claimed to have had total recall since the age of two. This presumably accounts for the vivid detail, including verbatim conversations, in his books.

Whenever archaeologists at the School complained of obtuseness on the part of the Greek Archaeological Service, which no doubt existed, and may still do, I would suggest that they reversed the situation and consider how their British *philotimo* (sense of pride) would be offended if Greek and other foreign archaeological schools were digging up Stonehenge, the Globe Theatre, or the Roman Wall (all modest indeed when compared to the archaeological heritage of ancient Greece), but they seemed not to get the point. Moreover, the School has not always been tactful in its relations with the host country. David Wallace, who was a Student at the School on the eve of World War II, recalled hearing a British ambassador assure a gathering at the School of several hundred distinguished Athenians that, in his opinion, 'the spirit of Ancient Greece had long since fled from the mountains of Greece and had taken refuge in Oxford and Cambridge'. It would appear that this memorable insult was uttered by Sir Sydney Waterlow, the minister in Athens between 1933 and 1939 and no mean classicist himself.

The director during our stay in 1966–7, A.H.S. Megaw, was a gentlemanly though distant individual and seldom impinged on the life of students. It was to him that I owed an introduction to Sir Harry Luke (Lukach), a couple of years before he died at the age of 85. A former member of the Colonial service, he was the prolific author of books of Levantine interest and was a living link with the Ottoman past. We had many more dealings with the School's secretary, Jane Rabnett, than with the director. A devout Catholic, she was disconcerted when the Vatican Council decreed that Catholics were no longer obliged to eat fish on Fridays. For a time there was confusion in the School's catering arrangements, until the sensible decision was taken to continue to serve fish on that day of the week. Her general outlook on life was epitomised by her reaction to a request to find a place on an archaeological dig for an undergraduate. By the time it was received all the places for volunteers for the summer digging season had been filled. But Jane insisted that, despite this, an effort should be made to slot him in. After all, he was the son of a bishop. One morning in May 1967, almost exactly a month after the Colonels had seized power in a coup, Jane came into the Finlay Library to announce that King Constantine had produced a male heir. 'I do hope this will do some good,' she remarked *à propos* the fraught political situation.

Most of those at the School in 1966/7 were prehistoric archaeologists, a specialism which left its mark on the general atmosphere, although as individuals they were pleasant enough. Life was made distinctly less pleasant than it might have been by the malevolent presence of the assistant director, Mervyn Popham, about whose role in Cyprus during the EOKA struggle dark rumours circulated. According to the Dictionary of National Biography he had some grim duties on the island, while he suffered from 'intermittent periods of dark depression'. Part of his problem was that he was older, almost 40, than he should have been for what was a relatively junior post, and this may have been one of the things that seem to have embittered him. His misanthropic and misogynistic persona made Mary Jo's work as a librarian unnecessarily difficult, as he was her immediate boss.

Another trial in the somewhat claustrophobic and inward-looking School was the presence for a good part of the winter of Peter Levi. At that time still a Jesuit, he was wintering in Athens allegedly for health reasons, although this did not prevent him from puffing away on fat and pungent cigars in the common room. He was undoubtedly a clever man, and Mary Jo assures me that he was an excellent poet, but his snobbery, name-dropping (he was forever rattling on about his friendship with the poet George Seferis) and general pseudery were particular irritants in the necessarily rather restricted life of the School. The atmosphere was that of an overmanned lighthouse which called for care not to rub people up the wrong way. Levi's sycophancy towards Seferis knew no bounds. In his autobiographical *The Hill of Kronos* (1980) he wrote that 'I venerated him then as an immensely great poet; later I came to love him as a friend, almost as a father, and to respect and admire him more than I can express.' His adulation was reflected in such ludicrous *aperçus* as 'there is a sense in which he virtually invented modern Greek, both in prose and in verse', a fatuous assertion coming from the pen of someone who came within an ace of being appointed lecturer in modern Greek at Oxford in the early 1980s.

One of Levi's more bizarre claims was once to have eaten a 'particularly delicious' (a characteristic Leviism) fig from a box given to Seferis by Mr Eugenides, the Smyrna merchant 'unshaven, with a pocket full of currants/C.i.f. London: documents at sight'. This was accompanied by a pained note begging Seferis to intercede with T.S. Eliot to stop writing about him as he had done in *The Waste Land*. It appears that Eliot had a real-life Eugenides in mind but he had died in 1954. This may have been Eugene Eugenides, for many years a business partner of John Langdon Rees, a member of a well-known Levantine mercantile dynasty. But Levi, who believed the case of Mr Eugenides to be a parable of Anglo-Hellenic relations at the time, was never someone to allow the facts to stand in the way of a good story, or what he believed to be a good story, which was not always the same thing. While in Athens, Levi had a 'mad flirtation' with Miranda Rothschild, a member of the banking family. Nicholas Shakespeare in his life of Bruce Chatwin tells of Rothschild sitting in Floca's, the fashionable Athenian *zakharoplasteion*, 'plunging her cake into a glass of icy water' and looking up and seeing a 'beautiful-looking Jesuit, like an icon, thin as hell', with whom she fell platonically head over heels in love.

Another irritating aspect of life at the School was that we sat in order of seniority when taking meals. Necessarily, we found ourselves very low in the pecking order (and appear to have been virtually alone among those at the School not to be invited to a reception at the British Embassy). We put up with these tiresome eating arrangements on the assumption that this was a convention that had existed from time immemorial. Only when Helen Waterhouse's history was published to mark the centennial of the School in 1986 did we learn that this was in fact an 'invented tradition' of recent origin. In earlier times, the assistant director or senior student sat at the head of the table, which was reasonable enough, and everyone else sat in no particular order. Our time at the School appears to have coincided with the dying days of this annoying insistence on sitting in rank order, a practice that seems to have irritated others as well as ourselves. For Waterhouse notes that the visiting fellow in 1968, two years after our sojourn, recorded that 'after consultation [...] it was agreed that formality as to dress, processing in and out and seating positions should be relaxed for lunch'. They were, however, to continue for a time at least, for dinner.

In the spring of 1967, J.D. Beazley, the great expert on ancient vase painting, visited the School, where he had been a Student in 1907, on what was almost certainly his last visit to Greece. He died three years later at the age of 85. We had temporarily to vacate our room to make way for the elderly, bird-like figure, who was accompanied by a battleaxe of a wife. We did not particularly mind giving up our room for the great man. But we, and others, were more than mildly inconvenienced by the way in which Lady Beazley stood guard over the communal facilities while her husband engaged in his protracted morning ablutions uninterrupted. These took an unconscionably long time. Lady Beazley's dragon-like behaviour while at the School was in keeping with her reputation in Oxford. Russell Meiggs, the Balliol classicist, has recorded that a knock at the door of the Beazley residence would be followed by the opening of a shutter: 'one faced a glittering eye, before entry was allowed; and the door was not always opened'.

However, deliverance was at hand from the petty irritations of life at the School, and particularly from the dread prospect of having to play charades at Christmas. This was in the form of the incredibly cheap tickets, provided you were under 26, offered by Türk Hava Yolları on their largely empty flights between Athens and Istanbul. On one of these visits to Turkey, we were the only visitors to Troy on a brilliantly sunny winter's day. On the same trip, we also tried to visit Imvros, one of the two Turkish islands straddling the entrance to the Dardanelles. Imvros in the early 1960s still had a majority Greek population. In 1960 some 5,500 Greeks lived on the island, down from the 9,500 recorded in 1912. The Turkish population in the same year, 1960, numbered barely 300. By the mid-1960s, however, pressures on the ethnic Greek islanders, which were to lead to the virtual extinction of the community, were at their height. Recurrent crises on Cyprus had led to reprisals against the Greek inhabitants of the island and the neighbouring island of Tenedos. In 1964, Greek language schools were closed, so that many islanders with families took the road to exile. In 1970, the islands were officially renamed Gökçeada and Bozcaada: Greek village names were changed, so that Schinoudi became Dereköy and Glyky, the seat of the Greek metropolitan, became Eski Bademli. Agricultural land was expropriated, while the establishment of an agricultural open prison gave rise to many problems. Ethnic Turkish settlers from various parts of Turkey were settled in large numbers. By 1990, the Greek population of Imvros was down to 300, while there were over 7,000 Turks on the island.

In 1967, the year in which we tried to visit Imvros and Tenedos, special permission was still needed to visit the islands, and the Turkish authorities clearly had a policy of discouraging visitors. We met with the *valı* of Çanakkale in a vain attempt to gain the necessary authorisation. He offered us coffee and was charm itself but it was clear that no amount of pleading was going to get him to change his mind. It was emphasised that only if we had relatives on the island would permission be granted. Some 40 years later, however, Mary Jo and I were able, in June 2008, to visit Imvros in quite other circumstances.

The restrictions on visiting the islands had been rescinded in the 1990s and our trip was arranged by a former graduate student of mine, Alexis Alexandris, who was by then Greek consul-general in Istanbul and an authority on the sad fate of the Greek minority in the Turkish Republic, which had been the subject of his doctoral thesis. The trip was fascinating, if dispiriting. The Greeks of Imvros are for the most part elderly and number barely 250. Many of the buildings that had housed Greek schools are in ruinous state, although a number of the Greek churches on the island have been beautifully restored. When the Islamist Turkish prime minister, Recep Tayyip Erdoğan, visited the islands not long ago, he was thanked by a prominent member of the Greek community for facilitating these restorations. Erdoğan replied that there was no question of thanking him. He was under a religious obligation to permit the restoration of Christian religious buildings, a welcome restatement of the relatively tolerant mores of the Ottomans. Whether this relatively tolerant attitude towards non-Muslim minorities will survive the draconian crackdown on internal dissent following the attempted military coup of July 2016 remains to be seen. In recent years, hundreds of Imvriots scattered throughout the world have returned to the island to celebrate the feast of the Dormition (Assumption) of the Virgin on 15 August.

The most dramatic event of our time at the British School occurred in April 1967 when we had the unusual experience of living through a military coup d'état. This was a development which both put paid to my hopes of completing my thesis in a timely fashion and led to a significant shift in my research interests. We had arrived in Athens in the autumn of 1966 at a time of endemic crisis in the Greek political system. This had been precipitated by the young King Constantine's ill-advised policy of conniving in the ousting, in what came to be known as the *Iouliana* (the July events) of 1965, of the centrist government of Georgios Papandreou, who had held out the promise of ending the monopoly effectively enjoyed by the right since the 1946–9 civil war and of liberalising an authoritarian political system. This ushered in 18 months of political turmoil which culminated in the April 1967 coup. Carried out by a group of crazed army officers, it ushered in seven years of military rule, at once brutal, anachronistic and absurd. On arriving in Greece, I was not particularly interested in, or knowledgeable about, the volatile state of current politics, and for some months carried on my rather recondite researches largely oblivious to what was going on, often noisily, in the streets outside. Gradually, however, I began to concern myself with what was happening.

This interest was fostered through our friendship with Nikos Oikonomides and his wife, Elisavet Zachariadou, a Byzantinist and Ottomanist respectively.

Both were attached to what was then the *Vasilikon Idryma Erevnon*, the *Royal Research Foundation*, but subsequently became the *Ethniko Idryma Erevnon*, the *National* Research Foundation. They made us aware of the seriousness of the situation and invited us to some meetings of the *Omilos Alexandrou Papanastasiou*, named after a (mildly) radical interwar politician. Under the junta, members of the Papanastasiou Society were to form the nucleus of an important resistance group, *Dimokratiki Amyna* or Democratic Defence. These gatherings were subject to aggressive heckling by ultra-right-wing hooligans. Another boisterous meeting, which reflected the tense atmosphere of the times and which we attended, was described as a gathering of the Cretan Students, Association (some of whom appeared rather elderly). This was addressed in flamboyant style by Andreas Papandreou, who had returned to Greece from a successful academic career in the United States and who had, for a time, been a minister in his father, Georgios' Centre Union government. Andreas was to be the principal bugbear of the junta that was soon to seize power.

Although the political atmosphere was febrile and mildly threatening, it was nonetheless a profound shock to discover on the morning of 21 April 1967 that the army had taken over the country, ostensibly to thwart a non-existent communist conspiracy to seize power.[3] The atmosphere at the School that day was odd. We first learned that something had happened from one of the maids, reinforced by the martial music coming over the radio. Soon a notice went up on the door of the School saying that anyone leaving the School premises would be liable to arrest or being shot. Mary Jo and I took this to be an invitation to make a break for it and we went out into the largely deserted city. Many of the few people on the streets seem to have been engaged in panic buying and there was a run on food in the shops. There were a number of tanks on the streets.

As the atmosphere grew increasingly eerie we returned to the School for lunch. The turnout was much larger than normal and included a rotund clergyman archaeologist, on whom we had never previously set eyes, who proceeded to stuff his pockets with fruit. One student had an American fiancée, but, because she was not actually staying at the School, she was not allowed to take lunch. In the afternoon, a foursome from the British Embassy came up to play tennis on the court shared with the American School of Classical Studies. This seemed to give the lie to the widespread belief in Athens that the coup had been orchestrated by the notorious and purportedly all-powerful British 'Intelligence Service'. But perhaps such a display of nonchalance was intended to provide cover for foul deeds. At the time, and subsequently, I have blithely assured Greek friends that the British could not have been implicated in the 1967 coup, not least because they would scarcely have backed such a trio of buffoons as Colonels Papadopoulos, Makarezos and Pattakos, the masterminds of the putsch. Now I am no longer so sure, following the revelation that, in 1976, the British government was prepared to contemplate a 'surgical coup' to prevent the communists coming to power in Italy. Characteristically, the British Council's contribution to the crisis in Greece was to offer a lecture on sport and the training of character.

On the first night we could hear the sound of guns being fired (in the air, as it subsequently transpired) but the restriction on movement applied only for the day of the coup and thereafter we could move about freely. The attitude to the coup in the School might have been described by Gibbon as one of supine indifference. Indeed, there was a degree of unwholesome rejoicing when Ioannis Kondis, the head of the Archaeological Service, who had a reputation for obstructiveness, was thrown out by the Colonels, as the conspirators soon came to be known, and replaced by Spyridon Marinatos, who had been appointed to the Archaeological Service and to a chair in archaeology at the University of Athens during the pre-war Metaxas dictatorship. His early career is unlikely to have been impeded by the fact that he originated from the same island, Cephalonia, as Metaxas. On the first anniversary of the coup Marinatos was to deliver a spirited panegyric in defence of the 'Revolution of the 21 April 1967' before the Academy of Athens.

The redoubtable Marion Pascoe, who had been a Student at the School in the 1930s, had a rather similar experience of the School during the Metaxas years. Not only did she encounter complete indifference to the Metaxas dictatorship but also the view that it was no more than the Greeks deserved. After the war, she was to marry General Stephanos Saraphis, the wartime military commander of the communist controlled resistance army ELAS whom she had first met when he had been sent into exile on the island of Milos by Metaxas. Not long after the 1967 coup, Joan Hussey, a frumpish and portly Byzantinist who taught at the University of London arrived at the School. She declared herself in favour of the Colonels on the somewhat unlikely ground that young Greek men no longer pinched her bottom. She was at the time preparing her calendar of the papers of George Finlay, the great historian of post-classical Greece, and was permitted to take the papers backwards and forwards to London in a bulging briefcase, which scarcely seemed a sensible way of treating such a valuable archive. This caused difficulties for anyone else, myself included, who wanted to look at the papers.

During our stay in Athens we had a close friend in George Frangos, a Greek–American who was working on a ground-breaking Columbia University thesis about the *Philiki Etairia*, the 'Friendly Society', that had laid the groundwork for the 1821 Greek uprising against the Turks. With George, we started to do what we could to alert the outside world to the wretchedness of the situation after the coup. One might have thought that this would be self-evident, but there were individuals like the one-time left-wing Labour MP, Francis Noel-Baker, who from the outset had been prepared to make excuses for the junta. Ironically, Noel-Baker had been one of the first MPs to question lobbying by fellow MPs on behalf of business interests. A self-styled philhellene, he owned an extensive estate in Euboea and lived in considerable style, with he and his guests dressing for dinner.

His case is an interesting one. As a young member of the Special Operations Executive during World War II, he was one of the relatively few in the organisation to manifest sympathy for the communist-controlled EAM, the National Liberation Front, which was much the largest resistance organisation in occupied Greece, and for its resistance army, ELAS. It should be noted, however, that he did not spend time in occupied Greece and therefore had no firsthand experience of EAM/ELAS rule, which could be harsh. During the period of the junta he became an advocate for the military regime. He made a nuisance of himself, for instance, by accusing the BBC Greek service of lack of impartiality in its coverage of military rule. I remember drawing the attention of Monty Woodhouse, who had commanded the wartime military mission to the Greek resistance and was, during the dictatorship, a Conservative MP, to the apparent inconsistency in Noel-Baker's support for the far Left during the occupation and his support of the far Right during the Colonels' regime. Woodhouse replied that there was no such inconsistency. To protect his property interests in Greece, Noel-Baker in both instances was simply backing what he (mistakenly) thought would be the winning side. After the downfall of the junta in 1974, the local villagers demonstrated against him for offering aid and comfort to the Colonels and there were calls for the expropriation of his property. The British Embassy was in the habit of sending someone down to observe the demonstrations and protect his interests, a move which appeared to me to be an unwarranted intervention in Greece's internal affairs.

When we returned to the UK in the summer of 1967 I went to see Noel-Baker in the House of Commons in an effort to get him to modify his views. The meeting was not a success. In her memoir, his wife, Barbro, loyally sought to exculpate him of his pro-junta reputation. She maintained that he had acquired this solely because, having flown from London to Athens on the day of the coup, he had met with the Colonels (it is rather surprising that they did not have more pressing business to attend to) and, in a subsequent interview with the BBC, had said that there had been no bloodshed, that life carried on as normal, and those who had booked holidays should experience no problems. But Noel-Baker, at the time chairman of the Anglo-Greek Parliamentary Group, consistently sided with the Colonels and seldom passed up the opportunity to criticise those who did not share his roseate view of the junta. When the barrister Anthony Marreco returned from Greece in 1968 with irrefutable proof of police torture of political prisoners, Noel-Baker was quick to attack him for speaking no Greek and not knowing the country. He was to develop a friendship with the most buffoonish of the troika of Colonels who misruled Greece, Brigadier Pattakos, who was a visitor to the Noel-Baker estate at Achmetaga.

Within a day or two of the coup, John Morgan, a reporter for the BBC Panorama programme, showed up in Athens. Somehow we came into contact with him and helped to chaperone him around. A voluble and agreeable, although somewhat discombobulated, character, he had lost his contacts book in a nightclub. We were able to steer him to have dinner with Nikos and Veta Oikonomides, where he received a highly perceptive briefing on the background to the coup. In doing so, we tried in an amateurish fashion to put off anyone following him by changing taxis and walking him the long way round through the streets. The Oikonomides were able to fill him in much more thoroughly than we could have and Morgan seemed to develop a good grasp of Greek realities in a creditably short space of time. What he did with his newfound knowledge of the Greek political scene I do not know, although he maintained an interest in Greek affairs and we shall encounter him again in the next chapter.

One of the early pronouncements of the putschists was that not only were Greek citizens not allowed to leave the country for a few days but that the ban applied also to those deemed to be of Greek descent. This prohibition encompassed George Frangos, despite the fact that he was a US citizen and that no member of his immediate family had ever been a Greek citizen. His father, an Orthodox priest, had been born on the island of Imvros and, before he emigrated to the United States, had been a Turkish national. The Greek authorities had also refused to accept the validity of George's civil marriage in the United States, as non-religious marriages at that time were not recognised in Greece. The US Embassy seemed not to be the least concerned with this blatant discrimination against their nationals. Nor did they demonstrate any concern when a couple from Mary Jo's hometown deplaned in Athens en route to the United States following a visit to India. The wife was extremely ill and in hospital for several weeks. She received good care, for which no charge was made, and the elderly husband was even himself given a bed at the hospital. The Greek medical authorities, in fact, behaved very humanely. The same could not be said of the US embassy. It proved impossible to get further than the locally employed Greeks or Greek–Americans who demonstrated not the slightest interest in the serious problems faced by two of their nationals, who had the misfortune of not having any influential contacts in the US who could put pressure on the embassy to offer assistance. We were told that, at that time, the British embassy by contrast paid weekly visits to any of its nationals who ended up in hospital in Greece.

In the early summer of 1967 I made my first visit to Mount Athos. Soon after arriving there, I met up with a young Greek who was about to emigrate to New Zealand. He was in effect bidding farewell to his homeland at what was probably the last period in the history of Greek emigration when it must have seemed that there would be few opportunities for long-distance migrants to return to their *patrida*, or homeland, from the New World or Australasia. I have sometimes wondered how he fared in the Antipodes. Over the course of a week, we visited five monasteries, Zographou, the Bulgarian monastery, Vatopedi, Aghia Lavra, Panteleimon (the Russian monastery which at that time appeared to be on its last legs as, indeed, did the Holy Mountain in general) and, finally, Dionysiou. We made our way on the marvellous network of well-tended, but not necessarily well-signposted, paths that linked the various monasteries. Sometimes we took the caique that was the easiest way of visiting those monasteries bordering the sea. My companion had no time for the Colonels' dictatorship and we both found our time on the Holy Mountain a welcome refuge from the brutal idiocies of the regime that were already beginning to manifest themselves.

I had a specific objective in visiting Vatopedi. This was to examine two examples of Protestant religious tracts printed in Greek on behalf of the Religious Tract Society at the press of the Ecumenical Patriarchate in Constantinople in 1818, a remarkable coup on the part of the missionaries involved. The library in London of the Religious Tract Society had been destroyed during World War II and it appeared likely that these two, the Reverend Legh Richmond's *The Negro Servant* and *Extracts from St. Chrysostom on the reading of the Old and New Testament*, were the only two extant copies. After protracted negotiations with the librarian I finally managed to see these and make notes.

It has become a cliché to assert that the monasteries of Mount Athos afford a living link with Byzantium. This was certainly more true at the time of my first visit than at the time of my next in 1998. In 1967, there was only one motor-powered vehicle on the peninsula, an ancient bus which took pilgrims from the landing stage at Daphni to Karyes, the administrative centre of the complex of monasteries that comprise the Holy Mountain. By 1998, motor transport, in the shape of minibuses and 'Mini Moke' type vehicles, was much more common. (At least there was a certain serendipity in the presence of Mini Mokes on Athos, as the Mini had been designed by Alec Isigonis, a

Greek born in Smyrna.) In 1998 I should have realised that I would encounter major changes. The boat taking pilgrims from Ouranoupolis to Daphni was no longer a diminutive caique but a substantial ferry. Moreover, virtually none of the pilgrims were sporting the hiking boots and rucksacks that were *de rigueur* in 1967 for pilgrims but were toting holdalls and in many cases wearing smart city shoes which would scarcely have lasted a day on the paths as they were in 1967. This was because many of the larger monasteries were now accessible to wheeled traffic and hardly any walking was required. As a result, the network of paths had been allowed to decay. Many were overgrown and I should have been loath to tackle these without a companion. It would have been easy to sprain an ankle, or worse, and the chances of coming across other users, whether monastic or lay, in the remoter areas would have been slight, whereas in 1967 there was always some traffic on the paths. In the new millennium, steps are under way to clear these paths; an initiative which, characteristically, appears to derive from Anglo-Saxon rather than Greek pilgrims.

I was glad, therefore, in 1998, to link up with the US consul-general in Thessaloniki and one or two others who were keen on doing as much walking as possible. The presence of the consul-general ensured that we received VIP treatment. At Vatopedi, for instance, we were housed in a comfortable refurbished dormitory, with newly installed and excellent plumbing, including flushing lavatories. These contrasted with the rickety holes in the floor, perched in many cases over a vertiginous drop, that I had encountered in 1967. It was even possible to have a hot, or at least lukewarm, shower. We may well have been given the red carpet treatment, but presumably Prince Charles, who has visited Athos more than once, has been treated with even greater consideration. He has emerged from these comfortable retreats to issue manifestos much influenced by the writings of Orthodox convert and environmental guru Philip Sherrard, with whom I shared an office at King's College for a number of years. In these Cnut-like philippics (no pun intended), Charles inveighed against materialism and the degradation of the environment, although he himself leaves behind a massive carbon imprint as, accompanied by two bodyguards, he is given to arriving on a fuel-guzzling luxury yacht belonging to a hugely rich Greek shipping magnate.

Perhaps the biggest change between 1967 and 1998 was the adoption by all the ruling monasteries of the coenobitic rather than the idiorrythmic system of governance. The idiorrythmic system had grown up in the late Byzantine Empire and provided that monks could retain some of their worldly resources. One or two of the monasteries in 1967 had a small shop where one could buy food to supplement the excellent, and very healthy, Athonite diet. Under the coenobitic, or 'common life' system, which now prevails throughout the 20 monasteries, monks live in common and are held to their vows of poverty. One by-product of the resurgence of the coenobitic system has been a growth of Orthodox fanaticism. At some of the monasteries, for instance, non-Orthodox visitors are not now allowed to eat alongside the Orthodox. Notoriously, in Esphigmenou, the monks decline to pray for the Ecumenical Patriarch. European feminists have a point in agitating for access to the Holy Mountain on the grounds that their taxes contribute towards EU funding for restoration projects which they are unable to visit. Moreover, it is a curious anomaly that foreign clergymen who wish to visit the Holy Mountain, which, of course, lies within the territory of the European Union, must secure the permission of the Ecumenical Patriarch, a citizen of a country, Turkey, which is not a member state of the EU.

In 1967, at the end of our eight months in Greece I still had no job but I was fortunate to be awarded a one-year research fellowship by the Carnegie Trust for the Universities of Scotland to work on aspects of the Greek Enlightenment during the decades before the outbreak of the War of Independence in 1821, a subject in which I had become interested during our time in Greece. This would keep the wolf from the door for another year. Meanwhile, Mary Jo would be able to finish her diploma in librarianship at University College, London.

2

The Colonels and the stage army

'Young people of Greece ... You have enfolded Greece in your breasts and your creed is the meaning of sacrifice, from the time of the "Come and take them [weapons]" of Leonidas, later of the "I shall not surrender the City [Constantinople]" of Constantine Palaiologos, of the "No" of Metaxas and, finally, of the "Halt or I shoot" of 21 April 1967 ...'
—Brigadier Stylianos Pattakos (1968)

For the next seven years while the Colonels remained in power, as I embarked on my academic career, I was at the same time much involved with the effort to draw attention to their iniquities and absurdities. During the period of the dictatorship I was a frequent broadcaster on the BBC Greek Service, the BBC World Service and the BBC's domestic transmissions. When the Greek Service wanted someone to be nasty about the Colonels they would call on me, or Monty Woodhouse, the Tory MP for Oxford. Monty's strictures carried particular weight, for not only did he know Greece very well but his conservative credentials were impeccable. This made it difficult for anyone to argue that he was a leftist agitator. He was one of the few Conservative MPs who was prepared to take a public stand over the regime of the Colonels. However, the Foreign Office, whichever government was in power in Britain, was determined to maintain a 'good working relationship' with the junta and was given to leaning on the BBC Greek Service to tone down its coverage of the dictatorship. One of its complaints was that it called too frequently on what it dismissed as the 'stage army' of Woodhouse and Clogg for comment on Greek affairs.

On our return to London from our eight months in Greece, Mary Jo and I soon came into contact with many of those engaged in blackening the junta. There were numerous committees, fundraising events (one of those that I remember was a fundraising dinner attended by a youthful Mia Farrow) and demonstrations. Another actress, Peggy Ashcroft, was, as I recall, an enthusiastic supporter of the North London Group for the Restoration of Democracy in Greece, which normally met in the Bird-in-Hand pub in Hampstead. We took part in many of these protests and I made one or two of my oldest Greek friends not inside the Greek Embassy but while demonstrating outside it.

Someone who was an indefatigable powerhouse of anti-Colonel propaganda and whose part in the campaign has not been sufficiently recognised was the diminutive and hyperactive George Yannopoulos, an economics lecturer at Reading University. Mark Dragoumis, another anti-Colonels activist, while conceding that George had opposed the junta, described him as 'far more interested in what he could do after its downfall than in actually trying to bring it down'. In my view this is a thoroughly unfair characterisation of someone who laboured night and day to blacken the regime's name. At this time, George was close to Andreas Papandreou, who was to be released from jail by the junta and allowed to leave Greece early in 1968, following pressure from the US administration. Papandreou, before returning to Greece in the early 1960s, had been chairman of the Department of Economics at the University of California at Berkeley. Before that he had been a postgraduate student at Harvard, had taught subsequently at the University of Minnesota, and had many friends among the US academic economist fraternity. Among these was the Harvard professor J.K. Galbraith who, in his memoirs, recalled that Andreas was a good economist and an even better academic politician. He also put on record Lyndon Johnson's characteristic message to 'those Greek bastards to lay off that son-of-a-bitch – whoever he is'. George subsequently had a serious falling out with Papandreou for reasons which I never fathomed. He ended up aligning himself with his fellow Cretan, the conservative politician Konstantinos Mitsotakis, who, like Yannopoulos, had started out in the centrist Venizelist *parataxis*, or political family, before moving to the right.

George was an inexhaustible source of often scarcely credible stories about the chicanery and obscurantism of the Colonels and their foreign apologists. For a time he published the *Greek Observer*, a monthly magazine which had both an impressive advisory board and a key financial backer in Sonia Orwell, the widow of George Orwell. A valuable source for the campaign against the Colonels in London, where she was in exile during the dictatorship, is the diary, published in Greece in 2007, of the journalist and writer Maria Karavia, although she has much more to say about the opposition activities of right-wingers than those of left-wing persuasion.[1] A characteristic lineup of the usual suspects in the anti-Colonels' campaign was a brains trust on 'Greece Today' held at Regent's Park College in Oxford in March 1973: Eleni Vlachou (the publisher of *Kathimerini*, the conservative newspaper which she closed down rather than publish under the Colonels' censorship); George Yannopoulos; Yannis Andrikopoulos, a former president of the (Greek) National Union of Students; and myself. The chairman was Christopher Lake, the vice-chairman of the League for Democracy in Greece, which had communist affiliations. A collection was made in aid of the Greek Relief Fund, which was an offshoot of the League.

Occasionally, such proceedings would be enlivened by someone prepared to put the case for the junta. One such rare apologist was Judge Gerald Sparrow, a barrister, author and one-time judge in Bangkok. He took part in a meeting organised by Amnesty in Sevenoaks in December 1969. He was subsidised for his efforts by the Greek Embassy and I subsequently came across the report on the meeting that he submitted to his paymasters. Eleni Vlachou, he reported, was 'much more subdued than usual', while Anthony Marreco, the barrister who had produced convincing evidence that the regime practised torture, seemed to Sparrow to be 'dangerous'. He dismissed me as 'a well-meaning, woolly teacher-type engrossed in his subject'.

George Yannopoulos was heavily involved in the invitation to Melina Mercouri to lead the large anti-Colonels' rally in Trafalgar Square planned for the first anniversary of the April 1967 coup. The larger-than-life star of *Never on Sunday*, probably the best-known Greek film star ever, and, in the view of the Foreign Office, 'a declared communist', was a fierce and effective, if erratic, critic of the junta, instantly generating masses of publicity wherever she went. After the downfall of the junta she became minister of culture in Andreas Papandreou's PASOK government. In 1968, she laid a wreath at the statue of Byron in Park Lane, and duly generated, through an impassioned speech at the Trafalgar Square rally, the hoped-for publicity for the anti-Colonels cause. Overall, her descent on London gave a much-needed boost to the anti-Colonels' campaign and we all considered it a triumph. She had stayed in some style in a suite, appropriately decorated in blue and white, the national colours of Greece, at the Grosvenor House Hotel on Park Lane. There Mary Jo and I had duly paid court to her amid a chaotic scrum of admirers. She stroked my thigh, a move by which I was mildly flattered until I noticed that she was stroking the thighs of pretty well every other male crammed into her suite.

If Melina's visit to Britain in April 1968 gave a welcome boost to the anti-Colonels campaign, a later visit to London narrowly avoided being a PR disaster. The organisers of this visit had failed to establish in advance who was to pay her hotel bill. On the day she checked out I was rung up by a frantic Yannopoulos who said that Melina had left with the bill unpaid and that the hotel manager was threatening to tip off the *Evening Standard* if it was not settled by six o'clock. This, of course, would have been a serious blow to the cause. George was therefore organising a whip round to pay her substantial bill. In the end, thanks mainly to one or two of the London shipowners who were hedging their bets by giving *sub rosa* support to the anti-junta campaign, George was able to pay off the bill in the nick of time. Some thought should clearly have been given to the question of who would pick up the tab for her visit and the delicate matter discussed with Melina in advance of her arrival.

The junta had stripped Melina of her Greek citizenship. This had prompted her to write her characteristically ebullient autobiography *I Was Born Greek* (1971), which I reviewed in the *Times Literary Supplement* (*TLS*). I could not resist submitting to Private Eye's *Pseuds Corner* the passage in which she recalled an improbable encounter with a fisherman on the island of Spetses 'lightly perched on a plodding donkey' while reading Proust. I had begun writing for the *TLS* at the invitation of the editor, Arthur Crook, after I had taken issue in the letters column with a much too favourable review of Kenneth Young's apology for the Colonels, *The Greek Passion* (1969). Reviews at that time were anonymous, but the *TLS* some years ago, with the permission of those reviewers still alive, produced a key to the authors. Apparently only a handful of reviewers objected to their identity being released. This particular review turns out to have been written by the classicist Peter Green.

Young, a former editor of the *Yorkshire Post* and political adviser to Beaverbrook Newspapers, advised the junta on press legislation. When Maurice Fraser, about whose activities more later, had made his pitch in the summer of 1967 for the contract as the regime's PR man in Europe, he wrote that he would wish to explore 'the possibility of sponsoring a historian or author of international repute to write a contemporary history of Greece. This could be arranged in the utmost secrecy and would be useful in dismissing the past, intellectually' (whatever this might mean). It is known that the Oxford historian, Hugh Trevor-Roper, forever remembered for his authentication of the forged Hitler diaries, was approached as a possible author, but he turned the proposal down. Could it be that Young's book was commissioned by the Colonels to dismiss 'the past intellectually'? We shall probably never know, but the junta must in any case have been pleased by *The Greek Passion*. One of Young's more preposterous claims was that Margaret Papandreou, Andreas Papandreou's second wife, was of Bulgarian descent, the Bulgarians being, after the Turks, Greece's greatest enemies in the eyes of the Colonels.[2]

One of Young's obligations as a press adviser to the junta was to advise on new laws on 'defamation, libel and so forth', although, ironically, he was himself to be at the receiving end of Britain's draconian libel laws, as they were at that time, as a result of writing *The Greek Passion*. Takis Lambrias, a Greek journalist who spent much of the period of the junta in exile in London and who was very close to the exiled politician Konstantinos Karamanlis, a former prime minister and future president of Greece, dismissed, in the émigré journal which he edited, Young's book as an extended bread-and-butter letter for the hospitality he had received from the junta. Young successfully sued him. But he was in turn successfully sued by Austen Kark, at that time the head of the South European section of the BBC External Services. The offending passage read 'since the Greek domestic radio omitted anything remotely detrimental to Government policy and the B.B.C. anything remotely favourable – while the Communist satellites broadcast lies – the Greek public became singularly ill-informed'. Someone else who sued was Anthony Marreco, a barrister who had produced, on behalf of Amnesty International, convincing evidence of the systematic torture of political prisoners. I wrote a long critique of Young's book at the behest of Derek Clogg (no relation) of Theodore Goddard, one of the solicitors involved in the litigation.

I was delighted when Young's publishers, Dent, capitulated and the book was withdrawn from circulation. Marreco received a substantial sum by way of damages. But, in hindsight, I think it was a mistake for Kark to sue for defamation, not least because there was no mention in Young's book of him by name. Journalistic dog should not bite journalistic dog. However, I believe that I may have ultimately been partially responsible for the issuing of writs. For I had been asked to review the Young book for the BBC Greek Service and, as I remember, it was I who first alerted Kark to the offending passage. Young subsequently complained that, as a consequence of the libel actions, his book was kept under lock and key alongside the British Library's holdings of pornography. Even now, getting on for 50 years after publication and after the deaths of both the defendant and the plaintiff (Austen Kark sadly died in the Potter's Bar railway accident in 2002), the book continues to be designated as 'special material' and can only be consulted under supervision.

I also reviewed David Holden's *Greece without Columns: The Making of the Modern Greeks* (1972), another, albeit more sophisticated, apology for the junta, in the *New York Review of Books*. Holden's basic line was that while military dictatorship might in general be thought to be undesirable, nonetheless the Greeks are such an unregenerate and incorrigible rabble that the rigours of martial law were the only means of keeping them in line. His book showed a rather poor grasp of the modern history of Greece and his style was at times over the top, as when he wrote that 'like the illegitimate child of some hedgerow affair, modern Greece was born out of, and into, the politics of irresponsibility'. This was strong stuff, and as Holden was chief foreign correspondent of the *Sunday Times* there was a danger that his views might be taken seriously. I was subsequently interviewed by Holden on the World Service of the BBC and, although my review had been highly critical and he presumably knew about it, he was perfectly civil. A few years after his book appeared he was murdered in Cairo in circumstances which to this day remain a mystery. After it had been published in the *New York Review of Books* my review was reprinted verbatim in the English-language *Athens News*, which was a constant thorn in the flesh of the Colonels. This was an indication of the way in which the regime was prepared to tolerate criticism in foreign-language publications and newspapers, which circulated freely in Greece throughout the period of the dictatorship. Newspapers published in Greek in Cyprus, and hence not subject to the junta's censorship policies, were, however, banned.

I also crossed swords in the pages of the *Times Literary Supplement* with Lady Amalia Fleming, the Greek widow of Sir Alexander Fleming, the discoverer of penicillin. Our relationship was always somewhat difficult as she had convinced herself that I had infiltrated anti-junta circles at the behest of British intelligence. Her anti-Colonels' book, *A Piece of Truth*, appeared in 1972, as did Holden's polemic. This was a deeply felt account of her courageous activities in Greece during the first four and a half years of the dictatorship, but contained some manifest exaggerations. When I pointed some of these out in my (at that time necessarily anonymous) review, a rather dispiriting and nit-picking correspondence in the columns of the *TLS* ensued.

One of the books that I was asked to review for the *TLS* by Arthur Crook was *Vérité sur la Grèce*, published anonymously in Lausanne in 1970 and written by an opponent of the Colonels living in Greece. This seemed to be an eminently fair-minded critique of the dictatorship, well documented throughout and mercifully free of the hyperbolic rhetoric of many anti-junta publications. I gave it a very favourable review, praising the author for writing 'with a wealth of information, a clarity, a sobriety and a detachment truly remarkable when one considers the circumstances in which the book was written'. One consequence of this was that I received a letter from Tom Rosenthal, soon to become managing director of Secker & Warburg, asking whether I might translate the book. His letter had been forwarded to me by Arthur Crook. The review being anonymous, Rosenthal did not know whom he was addressing and wrote, *inter alia*,

> if it turns out that we know each other already or that you are a man, or indeed woman, of some celebrity then please forgive the inevitable fatuity of much of this letter, but since I do not know who you are I have to write to you in these possibly idiotic terms.

Rosenthal's letter highlighted the unsatisfactory nature of the practice of anonymous reviewing.

By the time I received Rosenthal's letter I had already agreed to translate the book for Chatto and Windus, and to supply an introduction bringing events up to date. Peter Calvocoressi, a member of a prominent Anglo-Greek family which, like so many, was of Chiot origin, had until very recently been a partner in Chatto and I suspect that he had something to do with the commissioning of a translation. The anonymous author turned out to be Rodis Roufos, a diplomat and author who, as a young man, had taken part in the wartime resistance, and who had been dismissed from the diplomatic service by the junta. I translated it by dictating a rough first draft of the translation while Mary Jo typed this. Having a better formal knowledge of English grammar than me she was able to suggest many improvements, as she has done with most of my writings. In going through the text we decided that if the book was to have the maximum impact then one or two excisions would be necessary. One of these was that the musical taste of the Colonels resembled that of provincial grocers replete with rich food and resinated wine, which appeared to us as rather snobbish and needlessly insulting to grocers. Rather incestuously, the dust jacket of the translation, entitled *Inside the Colonels' Greece*, the author of which was given simply as 'Athenian', reprinted a substantial chunk of my *TLS* review with no indication that I was the author of this as well as the translator of the book. The cover reproduced a striking picture of a sinister-looking trio, consisting of Colonel Ioannis Ladas, the secretary-general of the Ministry of the Interior; one of the regime's hard men, General Odysseus Angelis, Commander-in-Chief of the Armed Forces, and Inspector Vasilis Lambrou, a notorious torturer and the deputy head of the Athens Security Police.

The approach that I had from Tom Rosenthal did, however, lead to a book published by his own firm, Secker & Warburg, in the same year as *Inside the Colonels' Greece*, 1972. This was *Greece Under Military Rule*, an anatomy of the dictatorship, which I co-edited with George Yannopoulos. It contained 12 chapters, four written by Greeks still living in Greece, three of them writing under their own name. These were Yanko Pesmazoglou, the former deputy governor of the Bank of Greece, on the economy; Rodis Roufos, the author of *Inside the Colonels' Greece*, on culture; and Alekos Xydis, a former diplomat, on foreign policy. The fourth, Alexis Dimaras, a PhD student of mine, wrote, under the pseudonym N.N. (Nescio Nomen), on education. The remaining chapters were written by Monty Woodhouse on the historical context; George Zaharopoulos on the army; Eleni Vlachou, the former publisher of *Kathimerini*, on the press; George Yannopoulos, on the consequences of the coup for workers and peasants and on the domestic opposition to the regime (two contributions); Arne Treholt (who was subsequently revealed to be working for the KGB and about whom more later), Norwegian Institute of International Affairs, on the European reaction to the dictatorship; Maurice Goldbloom, formerly of the US Economic Mission to Greece, on US policy towards the junta; and myself on the ideology, such as it was, of the regime. What greatly helped to give the book authority and credibility in Britain was the contribution by Monty Woodhouse. Not only was he one of the few Conservative MPs to take an active stand in opposition to the dictatorship, but he was a former junior minister and erstwhile director of Chatham House (the Royal Institute of International Affairs), and someone whose knowledge of Greece went back to the German, Italian and Bulgarian occupation and, indeed, before. His contribution made it difficult for apologists for the regime to dismiss the book as the work of left-wing agitators. It was not only widely distributed but extensively and well reviewed. Each contributor received the princely fee of £20.

A comprehensive bibliography of books on the Colonels' Greece was compiled by Yannis Yannoulopoulos, at that time a postgraduate student in history in London and subsequently a distinguished historian of modern Greece. After the downfall of the Colonels he was one of the translators of *Greece Under Military Rule* into Greek as *I Ellada kato apo stratiotiko zygo* (1976). When translating my own contribution on the so-called ideology of the 'Revolution of 21 April 1967', rather than re-translate into Greek my translations into English of Papadopoulos' tortuous and garbled *katharevousa*, or archaising Greek, he wanted, as a conscientious translator, to quote from the original texts which had appeared in several volumes under the title *To Pistevo Mas* (Our Creed). These had been distributed in vast quantities under the junta but, on the downfall of the regime, had mostly been destroyed and rapidly became quite hard to find. As Yannoulopoulos went to various libraries seeking copies, he was acutely conscious of suspicions on the part of the librarians that he must be someone who was nostalgic for the dictatorship, as they were unable to conceive of any legitimate reason to consult these turgid texts.

In the course of editing the book, George Yannopoulos, my co-editor, was a regular visitor to our house in Crouch End where we put in long hours to get the book into publishable shape. Like good middle-class parents, Mary Jo and I had striven to keep our daughter, aged about two and a half, in ignorance of forbidden fruit in the shape of chocolate. This effort was torpedoed when George arrived one day with a huge box of chocolates which he presented to Rachel. We had not the heart to deprive her of them, and after George had left she declared that she would like to go to live with him.

Greece Under Military Rule was 'adopted' by Lord Sainsbury of the supermarket chain, whose interest in Greek politics had apparently been kindled by a chance encounter with Rodis Roufos while swimming during a holiday in Greece. Not only did he sponsor a splendid launch party in the Cholmondeley Room at the House of Lords, attended by luminaries such as Roy Jenkins, but he bought up a substantial number of copies of the book for distribution to 'opinion-makers' and public libraries. This explains why, of all the books published about the Colonels, this is nowadays much the easiest to find in second-hand book shops.

Following the publication of the two anti-junta books, I had a spat with the British Council after I had discovered that, while the Council's library in Athens gave shelf space, perfectly justifiably, to David Holden's jaundiced apologia for the Colonels, *Greece without Columns*, it refused to stock either *Inside the Colonels' Greece* or *Greece Under Military Rule* on the ground that they were politically polemical.

Besides regular broadcasting on Greek affairs, I also wrote a number of articles and reviews on Greek-related subjects. Of one or two of these I am no longer entirely sure that I am the author as they were published anonymously. A long piece on the havoc wreaked on Greek education by the Colonels, in which I was much interested, and about which Nikos Oikonomides had sent me invaluable material, was published in two instalments in Eleni Vlachou's émigré journal, the *Hellenic Review*. It reads very much as though I had written it but I cannot, after getting on for 50 years, be entirely sure. In 1968 I was asked by Robert Browning, professor of classics at Birkbeck College, to consider stationing myself in Greece as a kind of full-time observer of the human rights situation on behalf of Amnesty International and others. I regretfully had to decline as I had a rather urgent need to find a job in the UK, and someone else took up the post. I did, however, go on a mission for Amnesty to observe a trial of some opponents of the regime, but this was postponed at the last minute, after I had arrived in Athens. Nonetheless, I was able to make contact with some of the lawyers involved and acquired some useful material about the most recent brutalities and absurdities of the junta.

Needless to say, my contacts with the Greek embassy in London during the seven-year dictatorship were non-existent. When, however, I received an offer from the regime of a donation of books for the Burrows Library at King's College, one of the richest collections of books on Byzantine and modern Greece in the United Kingdom, I accepted. My rationale was that even if the books consisted solely of pro-regime propaganda, and included some or, indeed, all of the seven or so volumes of Papadopoulos' *To Pistevo Mas*, his ranting and often scarcely intelligible speeches, they would all be part and parcel of the historical record, and that, at the least, we should not have to pay for them. Where, for instance, would one now begin to look for these unbelievably turgid speeches, of which huge quantities were printed, although most of the volumes seem now to have disappeared without trace? The University of Birmingham, where modern Greek was also taught, took the line that it would not accept the Colonels' tainted largesse. This was a principled, but, in my view, pointless decision. In the 1980s, I was bombarded with parcels of books from Ceauşescu's Romania, mostly on historical topics. Some were overtly propagandistic. Most were infused with the mandatory nationalist bias. Some were serious works of scholarship. Academic boycotts may sometimes be justified, but it is difficult to imagine any circumstances in which books should be boycotted.

Towards the end of the seven years there were slight but possibly significant signs that the Greek embassy was hedging its bets. In 1974, the year in which the Colonels' regime imploded, for instance, I received, for the first time during the years of the dictatorship, an invitation to the annual independence day reception on 25 March at the embassy. Naturally, there was no question of attending, although I did have lunch with a member of the embassy staff whose heart was clearly not in offering a defence of the regime.

Not long after the downfall of the Colonels' regime, I wrote a *Short History of Modern Greece* (1979). This was not technically part of a series, but similar volumes published by Cambridge University Press had boring, non-pictorial covers. I decided to break with tradition and use a striking cover to help sell the book. I chose a dramatic photograph of Konstantinos Karamanlis being sworn in as prime minister at four o'clock in the morning of 24 July 1974 by the Archbishop of Athens, Serapheim, in the presence of the General Phaedon Gizikis, the junta-appointed president, following Karamanlis' dramatic return to Greece on the implosion of the junta. The picture constituted a kind of secular icon as it depicted the trinity of the civil power, Karamanlis; the military, Gizikis; and the church, Serapheim. The archbishop's crozier cast a shadow over the face of Gizikis, a sinister-looking figure wearing dark glasses in the middle of the night. In the officially released photograph of the swearing-in ceremony, Gizikis is not visible. Only his shoulder can be glimpsed so he could have been taken for a policeman.

When the book was published, Aleko Xydis, art historian, former diplomat and a tireless opponent of the Colonels whom I had come to know well during the years of the dictatorship and who had contributed a chapter to *Greece Under Military Rule*, reproached me for having chosen a cover designed to flatter Karamanlis. This had certainly never been my intention. Nor, indeed, was it the case. The reality was, as I heard from an unimpeachable source, that when Karamanlis, who was about to elevate himself to the presidency at the time of the book's publication, saw the cover he was not at all pleased to be shown being sworn in under the aegis of a prominent member of the military regime, whose wretched legacy he had so energetically, and successfully, sought to clear up.

One of the more agreeable consequences of involvement in the anti-Colonels' campaign in London during the long years of the dictatorship was an association and friendship that developed with Paul Foot of *Private Eye* and *The Socialist Worker*, a connection that was to prove useful in subsequent years when exposure in the *Eye* was called for in respect of academic skulduggery or Western hypocrisy over Chechnya. Foot was the son of Hugh Foot, the last colonial governor of Cyprus, and had spent part of his childhood on the island. This had given him a particular interest in Cypriot and Greek affairs. One of the last stories that I gave him, just a few weeks before his death in 2004, was that the camp in Iraq known as Camp Bucca, where detainees had been abused by the US military police, was not an Arab toponym as it vaguely sounded but had been named after a New York fireman who had died in the 9/11 conflagration. This reflected an attempt to reinforce in the minds of the US soldiery and public a spurious link between Saddam Hussein and al-Qaeda. Paul duly drew attention to this underhand ploy in his column in the *Guardian*.

Over the seven years of the dictatorship a steady stream of pieces, frequently quite detailed, knocking the Colonels appeared in the *Eye*. It was good also to have an occasional go at British apologists for the junta. More often than not these were classicists such as Denys Page and Hugh Lloyd-Jones, who translated their distaste for modern Greeks and modern Greece into support for the junta. In most cases these stories were based to a greater or lesser degree on information which I passed to Paul, and which, in turn, had often been given to me by George Yannopoulos, who had a seemingly endless supply of frequently convoluted and sometimes fantastic, but invariably accurate, stories of military chicanery and obscurantism. These contacts resulted in the odd invitation to the notorious, highly entertaining but scarcely boozy *Private Eye* lunches at the Coach and Horses pub in Soho.

One of the earliest pieces to be published in *Private Eye*, indeed one of my earliest publications ever, was a translation that I had made of a decree issued in March 1968 by Brigadier-General Photios Ganasoulis, the military commander of Southern Boeotia. This perfectly illustrated the mindless idiocy of the junta and its minions. It forbade the uttering at the traditional celebration of the *Vlachikos Gamos*, or Vlach Wedding held in Thebes every Clean Monday, the beginning of the Orthodox Lent, of 'unseemly and filthy words and phrases' such as 'fuck', etc. These words, which the general deemed to offend against sexual modesty and morality, in the past had led to the disruption of the public peace and the creation of mutual discord at a ceremony that always attracted large crowds. The proceedings, so the general decreed, were to be tape recorded and transgressors would be punished.

While on the subject of the linguistic obsessions of the general, I might mention that when, some years later, Londoner's Diary in the *Evening Standard* had an item playing, rather childishly, on the name of the retiring Dutch ambassador, Robert Fack, I, no less childishly, informed the diary hacks that Romanians could not wait for an official visit from Michael Foot, at that time leader of the Labour Party. They would then have the opportunity of chanting, as the motorcade swept by, 'Foot–Ceaușescu', the Romanian *fut* being derived from the Latin *futuere*, the word that had so exercised General Ganasoulis. The *Evening Standard*, with more than a little hyperbole, wrote that the Labour leader's name provoked gales of laughter in Romania. By an odd coincidence, on the day the item appeared in the *Evening Standard* I bumped into the other Michael Foot, M.R.D. Foot, the historian of the Special Operations Executive, at East Finchley tube station. I gleefully showed him the paragraph in the diary about Foot–Ceaușescu, but he was not amused.

Quite a number of the stories that appeared in *Private Eye* were too hair-raising for the mainstream press, but Foot could always be relied on to write them up in a careful fashion and none provoked even a hint of legal action. One of the most entertaining of these pieces did not relate to Greece at all but rather to the rather shocking degree of deference shown towards Lyudmila Zhivkova by St Antony's College, Oxford, where I was to wash up in the 1990s. She was the maverick (and more than a little dotty) daughter of the predictably unpleasant Bulgarian communist party boss, Todor Zhivkov. The story, which was leaked to me by a student at the all-graduate college, went as follows. The college, wishing to enrol a postgraduate student from Bulgaria, had solicited from the Bulgarian Academy of Sciences a short list of three suitably qualified students, from which it would choose one. The thinking was that all three nominees would, by definition, be deemed to be acceptable to the ruling communist party but the college would be able to exercise at least a small margin of discretion. After some considerable delay the short list arrived, with a single name on it, that of a Mrs Zhivkova. The college supinely agreed to admit her. No one apparently had the wit to ascertain whether she might possibly have some connection with Zhivkov.

A few days before the beginning of the 1969 Michaelmas term, the college received a frantic call from the Bulgarian embassy asking what arrangements had been made to receive the daughter of the first secretary of the Bulgarian communist party. Did they know that she was to be accompanied by her husband? This was a virtually unheard-of privilege for academics from the Eastern Bloc, as the authorities, always fearful of the possibility of defection, usually preferred to keep one spouse back in the home country as a hostage. Panic had then ensued in the college. The rather spartan room that had been reserved for Zhivkova was deemed to be inadequate, and arrangements were hastily made for the couple to be given a much more salubrious flat in one of the college houses on the Woodstock Road. In this she was installed with her water-polo-playing husband and her formidable train of luggage, containing, in contrast to that of her fellow students, many changes of costume.

Zhivkova spent much of her time in Oxford browsing through antique shops in the Cotswolds. Her father, Todor, was apparently not best pleased with the amount of money from the sums he had purloined from the Bulgarian people that she spent during these buying sprees. Towards the end of her agreeable sojourn in Oxford it was arranged that Zhivkova, who was an historian of sorts, should give a seminar on the development of Bulgarian historiography. Students were urged to attend by the senior tutor. A group of dissidents from the BBC's Bulgarian service came up for the seminar. So, too, did a large claque from the Bulgarian embassy, including the ambassador who, in the words of *Private Eye*, greeted the lecture 'with almost hysterical rapture'. A principal theme of Zhivkova's presentation were the wholly beneficial consequences of the arrival in her country of the Soviet army in 1944.

At the end of her presentation there were a couple of perfunctory questions, before someone had the presumption to ask Zhivkova why, if Ohrid was, as she maintained, such a central part of Bulgaria's cultural heritage, it was currently situated in Yugoslav Macedonia. At this point a flustered chairman brought the proceedings to a rapid halt, with an effusive vote of thanks for Zhivkova, who then proceeded to present the college with a picture, which appears to have sunk without trace. Paul Foot concluded his piece with the snide comment that any link between what went on at St Antony's and political priorities at the Foreign Office was entirely coincidental. A fellow of the college subsequently told me that, during Zhivkova's unproductive sojourn in Oxford, he was approached by a bowler-hatted emissary from the 'Ministry of Defence', who sought his help in 'getting alongside' Zhivkova while she was in the UK. He sent the 'Colonel' on his way. The basic facts of the Zhivkova story were never denied and indeed its appearance in the *Eye* must have caused quite a stir, for reference was made to the piece when the history of the college's first 50 years was published some 30 years later in 2000.

Subsequently, following her early and somewhat mysterious death, a Lyudmila Zhivkova visiting fellowship was established to commemorate her unmemorable stay at St Antony's. This was funded by Robert Maxwell, the crooked publisher, *inter alia*, of grossly sycophantic biographies of Lyudmila's father and of the even more tyrannical Nicolae Ceaușescu. He was also the publisher of Elena Ceaușescu's plagiarised doctoral thesis, about which more later. In 1982, a year after Zhivkova's death, Maxwell published a weirdly entitled book dedicated to her rather peculiar thoughts. This was entitled *Ludmila Zhivkova: Her Many Worlds: New Culture and Beauty: Concepts and Action* and published to coincide with the establishment of the Lyudmila Zhivkova International Foundation which sought to popularise her 'noble ideas and undertakings'. Maxwell in his own contribution to this overblown puff, maintained, somewhat sinisterly in hindsight, that he had been the last foreigner to see Zhivkova alive. All those, he maintained, who came into contact with Zhivkova during her time in Oxford had been 'immensely impressed' by her dedication, determination and originality. Her voluminous and various writings were listed in the bibliography and included a volume, no doubt largely or wholly written by some distinguished scholar on her behalf, on the Kazanluk tomb.

I was given a copy of this handsomely produced volume by the father of a Bulgarian academic whom I had got to know, and it was delivered to our modest Crouch End home in a large Bulgarian Embassy Mercedes. It was accompanied by a rather good bottle of home-distilled plum brandy. This occurred not that many years before Georgi Markov, a member of the Bulgarian service of the BBC, was murdered on Waterloo Bridge, on the birthday of Todor Zhivkov, by a Bulgarian secret service agent armed with a poisoned umbrella. Had the bottle of slivovitz arrived after the 1978 assassination of Markov I should have had little option but to pour it down the sink.

The collapse of communism put paid to the Zhivkova fellowship at St Antony's. The Robert Maxwell fellowship in politics at Balliol College, however, survives unscathed. Indeed, Ian Robert Maxwell (born Jan Ludvik Hoch, the original 'bouncing Czech') is commemorated in the college's bidding prayer, which is intoned by the Master on the feast of St Catherine of Alexandria, the college's patron saint. The Robert Maxwell fellowship was established at Balliol in 1965, hopefully before he started plundering the *Daily Mirror* pension fund. Any connection between Captain Bob's benefaction for the 'furtherance in virtue, and increase in learning' at the college and the fact that three of his children, sons Ian and Kevin and daughter Ghislaine, secured places at Balliol is no doubt purely coincidental. I once heard an Oxford vice-chancellor say on Radio Oxford that, in all his years at the university, he had never once heard of a case where money had secured a much sought-after place at Oxford. He must indeed have led a very sheltered life. I was told by someone in a position to know of a very rich Greek securing a place for his son at St Peter's College in return for a very large donation. Confirmation that places are on offer if the price is right was afforded by the case of a fellow of Pembroke College, who, in 2002, told a *Sunday Times* reporter posing as a banker that, in return for a benefaction of £300,000, there was a distinct possibility of his (non-existent) son being offered a place, provided the matter was kept totally confidential. Such deals had apparently taken place in the past. The Fellow in question resigned immediately when the story broke.

During the Colonels' dictatorship, I was asked by Lady Amalia Fleming to find a place at Balliol for the son of the prominent Greek communist, Nikos Beloyannis, who had been executed in 1952 after he had returned clandestinely to Greece soon after the end of the civil war, at a time when the communist party was still illegal. She was fearful that the son would be given a hard time if he remained in Greece and was obliged to carry out his military service. Balliol was prepared in principle to offer him a place, without a Maxwell-style dowry, subject to his academic qualifications being up to scratch. But Lady Fleming was unable to provide a financial guarantee that his expenses would be paid and the offer fell by the wayside.

Another regular contact was John Barry of the *Sunday Times* Insight team. I was able to feed him with stories, some of which came from Nikos and Veta Oikonomides. Before leaving Athens we had arranged a simple code with them. Anything sent would be addressed to Mary Jo in her maiden name. To be certain of its authenticity it would be headed with a number followed by a word. The number would be a page number taken from Joan Hussey's *The Byzantine World*, copies of which we both possessed, and the word would be the first word on that page. It seemed appropriate to put a book by an enthusiast for the junta to good use. Among the stories that were published was the stripping by Columbia University of the PhD in economics awarded to Constantine Thanos, the deputy-governor of the Bank of Greece and a junta appointee. Thanos had replaced Yanko Pesmazoglou, who had resigned as deputy-governor when the Colonels seized power, as had the governor, Xenophon Zolotas. Yanko was subsequently to become a good friend and another of my mentors on Greek politics. Shortly before the coup, the historian C.W. Crawley, an authority on the diplomatic background to the Greek war of independence whom Pesmazoglou had known when a student at Cambridge, had been staying at the British School. Pesmazoglou had lent Crawley his car and chauffeur to make a trip to Delphi, Crawley had asked us if we wanted to come along, which we did. But we did not meet Pesmazoglou himself until after the coup.

The friendship with John Barry had a fortunate outcome, for when we moved from Edinburgh to London in 1969, by now with a seven-month-old baby, Rachel, it was he who suggested that we house-hunt in the then distinctly unfashionable Crouch End, where he himself lived. We were able to purchase a run-down but serviceable and, eventually, habitable house on a starting lecturer's salary. Such a house would now be way beyond the reach of someone starting out on an academic career or even to an established professor. A few years ago I enquired of Margaret Hodge, then the Labour minister responsible for higher education, whether university teachers would be eligible for subsidised housing of the kind in theory available to some key workers such as teachers, nurses and ambulance drivers. I was told that they would not, not even for the Portakabins which Ken Livingstone, the mayor of London, was planning to stack on areas of waste ground in the less salubrious parts of London to house individuals deemed to be socially useful. No sooner had we departed from Crouch End in 1980 for the supposedly greener pastures of Muswell Hill, than Crouch End became the fashionable haunt of people in the media, who were in the fortunate position of being able if not to talk up, then to write up, the value of their real estate. So many therapists have established themselves in the area that it is known by some as 'Couch End', just as Muswell Hill is sometimes referred to as 'Muesli Hill'.

Much the greatest anti-Colonels' coup with which I had a direct involvement was the wrecking of the regime's effort to acquire respectability through an expensive PR offensive. The campaign against the junta had, in general, proved highly successful. One of the relatively few to look with favour on the regime was Alistair Horne, the military historian whom I was later to encounter at St Antony's, where he had founded the Alistair Horne fellowship and was an honorary fellow. He was among those impressed by Colonel Papadopoulos' word as 'a Greek, a soldier and an officer'. In a letter to the *Daily Telegraph*, written shortly after the first anniversary of the coup, he plaintively bemoaned the fact that it was virtually impossible to get anything published in Britain that was not 'actually defamatory of the Colonels'. Some exaggeration here, surely. Likewise, Peter Green, in his *Times Literary Supplement* review of Kenneth Young's *The Greek Passion*, complained that 'the volume of world protest over the Colonels' coup in Greece far exceeds that generated by any other takeover'. But Horne and Green did have something of a point. Few regimes in the postwar period have been the subject of such persistent, informed and hostile comment as the junta. But the anti-Colonel campaign received a major setback in 1968 when the Colonels hired a PR man to spruce up their image. The individual concerned was Maurice Fraser, who was reportedly Egyptian-born. Eleni Vlachou, the Athenian newspaper proprietor, records that he was married to a Greek, understood the language and operated out of luxurious offices in Fleet Street. He also had offices in a number of European capitals.

Certainly the junta's public relations effort in the early months had been pitifully inadequate and needed a complete revamp. Characteristic of these feeble efforts was a bulky illustrated pamphlet published, in English of a kind, on behalf of the Panhellenic Confederation of Reserve Officers. This was entitled *Why did the Revolution of April 21 1967 take place?* and purported to explain the reasons for the army's intervention. Francis Noel-Baker, the Labour MP and apologist for the junta, was quoted as saying that

> those, who called the army people and their friends fascists, are mistaken. One has to remember that the parliamentary institutions had been abolished during the last two years. The State's functions remained inactif [*sic*]. The parliamentarism reached to an impass [*sic*], and the Constitution was transgressed.

Talking of the political turmoil that preceded the coup, the pamphlet continued that the 'plot was covered by a patriotic mask; the secret purposes were covered by incoherence; our national humiliations were beautified by beautiful speeches the conspiracies against the regime took place into the political secret places'. The communists had controlled 'the beds of public hospitals, the licences of trifle-sellers, even the frozen chickens'.

The ludicrous nature of such publications demonstrated that Fraser clearly had his work cut out in the effort to burnish the junta's image, but despite one or two glitches, such as referring in a handout to the 'Greek junta' rather than the 'National Revolutionary Government', he quickly showed his mettle and brought off what, in PR terms, must be seen as a major coup. This was the organisation, in April 1968, on the first anniversary of the Colonels' takeover of a 'fact-finding' visit to Greece by an all-party group of British MPs, accompanied by their wives. The visit initially got off to a shaky start from the junta's point of view. The Greek press, at the time subject to stringent censorship, was apparently unaware that the MPs were official guests and attacked them as 'self-appointed investigators' and 'leftist agents' who had no doubt voted to legalise homosexuality. Papadopoulos later apologised personally to the MPs for the onslaught. At the end of their week-long visit, however, the five MPs declared that they had been assured that the junta intended to move towards democratic government.

These assurances had included Papadopoulos' word of honour as 'a soldier and an officer' (a naive reliance on which they shared with Alistair Horne) and they believed this indeed to be his intention. While the key question was when democratic government would be restored, they were against the economic isolation of Greece. Already by this time well-founded allegations of torture and ill treatment by the junta had begun to circulate.

The five concluded, however, that while there might have been isolated cases, particularly in the early days, they found it difficult to distinguish fact from propaganda. Nonetheless, they were confident that there had been no direction of cruelty from the top, and had received assurances that what they termed 'cases of individual zeal' by lower-ranking officers would be dealt with. Two of the party, Gordon Bagier (Labour) and Russell Johnston (Liberal), had stayed on in Greece and visited political prisoners held in the Partheni camp on the island of Leros. One of the prisoners had complained of a broken nose and broken ribs. The MPs interviewed the army major accused of this maltreatment. He duly denied the allegations. Bagier declared that 'we believe the officer was telling the truth' (again a curious reliance on the word of an officer, not least coming from a Labour MP sponsored by the National Union of Railwaymen). The two had revised their view of the Greek regime 'for the better' and declared that they were now convinced that it was more popular than they had been led to believe by biased reporting in the press and by the BBC. None of those who had approached them in the streets of Naxos, for instance, had anything but praise for the government.

On returning to Britain, Johnston, for many years the Liberal Party's spokesman on foreign affairs, wrote up in the *Guardian* his impressions of a visit made 'at the invitation and expense of the Greek military government', impressions which were contrary to 'the whole tenor' of reporting in the British press. The Greeks he had encountered, among whom were a hotel doorman and two souvenir sellers, had been supportive of the junta. He believed that those who had launched the coup had done so not because they wanted power but because they wished to forestall a breakdown of government. Stories of 'unrelieved tyranny and repression' had been grossly exaggerated: 'It is not,' he concluded, 'a harsh regime'. Fraser, and indeed Papadopoulos himself, must have been delighted with the article. It was clearly hoped to repeat this success when, in September 1968, a spurious referendum was held on the Colonels' proposed new constitution. According to the British Embassy, some 13 British MPs arrived in the Greek capital as 'observers'. While most of these were there just for the freebie, a handful was genuinely interested in establishing whether the procedure could be called democratic.

On this occasion, however, the farcical nature of the 1968 referendum on the Colonels' constitution was to be completely overshadowed, in Britain at least, by the furore that developed after a report (the fifth), dated mid-June 1968, which Fraser had submitted to Papadopoulos and which had subsequently been leaked. This leak was to have devastating consequences for the regime's attempt to win friends and influence people in Britain. By a fortunate chance I was involved from the outset in the unravelling of the junta's PR campaign.

One morning, towards the end of September 1968, I was having a coffee, as I did from time to time, with Eleni Vlachou in her London office near Selfridges, conveniently situated for Oxford Street, a traditional magnet for Greeks on shopping expeditions. Eleni's *liméri*, her lair, was the centre of a spider's web of anti-junta intrigue and gossip such as would have delighted that arch-intriguer, Compton Mackenzie. She had been the courageous publisher of the conservative *Kathimerini*, the nearest thing that Greece had to a newspaper of record. When the Colonels seized power she had immediately shut the paper down in protest and had smuggled herself out of Greece. From her base in London, Eleni ran a very effective campaign against the Colonels. Telegenic, well connected, with an impressive command of English and an instinctive understanding of what was required to win over a British audience, she proved, with her acerbic wit, to be a very effective thorn in the side of the regime. I remember her disdainful aside when the establishment of the *Elliniki Etairia*, a kind of Greek National Trust, was announced in 1972. One of the *Etairia*'s principal concerns at the time was the fate of the pelicans of Lake Prespa on the Albanian border. She could not, she said, get worked up over the plight of pelicans when human beings were being routinely tortured by the junta. One happy consequence of her London exile was that I was able to arrange for extensive runs of rare nineteenth-century Greek periodicals that had been kept in the Athens offices of *Kathimerini* to come to the library of King's College.

As I was leaving Eleni's office, she casually mentioned that she had just received a document from Constantine Karamanlis, the once and future prime minister and president of Greece. He was at that time, like Eleni, living in exile, although in Paris, from where he delivered the occasional blast against the junta. An anti-junta mole in Papadopoulos' office in Athens had apparently filched the document from the dictator's desk, photocopied it and sent the copy to Karamanlis. He had forwarded it to his old friend Eleni. She asked me to translate the document from the Greek for publication in the *Hellenic Review*, the sprightly but low circulation émigré journal that she edited. There was no hint of urgency in her request, but on reading through the document on the bus back to the British Museum Library in which, as a graduate student, I practically lived at the time, I almost fell off my seat with excitement. For the document proved not only to be a Greek translation of one of Maurice Fraser's reports to his paymasters in Athens but appeared to indicate that the junta had, albeit at one remove, a British member of parliament in its pay.

Eleni's memory was on shaky ground when she wrote in her memoirs that she had approached Harold Evans, the editor of the *Sunday Times*, with the document. Her account of the whole affair is in fact somewhat confused, and for once it appears that her instinct for a good journalistic story had failed her. For I distinctly remember dashing into the British Museum to telephone her to ask whether I might take the document round to my friend, John Barry, a pillar of the *Sunday Times* 'Insight' team. She readily agreed and John quickly grasped its potentially explosive nature. Such was the significance of the report that it was important that the translation be as accurate as possible. I therefore got hold of Alexis Dimaras, at that time teaching at Sevenoaks School and soon to be my first graduate student, and asked him to come round to the *Sunday Times* offices in Gray's Inn Road and help me ensure that the translation into English was as faithful to the original as possible. Thanks to our efforts, we produced a translation so convincing that Fraser, as I subsequently heard, thought that the paper had got hold of a copy of the original English text rather than the Greek translation. This confusion did no harm as it made the search for the courageous mole who had leaked the document to Karamanlis correspondingly more difficult.

For the next two weeks or so, just as I was about to take up a lectureship in modern history at Edinburgh University, I spent virtually every day either at the *Sunday Times* or in the High Court, helping the 'Insight Team' with the Greek background to the story. On the night when the *Sunday Times*' revelations appeared I had an interesting glimpse of the deference paid by journalists to the then all-powerful Fleet Street print union workers, who were jealous of their control over every aspect of the 'hot metal' process of newspaper production. I was able to take the pages, almost literally hot from the press, round to the BBC Greek Service in Bush House to be broadcast in its midnight transmission.

Maurice Fraser's reaction when he first learned that we had got hold of the report ensured that this was a story that would run and run. For he successfully applied for a High Court injunction restraining the *Sunday Times* from publishing the report, or even making reference to its contents, in its issue of 22 September, exactly one week before the referendum on the Colonels' so-called 'constitution'. The injunction was served on the editor, Harold Evans, just four hours after it had been granted and less than an hour before the presses were ready to roll with that Sunday's paper. The granting of an injunction necessarily added an aura of mystery to the proceedings and quickly transformed what might otherwise have been a scandal with a short shelf-life into a political *cause célèbre* of major dimensions. A statement issued by the *Sunday Times* maintained that, following the injunction, 'newspapers, television and radio in this country and abroad had shown the keenest interest in the story'. Even *Pravda* had a piece on the emerging scandal entitled 'Greek machinations'.

The *Sunday Times* was determined to contest the injunction 'with the utmost vigour' on the ground that it raised a major principle of press freedom, a cry taken up by other newspapers. A welter of litigation in the matter of *Fraser v. Evans and Others* thereupon ensued. In the following week the injunction was continued, albeit in a modified form, in the High Court. The judge held that it was impossible to escape the conclusion that the document that had found its way into the hands of the paper was at some stage surreptitiously and improperly obtained, although, he piously added, it had never at any time been suggested that the defendants themselves (i.e. the *Sunday Times*), or any of their agents, were guilty of any impropriety. I wonder if I would have been deemed in the view of the judge to be an agent of the paper or a miscreant? No doubt the latter. He added bizarrely that he was not satisfied that the matters contained in the report, which included the suggestion that the junta had a British MP in its pay, albeit at one remove, could be 'properly characterised as iniquitous', as counsel for the *Sunday Times* had argued.

The *Sunday Times* immediately appealed against the decision to uphold the injunction and three appeal court judges were asked to cut short their vacation to hear the appeal. Meanwhile, the Press and Information Office of the Greek Embassy in London announced that the junta had decided some two weeks previously not to renew Fraser's contract, which was due to expire at the end of the year. *The Times* described it as the biggest public relations contract of any foreign government in Britain. In Athens, the junta confirmed that it would not be renewing what the *Guardian* termed its £100,000 a year (roughly the equivalent of £1,500,000 in 2016) contract with Maurice Fraser and Associates 'in its present form' after December 1968.

The next, and sensational, development in the affair was the revelation, in the following Sunday's *Observer*, by Ivor Richard, Labour MP for Baron's Court, of parts of the report, and in particular of the claim that among 'persons now employed in the organisation of our London office' was 'a British MP working behind the scenes with the object of influencing other British MPs. We must protect the identity of the British MP because this would expose him. But his name is at the disposal of the Prime Minister' [i.e. Papadopoulos]. This passage is not identical either with the Clogg/Dimaras translation or with the official English version of the fifth report, published in the *Sunday Telegraph* on 6 October. Who could have leaked yet another version of the report to the *Observer*? Could it have been Eleni Vlachou? Ivor Richard went on to state that

> this document, on the face of it, discloses a most serious situation and one which appears to involve parliamentary privilege, because if the document is accurate one of my colleagues in the House of Commons is being paid to influence the opinions of MPs and he has not disclosed this interest.

This seemed to him to constitute 'improper conduct quite contrary to the practice and spirit of the House of Commons'. He therefore intended to raise the matter in parliament as soon as he was able.

On the same day, the *Sunday Telegraph* published a 'Close Up' feature, its imitation of the *Sunday Times*' 'Insight' column, on Fraser. This was entitled 'Man who wins friends for the Greek Colonels'. The article paid tribute to the speed and effectiveness of Fraser's work on behalf of the junta. It also claimed that Fraser had once worked for the same *Sunday Times* 'Insight' team that was now seeking to expose his activities, and also for the British government information services and the *Sunday Telegraph*. He had also worked for the public relations firm Lex Hornby and Partners, which had the even more daunting task of promoting a favourable image of the German Democratic Republic.

On 2 October, the Court of Appeal began hearing the *Sunday Times*' appeal against the modified injunction restraining the publication of Fraser's fifth report. Counsel for the paper argued that it was

> a matter of public importance that the methods used by a British public relations consultant to influence public opinion in the United Kingdom and members of parliament in favour of a foreign government which employed him should be made known.

He went on to claim that the paper was being constrained by issues of breach of confidence and copyright from 'doing what it was constitutionally their right to do at their own risk, namely, publish and be damned, subject to what a jury might think of it if the plaintiff chose to bring an action on what they published'. The following day, the three Appeal Court judges declined to continue the injunction. They held that

> though Mr Maurice Fraser, the author of the report, was under a contractual obligation of confidence to the Greek Government, that Government had no corresponding obligation of confidence to him and they alone had the *locus standi* to complain against any proposed publication.

In his judgement, the grandstanding Master of the Rolls, Lord Denning, said that

> in the end what it came back to was: there were some spheres of activity in which the public concern was such that the newspapers, the press, and indeed everyone might be entitled to make a matter public. Freedom of speech and expression was the foundation of that. The *Sunday Times* had asserted that in the present case they were acting in the public interest and therefore should not be restrained. That was

a matter the Court could not prejudge by granting an injunction against them. The injunction that had been granted should be lifted and the *Sunday Times* should be allowed to publish the article at their risk.

If the paper were guilty of libel, breach of confidence or copyright that could be determined in an action in the courts and damages awarded against it. 'But it was not a case for granting an interim injunction in advance of an article when the court did not know what it would contain.' The way was now open for the *Sunday Times* to publish at its own risk, although with the various leaks that had occurred during the intervening fortnight there was some prospect that it might not have anything very startling left to say, particularly as on the evening of the Appeal Court judgement the Greek regime itself had released the text of the report.

At the same time, articles were being written by newspapers without access to the report on the need for a register of the outside interests of MPs, particularly after Ivor Richard's announcement of his intention to table a motion asking the House of Commons to appoint a select committee to investigate and report on the activities of Maurice Fraser Associates and 'their relationship with members of this honourable House in connection with the affairs and activities of the present Greek Government'. This renewal of interest in the question of MPs' outside interests, however, by no means met with the approval of all MPs. One Conservative member, Tom Iremonger (Ilford North), for instance, denounced recent moves by Liberal MPs to secure voluntary disclosure by MPs of company directorships and other sources of outside income as 'vulgar exhibitionism'.

On Sunday 6 October, the much-trumpeted revelations of the *Sunday Times* appeared. All three broadsheet Sunday newspapers, the *Sunday Times*, the *Sunday Telegraph* and the *Observer*, devoted considerable attention to Fraser's activities and to the broader issues raised by the phenomenon of political public relations. All three devoted leading articles to the issue of press freedom raised by the initial granting of an injunction to Fraser. A surprising development was the *Sunday Telegraph*'s publication, as a spoiler, of the complete original English text of Fraser's controversial fifth report. The *Sunday Times* devoted a lengthy and somewhat involved article to an account of Fraser's activities, including a digression into a rather baffling piece of Greek intrigue involving Zapheiris Pappas, secretary of the Greek Shipping Co-ordination Committee, which reflected the interests of Greek shipowners based in London, and Colonel Aristides Voulgaris of the Directorate for the Enlightenment of Foreign Public Opinion in Athens. Pappas, a former director of the Piraeus security police, was apparently anxious that one of his own nominees, who could 'do the work of ten Frasers', be given Fraser's public relations contract. It is worth noting in parenthesis that the Association of Greek Shipowners had made Colonel Papadopoulos its president for life, an office which he presumably continued to hold until his death in prison in 1999. When writing about the Colonels I have frequently mentioned this fact, for it affords a striking demonstration how closely many of the shipowners were in cahoots with the junta.

As comprehensive an account as is available of Fraser's energetic endeavours in promoting the Colonels' cause is to be found in the 'authorised' version of his report as it appeared in the *Sunday Telegraph*. There are, for instance, no fewer than 35 entries under the general heading of 'Results', and these indicate an extraordinary range of activity, from negotiating British participation in the 'Olympiad of Song' (whatever that may have been) and the issuing of press releases, to claims that Fraser had made approaches to influential political personages. Fraser's own account of his initatives was in a number of cases hotly contested by the persons concerned. Result ten, for instance, reads:

> We made contact with Dr Puttkamer in Germany, personal assistant to Foreign Minister [Willy] Brandt, and a friend of our Director in Bonn. Dr Puttkamer has made it clear to us that he is quite prepared to be persuaded that the Greek government's intentions are honourable and to report this to Herr Brandt. At the time of writing he is trying to persuade Herr Brandt to let him visit Greece to see for himself, and I must stress that this visit would have to be carried out in secrecy so as not to compromise Dr Puttkamer or Herr Brandt.

The *Sunday Telegraph* 'Close Up' team, arch rivals of the *Sunday Times* 'Insight' team, contacted Jesco von Puttkamer who, they said, was nothing to do with foreign minister Brandt but was the editor of the Social Democrat weekly *Vorwärts* and, subsequently, West German ambassador to Israel. Von Puttkamer vigorously denied the account in the fifth report. According to the 'Close Up' team, he said that, in June 1968, he had been approached by a Herr Finkel, one of Fraser's men in Bonn, who had offered him and his wife a free trip to Greece. 'I said to him, "Are you mad?" I told him to read my paper. There he would find out what we thought of the Greek military junta.' A week later the persistent Herr Finkel was back again, this time with the suggestion that the trip could be made in secret. '"I would only be expected to make a private report to the party leader, Herr Brandt," Puttkamer told us.' The offer was declined.

One of the listed results (number 22) referred to an invitation to Lord Thomson, the proprietor of the *Sunday Times* and *The Times*, 'to interview the Prime Minister [Papadopoulos] and to see if he can be of any assistance in regard to television'. The [Daily] *Times* claimed that Lord Thomson, on receiving the invitation, had immediately declined it. But the *Sunday Telegraph* reproduced the text of Fraser's correspondence with Lord Thomson, although this was not printed in the paper's first edition which rolled off the presses in the early evening of Saturday. This showed that Thomson's refusal was not quite as forthright as *The Times* had claimed, for he had concluded his letter: 'I think it could be possible next year if it is still your wish that I should go at that time.'

Under the heading of plans (number ten), Fraser claimed that 'We are in the process of making approaches to a head of the BBC through a third party with a view to trying to tone down the hostility that has been shown.' What was meant by this remark is not completely clear, but the Athens regime always showed itself to be extremely sensitive to the broadcasts of foreign stations, particularly those broadcasting in Greek from Western Europe, such as Deutsche Welle and, above all, the BBC in view of its high reputation in Greece dating back to the Axis occupation. The mention of a third party may have been a reference to Francis Noel-Baker, the Labour MP who owned an extensive property in Greece, and who had certainly sought to put pressure on the BBC Greek Service to tone down its coverage of Greek affairs. Documents in the Public Record Office demonstrate that, at much the same time as the Fraser affair, Noel-Baker had complained that the BBC Greek Service was 'too unsympathetic to the present regime'. Noel-Baker's views appear to have been shared by the British Embassy in Athens.

Undoubtedly, however, the item that aroused most interest in the fifth report was Fraser's claim to have in 'the organisation in London […] a British M.P., Lobbiest' [*sic*]. The English original of the report continued, 'We have to disguise the identity of the British M.P. who is our lobbiest as this would compromise him. His name will be made available to the Prime Minister.' Understandably, whoever translated the fifth report into Greek had some difficulty with the term 'lobbyist' and, reasonably enough, given that there is no Greek equivalent for the word, paraphrased rather than translated it as someone who '*ergazetai paraskiniakos me skopon na epireasi allous Anglous vouleftes*': ('works behind the scenes with the aim of influencing other English [*sic*] members of parliament'). Fraser categorically denied to the *Sunday Telegraph* that 'a British M.P. is working for me behind the scenes to influence people'.

A number of the free-loading MPs who had been to Greece to observe the referendum on the 'constitution' (although not the MP in question, whose identity at this stage was still unknown) doubted whether Fraser had an MP working for him, and denied that they themselves were involved. One of these, Anthony Buck (Conservative, Colchester), who had been a member of the initial 'fact-finding' mission, pertinently commented that 'it seems to me there is a double standard here with all this fuss. What about MPs' visits to Iron Curtain countries?' Buck had a point. Many of the calls for the international ostracism of the Colonels came from those concerned to strengthen ties with the tyrannies of Eastern Europe. Harold Wilson, for instance, would scarcely have thought it politic to say about Greece what he said in the summer of 1973 about the Soviet invasion of Czechoslovakia in 1968, namely that it was time to let bygones be bygones. Indeed, one of the first acts of the Labour government following its victory in the first 1974 election was to cancel a courtesy visit to Greece by the Royal Navy.

Although the *Sunday Times* had adopted a censorious attitude towards Fraser's activities, Victor Lewis, a past president of the Institute of Public Relations, of which Fraser was a member, said that he could see nothing wrong or unprofessional in Fraser's conduct. Lewis declared that it would not be unprofessional conduct for a PR man to pay an MP to 'work behind the scenes in order to influence other MPs'. 'I can on the evidence of today's reports,' he was reported as saying, 'see nothing irregular in the activities of Maurice Fraser Associates. There is nothing to suggest that he is in breach of the code of professional conduct under which he operates as a member of the Institute.' In the event, however, Fraser announced his intention to resign his membership of the Institute after its council, following hearings before its disciplinary committee, decided to suspend his membership.

The immediate furore over Fraser's activities soon died down, but public interest continued to be focused on the question of MPs' outside interests, and particularly their links with public relations firms. Fraser himself took part in this debate in a letter to *The Times*. He concluded

> let us be quite clear about this, that when the prime minister of a country which is opposed to your client's country openly gives money to one of your client's opposition leaders and that leader has himself declared that he intends civil war in your client country, then you cannot meet such a problem by sitting around drinking tea while your secretaries roll out press releases, even if the facts you put out are truthful.

'Truth,' he continued, 'must be used as a weapon in combat because we are not selling washing powder but dealing with such matters as people's lives, nations' views and the direction of alliances.' Fraser was presumably referring here to Olaf Palme, the prime minister of Sweden, and to Andreas Papandreou, who had briefly settled in Sweden after he had been allowed by the junta, in somewhat mysterious circumstances, to leave Greece in early January 1968, and who was threatening to mobilise armed resistance against the junta, although, in the event, this never materialised.

Interest in the activities of Maurice Fraser and Associates then subsided, to be revived a few months later in a further flurry of media publicity. This was to lead to the establishment by the House of Commons of a select committee to inquire into the whole question of members' outside interests. In mid-February 1969, an investigation by the Thames Television *This Week* programme into Fraser's activities was halted by a writ alleging libel against the *Sunday Times*. Eventually, a truncated version of the programme was shown following discussions between the Independent Television Authority, the body responsible for regulating independent television, and Thames Television and its lawyers. Two sections of the programme had been excised. One dealt with an inquiry, partly financed by Maurice Fraser and Associates, into business opinion about the regime carried out by P.A. Management Consultants. The second was an interview with a former employee of Fraser, Howard Preece, a onetime member of the parliamentary staff of the *Daily Mirror* and a former president of the Oxford Union. In the course of this interview, Preece had apparently given the name of the MP who had been retained by Fraser. The Independent Television Authority, apparently on the ground that the matter was now *sub judice*, insisted on the deletion of this item. Nonetheless, in an unscheduled aside at the end of the programme, John Morgan, the presenter, whom, as we have seen, I had encountered in Athens a few days after the 1967 coup, made it clear that *This Week* had evidence of a connection between Maurice Fraser and a specific MP.

The screening of the programme in turn prompted Gordon Bagier, Labour MP for Sunderland South, to issue the following statement:

> Suggestions have been made in the Press and on television that a British MP has received payment from the present Government of Greece to influence opinion in Parliament and in the country. I understand that my name has been widely mentioned. It is true that I visited Greece last Easter and in September 1968 to observe the referendum and that these visits were arranged by the public relations firm of Maurice Fraser and Associates. On each occasion I went with other MPs.
>
> Last May I was invited by Maurice Fraser and Associates to accept a retainer as parliamentary consultant. I was to receive a salary and commission on any new business which resulted in contracts. The business was to be in the field of public relations. I accepted the offer and acted as consultant until October 1968 when I resigned.[3] At no time did Maurice Fraser and Associates ask me to take any action in Parliament or outside on behalf of the present Greek Government. I have made no speech in the House with reference to the situation in Greece, nor have I made any representations to any Government Department.

> I have not used my position as an MP to further the interests of the firm of Maurice Fraser and Associates. There are many MPs who combine their membership with business or professional activities outside and this does not in any way affect their conduct as members.

The *Sunday Telegraph*'s political correspondent, Ian Waller, revealed that Bagier's retainer had been £500 per annum, plus 10 per cent of the value of any new business that he attracted to the firm. An MP's parliamentary salary at this time was approximately £4,000 per annum. My own starting salary as a junior lecturer at Edinburgh University in 1968 was £1,470 per annum, the lowest point on the lecturer scale. Bagier's fee, although generous by academic standards, appears to have been relatively modest by the standards of parliamentary consultancies. Some years later, for instance, Brian Walden, Labour MP for Birmingham All Saints, was reported to be receiving more in the shape of a retainer from the National Association of Bookmakers than his parliamentary salary.

In the wake of the furore over the *This Week* programme, Maurice Fraser and Associates issued a statement which, *inter alia*, declared that 'we have repeatedly been asked about an MP and have categorically denied that there was any MP in the pay of the Greek Government'. 'Had we had anything to hide', he continued,

> we would have personally paid the MP secretly in cash. Instead he had a proper contract. It will be said that we should not therefore have described him as a lobbyist. This is perfectly true. He should in fact have been described as a parliamentary consultant. But we were working at tremendous speed at the time and in Greece the word lobbyist is only understood in a broad sense.

Fraser insisted that at no time had he ever described Bagier as an 'MP working behind the scenes to influence other M.P.s', and expressed the hope that those who had said so would have the decency to retract their statements. On the face of it this was a puzzling request given that the official Greek version of Fraser's fifth report made unambiguous reference to an MP working in precisely such a capacity. But the answer presumably lay in his being unaware of the way in which 'lobbyist' had been translated by one of his employees into Greek.

Bagier strenuously denied misusing his position and received the full backing of his constituency party. The 'club culture' prevailing in the House of Commons, which made MPs so resistant to the introduction of any kind of register of their outside interests, is strikingly illustrated in the words of comfort offered by the Liberal MP David Steel, subsequently leader of his party:

Mr Gordon Bagier, Labour MP for Sunderland South, is as pleasant a fellow as one would wish to meet in the House of Commons. It is difficult to imagine him involved in skulduggery of any kind. He was unwise to accept the £500 from Maurice Fraser and Associates, the Greek Colonels' PR man in Britain, but there is nothing more to it than that.

But then the future leader of the Liberal Party seemingly had no qualms about presenting the Romanian dictator Nicolae Ceaușescu, as unpleasant a fellow as one would wish to meet anywhere, with one of his own labrador's puppies. Ian Waller, the political correspondent of the *Sunday Telegraph*, perhaps had the measure of Bagier when he wrote that the MP was 'more sinned against than sinning; a man caught up in an alien world that the more sophisticated would have steered clear of'.

By now the momentum for some move by the government for an inquiry into the question of MPs' outside interests, and the rules and conventions of the House of Commons in declaring such interests, was irresistible. The prime minister, Harold Wilson, soon after the *This Week* programme was broadcast, recommended that a select committee be set up to inquire into the whole matter, and such a committee duly came into being in May 1969. The committee heard evidence from Colin Mann, a past president of the Institute of Public Relations. Mann reported that the Institute's disciplinary committee had found Fraser not to have employed any MP as a lobbyist 'with the object of achieving a specific end.' Rather he had been employed as a consultant to advise on parliamentary matters. The parliamentary select committee ranged widely in the evidence which it took, but its principal recommendations were scarcely far reaching. It rejected the idea of a register, open to public inspection, of the outside interests of members of parliament, along the lines of the register that had already been voluntarily adopted by the Liberal Party. Instead, it limited itself to recommending that the House of Commons adopt two resolutions, which together would comprise a code of conduct for members of parliament.

These were amplifications of earlier resolutions calling on members to disclose, in parliamentary proceedings, 'any relevant interest or benefit of whatever nature, whether direct or indirect' and forbidding the advocacy of 'any bill, motion, matter or cause for a fee, payment, retainer or reward, direct or indirect'. Although the committee's recommendations were essentially a damp squib, there was subsequently a decline in the number of MPs accepting freebies dangled before them by PR firms acting on behalf of unappealing foreign governments. Moreover, in the wake of the contretemps over the activities of Maurice Fraser and Associates, the Greek regime, having so comprehensively burned its collective fingers, placed little emphasis on this particular method of gaining a more sympathetic hearing in Western political circles. Perhaps predictably, the select committee on this occasion failed to come to grips with what was, and indeed remains, a serious problem, and chose to kick the whole issue into the long grass.

Such a compulsory register did come into existence a few years later, following another, much greater scandal, the Poulson affair. This claimed Reginald Maudling, the Conservative Home Secretary, among its victims. The case of the bent architect and the greedy Tory politician put pressure on parliament to put its house at least partially in order, although it was not until 1994, following the inquiry by Lord Nolan into standards in public life, that MPs were barred from being 'paid lobbyists' of the Bagier variety. It is difficult to think of a single positive contribution made by the Colonels during their seven-year misrule (even their attempt to regulate the chaotic Athenian taxi system foundered) but, indirectly at least, they did help to clean up British public life. For Papadopoulos could in some sense be considered as the grandfather, or should I say godfather, of the present compulsory register of members' interests in the British parliament. And if Papadopoulos is the godfather of the register, then I might somewhat immodestly claim to be its midwife.

I did not have much contact with the British embassy in Athens during the period of the Colonels' misrule. I did, however, occasionally have an agreeable lunch with Roger Tomkys while he was head of chancery at the embassy. Following a distinguished diplomatic career, he subsequently became Master of Pembroke College, Cambridge. I got the impression that he had been detailed to keep in touch with those such as myself who made no secret of their hostility towards the Colonels. One day in the early seventies, Tomkys telephoned me in my modest Omonoia hotel with an invitation to meet our man in Athens, Sir Robin Hooper, to discuss the current situation. As a relatively young lecturer I was mildly flattered by this approach and duly went to see him. As far as I have been able to establish this meeting took place at ten o'clock on the morning of 21 April 1972, oddly enough the fifth anniversary of the Colonels' seizure of power in 1967.

I hoped that we might have a sensible discussion about the situation and, in particular, about Britain's pusillanimous official line towards the junta with which it sought to maintain a 'good working relationship'. Such hopes, however, were soon to be dashed. For scarcely had I sat down than Hooper proceeded to berate me for agitating against the Colonels. Some of my anti-Colonel contacts were, so he said, regarded by his Greek friends as little more than criminals. He mentioned by name Professor Georgios-Alexandros Mangakis, who had been sentenced to 18 years in prison as a member of the resistance group *Dimokratiki Amyna* (Democratic Defence). Just a few days before our meeting Mangakis had been temporarily released on grounds of ill health and whisked out of Greece on a German military transport, seemingly with the connivance of Papadopoulos himself. I was somewhat taken aback by Hooper's outburst as I do not recall ever having met Mangakis, although I certainly admired the courageous stand that he had taken. Hooper then proceeded to tell me how, when posted to NATO Headquarters in Brussels in the early 1960s (he had served as Assistant Secretary-General (Political) at NATO between 1960 and 1966), he had witnessed at firsthand how de Gaulle had saved France. Puffing away at his pipe, he assured me that Papadopoulos had likewise been the saviour of Greece, and that I should make no mistake about it. It rapidly became clear that our conversation was going nowhere so, as the saying goes, I made my excuses and left. Hooper's parting remark was that I must come and have some 'grub' some time, although, mercifully, this rather half-hearted invitation never materialised.

The opening of the Foreign Office papers for the period of the Colonels' dictatorship revealed the depth of Hooper's hostility to the Greek Service of the BBC. In his annual report for 1973 to the Foreign Secretary, Sir Alec Douglas-Home, he wrote of the bad press outside Greece which the regime continued to receive:

> the anti-régime lobbies (in which I include the Greek Service of the BBC, which appears to be pursuing, on Government money, a policy which bears little resemblance to the one which you, Sir, pay me to carry out) were hard at work.

Back in London, soon after my dispiriting encounter with Hooper, I met with Monty Woodhouse, then MP for Oxford, at the House of Commons. Knowing that I had recently been in Athens, Monty asked me for my impressions. *Inter alia*, I told him of my rather one-sided encounter with Hooper. I thought no more about the matter until a curious incident more than three years later. In November 1975, the Greek Embassy in London organised a Greek Month to celebrate the downfall of the Colonels the previous year, and as part of the programme I found myself chairing a panel on contemporary Greek literature. As I knew almost nothing of the subject, I was a little nervous about the evening. I was even more so when told that one of the panellists, Costas Tachtsis, author of an excellent novel, *To Trito Stephani* (The Third Wedding), might turn up dressed as a woman. In the event he did not turn up at all.

In the midst of the various cultural events there was a rather grand reception at the Savoy Hotel, which had turned its hand to Greek cuisine for what I take to have been the first, and devoutly hope was the last, time. Its version of a *horiatiki salata* had to be tasted to be believed. In the crowd I spotted Robin Hooper, by this time retired from the Foreign Office, and by now chairman of the Anglo-Hellenic League, the somewhat snooty organisation that endeavoured, not altogether successfully, to promote cultural relations between Britain and Greece. He was on his own and looking rather at a loose end, as indeed Mary Jo and I felt ourselves to be amid the usual throng of shipowners and their bejewelled and befurred spouses. So I went up to introduce Mary Jo to him. As I sought to do this, he turned his back on us and stormed off. I was naturally taken aback by such rudeness. So I followed after, tapped him on the shoulder and asked him what the problem was. He replied that he did not speak to people who betrayed confidences. At first I had no idea what he was talking about, but he then went on to complain that Woodhouse had referred to his equation of Papadopoulos with de Gaulle in a speech in the House of Commons. Not being an obsessive reader of *Hansard*, I replied that this was news to me, which indeed it was, and that was about the sum of our conversation. At no stage during our brief encounter did he deny having made such a fatuous comparison. I can understand that Hooper might have felt peeved, but I had not leaked the story to Monty with the intention that he should publicise Hooper's views. However, I cannot in all honesty say that I was heartbroken that this absurd assessment had been placed on record, although, so far as I am aware, the story got no further than *Hansard* and was not picked up by any of the papers, which were usually ready to have a go at Foreign Office stuffed shirts whenever they made fatuous comments.

Monty did not make the speech in question until June 1973, well over a year, by my calculation, after our chat. He was reported in *Hansard* as saying that 'I am told that our Ambassador in Athens has explicitly compared Papadopoulos with de Gaulle', adding, in characteristic fashion, that 'I do not believe that he did that in order to insult the memory of the French President.' He never told me of this speech, although he did make brief reference to it in his 1982 autobiography, *Something Ventured*. As I was to discover only in 2004, when a former student of mine, Viron Karidis, came across the correspondence among newly released documents in the Public Record Office, the Foreign Office had duly notified the Athens embassy of Woodhouse's comments a few days after the debate. In a 'personal and confidential' letter in reply, Hooper wrote to the head of the South European Department, that he had no idea where Woodhouse had got the story, although my name came to mind 'as a possibility'. If I am right in thinking that my meeting with Hooper took place in April 1972, the only time, so far as I remember, that I spoke to him apart from our brief encounter at the Savoy, it seems odd that he should have thought of me as a possible source some 15 months later unless he had some recollection, however dim, of a conversation along the lines that I recalled. At the Savoy, Hooper had simply assumed, correctly as it happens, that I must have been Woodhouse's source. The fact that he never accused me of distorting the thrust of our conversation at the embassy, but rather of revealing it to a third party, would appear to confirm that he had indeed uttered the name of de Gaulle in the same breath as that of Papadopoulos during our brief, dispiriting and one-sided encounter.

Indeed, he conceded as much in his letter to the Foreign Office when he went on to say that

> there are obvious parallels between the present Greek regime and the seamier side of Gaullism, and after six years' experience of the latter, it would be odd if I hadn't from time to time drawn them. No doubt I have on occasion said to visitors [...] that Papadopoulos has a highly developed Messiah complex [...] and that like de Gaulle, he may see himself as the national leader sent by Heaven to clear up the mess.

Nonetheless, he emphasised, 'the idea that anyone who has been exposed to both could possibly put Papadopoulos and de Gaulle in the same class is too absurd to refute'. While he regretted that Woodhouse had had the wool pulled over his eyes, he did not take the matter 'too tragically' and would refrain from making 'pompous noises about the ethics of making innuendos under parliamentary privilege against those who have no right of public reply'. It does not seem to have occurred to him that I had no right of reply, either public or private, to his holding me up as 'an example – and a warning – of how totally unscrupulous some of the opponents – both British and Greek – of the [Colonels'] regime can be in twisting, misrepresenting, and quoting out of context to suit their own ends'. This was some charge to level at someone who makes his living as an historian.

It seems scarcely credible that Hooper should have espoused such a view of Papadopoulos, but this was apparently not the only occasion on which he expressed disconcerting views about the Colonels. I remember speaking of my brief encounter with him to Nigel Clive, a friend who had parachuted into Greece on behalf of SIS in 1943, married a charming Greek, and worked for the Secret Intelligence Service for many years after the war. I said that he must have found it difficult to credit what Hooper had said to me. Not at all, he replied, it was absolutely in character. He recalled that on the night that Karamanlis returned to Greece on the implosion of the junta in July 1974, he was having a drink on the Embassy terrace with Hooper and a very prominent American journalist. As they watched the vast and delirious crowd assembling to greet Karamanlis returning to Greece like some *deus ex machina*, Hooper expressed the view that the Greeks would live to regret the collapse of the Colonels' regime. Clive could scarcely believe his ears and spent an anxious few days fearing that the journalist would quote Hooper in his paper, but he did not do so.

As I have often quoted in various publications some of the more pungent comments to be found in the Foreign Office papers in the Public Record Office, I can scarcely complain of Hooper's outburst. Indeed, not long after my bollocking by Hooper, I was harangued at considerable length by another Foreign Office panjandrum, David Balfour. This was for having the temerity to quote from the abusive, and wholly unwarranted, attacks of Rex Leeper, when ambassador to the Greek government-in-exile in Cairo in 1943, on another old friend of mine, Brigadier Eddie Myers, Woodhouse's predecessor as commander of the military mission to the resistance in occupied Greece. These were contained in letters penned by an overwrought Leeper, in the torrid heat of a Cairene summer, to the deputy permanent under-secretary at the Foreign Office, Sir Orme 'Moley' Sargent, a man who manifested a marked reluctance to serve overseas. I had come across these in the great flood of documents relating to World War II that were released to the Public Record Office in 1972 and had published some of the juicier outbursts in my contribution to the proceedings of the 1973 Cumberland Lodge conference on Britain and the wartime resistance in Greece and Yugoslavia. At the conclusion of his long, one-sided, choleric and unprofitable harangue over the telephone, Balfour declared that he was going to 'report' me to the Foreign Office for quoting from 'most secret and personal' letters, which, as I continually, but to no avail, sought to impress upon him, were, by the 1970s, freely available in the Public Record Office. I do not know if he carried out his threat, but if he did then there is presumably yet another unflattering letter about my caddish behaviour lurking somewhere in the recesses of the FCO.

Balfour was an exotic character with a strong physical resemblance to Edward VII. He had undergone several metamorphoses in the course of his long life: from Catholic priest to Russian Orthodox monk; from Greek Orthodox parish priest and confessor to King George II of Greece and the Greek court to army officer; and finally to diplomat, latterly serving as chief interpreter to the Foreign Office. Not altogether surprisingly, he was widely believed in Greece to be working for the devilishly cunning 'Intelligence Service'. Indeed, I was once told, in all seriousness, by a woman in Athens at a gathering organised by the BBC Greek Service, that Balfour had been raised from the age of five, in the manner of a janissary, with a view to future service on behalf of the 'Intelligence Service'. This hardly seems to have been the style of the Secret Intelligence Service. Yet many Greeks, among them Professor Nikolaos Louros, a highly distinguished doctor, were convinced that Balfour was a *praktoras*, or agent, and deplored the use of the institutions of the church by international espionage. (Louros, incidentally, once told me that, having assisted at the birth of Melina Mercouri, he could reveal that she was somewhat older than her publicly proclaimed age.) In retirement Balfour became the oldest individual (at the age of 75) to be awarded an Oxford DPhil, for a thesis on the fifteenth-century Byzantine archbishop, Simeon of Thessaloniki.

Prior to my unhappy encounter with Hooper I had had occasional contact with the British Embassy. On one occasion, I accompanied the press officer to the site of the purported assassination attempt by Alekos Panagoulis against Papadopoulos on 13 August 1968. This occurred when there was a small explosion aimed at Papadopoulos' heavily armoured Lincoln Continental (once the property of Kwame Nkrumah of Ghana) near a culvert on the coastal road not far from his summer residence in Lagonisi. Having checked out the scene of the attempt, I subsequently wrote for Eleni Vlachou's *Hellenic Review* a detailed account exposing the many contradictions in the official version of what had happened given by the regime's spokesman, Viron Stamatopoulos. This was given the byline of 'Our Athens crime reporter'. By contrast, I had only one, unsatisfactory, encounter with the US Embassy in Athens during the *eptaetia*, the seven-year dictatorship. This was in 1973 when I was invited to lunch (which consisted of a miserable sandwich) by a rather boorish official who repeatedly asked me whether Eleni Vlachou was sending money to the students who, in February and March, had occupied the law faculty of the University of Athens in protest at the lack of democracy. I had not the slightest idea whether she was or was not, and replied that I thought it unlikely. It seemed to be quite beyond the wit of US diplomats to imagine that the students themselves might have begun to demand an end to the dictatorship without needing incitement or money from abroad.

One of the still unresolved mysteries of the period of the Colonels' dictatorship is the brutal murder in a beachside suburb of Athens in October 1971 of Ann Chapman, a young British freelance radio journalist. I never met Chapman. Indeed, the first I heard of her was when I read of the sad murder in the British press, where it was given wide publicity. Attempts, however, were subsequently made to link my name to some of the various conspiracy theories to which the affair gave rise. Just before departing for Athens, Chapman had apparently told her mother that she was on to a big story that would ensure her a worldwide reputation as an investigative journalist. After her death, all kinds of rumours circulated of her involvement in anti-junta resistance activities and it was in these that I was supposedly implicated. Particular significance was attached to the fact that her visit to Greece coincided with that of Spiro Agnew, the subsequently disgraced Greek–American vice-president in the Nixon administration, who was visiting his ancestral homeland. A semi-literate Greek labourer was convicted for what was declared by the Greek authorities to be a squalid, sexually motivated, murder, wholly devoid of political overtones. Her distraught father, Edward Chapman, understandably became obsessed with finding out the truth behind his daughter's murder, and his tenacity kept the case in the public eye for many years.

One of those who took up the story was a Greek journalist and historian, Giannis Andrikopoulos, who had been active in anti-Colonel activities based in London and has subsequently established a 'new age' holiday centre on one of the Greek islands. During the period of the dictatorship I had had a passing acquaintance with him. One day in the early 1980s he came to see me in my office at King's College and began to ask questions which appeared to link me with various members of the anti-junta resistance who might have been involved in despatching Ann Chapman on the mission which culminated in her death. He was particularly interested in Martin Packard, a naval officer who had served in Cyprus in the early 1960s, was Greek-speaking, married to a Greek, and was reputed to have been a squash partner of ex-King Constantine. Andrikopoulos' questions and remarks were fantastic and were aimed at implicating me in some obscure way, which I never fully understood, in the '*ypothesi Chapman*', the Chapman affair. It was not long before I (figuratively) threw him out of my office, saying that if he wrote anything linking my name to the affair I might have to make life difficult for him. How I was going to deliver on this threat I had no idea, but my blood was up.

Anyway, not long afterwards, Andrikopoulos wrote a series of, to me at least, incoherent articles in January 1983 for the Athenian newspaper, *Eleftherotypia*, under the general heading 'The [British] Intelligence [Service] "shopped" the resistance to the junta: the dirty and traitorous stand of "Group C" towards the Greek resistance organisations'. This article duly referred to me, albeit not by name. The offending passage read as follows:

> a Greek-speaking Englishman, a London University professor, who warned me that if I mentioned his name in the course of this investigation, or his 'brief' connection with Packard, then he would 'make my life hell in England', told me that Packard as head of the 'Greek' section of the Intelligence Service had, at first, close

links with the deposed King Constantine. Among other things, he said that they had played 'squash' together in Rome.

This record of our brief conversation is accurate only in part. I had indeed attempted to put the frighteners on him to ensure that my name was kept out of whatever wild allegations he was planning to publish. I had mentioned that Packard and Constantine had played squash together, although I believed that these games had taken place in Athens rather than in Rome. I had this information, such as it was, not from Packard himself but from George Yannopoulos. Whether it was true or not I do not know, but it had always stuck in my mind. But I had certainly not said or implied that Packard was 'the head of the "Greek" section of the Intelligence Service'. In fact, I should have thought that extremely unlikely. Ironically, because Andrikopoulos described me as a London University 'professor', which at the time I was not, not many made the connection with me. Indeed, I was told by a former student that the 'London University professor' was assumed to be Douglas Dakin, a professor of history at Birkbeck College and the author of a number of books on the modern history of Greece. Dakin was a dyed-in-the wool conservative, a friend of Spyros Markezinis, the only significant figure among the old politicians willing to collaborate with the Colonels, and a most improbable candidate for any involvement in émigré politics or resistance activity.

If Andrikopoulos did not dare mention me by name, he showed no compunction about blackening Packard's. He believed that the 'resistance' organisation with which Chapman had been in touch was called 'Group C', 'the "Greek" section of British Intelligence', of which, so he alleged, Packard was the head. Andrikopoulos maintained that Packard had declined to meet him when he had telephoned him in 1976, but he had been described by people who knew him as 'a fiendishly clever man of outstanding ability, minimum moral standards and with a formidable social side and also a megalomaniac'. Andrikopoulos claimed that whenever, in the course of his investigations, he had mentioned Packard's name, it had aroused nothing but fear. Andrikopoulos also maintained that when, in 1976, he had contacted Makis Arnaoutis, ex-King Constantine's aide-de-camp, Arnaoutis had described Packard as 'scum'. But in 1982, Arnaoutis had claimed not to know Packard.

Packard, unsurprisingly, was not best pleased by this absurd torrent of abuse and sued Andrikopoulos for libel, taking advantage of restrictive British libel laws which allowed such action on the ground that a few copies of *Eleftherotypia* circulated in Britain. Andrikopoulos chose to defend himself in person and Packard was awarded £450,000 in libel damages in 1987, apparently the highest such award made in the UK up to that time. But Andrikopoulos, apart from a token payment, could not pay up and Packard was left with most of his own substantial legal costs. If Andrikopoulos had mentioned me by name in the *Eleftherotypia* articles then I might, too, have had grounds for legal action and might have secured a massive award of damages, although any victory in the courts would have been, like Packard's, a Pyrrhic one. In a bizarre footnote to the story, the CIA in 1994 attempted to convince the British government that Packard was spying for the Russians. He was summoned to the presence by MI6, shown 'a huge volume of missives' sent by the CIA, purporting to demonstrate 'compelling and incontrovertible evidence' for its charge. MI6 was not impressed by the CIA's claims.

Later in the 1980s, I experienced another uncomfortable and similarly short-lived interview about the Chapman affair. This time my would-be interviewer was Richard Cottrell, Conservative member of the European Parliament for Bristol and Bath. He was a former TV journalist and the author of *Blood on their Hands: The Killing of Ann Chapman* (1987), a book, incidentally, which was bitterly criticised by Chapman's father, Edward. Cottrell came to my office at King's and began asking questions in a somewhat aggressive fashion about my purported involvement in the Ann Chapman affair. I had offered him a cup of coffee but before this had even been half-drunk Cottrell, like Andrikopoulos, was on his way and I heard no more from him. I should have thought that he might have learned from his experience as a TV journalist that it is almost always more productive to try and get alongside those you are interviewing rather than adopting the blustering manner he demonstrated when he came to see me. Although I had no inside knowledge of the Chapman affair, I should have thought it highly unlikely that she was murdered because she was privy to the work of the Greek resistance or, as Cottrell suggests, because she had become aware of high-level deals involving the partition of Cyprus being discussed with the Colonels by Richard Nixon's vice-president, Spiro Agnew, who was at that time in Athens. Brutal though the junta was in its treatment of Greek opponents, it was not in the habit of physically harming foreigners. But the real circumstances of, and motives behind, the sad murder of Ann Chapman remain a mystery.

Although I scarcely hid my anti-dictatorship views under a bushel, I never experienced any difficulty in getting into Greece while the Colonels were in power, although my brother, John, was briefly taken to one side at Athens airport by immigration authorities, apparently under the impression that he was me. It was always at the back of my mind, however, that I might be stopped, although, at worst, I would have been denied entry, which says something about the nature of the dictatorship. My involvement in anti-dictatorship activities would presumably have earned me a file in the voluminous archive of the *Asphaleia*, the Greek security police. But regrettably this archive was deliberately destroyed by the government in the 1980s despite the vociferous opposition of many historians in Greece who were alarmed at the prospect of the loss of this priceless historical resource.

Once, I remember, I arrived in Athens with a plane load of Everton supporters (in the days when English football supporters were reasonably well behaved) whose team was playing a match in Greece. As they got off the plane they started chanting 'Everton, Everton', I joined in and we were all whisked through immigration with the barest minimum of formalities. In 1973, however, when I travelled with Mary Jo, Rachel and our one-year-old son, Nathan, to Greece, I thought that the security police had at last caught up with me. We were travelling on a cheap night flight, and, as we were queuing up to go through immigration at the rather run-down Ellinikon airport, a policeman came up to us and marched us to the front of the queue. This was it, I thought: there was going to be trouble ahead. In fact, all the policeman was doing, in characteristic Greek fashion, was giving us priority as we were carrying a baby. Incidentally, during this trip we had lunch with Yanko and Miranda Pesmazoglou, just a few days after Yanko's release from imprisonment in the notorious EAT/ESA military police headquarters. Miranda served wonderful chocolate ice cream; Nathan's eyes nearly popped out of his head, and, for the first time, he began to feed himself.

The military regime finally collapsed under the weight of its own incompetent belligerence in July 1974, following its short-lived overthrow of the President of Cyprus, Archbishop Makarios, a putsch which provoked the Turkish invasion and occupation of the north of the island that has lasted ever since. Makarios was rescued by a British helicopter, flown to Malta, and quickly made his way to London and then to New York. The large Greek Cypriot population in North London, many tens of thousands strong, was, unsurprisingly, in turmoil. Soon after Makarios' return to London from New York, the presenter of the BBC's World at One programme called on a member of the Greek Cypriot community to issue an appeal for calm in Greek, the first and only time I ever heard someone speaking in Greek without a translation on BBC domestic radio. This was some way from being an appeal for calm, and the speaker ended with a stirring call for the London Cypriots to rally around the deposed president, saying '*Oloi sto Pratt Street*' (everyone to Pratt Street). This was the street in Camden Town, at that time an area with a larger Greek Cypriot population than it has now, where the Archbishop was about to speak in *Agioi Pantes* (All Saints), an Anglican church that had been made over to the Orthodox.

I immediately raced down the short distance from Crouch End to Camden Town and managed to get into a church that had probably never been as crowded in its history. Not only was the chancel full to bursting but so were the galleries. It would certainly never before have experienced such an emotionally charged and explosive atmosphere. I was standing only a few feet from the Achbishop and seemed to be the only non-Greek there apart from the Archbishop's Special Branch minder (who looked uncannily like my brother, John). Understandably, he looked decidedly nervous in such a volatile atmosphere, not least because he had no view of what was going on in the balcony overhanging the Archbishop's throne. The Archbishop of Thyateira, Athinagoras Kokkinakis, the head of the Greek Orthodox Church in Britain, introduced Makarios, but, as he was considered to have been a supporter of the junta, his words were punctuated with cries of '*Exo oi prodotes*' (out with the traitors). The Special Branch man looked mightily relieved when Makarios had given his rousing speech and the church began to empty. This seemed a fittingly dramatic end to the seven-year dictatorship as it had been experienced in Britain.

There was a curious tailpiece to the excitements of the *eptaetia*, the seven-year dictatorship. In November 1983, I received a telephone call from the Greek Embassy in London inviting me at short notice to attend a gathering in Athens, with all expenses paid, of *xenoi philellines antistasiakoi*, the foreign philhellenic 'resisters' who had been active in campaigning against the junta, to mark the tenth anniversary of the student occupation in November 1973 of the Athens Polytechnic. This, although brutally repressed, had marked the beginning of the end for the dictatorship. I rather got the impression that I had been invited to take part because another invitee had dropped out at a late stage. This feeling was strengthened when I found that I was, as I remember, the only member of the British contingent travelling in business class on the Olympic Airways flight. Those invited from Britain included Monty Woodhouse; Anthony Marreco, the barrister whose investigations on behalf of Amnesty had demonstrated that torture was routinely practised by the junta; Benedict Birnberg, a solicitor; Peter Thompson, a poet, writer and journalist heavily involved in the European–Atlantic Action Committee on Greece; Sir Hugh Greene, the former director-general of the BBC and the chairman of the European–Atlantic Action Committee which focused exclusively on bringing pressure on the Greek dictatorship; and George Forrest, a classicist at Wadham College, Oxford.

As I remember, Diana Pym, an elderly stalwart of the communist-inspired League for Democracy in Greece, was also a member of the group. Hugh Greene was a bear of a man, well-built and well over 6 ft tall, and known to readers of *Private Eye* as Sir Huge Greene. It did briefly cross my mind that I should do the decent thing and offer to exchange my business class seat for his cramped seat in economy. But then I thought that he would have had many more business class trips during his life than I ever would, and I rather selfishly hung on to my more commodious seat.

Incidentally, I have always had something of a soft spot for Olympic Airways, or *Olympiaki Aeroporia*. Known to some in Greece as *Olympiaki Talaiporia*, or Olympic Hassle, the airline always had a poor reputation. In my (distinctly minority) view this was undeserved. In the days when Olympic Airways had its own Greek check-in staff at Heathrow I was twice bumped up to business class by Olympic agents who had had to read the Greek translation of my *A Short History of Modern Greece* at university. Moreover, whenever I have returned from Greece my baggage has been crammed with books and seriously overweight. Books in Greece until recently were cheap, while Greek colleagues are very generous in handing out copies of their works, a practice which was not easy to reciprocate given the ridiculous price of some academic books published in Britain. A recent slim volume of conference papers to which I contributed was priced at £95. Whenever the Olympic check-in agent began to mention excess baggage charges, I needed only to say that my bags were full of books to promote the image of Greece abroad, which had more than an element of truth, for them to be waived. Olympic must surely have been the only airline in the world to demonstrate an appropriate appreciation of the worth of historians as opposed to celebrities.

The 1983 Polytechnic commemoration proved to be a surreal occasion. The participants, who included such luminaries as the economist Kenneth Galbraith, were mainly housed in the King George II hotel in Syntagma Square. Theoretically a luxury class hotel, it had fallen somewhat on hard times. Its extraordinary Tudor Room, however, still offered a spectacular view of the Acropolis. Every morning I would be woken at about 6.00 am by a shouting match in the corridor outside. Apparently, Andreas Papandreou's recently installed PASOK government had engineered the takeover of the hotel by a workers' cooperative, who were arguing at this early hour as to who should do what on their shift. There was an unending succession of receptions and grand dinners, at heaven knows what cost to the Greek taxpayer. At one of these, water began to gush from a broken pipe in the ceiling perilously close to the table where the *episimoi*, or dignitaries, were sitting. Papandreou himself attended many of the manifestations of what cynics dubbed '*I exegersi tis Grande Bretagne*' ('the uprising of the Grande Bretagne'). This was the legendary luxury hotel which adjoined the King George II and where some of the lavish receptions took place. Papandreou was not a visible presence throughout, for, on 15 November, in the middle of the Athens jamboree, the 'Turkish Republic of Northern Cyprus' declared itself independent and the prime minister was called away to deal with the ensuing crisis.

Meanwhile, we were supposed to be among the leaders of a massive protest march to mark the anniversary of the Polytechnic uprising, chanting all the while 'the people united will never be defeated'. These annual demonstrations inevitably, and at times violently, culminated at the US embassy on Vasilissis Sofias. Anthony Marreco and I opted out of this particular event and walked in the opposite direction to pay our respects to Eleni Vlachou and Maria Karavia, doughty members of the 'anthellenic' community in London during the dictatorship, in the offices of *Kathimerini* in Sophokleous Street. We passed a group of Libyans taking part in the march. It was difficult at first to catch what they were chanting, but it turned out to be 'down, down, USA'.

One pleasing event was a ceremony in the University of Athens at which we were presented with certificates by the Association of Imprisoned and Exiled Resisters between 1967 and 1974 in recognition of our supposed contribution, and that of our compatriots, to the overthrow of the dictatorship and to the restoration of democracy in Greece. The certificate reproduced the bloodthirsty decree of Demophantos of 410 BC. This declared that those seeking to overthrow the Athenian democracy and establish a tyranny or holding office under such a tyranny could be murdered with impunity. For some reason I was deemed by the organisers of the gathering to be a journalist, and so, for the next 17 years, I received through the post three or four times a week the bulletins of the Athens News Agency. I tried more than once to stem the tide, but without success. Help was at last at hand when, with the beginning of the new millennium, the bulletins went online.

Each of the participants in this most agreeable (and expensive for the Greek taxpayer) of junkets received a list of all those who had been invited. Leafing through this I saw, among the Norwegian contingent, the name of Arne Treholt, who had contributed a chapter to the book that George Yannopoulos and I had edited on *Greece Under Military Rule* and which had been published in 1972. His had been a rather weak piece, which had required extensive editing, on the European reaction to the Colonels' dictatorship. Treholt had been included at the urging of Andreas Papandreou, to whom, at the time, George, and indeed Treholt, was close. I had also acquired a copy of Treholt's *Marketakis og juntaen* (Marketakis and the Junta) (1969) for the Burrows Library at King's College. This was an account of skulduggery and derring-do at the 1968 Strasbourg hearings of the European Commission of Human Rights of the Council of Europe on torture in Greece. It recounted the case of two Greeks brought to Strasbourg by the junta to testify that they had not been tortured despite reports to the contrary. They had then defected and testified that they had in fact been tortured, whereupon one of the two had redefected to the Colonels. It was the only book in Norwegian in the library's rich holdings on modern Greece and, almost 50 years later, lies unread. The book had a foreword by Andreas Papandreou, with whom Treholt had a close relationship, and at whose Kastri villa he was a frequent guest. I had never met Treholt in person, nor, I believe, had George. So naturally, while in Athens, I sought him out. This was not as easy as it sounds. I eventually ran him to ground and we had a brief chat about the days of the anti-Colonel struggle.

A few weeks later, in early 1984, the BBC television news one evening opened with the presenter saying, 'Top KGB agent arrested in Norway' with a picture of the culprit. It was none other than Treholt, who was named later in the programme as a real-life *praktoras* who had worked for the KGB. Prominent in the politics of the Norwegian Labour Party, he was close to a leading Social Democratic politician and fierce critic of the junta, Jens Evensen. At the time of his arrest Treholt was head of the press division of the Norwegian Foreign Ministry. I was subsequently able to get hold of the almost 200 pages long judgment, fortunately in English, of the Norwegian *Eidsivating* or Court of Appeal. This makes clear that Treholt was in contact with KGB operatives in Norway at the time he was writing his contribution to our book. One of these gave Treholt gifts of caviar, although the court ruled that 'this did not occur more often than is normal in diplomatic circles'. One of the tasks Treholt was charged with by his Soviet contacts before becoming a fully fledged agent was buying up some 50 copies of a book by Jens Haugland imaginatively entitled *Juntaen ut av Hellas* (Junta Get Out of Greece) and sending them to opinion makers.

I was relieved, however, to learn that Treholt became a fully paid-up KGB operative only in 1974, two years after the publication of *Greece Under Military Rule*. In 1985, Treholt was sentenced to a substantial prison term, although he was pardoned by the Labour government in 1992. I understand that in Norway the Treholt case has echoes of the Dreyfus affair, with some passionately championing Treholt's cause and considering him to have been the victim of a rightwing plot, and with others calling for condign punishment. Quite a number of books (some 17 in all) on the Treholt affair have appeared in Norwegian but these, unfortunately, are unintelligible to me. It was also a surprise to learn that Treholt, after the downfall of the junta, had worked for Iraqi intelligence.

By the time Treholt was exposed as a Soviet spy I was working on a history of the Special Operations Executive in Greece, for which I had to get a high level of security clearance, signed by Mrs Thatcher herself. It would have been embarrassing to have to admit to having a KGB agent contributing to one of my books had he already by then been working for, and earning substantial sums of money, from the KGB. I am glad to report that the relevant authorities took a relaxed view of the matter.

When the news came through of the downfall of the junta I remember taking a bottle of whisky for the BBC Greek Service to celebrate with. At this time I was on the Greek Service, World Service and the BBC's domestic services so often that I became rather exhausted and was glad to flee to the Wye Valley for few days with the family to escape the incessant ringing of the telephone. I scored quite a hit with the *Sunday Times* by confidently predicting that the Turks would invade Cyprus following the overthrow of Archbishop Makarios. I was privy to no inside knowledge but my conviction was strengthened by chats with a young Turkish Byzantinist, Melek Delilbaşı, who at that time was working in our department at King's and who, some 30 years later, was to become Dean of the Faculty of Languages, History and Geography of Ankara University. She was absolutely convinced that the Turkish army would invade, and I felt that, if someone as mild-mannered as she felt that there was no alternative to invasion, how then must the Turkish generals be thinking. And so it turned out. On the day of the invasion, 20 July 1974, I was telephoned at the crack of dawn by an admiring Bruce Page of the *Sunday Times* to be told that Turkish paratroops were landing in the north of the island and that my earlier pontifications and prognostications had turned out to be correct.

In September 1974, some five weeks after the downfall of the Colonels, I paid a research visit to Greece. The political atmosphere in Athens was still electric. I remember attending a huge demonstration in Plateia Klafthmonos with the crowd continually chanting 'Doste ti hunta sto lao' (hand over the junta to the people). I naturally called on Takis Lambrias, a journalist whom I had got to know in London during this exile under the Colonels. A close confidant of Karamanlis, he was the minister responsible for the press in the first post-coup government. He was frantically busy and I had to wait quite some time for an audience. But when I did get to see him Takis asked me where I was staying. I mentioned that the name of a rather modest hotel near Omonoia Square. Why do you not move into the Grande Bretagne (probably the most luxurious, and certainly the most famous, hotel in Athens), he asked. He then asked me whether I intended to travel anywhere else in Greece. I said that I was hoping to go to Corfu to interview Lord Glenconner, who had been the head of SOE in Cairo during a critical stage of the war and had a house on the island. Right, he replied, let us take care of your visit. I was somewhat taken aback by this proffered largesse but, after a quick telephone call to Mary Jo to discuss whether my conscience could allow me to accept such hospitality, I agreed to be an official guest of the Greek government and I spent a few days in an almost deserted Grande Bretagne where often the only other diner was the American-born wife of a prominent Greek ship owner, who frequently seemed the worse for wear. In Corfu I was put up in the equally deserted but extremely comfortable five-star Corfu Palace Hotel, having narrowly managed to avert being officially welcomed to the island by the *nomarch*, or prefect. I had the hotel's swimming pool pretty much to myself. One morning I felt a strange sensation of the water lurching. It turned out that the hotel staff had decided to drain the large pool but had not troubled to inform guests, of whom I was about the only one.

At this time I was becoming seriously interested in SOE's wartime involvement in Greece, so it was fascinating to meet Lord Glenconner who had been so closely involved in its affairs in the Middle East. He lived in a wonderful house by the shore in a secluded bay on the west of the island. I put my foot in it somewhat by asking whether a painting on the wall was a real Fragonard. It was. Rather sadly, he told me that he much regretted not having purchased the whole of the bay in which his house was situated as, during the summer months, he was plagued by the thumping sounds emerging from a nightclub built on the part that he did not own. Repeated complaints to the authorities had got him nowhere, and he had been advised that the only way that he could counter the mindless din was to buy a machine to simulate the sound of waves crashing on the shore. And this when his house was within sound of the real sea.

3

Sancte et sapienter. King's College and the School of Slavonic and East European Studies

'It was never so easy to get a job as a paid, professional historian as it was in the second half of the 1960s.'
—Richard Evans, *In Defence of History*

'[In the late 1960s] new staff [in history at the University of Edinburgh] were not always up to scratch.'
—Geoffrey Best, *A Life of Learning*

The alarums and excursions of the propaganda war against the Colonels were all very well, but, with my research fellowship of the Carnegie Trust for the Universities of Scotland due to end in the summer of 1968, I was faced with the urgent need to find gainful employment, if at all possible in the academy. I have no doubt that Richard Evans is correct in saying that at no time was it ever easier to get an academic job in history in the United Kingdom than in the second half of the 1960s, although this did not appear so to me at the time. I was not working in a mainstream field and I did not have much luck with my various applications. What I found most discouraging was that some universities, among them, as I remember, the University of East Anglia, often could not even be bothered to send an acknowledgement that they had received an application, so that I could never be certain that it had even arrived. But just as I was considering applications to the University of Khartoum and the newly established La Trobe University in Melbourne (which, had it been successful, would have enabled me, if not Mary Jo, to qualify as a 'ten pound Pom', eligible for a highly subsidised passage to Australia), at least temporary salvation proved to be at hand.

The University of Edinburgh had advertised a post in modern European history. True, it was only a temporary post, but it was a cut above the normal as it was for two years rather than the much more usual one. Universities had not yet cottoned on to the scam of hiring staff for nine months only and thus not paying them during the long vacation. I duly applied for the job, was interviewed and, to my great relief, appointed. We bought a not very attractive flat in Marchmont, just across the Meadows from the university. Why we should have done this, and incurred hassle and legal costs, when the post was only a temporary one is, in retrospect, not clear. Mary Jo, by now having acquired her diploma in librarianship from University College and pregnant with our first child, Rachel, was able for a time to continue her work on compiling a bibliography of pre-Islamic Iranian studies, under the supervision of J.D. Pearson. Her stipend was paid by the Princess Ashraf Foundation, headed by the twin sister of the Shah.

It was agreeable to be back in Edinburgh, but the post called for expertise in eighteenth-century European history, which was not a period with which I had any great familiarity so I had something of a struggle to get up to the mark. I notionally shared a room with Professor D.B. Horn, one of the panjandrums of the history department with a formidable reputation as an eighteenth-century diplomatic historian. As he reached retirement age, he was working on a history of the university. He very seldom used his office so I had the almost exclusive use of a professorial room. Horn was a thoroughly decent man, although remote. According to departmental lore, when Denys Hay, the medievalist, arrived in Edinburgh soon after the war and attended his first departmental meeting, he overheard someone ask Horn whether he would like to meet the new member of his department, to which Horn had replied 'no'. In the course of the year a permanent post in the modern history of Europe became available. I was not appointed to it. That was understandable, as my heart was not really in the study of mainstream European history, but it was rather galling that the job went to an amusing but lightweight charlatan, who had the wit (and the wherewithal) to wine and dine senior members of the department at Edinburgh's Café Royal. One of those who took some time to get the measure of this character was Geoffrey Best, whose *A Life of Learning* (2010) affords a quirky, albeit entertaining, account of his time as a professor at Edinburgh and subsequently at the University of Sussex. The individual concerned, Best eventually realised, 'was seen through and laughed at by the cleverer students'.

The bad news that there was no possibility of achieving *monimotita*, as the Greeks term the nirvana of permanent (and above all pensionable) employment, coincided with the birth of Rachel in the Elsie Inglis Memorial Maternity Hospital at the foot of the Royal Mile, a Dickensian institution now thankfully closed down. Only later did I discover who Elsie Inglis was, namely the moving spirit behind the Scottish Women's Hospitals, which, after being rebuffed by the stuffed-shirts of the War Office, served in Romania and Serbia during World War I. As I knew from personal experience, the remedy for most, if not quite all, ailments advocated by Scottish doctors and nurses, at least until the 1960s, consisted of copious draughts of bracing, preferably freezing, air. Despite the fact that the Serbs, like many of the Balkan peoples, the Greeks included, had a morbid fear of draughts, these Scottish battleaxes acquired a unique place in the affections of the Serbs. A number of them married Serbs and were still alive in the 1960s.

Scottish nationalism is, we are continually assured by the Scottish National-al Party, a civic nationalism, so, in theory, Rachel should, by virtue of her birth in the Elsie Inglis, have a good claim to Scottish citizenship if, or rather when, it eventually materialises. The reality is, however, rather different. When she was applying to university, knowing how much Mary Jo and I had enjoyed our student days in the city, she gave Edinburgh as one of her choices. She wanted to read Russian at a time when many universities were having difficulty in attracting students for degrees in that particular subject, but she was turned down out of hand. It subsequently transpired that she had fallen victim to a hidden *numerus clausus* operated by the university. The previous year, English entrants to the Faculty of Arts had, for the first time, outnumbered Scots, and a fair number of these were products of public schools. Some of these were high-spending 'hooray henrys' who, understandably, had got up the noses of the more reserved natives. I had some sympathy with the agitation to preserve the distinctive Scottishness of the university, but little with the method used to keep the perceived 'English' hordes at bay. This was to impose a blanket ban on applicants who registered an intention to take a gap year (how much more elegant is the German expression *Wanderjahr*) between leaving school and entering university. As almost all those who intended to take a gap year were English, it was they who were mainly affected, although the ban was not revealed at the time. This seemed an underhand way of managing the problem and there was much controversy in the columns of *The Scotsman* about the issue. Thereafter, I was somewhat less enamoured of the University of Edinburgh.

Best, who taught at Edinburgh in the later 1960s and early 1970s, writes of the resentment of some of his Scottish colleagues at what he terms the 'irreversible Anglicisation' of the History Department. When he spoke in praise of the university's cosmopolitanism, he was told by a member of the (separate) Scottish History Department 'It's not cosmopolitan, it's colonial.' On decamping for 'Balliol by the sea', as the University of Sussex was then satirically known, he was told by several English members of the department that they envied him the chance of getting out. But during my time as an undergraduate and, briefly, as a lecturer I was not aware of this undercurrent of nationalist resentment.

Just as I was coming to terms with the need to begin over again the dispiriting search for a permanent job, which had now taken on a new urgency with the arrival of Rachel, possible salvation seemed at hand with the emergence of two lectureships at the University of London. One was precisely in my chosen field, modern Greek history, or as I prefer it, the modern history of Greece. The other was in the history of the Orthodox Church. These were among the last of a series of posts established at the School of Slavonic and East European Studies (SSEES) in the wake of the Hayter Report of 1961 into provision in Oriental, Slavonic, East European and African Studies in British universities. Posts had already been established in the medieval history of Orthodox Eastern Europe, the history of the East Baltic lands, Hungary, the Czechs and Slovaks, Central Europe with special reference to Poland, the South Slavs, Bulgaria and Romania (I had thought of applying for this last post as I had a considerable interest in Phanariot Greek rule in the Danubian Principalities in the eighteenth century and had taken some classes in Romanian at SSEES with Eric Tappe, but I had been warned that I would be wasting my time if I did so. This was a pity, as the person appointed fairly rapidly lost interest in Romania and its history). It was proposed to complete the picture with the two new posts in the history of modern Greece and of the Orthodox Church. They were, however, to be joint posts, shared between SSEES and King's College.

The School of Slavonic Studies had originally been founded at King's College in 1915, and the college archive still contains the brief exchange of letters between Professor R.W. Seton-Watson, the eminent historian of Eastern Europe, and the principal, the classicist Ronald Burrows, with Seton-Watson suggesting the establishment of such a School and Burrows wholeheartedly approving, and replying that there was a spare room where it could be housed. King's had given an academic home to Tomáš Garrigue Masaryk, the effective creator, and first president, of Czechoslovakia, at this time a political émigré in London. In 1915, he gave an influential lecture on the question of small nations in the European crisis to mark the opening of the School, where he was appointed to a lectureship. During World War I there was a clear political as well as academic motive in establishing such a School as, conveniently, the oppressors of the subject peoples of Eastern Europe were, in most instances, the Central Powers, with which the Entente was locked in combat. When SSEES became an independent institution within the University of London in 1932, post-classical Greek studies remained at King's. This was presumably out of deference to the memory of Principal Burrows and because King's had a large classics department whereas SSEES had none. In so far as anyone had an interest in the modern history of Greece at that time, its study tended to be the hobby of classicists, of whom Burrows was one. Burrows had presided over the growth of Slavonic and East European studies at King's but, as we shall see, he was a rather naive philhellene who always had a particular interest in, and affection for, the modern Greeks. Hence, in 1969, it had been decreed that the two posts should be shared with King's. The partial assignation of the post in Orthodox church history to King's made sense in that it had a large Department of Theology.

I applied for both lectureships for, besides my work on Greek history, I had done a fair amount of work on the history of the Orthodox Church and, in particular, on the negative reaction of the Orthodox hierarchy to the ideas of the Enlightenment and the French Revolution as these began to have some resonance in the Greek world. One of my earliest articles had been an annotated translation of the *Patriki Didaskalia*, or Paternal Exhortation, published in Constantinople at the press of the Ecumenical Patriarchate in 1798. Attributed to Anthimos, the Patriarch of Jerusalem, this was a fierce denunciation of the new-fangled ideas of liberty emanating from France. Indeed, Anthimos went so far as to argue that God had raised up the Ottoman Empire so as to preserve the Orthodox faith unsullied by contamination with popery and 'Luthero-Calvinism'. My application for this particular post was something of a long shot and not taken very seriously. Clearly, the post in the modern history of Greece was more up my street. The process of applying was rather nerve-racking, for not only was this the first academic position to be created in a British university in the field, but there was a strong chance that it would be the last, and so it turned out when King's College abolished the post in 2011. I was lucky enough to be appointed in the face of some very serious competition in the shape of Michael Llewellyn Smith, who went on to have a stellar career in the Foreign and Commonwealth Office, ending up as Ambassador in Athens, while producing excellent work on modern Greek history. I had the impression that what swung the decision with the King's representatives on the board was the feeling that I would be a useful adjunct to the history department at King's in view of my year's experience of teaching at Edinburgh.

This meant that I left Edinburgh after barely nine months of my two-year appointment, and so we returned to London and to the Greek émigré world that I had found so intriguing. Douglas Dakin, an historian at Birbeck College, about this time counselled me, in a well-intentioned fashion, not to become too closely identified with the anti-Colonel cause as this might adversely affect my academic career. This was advice that I happily ignored. Dakin, a man of pronounced conservative views, was one of the few British academics at that time with a serious interest in modern Greek history. This had been inspired by wartime service in the Middle East when he had acted as a liaison officer with units of the Greek air force. As I remember, in the 1960s he had been sued in the High Court by an Indian student, who claimed that his academic record had suffered because he had bowled Dakin out in a college cricket match.

Although I was greatly relieved to have what was likely to prove a permanent position in the field in which I had the most expertise and interest, and was much looking forward to promoting the subject, the job proved to be somewhat problematic. The basic difficulty was that not only was the post split between SSEES and King's but, initially, I was divided among three departments, the history department at SSEES, the history department at King's, where there was no expertise, and little interest, in east European history, and the embryonic department of Byzantine and Modern Greek Studies at King's. This was an inherently unsatisfactory situation as, not suprisingly, each department failed to make allowance for my obligations in the others. In the event, I was not a member of the King's history department for long, as my efforts to develop modern Greek studies at King's were inevitably focused in the emerging department of Byzantine and Modern Greek Studies. Post-classical Greek studies at the college at the time were in abeyance, for there was no Koraes professor then in post after Cyril Mango's departure for Oxford.

The nucleus of our small department, besides myself, consisted of Philip Sherrard, who had been appointed to the lectureship in the history of the Orthodox Church. Philip proved to be a pleasant if somewhat distant colleague. Seventeen years older than me, Orthodox by religion, twice Assistant Director of the British School at Athens, he had held research positions at Chatham House and St Antony's College, Oxford. In Greece he owned a substantial property on the island of Evia in the form of an abandoned mine and its associated housing. There he lived a contemplative life without telephone or electricity. He was not so much a specialist in the history of the Orthodox Church as an Orthodox theologian, with strong interests in modern Greek literature, of which he was a noted translator. He has been described as 'perhaps the most potent and prophetic voice on behalf of the Church's vocation to heal the earth in Orthodox theology'. After his death in 1995 (he was buried in an Orthodox chapel which he had built on his property) he became a posthumous guru of Prince Charles. Philip had very little to do with SSEES and, indeed, was not a very visible presence at King's. There we shared a room, and were both rather alarmed that a chimney outside the window bore the nuclear radiation hazard warning sign. When we queried this rather unsettling feature, the college's response was simply to paint out the sign.

Sherrard and I soon realised that there would be little future for modern Greek studies either at King's or at SSEES if there were no provision for instruction in Greek language and literature of the kind that was available at SSEES for all the other languages of the Balkans, with the single exception of Albanian. We therefore began an agitation for such an appointment. Although money was still, just about, available for such new posts (it was not until 1975 that Tony Crosland, a member of the Wilson government, famously declared that the party was over in terms of government expenditure), it was nonetheless difficult to try to get both institutions to prioritise such an appointment in a field that, to King's at least, must have appeared peripheral. But, after much huffing and puffing, which included Sherrard and me lobbying the principal of King's, General Sir John Hackett, a classicist and historian by training (he was president of the Classical Association in 1970-1) and someone fairly sympathetic to the cause, such a post was created. Hackett, sporting a Homburg and a rolled umbrella, once famously joined a student march carrying a placard reading 'More pay for principals.' Fearing that the demonstration might end in trouble, he bailed out before the end into the chauffeur-driven car which he had negotiated as part of his remuneration as principal. His predecessor, Sir Peter Noble, used to travel to work by bus.

Like Sherrard's and mine, the new post was shared between SSEES and King's. To this Peter Mackridge was appointed in 1973 and modern Greek was taught in the college, and indeed in the university, for the first time since the early 1920s, when the Greek government had withdrawn its subsidy for the teaching of the language in unhappy circumstances that will be explained in the next chapter. Donald Nicol, who had previously taught at the University of Edinburgh, where we had briefly been colleagues, had by this time been appointed to the Koraes Chair of Modern Greek and Byzantine History, Language and Literature in 1970 so we now had a (just) viable nucleus with which to establish a department of Byzantine and Modern Greek Studies.

Despite the manifest problems associated with holding a joint post, there was one considerable advantage in holding a Hayter lectureship at SSEES, namely access to lavish funding for research trips abroad. This was quite disproportionately generous in relation to modest academic salaries. During the summer vacation of 1970, for instance, I received £358 for a 37-day research visit to Romania, Bulgaria and Greece at a time when my annual salary was under £2,000. It seemed rather absurd, albeit agreeable, that at a time when much of our free time was spent in fixing up with own hands a dilapidated house in Crouch End because we could not afford a builder, I should for a month or so be able to travel in some style in the Balkans. Moreover, unlike most of my SSEES colleagues, whose research took them to communist countries, I could legitimately claim for travel to Greece where, despite military rule, conditions were nothing like as grim as in the Eastern Bloc countries. There was no problem about getting grants for travel during both the Easter and summer vacations. Even in 1974, when Britain was experiencing the deprivations of the 'three-day week' and the economy appeared to be near collapse, I received almost £500 for a research trip to Romania and Greece. On this particular trip I got a clearer understanding of how the Eastern Bloc regimes had seemingly done away with unemployment when I went for a coffee in the buffet of the Keleti station in Budapest before taking the night sleeper to Bucharest. I was the only customer and was serenaded by a quartet which included a cimbalom player. On returning from our Hayter-funded travels we had to produce receipts to justify our expenditure. I remember asking for a receipt at the restaurant of the Lido hotel in Bucharest, to which the waiter obligingly replied, 'How many do you want?'

In Romania, I was pleased to make the acquaintance of a number of scholars with interests in the Orthodox commonwealth that had coexisted alongside Ottoman rule in the Balkans. These included Mihai Berza, the director of the Institut d'Études Sud-est Européenes, and two researchers at the Institute, Alexandru Duțu and Cornelia Papacostea-Danielopolu, with whom I had a number of research interests in common. By the time I was researching in Romania, a number of scholars of 'bourgeois' background (Cornelia Papacostea was the daughter of the distinguished Balkanist Victor Papacostea) had been rehabilitated to the extent of being permitted to work in research institutes if not in universities. They were charming and civilised company, although often living in reduced circumstances, and afforded a glimpse of the old Romania that had existed before the sheer nastiness of the postwar communist regime. In the early 1970s, the megalomania and paranoia of the Ceaușescus had not yet plumbed the depths that they did in the 1980s and, if one had a certain amount of money, which thanks to the Hayter fund I did, one could eat quite well. I remember one day having lunch in the dining room of the best hotel in Bucharest, the Athénée Palace, next to a table containing much of the exiled leadership of the Communist Party of Greece (KKE), at that time still an illegal organisation in Greece itself.

By the end of the 1980s, of course, food shortages were endemic and I remember being repelled by the unappetising slabs of raw meat on sale in the hard currency shop in the Intercontinental Hotel in Bucharest. This was but one of the obnoxious aspects of the Ceaușescu regime: if one had hard currency one could purchase a range of Western food and drink and consumer goods. One would see people gazing longingly through the door at what was on display. Paradoxically, it was in Ceaușescu's Romania in the early 1970s that I received the only payment I have ever received for a research article. I was taken by a colleague one day to a dingy basement in the Writers' Union. There a cashier handed me quite a respectable sum for an article that I had published in the *Revue des Études Sud-est Européennes*. The problem I now had was that there was nothing on which to spend a pile of Romanian *lei* and it could not be taken out of the country. But, quite by chance, I came across one of the very few objects of high quality, a set of doll's house furniture, decorated in the traditional style. This made an excellent present for Rachel.

I found that many of the Romanian scholars with whom I came in contact were Greek-speakers. A knowledge of Greek more than once came in useful outside Greece in the course of my Hayter travels. On one occasion I visited Varna, the Black Sea port not far from Zlatni Piasaci, the 'Golden Sands' resort on the Black Sea coast. This had been put on the map by the miners' leader, Arthur Scargill, who had famously declared, after a holiday in the workers' paradise that was Bulgaria, when he had had to wait two hours for his dinner, 'If this is communism they can keep it.' An objectionable woman in the Balkanturist office told me that there were no rooms in Zlatni Piasaci with the exception of a suite in what was presumably the best hotel in the resort. This would cost $100 or so, a large sum in the early 1970s, even to someone travelling on the bounty of the Hayter fund. I said that I would sleep out on the beach, whereupon she threatened to send for the police and have me arrested. The phone then rang and she started chatting to a friend in Greek. When she finished I spoke to her in Greek, and, all smiles, she fixed me up with perfectly satisfactory accommodation at a tenth of the price she had quoted earlier.

In 1975 I received a grant to enable me to visit Albania, probably the first such visit paid for with Hayter funds. I was particularly interested to learn something of the fate of the Greek minority in southern Albania, or Northern Epirus as the Greeks call it. I had to go as part of a package tour as individual travel was not permitted. Some of the members of the British group with which I initially travelled consisted of people for whom the Costa del Sol had become, in the economic crisis of the early 1970s (this was only a year after the three-day week), too expensive for holidays. They were wont to complain of the impossibility of buying the *Sun* or the *Daily Mirror* on the beach in

Durrës. By good fortune, our British group was slightly too large to fit comfortably into a single bus and so two us were hived off and placed with a group of Dutch Marxist–Leninists, devotees of Enver Hoxha, the Albanian party boss. My travelling companion was an engaging character who, despite working for the *Reader's Digest*, had marked leftward leanings. He told me that he had an acquaintance with a member of the Chinese Embassy in London who, alongside other 'diplomats' bearing improvised weapons, had caused a stir at the height of the Cultural Revolution by emerging into Portland Place wielding an axe. It seemed that we had been selected as ostensibly more 'politically mature' than the rest of the British party.

Being with Dutch fans of Hoxha meant that we gained a much better insight into the realities of life in Albania in the 1970s than we would have done with an ordinary tourist group. While we did not get to follow the entire itinerary of the Marxist–Leninists, we were able to take part in visits to collective farms and factories which were not on offer to those in the tourist parties. In Gjirokastër (Argyrokastro) it was a pleasant surprise to encounter a small band of itinerant street musicians, playing traditional Epirot melodies. At a textile mill in Korçë (Korytsa) I was interested to notice how many of the names of the workers who had clocked in appeared to be of Vlach origin. Many of the Vlachs, widely distributed in the Balkans, spoke a variant of Romanian. One day we visited a group of Albanian students, who had supposedly 'volunteered' part of their summer vacation to work on the construction of the Pogradeci to Prrenjas railway. We sang a couple of anthems in praise of Hoxha and the construction of socialism and engaged in some, entirely token, work on building a railway embankment before being presented with Young Pioneer scarves, adorned with the regime's logo of pickaxe and rifle. We then piled back into our bus for a rather good lunch in Pogradeci, leaving the bemused students to their seemingly not very energetic labours. In Korçë, we were taken to the museum dedicated to Hoxha in the house in which he had been born. Various artefacts allegedly connected with the great leader were on display, including the boots he had worn as a partisan commander. These appeared to be in too pristine a condition ever to have had much contact with Albania's rugged terrain. I found these secular relics fascinating, just as, in 1966, on the fiftieth anniversary of the Easter uprising in Dublin, I had been intrigued to find the starting handle of The O'Rahilly's car that had been used in the Howth gun-running of July 1914 reverently displayed in the National Museum of Ireland.

Although deemed 'politically mature', our group, despite its touching devotion to Hoxha as an icon of Marxism–Leninism, was nonetheless carefully shepherded everywhere, as were the tourist groups. In Sarandë (Agioi

Saranda) we were taken on a walking tour of the town. As we passed what seemed to be the only bookshop, I noticed that it opened at 8.00 am. The following morning I skipped breakfast and the numerous taciturn Albanian honeymoon couples in our hotel, and made for the bookshop, arriving a minute or two after it had opened. As I had hoped, there was no one there apart from the man who was in charge. Knowing precious little Albanian, I spoke in Greek. He replied delightedly, also in Greek, and we were able to have a chat. It was clear that, understandably, he was not going to volunteer anything to the discredit of Hoxha and the Albanian Party of Labour, and I certainly had no intention of asking any leading questions and possibly getting him into trouble. I did, however, ask whether he had any books in Greek and he enthusiastically dug out a copy of every publication that he could lay his hands on and I left with a dozen or so small and ill-printed books. These consisted of schoolbooks with poems in praise of Hoxha and the Party and a number of anti-religious tracts, as, some eight years previously, Albania, while in the throes of its own tightly controlled 'cultural revolution', had declared the country to be the world's first atheist state. These modest publications are probably now difficult to come by.

In Greece at the time there was much complaint about the plight of the Greek minority in Albania, and Hoxha's anti-religious decrees were indeed harsh. Nonetheless, the Greeks in southern Albania did at least have the formal status of a minority, unlike, for instance, the Slav-Macedonians in Greece. Unlike the latter, the Greeks of Albania did have school instruction in their maternal language up to a certain age in the minority areas, and had access, as we have seen, to a few publications in Greek. There were radio broadcasts in Greek and a weekly newspaper, the *Laiko Vima*, or People's Tribune. By contrast, only one book for the Slav-Macedonians has ever been published officially in Greece, a school textbook in the 1920s known as the *Abcedar*. But copies of this were soon destroyed, and the schools that had been promised for the Slav-Macedonians never materialised. The Greek minority in Albania undeniably constituted an oppressed group, but then all Albanians were brutally repressed.

In the course of the trip we encountered what appeared to be the entire membership of the Marxist–Leninist Party of the Faroe Islands. We also came across three members of the Socialist Party of Ireland, waiting patiently but in vain, day after day on the beach in Durrës, hoping for an audience with Enver Hoxha at which they intended to enlighten him on their solution to the problem of the Six Counties, namely the creation of an all-Irish workers' state. On the last night of our visit, by which time we had returned to our beachfront hotel in Durrës, we were treated to the bizarre spectacle of the various groups of Marxist–Leninist devotees from various parts of Western Europe treating the domestic staff of our hotel to an open-air display of anti-capitalist skits. These were intended to be in lieu of the tips which had been decreed to be a pernicious capitalist practice, although I have little doubt that our Albanian waiters, waitresses and chambermaids would have greatly preferred cash, or at least a few Western cigarettes, to what must have often seemed incomprehensible and obscure attacks on the world capitalist system. Only at the very end of the tour did an elderly couple in the British group reveal that the husband, a retired jeweller, had been to Albania once before, in the 1930s, when he had worked on the Albanian crown jewels for King Zog and had now returned to see how the country had developed.

When I arrived at the School of Slavonic and East European Studies in 1969 George Bolsover was the director. He had been appointed in 1947, and only in 1975, just short of a 30-year stint worthy of a Stakhanovite, did he retire. During the era of *perestroika* in the Soviet Union, Mikhail Gorbachev had sought to ensure that apparatchiks did not hold the same office for more than ten years. Bolsover was a good example of the wisdom of such a policy. To persist with the Soviet analogy, his tenure was the equivalent of Brezhnev's era of stagnation, and by the time I arrived at the School many of its junior (and not a few senior) members of the staff were in a state of incipient revolt against his directorship. Bolsover was probably the only academic administrator in the UK to return to the University Grants Committee the unspent balance of the quinquennial grant to the School instead of finding some worthy (or even unworthy) object on which to spend the money.

It was presumably this kind of behaviour that earned Bolsover the soubriquet 'Honest George' among his fellow academic apparatchiks. In the mid-1970s the School was contributing £3,000 a year out of its accumulated surplus to pay for the staffing costs of the Polish Library in London. This was undoubtedly a worthy cause, but surely a plausible object for expenditure of this magnitude could have been found within the School. Yet when one looks at what happened to the School after Bolsover's retirement, his unimaginative, defensive and inward-looking management had, in retrospect, a certain merit. I used to look on his regime as the academic equivalent of the reign of Sultan Abdul Hamid II. Abdul the Damned, as he was known in the popular prints, was on the Ottoman throne from 1876 until the Young Turk Revolution of 1909, only a few years longer than Bolsover ran SSEES. Just as Abdul Hamid's reign, tyrannical though it was, with hindsight had something to be said for it when compared with the fate of the successor states of the Ottoman Empire, so Bolsover's uninspiring directorship seemed rather attractive in relation to that of some of his successors.

Bolsover had a PhD in Russian history and had served in the British embassy in Moscow during the war. Rumour in the School had it that he had been parachuted into the School, *inter alia*, to purge Andrew Rothstein, the son of Theodore Rothstein, one of Lenin's closest associates. Rothstein, who lectured on Soviet institutions at the School, made no bones about his communist convictions. Indeed, he was one of the founding members of the Communist Party of Great Britain and was subsequently revealed to be an NKVD agent. When Bolsover and the then chairman of the School's council announced that Rothstein's contract would not be renewed, the decision was much criticised by some members of the School's staff, by the Association of University Teachers, by the Students' Union, and in the columns of the *New Statesman*. In his inadequate account of the affair, Ian Roberts, the author of the School's history, writes that a hearing of Rothstein's case was presided over by the Lord Chief Justice, who 'refused to give a ruling on the matter', which seems a curious outcome. Given my interest in the interface between academic and 'real' politics in the wake of my anatomy of the Toynbee affair (see Chapter 4) I had hoped, in retirement, to look further into the Rothstein affair. But when I enquired at the Marx Memorial Library in Camberwell, which Rothstein had run after being winkled out of SSEES, whether there was any chance of looking at his papers I drew a blank. Rothstein, who died in 1994, at the age of 96, had given his papers, as opposed to his books, personally to the archivist. They were embargoed for ten years after his death and are to be used as the basis for a biography. Meanwhile, it seems that no one else was to be allowed to consult them.

Bolsover, a Lancastrian and something of a professional northerner, had a line in non-PC jokes. The only one that I can recall is his tale of someone who had emigrated from Bradford as a young man and, in middle age, had returned to his birthplace, saying, 'When I left Bradford the buildings were all black and the people all white, but when I came back the buildings were all white and the people all black.' I remember one morning in 1975 in the men's room in Senate House, where the School was mainly situated, when Bolsover came in and said, 'At last, I see you've had your hair cut, Richard.' This was, of course, the height of the embarrassing era of long hair and even longer sideburns. 'Yes, Director,' I replied, 'and I'm going to charge the cost to the School.' Bolsover responded, as I had hoped, and said that I could not possibly do that. To which I replied that I was soon off to Albania on a Hayter grant and that the Albanians were famous for scalping hirsute foreigners at the airport (as well as banning the then fashionable drain pipe trousers, any which could not be taken off with shoes on). I said that it seemed reasonable to pre-empt such a humiliation by getting a hair cut in advance. In the event, although my hair was now pretty short, I was made to have a second hair cut at Tirana airport, but was somewhat reassured when the barber asked me in a whisper whether I had any American cigarettes. (I did not.)

This episode is immortalised by a friend and St Antony's colleague, Robert Service, in his *Comrades: A World History of Communism* (2008), although Bob does not mention me by name. Someone who does mention me by name in the acknowledgements to *Eastern Europe in the Twentieth Century – and After* (1997) is another good friend and Oxford colleague, Richard Crampton. He pays me a somewhat backhanded compliment in writing that Richard Clogg 'is perhaps the most exhausting and therefore the most rewarding of travelling companions', a view with which Mary Jo, in the early years of our marriage at least, would have concurred. I suspect that Dick's remark may be connected with my determination that we visit the church of the Bulgarian Exarchate (Dick is a specialist, *inter alia*, in Bulgarian history) in Istanbul in a rather grim section of the city not far from its Greek rival, the Ecumenical Patriarchate. As we ventured along the rundown streets, a man came running down a side street with blood pouring from his head.

Throughout the 1970s there was protracted navel gazing in SSEES over the striking imbalance between staff, of whom there were many, and students, of whom there were few, an unusual reversal of the norm in the university world. I taught a fair number of classes at SSEES, although these were often very small. More than once, my history special subject on the movement for Greek independence in the late eighteenth and nineteenth centuries attracted only one student. In the days before word processors, gobbets in Greek from contemporary sources had to be typeset in the traditional way for the final examinations at heaven knows what cost. One of the troubles with SSEES was that not only was the student body small, but the undergraduate students were, for the most part, not particularly interested in Russian or East European matters. This led to increasingly rancorous debates in the history department between those who felt that, students or not, SSEES should remain a centre of expertise in area studies and those who felt that, to attract more students, we should dilute the Russian and east European content of the curriculum by offering courses in mainstream European history.

By the 1990s it was apparent that Britain had need of a reservoir of academic competence in the complexities of Russian and east European history, economy and society not to mention expertise in the languages of the region, although few could have foreseen this in the early 1970s. It was argued by those keen to move away from the study of Eastern Europe that the absence of suitable textbooks made the teaching of east European history more difficult for students, few of whom had any knowledge of the languages of the region.

My suggestion was that we should ourselves provide more teaching material suitable for those without the requisite linguistic skills. I myself produced a collection of documents, many of them translated from the Greek. This, *The Movement for Greek Independence, 1770–1812: A Collection of Documents*, was published in 1976 as a volume in the series that the School had begun to publish in association with Macmillan. If more publications of this kind had been produced, then some of the difficulties that we encountered might have diminished.

During these rather pointless, and not infrequently acrimonious, battles I came to know and greatly respect Hugh Seton-Watson, the son of R.W. Seton-Watson, who had been instrumental in the creation of SSEES and was one of the pioneers of the academic study of Eastern Europe in the UK. Hugh was professor of Russian history, although he was always more interested in Eastern Europe than in Russia. When SSEES was swallowed up by University College in 1999, an architecturally striking building was purpose-built within the curtilage of the college. As it was under construction, I wrote to the then director to suggest that one of the seminar rooms, or something similar, be named the Seton-Watson room, in honour of the Seton-Watsons, father and son. The reply that I received was that there was a problem with my suggestion, for rooms were seen by University College as naming opportunities in return for substantial donations. As far as I know, no room has been named for the father and son, whose combined and distinguished service lasted for 67 years. This seems a pity.

A conference on 'Historians as nation-builders in central and eastern Europe', was organised at SSEES in honour of Hugh on his retirement in 1983, and the proceedings were published as a posthumous Festschrift in honour of a remarkable scholar. I was glad to have been able to organise a lunch for Hugh when he retired, with the principal of King's, Air Marshal Sir Neil Cameron, Donald Nicol and myself, to mark the end of the long and fruitful connection of the Seton-Watsons with King's. Hugh died in Washington DC in 1984. I happened myself to be in Washington at the time, working on the frequently troubled relations between the Office of Strategic Services and the Special Operations Executive, when he fell ill, but by the time I heard the news he was too ill to visit. At the subsequent memorial service for Hugh in the University Church of Christ the King in Gordon Square there were two speakers. One of these was Reggie Smith, the husband of the novelist Olivia Manning. The other was Professor James Joll. Smith, who was himself to die shortly afterwards, had clearly been the model for Guy Pringle in Manning's *Balkan Trilogy*. A thinly disguised Seton-Watson also appears in the first volume of the trilogy, *The Great Fortune*. Likened to 'a lecturer wholly confident in the magnitude of his knowledge', David Boyd combines clandestine derring-do on behalf of SOE with occasional bird watching in the Danube delta. For many years, while Hugh was still in harness at the School, I used to offer a modest prize for the first student in the course on the modern history of the Balkans to identify their professor. In the novels, Manning had brilliantly captured the febrile atmosphere of Bucharest and Athens in the early stages of World War II, and I was keen that students should read them.

Working out which character was based on Hugh was not difficult – Boyd's enthusiasm for bird watching was one of the give-aways. Manning points to the physical similarity between Hugh and Reggie and to their youthful radicalism. Both had seen Marxism as the only solution to the feudal mismanagement of Eastern Europe. Manning points to David's fluency in the languages of the region and has him thinking of flying to Sofia to pick up the second volume of Anna Karenina from the Russian bookshop in the city.[1] Hugh, after his time in Romania, with his vast knowledge of Balkan affairs, became a key member of SOE's Middle East headquarters, for which he once mischievously devised insignia for the organisation. His suggested crest took the form of a tasteful arrangement of 'Rackets and Balls'. Unfortunately, he never wrote about his time in SOE. Having witnessed at firsthand the subjugation of the countries of Eastern Europe in the aftermath of World War II, he was to exchange his youthful radicalism for a strong anti-communism. It was characteristic, however, that he should have maintained his close friendship with Reggie Smith, who remained an unrepentant Marxist, although he had resigned from the Communist Party of Great Britain in protest at the Soviet invasion of Hungary in 1956.

James Joll, the other speaker at Hugh's memorial service, was at the time a professor at the London School of Economics, having formerly been a fellow of St Antony's College, Oxford. Likewise of a radical cast of mind, he had sheltered Anthony Blunt when he was unmasked as a Soviet spy in 1979. When Blunt went to earth, with the British press in hot pursuit, Joll spoke about his friend on Radio Four. Although his name was not given, I immediately recognised his characteristic voice and fleetingly entertained the unworthy thought of tipping off one of the tabloids (for an appropriately fat backhander) that if they wanted to track down Blunt, which they were clearly desperate to do, then they should stake out Joll's flat. Incidentally, talking about the ease with which supposedly anonymous voices can be recognised, I found it strange, when a heavily disguised Radovan Karadžić was unmasked in Belgrade in 2008, that, seemingly for years, no one had recognised a voice which must often have been on the air waves during the Bosnian crisis of the 1990s.

That two such non-establishment figures as Reggie Smith and James Joll should have given addresses at Hugh's memorial service was typical of the man. His *Times* obituary recalled that Seton-Watson 'showed the impatience of those who do not suffer fools gladly'. This was true, but he was a man not only of quite extraordinary intelligence and profound learning but also of a fundamental decency of the kind that was not always evident at SSEES, at least at the time when I was associated with it.

Through much of the 1970s there were prolonged discussions about finding an answer to SSEES's woes in a possible merger with a larger, multi-faculty college in the university, as had been recommended in the Noble Report in 1971. The two most likely candidates were King's and Queen Mary College. Another possible solution that was discussed was a merger with the School of Oriental and African Studies. This would have made sense, although SOAS was an institution that at the time had problems of its own, and many that it shared with SSEES. King's was in many ways the obvious choice for a merger, as the School had its origins in the college in the early years of World War I. Donald Nicol, the Koraes professor, chaired a college committee to consider the implications of such a 'melding' of the two institutions. But the idea of a merger with King's did not appeal to many at SSEES or, indeed, at King's, particularly to those in the history department.

There was even less enthusiasm in SSEES for the idea of joining up with Queen Mary College (QMC). When the idea of such a merger was mooted there was understandable concern about ending up down Mile End Road, far from the central university precinct, and, in the preliminary discussions at SSEES, some rather dismissive remarks were made about Queen Mary. The powers that be at QMC appear to have got wind of these and we were sent a list of distinguished alumni of the College. This was headed by Marcia Williams (Baroness Falkender), Harold Wilson's long-time personal secretary and adviser, then at the height of her influence over the Labour leader.

Probably the best-known alumnus of SSEES is Jonathan Ross, renowned for reputedly receiving £6 million a year from BBC licence payers and for his suspension in 2008 for a foul-mouthed on-air rant. But judging by his autobiographical *Why Do I Say These Things* (2008), the experience seems to have meant little to him. Three times we are told that he went to university but this is not identified nor does he indicate what he studied. Nonetheless, in 2006 he was made a fellow of University College, London. This was another indication of the lack of interest in the subjects taught at the School and highlights the problem I have mentioned earlier which was a major factor underlying the eternal, time-consuming and, at times, stormy debates about the future direction of the School.

Nothing came of these protracted negotiations with other London colleges. Neither King's nor QMC proved enthusiastic about taking on such a top-heavy institution with so many staff and so few students. In 1973, for instance, the School had 171 undergraduates, 33 postgraduates and 53 members of staff, a far higher ratio of staff to students, I believe, than almost any other UK academic institution. SSEES soldiered on as an independent institution until it eventually merged with University College in 1999, a logical arrangement, if only on geographical grounds. A more cogent reason why the proposed mergers failed may have been that the putative host institutions had got wind of the fact that SSEES in the 1970s and early 1980s was an institution given, in the parlance beloved of communist polemicists, to 'factional struggle without principles'. In an attempt to explain this there was a theory, which, rumour had it, emanated from the student health service of the university, that small specialised institutions such as SSEES were particularly prone to this kind of factionalism. According to this, they were in effect sheltered workshops full of inadequate people who, instead of showing a healthy interest in such 'normal' subjects as medieval pipe rolls or Victorian sanitary engineering, plunged headlong into the study of 'deviant' subjects such as Ruritanian language, literature and history. Those of us who were not actually Ruritanian-born were in effect deviants, fleeing from reality by immersing ourselves in another culture. Another indicator of such alienation was a tendency to marry (and in the 1970s one did marry) an alien spouse, so that a British lecturer in Ruritanian language and literature would often have a Ruritanian spouse, or if a native-born Ruritanian then (s)he would have a British spouse.

Once, on the way by train to a congress of Soviet and east European studies in Garmisch-Partenkirchen, Frank Carter, who held a joint post at SSEES and University College in the geography of Eastern Europe, and I were talking about this notion over a cup of coffee in the restaurant car and drew up a list of those at the School who were married to aliens. This revealed a disproportionately high number, beginning at the top with Bolsover whose wife was Hungarian-born. Frank and I both fitted comfortably into this category. Constantine Karamanlis, the bluff Macedonian who governed Greece for much of the second half of the twentieth century, once unflatteringly described the country as a *terastio phrenokomeio*. If Greece was indeed a 'vast madhouse', then SSEES was a tiny one. I have to admit to contributing my share to the general cacophony of those years. SSEES was an institution housing too many articulate individuals, some of them, although learned, not over-endowed with common sense, and some of them with too much time on their hands.

As the years passed I found, as did many of my joint postholder colleagues, of whom at one stage there were as many as 11, the shared loyalties implicit in the arrangement increasingly irksome. The School of Oriental and African Studies had a number of such posts, and, in a submission in the 1970s to one of the endless reviews into the future of the University of London, had pointed out that a joint postholder will inevitably gravitate towards one of the two employing institutions, leaving the other one feeling it had 'got a bad bargain'. I necessarily gravitated towards King's because this was the natural locus of the study of the modern history of Greece in the university, and perhaps in the country. For it housed the splendid Burrows Library, named after the principal of the college who had been instrumental in establishing the Koraes chair. Invariably and inevitably, a joint postholder at SSEES was given the poorest accommodation, which always had to be shared with others. At one stage six joint postholders were obliged to share a single room, with the result that they were seldom seen there. In my case, being a joint postholder was a major inconvenience as SSEES and King's were at some distance from each other. Getting books and lecture notes in the right place at the right time was not always easy. More seriously, there were problems over promotion. As the universities were subject to an ever more severe financial squeeze in the 1970s promotion prospects were shrinking all round. But the hurdle of getting two institutions, at least one of which, and quite possibly both, may well have felt that they were not getting their money's worth from the individual concerned, to agree simultaneously to promotion proved difficult. For some unfathomable reason, alone among the joint postholders, any prospects of promotion that I may have had lay solely within the patronage of SSEES, whereas I spent most of my time at King's. At one stage, King's had recommended me for promotion three years earlier but SSEES had taken no action.

Matters came to a head with the sudden death, in 1980 at the age of 30, of Alan Ferguson, the lecturer in the history of the South Slavs. It emerged that he had committed suicide. One can never know with any degree of certainty in such circumstances what triggered the decision to take his own life, though he was certainly profoundly depressed by a broken engagement. Yet, as I well knew, he was also seriously unhappy in his work, and there was continual pressure to dilute his concentration on the subject that he had been appointed to develop. Alan was what we would now call a very private person, someone not easy to get to know, but he was a close colleague with whom I shared a room and I reckon that I knew him as well as anyone at the School. Alan's death followed the breakdown and subsequent lengthy hospitalisation of the lecturer in Bulgarian history. The fourth teacher of Balkan history appeared to have little interest in the history of Romania which he had been appointed to teach. All in all, the situation of south-east European studies at that time was not a happy one.

After much lobbying I managed to sever my formal ties to SSEES and my post was, in 1983, transferred to King's. A year earlier, I had brought out an edited volume, *Balkan Society in the Age of Greek Independence*. This was a collection of the papers delivered at a conference, held in October 1977, to mark the 150th anniversary of the battle of Navarino, the last great battle of the age of sail, in which a combined British, French and Russian fleet destroyed an Ottoman fleet in the bay of Navarino in the Peloponnese, thus ensuring that some kind of autonomous or independent Greece would come into being. (To my surprise, the naval attaché at the Soviet Embassy accepted an invitation to attend the opening lecture at the conference.) To this volume Alan Ferguson had contributed an excellent chapter on Montenegro. With the agreement of the other contributors, the modest payment due for each of our chapters was contributed to the fund set up to endow a prize in south-east European history in memory of Alan. I am glad to say that it is still in existence.

After the death of the Yugoslav president Tito in 1980, SSEES was involved in an ill-conceived attempt to establish a Tito fellowship at the School, exploiting the good will that existed in many British quarters, including in particular those on the right, towards the vain tyrant. But SSEES, above all, should have been aware that, whatever the relative liberalism of Tito after the break with the Cominform, the internal regime in early postwar Yugoslavia was as harsh, if not harsher, as anywhere in communist-dominated Eastern Europe. What if Aleksa Djilas, an academic and the son of Milovan Djilas, one of the leading dissidents in Tito's Yugoslavia, had applied for the Tito Fellowship? A Djilas as Tito fellow really would indeed have been something.

These are but some glimpses of the fascinating, if somewhat troubled, history of SSEES. It has employed some truly first-rate scholars and has contributed greatly to the professionalisation of the study of Russia and Eastern Europe in the United Kingdom. It had all the ingredients for an outstanding institutional history. There is, as we have seen, the story of the eviction of Andrew Rothstein, a committed communist, from his lectureship in Russian institutions in 1950 at the height of the cold war. There was also the extraordinary character of Dorothy Galton, appointed Secretary of the School in 1932, when it became independent of King's, a post she held for almost 30 years. She was the author, *inter alia*, of a *Survey of a Thousand Years of Beekeeping in Russia* (1971). The FBI seems to have believed that she was influential in effecting a reconciliation between Sir Bernard Pares, professor of Russian history at SSEES in its early years, and Stalin. An informant at the School described her to MI5 as a most unpleasant and seriously unbalanced woman and the only person in the place who makes a serious attempt at administration. She is by no means efficient, yet through her industry and her policy of interfering in every aspect of the school's activities, she exerts considerable influence.

She had been a friend of Prince Dimitri Petrovich Sviatopolk-Mirsky, an émigré and a great authority on Russian literature, who had been a teacher at the School. This Russian aristocrat underwent a Pauline conversion to communism while working on a book about Lenin and, disenchanted by life in Britain during the depressed 1930s, had made the fateful decision to return to the Soviet Union. Despite having the protection until he died of Maksim Gorky, Mirsky came under increasing threat as Stalin's paranoia grew. In 1937 he was arrested as 'a filthy Wrangelist and White Guard officer' and, two years later, perished in a Siberian labour camp at the age of 48.

In small fields such as mine a limited number of academics can have a disproportionate influence on public perceptions of the history and politics of a region. A classic instance of this is R.W. Seton-Watson, whose pro-Romanian, pro-Yugoslav and anti-Hungarian views powerfully influenced attitudes in the Foreign Office. Ian Roberts, in his history of the School, missed an opportunity to write frankly and entertainingly about the School and its often highly learned, not infrequently temperamental, and sometimes inadequate, teachers. When in the 1990s I levanted from London to St Antony's College in Oxford I made a rather half-hearted attempt to stimulate a more revealing account of the development of at least south-east European studies at SSEES, in which I had been particularly involved and about which I had some knowledge. Regrettably, nothing came of this.

An interesting, and somewhat disturbing, aspect of the School's early history, and an indication of how little governmental interest there was in Russian and east European studies, was the extent to which it was dependent on subsidies from governments in the region; for example, those of Romania and the newly established states of Czechoslovakia, Yugoslavia and Poland. When R.W. Seton-Watson, whose salary was initially paid by the Czechoslovak government, fell on hard times during the depression, both the Yugoslav and Romanian governments in 1940, independently of each other, offered a subsidy for his chair, the Masaryk Chair of Central European History, provided that he remained the professor. As late as December 1940, the Romanian dictator and loyal ally of Hitler, Ion Antonescu, maintaining that Seton-Watson was a good friend of Romania, rejected the suggestion of his Iron Guard (i.e. fascist) foreign minister, Mihail Sturdza, that the subsidy for his professorship be discontinued on the ground that he was a democrat who worked for British intelligence. This dependence on subsidy helps to explain, in part at least, the depth of R.W. Seton-Watson's hostility towards Arnold Toynbee, whose bitter quarrel with the Greek donors of the Koraes chair appeared to Seton-Watson, as we shall see in the next chapter, to threaten the whole edifice of subsidy by foreign governments on which the School had been built. Extraordinarily, the Hungarian government continued its subsidy for Hungarian language throughout World War II at a time when Hungary was aligned with the Axis, arranging for the money to be channelled through the Swedish Legation.

In 1983, I was appointed reader in modern Greek history at King's when my formal links with SSEES ended, although I continued to do a certain amount of teaching for the School. King's, in keeping with its origins as a religious counterweight to 'that godless institution in Gower Street', University College, was a conservative institution. Principals of the college were crown appointments, made on the recommendation of the prime minister. This resulted in a succession of principals whose achievements lay in the past: General Sir John Hackett, formerly Commander-in-Chief of the British Army of the Rhine; Sir Richard Way, formerly a senior civil servant and latterly Chairman of London Transport; and Lord (Neil) Cameron of Balhousie, former Chief of the Defence Staff. The premises of the college were somewhat antiquated. When I first began to teach there were still some hydraulically powered lifts in the older parts of the college and I was more than once challenged about using them as they were reserved for staff.

When I had first arrived in the college there was a prohibition against women students wearing trousers, while there were separate and very unequal common rooms for male and female faculty and a rather miserable mixed one. By contrast, SSEES, unlike most academic institutions at the time, had a respectable number of women in senior positions, among them Phyllis Auty, Olga Crisp, Georgette Donchin and Isabel de Madariaga. At the time of the student unrest of 1968, the principal, Sir John Hackett, attributed the calm that prevailed at King's, which contrasted with the turmoil across the Strand at the London School of Economics, to the fact that the college at the time did not teach the social sciences. By the 1980s there were indications that the college was a conservative institution with a large 'C'. Lord (George) Jellicoe, a Tory peer, was chairman of the Delegacy and its successor, the Council, from 1978 to 1986, while in the 1990s, Baroness Rawlings, an erstwhile Conservative member of the European Parliament and subsequently a Conservative member of the House of Lords, became chairman of the Council, a post she held for nine years. Lady Mayhew, the wife of the Tory attorney-general, was a member of the Council, as was John MacGregor, a Conservative MP and subsequently a Conservative peer. Labour or Liberal politicians appear to have been thin on the ground, if they were represented at all. I remember making myself somewhat unpopular at a meeting of the academic board when I spoke out against a proposal to accept money from the Thatcher government to introduce the teaching of 'enterprise studies'.

During the period of the dictatorship I had been a frequent contributor to the Greek Service of the BBC and had got to know well the successive programme organisers, Peter Frankel, Michael Williams and Paul Nathanail, together with Andrew Mango, at that time the programme organiser of the Turkish service and subsequently successor to Austen Kark as head of the South European service. These contacts and broadcasts continued after the *metapolitefsi*, the change of regime that followed the downfall of the Colonels, and I was eventually invited to act, on a part-time basis, as the stand-in *proistamenos*, or programme organiser, of the Greek Service. This proved to be a not particularly onerous job and one which was remarkably easy to combine with my obligations at King's. It took scarcely five minutes to exchange my room at King's for my office in Bush House, which housed the World Service and the External Services and which was barely a hundred yards across the Strand. There is actually a tunnel from King's to the church of St Mary-le-Strand which occupies a large traffic island in the middle of the Strand opposite the college. How convenient it would have been had it extended to Bush House. As it was, I could be teaching until a few minutes before 12 and still be able to attend the noon meeting of the South European section at which the running order of the various programmes would be established. After a few months it was suggested that I become the full-time programme organiser. This was an attractive proposition, not least because BBC salaries were considerably more generous than those of the university system. When I said that I did not want to give up my academic job, I was told there would be no trouble in keeping this while working full time for the BBC. This was an even more attractive proposition and I would have achieved the status of a *polythesitis*, someone holding down more than one job, so eagerly prized in Greece. I was sorely tempted, as on two salaries I would have been comfortably well-off, but, out of a sense of loyalty to King's, which proved a few years later to have been misplaced, I declined the offer, although I continued to work for the Greek Service for a number of years on a part-time basis, being paid by the shift.

The members of the Greek section were a very agreeable group, many of whom I had got to know during the years of the dictatorship. All were highly educated, many were aligned politically with the broadly Eurocommunist KKEes, the Communist Party of the Interior, which had broken with the sclerotic orthodox Communist Party of Greece, the KKE, which had never really de-Stalinised. At the time of the 1977 elections, there were high hopes that the KKEes, albeit contesting the election under another name, would do well in the poll. I made myself somewhat unpopular by predicting that the KKEes' share of the vote would be no more than 3 per cent. The party actually achieved 2.7 per cent, so my prediction proved highly accurate, to the mild chagrin of the KKEes supporters in the section. It was interesting having to find translations for words that simply did not exist in Greek. At the time of the train siege in Holland by South Moluccan militants in 1975, the section came up with 'Notioi Moloukoi' for 'South Moluccans'. The only occasion when I experienced a mini-mutiny in the Greek section was on the day that Elvis Presley died in 1977. I realised that, in Greece, Presley had perhaps not received the wild adulation that he had been accorded in the English-speaking world, but I nonetheless thought that we should make some mention of his death. This did not go down well with those in the section who had a lofty disdain for popular culture, at least in its American manifestations.

The only time I got into mild trouble with my superiors at Bush House concerned Albania. An item came through on the wires that someone calling himself Mr Mbret Leka had been arrested in Bangkok and his hotel room found to contain large quantities of weapons and ammunition. I know precious little Albanian but I did know that Mbret meant King. This sounded very much as though the person arrested was the Sandhurst-trained King Leka, who, as a babe in arms, had been whisked out of Albania at the time of the Italian invasion at Easter 1939 by his father and mother, King Zog and Queen Geraldine, and so it turned out. By the 1970s, Zog was long dead but Leka continued to plot the liberation of Albania and his return to the throne. I thought that our listeners in what the Greeks call Northern Epirus, that part of southern Albania with a sizeable Greek minority, would clearly be interested in this story, always assuming that anyone in Albania, the party *nomenklatura* excepted, could possess a short-wave radio capable of receiving our transmissions. (Wireless sets capable of receiving short-wave transmissions may have been thin on the ground, although I remember sitting one evening on the beach in Durrës during my 1975 visit to Albania and being able to pick up on a cheap transistor Vatican Radio broadcasting loud and clear in Albanian on medium wave for the Catholic minority in the north of the country. This was some years after Enver Hoxha, the Albanian party leader had declared Albania to be the first atheist state in the world and had viciously persecuted the Muslim, Orthodox and Catholic religious leadership of the country.) When Andrew Mango listened to the recording of our daily news transmission the next day he was alarmed lest 'Mr Mbret Leka' turned out to be an impostor and the real King Leka should sue the BBC for implicating him in clandestine arms purchases. I was instructed to make no more reference to this curious episode, so our putative northern Epirot listeners would have been left with only the first part of the story and would have learned nothing of its sequel.

I have always thought that someone could write a fascinating account of the Greek Service from its beginning just after the outbreak of World War II until its demise in 2005. For the duration of the wartime occupation the Greek Service used the peace time call sign of goat bells of Athens Radio. For much of the service's existence, British–Greek relations were in crisis and the Greek Service, funded as it was by the Foreign Office, had to steer a difficult course between not questioning official British policy, while at the same time not alienating its Greek audience, at one time sizeable. During the war many of the Greek members of the section were republicans appalled by the strength of Churchill's attachment to the cause of King George II. In consequence, Dilys Powell, at that time working for the Political Warfare Executive, fought numerous battles in an attempt to ensure that the section followed policy guidelines ultimately deriving from the Foreign Office. At the same time, the service came under fire from the Greek government-in-exile, based in London initially, and from March 1943 in Cairo, although it was always a marginal player in Greek affairs during World War II.

December 1944, when British troops were locked in fierce combat in Athens with former allies in the communist-controlled ELAS resistance army, proved to be one of the lowest points in Churchill's wartime administration and presented a real headache to those running the service. Within 18 months outright civil war had broken out and this did not end until the summer of 1949. Scarcely had the civil war come to an end than the campaign for the *enosis* of Cyprus with Greece had got under way, and the Conservative government then in power in Britain had unwisely declared that it could 'never' yield sovereignty over the island. This fuelled the EOKA campaign against British rule, masterminded by George Grivas. The granting of a qualified independence to the island in 1960 proved fragile. No sooner had peace of a kind returned to Cyprus than the Colonels seized power in Greece in 1967. This resulted in seven years of friction between the Foreign Office, which controlled the BBC External Services's purse strings and was anxious to preserve what it termed a 'good working relationship' with the junta, and a BBC committed to reporting the truth about a brutal, if absurd, dictatorship and to reflect the depth of anti-junta feeling in Britain. A book along the lines of Jeremy Bennett's 1966 study of *British Broadcasting and the Danish Resistance Movement 1940–1945* could be of great interest. Perhaps I should have written it myself, not least because at the time I was associated with the Greek Service a number of those involved with its early years were still alive to be interviewed.

I certainly enjoyed my association with the BBC and learned a lot about the contemporary Greek scene, although I am unable to shed light on a curious accusation made by the maverick Elias Petropoulos that the BBC's unique holdings of *rebetika* (underworld) songs had been pillaged by the 'Greek resistance movement' between 1967 and 1970. An additional, and not negligible, bonus was that working for the BBC gave access to its excellent canteen, which, as it largely catered for foreigners, was much superior to that at King's. Among other things, my *polythesia* enabled me to follow political developments during the exciting years after the collapse of the Colonels' regime in 1974, which saw the rise of Andreas Papandreou's populist, quasi-socialist PASOK party, or, as Papandreou insisted, 'movement', far more easily and closely than I could have done at King's alone. There was thus a considerable degree of academic as well as financial pay off from the BBC connection. I had access, for instance, to the despatches of the incomparable Mario Modiano, who for many years had been the Athens correspondent of *The Times* and who also filed copy for the BBC.

One extraordinary story of his that came through the teleprinter has always stuck in my mind, although it did not rate a mention in the British press, which had rather lost interest in Greek affairs with the downfall of the junta in 1974. In May 1981, a ceremony was held to mark the centenary of Kemal Atatürk's birth in Thessaloniki at the house in which he had reputedly been born and which now forms part of the Turkish consulate-general. This is home to a small museum in honour of the 'Father of the Turks', the name bestowed on Mustafa Kemal by the Grand National Assembly in 1934, the year in which all Turks were required to adopt surnames. The commemoration represented a welcome effort to improve the almost continuously poor climate in Greek–Turkish relations during the 1970s and 1980s. Assorted Greek and Turkish luminaries had gathered at the fine old Turkish building on Agiou Dimitriou Street but, alas, the hoped-for climate of mutual good will was rudely disrupted by a circus performer who began to buzz the consulate in a light plane, claiming that it was packed with explosives. Chaos inevitably ensued. The *episimoi*, as the Greeks would say, or bigwigs, were forced to disperse and the would-be kamikaze pilot returned to earth only when the police radioed that his family had been taken to the consulate. It proved to be no more true that the pilot's family had been corralled in the consulate as hostages than that the plane had been loaded with explosives. This tragi-comic episode had an even odder sequel. When the pilot was brought to trial, the public prosecutor, no less, successfully sought his acquittal on the ground that when a person's patriotic sentiments are aroused they can no longer be held accountable for their actions, thus adding 'crime national' to 'crime passionnel' in the legal vocabulary.

One result of the BBC connection was my writing of *Parties and Elections in Greece* (1987) for the small but enterprising publishing house of Christopher Hurst, who acquired over the years a considerable reputation as a publisher, *inter alia*, of books of Balkan interest. Christopher, whom I got to know well over the years, paid me the somewhat back-handed compliment of saying that I had written 'a dense book of greater solidity and stature than I had expected' in his entertaining, if rather idiosyncratic, memoir of a productive life in publishing. The modest sales of the book were boosted by the purchase of five copies by the Japanese embassy in Athens. Another indirect consequence of work for the BBC was that the extra income I received from the BBC in the late 1970s and early 1980s made easier the move from Crouch End to a larger house in Muswell Hill, one of the largest and best-preserved Edwardian suburbs in Britain, once home to impoverished intellectuals no longer able to afford to live in Hampstead but now a favoured abode of city slickers.

The BBC connection also enriched the short articles which I contributed every year for some 30 years to *The Annual Register*, which had been founded in 1758 by Edmund Burke and which continued to be published, seemingly because no one dared to bring an end to such a venerable publishing institution. Although a salutary task, it was not always easy trying to compress the previous year's events in Greece into 1,250 or 1,500 words, not least because successive editors applied very strict deadlines which required submission in January of the following year. I used to be particularly thankful when there had been elections in the previous year, because by the time I had described the campaign, outlined the platforms of the various parties, and given the results I would have used up a significant part of my word allocation. I began writing for the *Annual Register* by covering the events of 1970 and contributed a further 30 annual surveys, the last covering the events of the millennial year, 2000. I was never entirely sure what readership would find the *Annual Register* useful, although I found myself frequently referring to my own articles. I originally harboured the rather childish ambition to write for the *Annual Register* for half a century, thus probably becoming one of the longest-serving contributors, if not the longest, in its 250-year history. But I decided to throw in the towel in the year of the millennium. This was partly because the Greek political scene had by then become, as I used to tease Greek friends, rather boring, which had resulted some years earlier in my abandoning the effort to follow the convoluted twists and turns of politics on a daily basis, although towards the end of the first decade of the new millennium Greek politics became considerably less boring as the country teetered towards bankruptcy. It was also partly because I was feeling ever more oppressed during the Christmas holiday period by the need to produce my copy. Moreover, by the time I stopped writing for *The Annual Register* in 2000, I had long ceased working for the BBC.

The fee paid to contributors to the *Annual Register* was nugatory but we did receive a free copy of an expensive publication. The real reward was the annual dinner for the contributors, which I always found to be an agreeable occasion. At one of these, in 1975, at precisely the time that an International Monetary Fund team was ensconced in Brown's Hotel to oversee the bailing out of the British economy, which seemed in a state of near terminal decline, the *Annual Register* dinner was held at the same hotel. At the end of the meal bottles of various liqueurs were produced and left on the table, not a wise move when most of the diners tended to be impecunious but bibulous academics, least of all at a time when the pundits had been talking of the end of civilisation as we had known it. No one seemed much interested in the bottle of Kümmel, so Michael Leifer, an expert in south-east Asian politics at the London School of Economics, and I made a serious effort to drink it down. The combination of too much Kümmel and the large cigar that was also on offer proved too much for me and I passed out. The next year the dinner moved to the genteel surroundings of the Savile Club where the hospitality was less lavish. Whether our disreputable behaviour had contributed to this move I do not know.

One of the problems in my career has been that my academic interests have ranged too widely over the field of the modern history of the Greek people, from the Turkish-speaking Greeks of Asia Minor, who employed the Greek alphabet to write Turkish, to contemporary Greek politics. One of the subjects which particularly caught my interest in the 1970s and 1980s was Greece during World War II and, in particular, the role of the Special Operations Executive (SOE) in giving aid and encouragement to the wartime resistance. This interest had its origin in a conference held in July 1973 and organised by Phyllis Auty and myself on British policy towards wartime resistance in Yugoslavia and Greece. The occasion for the conference, which was held at Cumberland Lodge in Windsor Great Park, was the release, in January 1972, by the Public Record Office of the official government records for the whole of World War II, a blanket release from which, as was to be expected, the papers of the Secret Intelligence Service were withheld, as were those, with rather less justification, of the Special Operations Executive. Phyllis was reader in south Slav history at SSEES, and during the war had worked in the BBC's Yugoslav service and in the Political Intelligence Centre in Cairo. The idea was to discuss British policies in the light of the official papers and of the recollections of some of those who had participated in the formulation and execution of those policies. SSEES supported the conference with a generous subvention, putting its financial surplus on this occasion to good use, while we also had a useful grant from the Nuffield Foundation.

At this time, of course, many of the participants in the events which we wanted to discuss were still alive, although two of those who had taken part in the conference had died by the time the conference proceedings were published in 1975 in the SSEES/Macmillan series. These were Sir John Stevens, who, *inter alia*, had been on two missions to occupied Greece on behalf of SOE, and S.W. (Bill) Bailey, a pre-war engineer at the Trepča mines in Kosovo and the head of the British mission to General Mihailović's headquarters in 1942-3. After the conference, John Stevens invited me to a *tête à tête* over a splendid lunch at Morgan Grenfell, the merchant bank of which he was Managing Director. Others who attended the conference included Elisabeth Barker, head of the Balkan region in the Political Warfare Executive from 1942 to 1945 (and the daughter of a former principal of King's College, Ernest Barker); Stephen Clissold, Political Intelligence Centre, Middle East, 1943-4 and the British military mission to Yugoslavia, 1944-5; Basil Davidson, a liaison officer in Yugoslavia, 1943-4; F.W.D. (Bill) Deakin, the first British liaison officer at Tito's headquarters, 1943; Sir Alexander (Sandy) Glen, SOE in Yugoslavia and Albania and personal representative to Yugoslavia of the Commander-in-Chief, Mediterranean, 1943-5; N.G.L. (Nick) Hammond, a liaison officer in Greece, 1943-4; Sir John Henniker-Major, a liaison officer in Yugoslavia, 1943-4; Dame Patricia Hornsby-Smith, Personal Assistant to Lord Selborne, who as minister of economic warfare had for much of the war been responsible for SOE (after the war Selborne, somewhat paradoxically, became head of the Church Army); Kenneth Johnstone, Political Warfare Executive in Cairo, 1941-4; Sir Fitzroy Maclean, commander of the Allied military mission to Tito; E.C.W. (Eddie) Myers, commander of the British military mission to the Greek resistance, 1942-3; David Pawson, SOE in Greece, Istanbul and Izmir, 1941-3; Pamela Pawson, SOE in Greece, Istanbul and Izmir, 1941-4; Hugh Seton-Watson, SOE in Romania, Yugoslavia, Istanbul and Cairo, 1940-4; Bickham Sweet-Escott, Staff of SOE headquarters in London; George Taylor, Chief of Staff in 1940-3 to Sir Frank Nelson and Sir Charles Hambro, successive heads of SOE; and C.M. (Monty) Woodhouse, Eddie Myers' successor as Commander of the Allied Military Mission to the Greek Resistance, 1943-4. This was an impressive turnout, which was enhanced by the presence for a time of Major-General Sir Colin Gubbins, who had been the executive head of SOE from 1943.

This gathering afforded a fascinating insight into the world of clandestine operations in the Balkans during World War II and also into the ethos of SOE and kindred organisations. The entire proceedings could no doubt have been categorised as a wholesale breach of the draconian Official Secrets Act, but that is another matter. At dinner one evening I heard above the general hubbub Mary Jo declaring that she had been at Lakeview High School in Oregon. It transpired that her neighbours were talking about where they had been to school. Pretty well all of them had attended public schools (two, Nick Hammond and Sandy Glen, had been at Fettes) and formed part of the somewhat hermetic establishment world remarked upon by a shrewd Office of Strategic Services (OSS) (the approximate counterpart of SOE) operative with the Yugoslav partisans, Franklin Lindsay. He noted of the entourage of Brigadier Fitzroy Maclean that these 'British officials who were drawn to irregular operations seemed not only to have been together in early wartime operations but also to have had many many close school and family ties.' (Eddie Myers, for instance, married Bickham Sweet-Escott's sister.) By contrast, Lindsay himself, in three years service with OSS, had met only one person whom he had known before the war. SOE's operatives were often recruited on an 'old school tie' basis, with the principal locus of recruitment popularly believed to be the bar at White's Club. The fashionable law firm of Slaughter and May was also a favoured source of recruits, leading to the jibe that SOE was all May and no Slaughter. Recruiters to the organisation, in fact, seem to have adhered to the maxim attributed to Admiral 'Jacky' Fisher, who played an important role in modernising the Royal Navy in the years before World War I, that favouritism is the secret of efficiency.

Seven papers were delivered. Mine was the only one to be given by someone who had played no part in the events and, indeed, had scarcely been born at the time, but some of the most valuable insights came in statements rather than papers or in contributions to the discussion, ably recorded for us by the aptly named Nicholas Bugg of the King's College audio-visual department. One of the most striking of these statements was that of Fitzroy Maclean. This recorded the obstructiveness of SOE when Churchill, in the summer of 1943, decided to send him into Yugoslavia to report on the activities of Tito and the partisans. SOE's subterfuges apparently included forging a signal from General 'Jumbo' Wilson, the commander-in-chief in the Middle East, to say that Maclean was totally unsuitable for the job and an outright attempt by the legendary and eccentric Brigadier 'Bolo' Keble, Glenconner's Chief of Staff in SOE Cairo, to thwart Churchill's orders. Keble refused to show Maclean signals and files relevant to his mission. Rumours were spread, at SOE's instigation, that Maclean was an alcoholic, a homosexual and a coward. When it was finally accepted that he would be parachuted in, Maclean, wisely perhaps, did not take the first parachute that was offered to him.

Although I had already met Monty Woodhouse when he had delivered a paper at a seminar that I had organised at SSEES in 1971 to mark the 150th anniversary of the outbreak of the Greek war of independence (the papers were published by Macmillan in 1973 as *The Struggle for Greek Independence*), I had not at the time of the conference met any of the other SOE operatives who had been sent into Greece. (I avoid the absurd usage, Special Operations Executives, that is nowadays sometimes encountered to describe those enlisted in SOE.) I now had the opportunity of meeting John Stevens, Nick Hammond and Eddie Myers, all of whom had served with SOE in Greece. It was with some trepidation that I gave my paper on the troubled relationship between the Foreign Office and SOE over Greek affairs. This was entitled '"Pearls from swine": the Foreign Office Papers, S.O.E. and the Greek resistance', 'Pearls from swine' being the dismissive expression used by Rex Leeper, the Australian-born British ambassador to the Greek government-in-exile, to describe communications from SOE which crossed his desk in Cairo, where the Greek government-in-exile was located after March 1943. When, in August 1943, Myers accompanied a delegation representing the major resistance groups to the Middle East, fully intending to return to his duties as the commander of the British military mission, Leeper met with him for the first time in person and had immediately taken against him.

I included a number of extracts from Leeper's outbursts as he pursued what was looked on by SOE's enemies, and they were many, as the 'great war against SOE'. I felt distinctly uncomfortable as, sitting only a few feet from Myers, I read out some of the comments made about him:

> Myers has been to my mind a complete disaster [...] it is quite impossible to penetrate his skull [...] my blows seem to ricochet off his skull and disappear somewhere in thin air [...] I am completely convinced that he is a very dangerous fool, and [...] a fanatic for his own ideas.

The documents from which I quoted were new to Myers and, indeed, to the others at the conference. Mine was the chapter, which, when the conference proceedings were published by Macmillan, had so aroused the wrath of the retired Foreign Office functionary, David Balfour, that he threatened to report me to the Foreign Office for utilising private letters sent by Leeper to the Foreign Office which, with the release of the relevant papers, had become freely accessible in the Public Record Office.

I need have had no qualms about revealing the depth of Leeper's animosity towards Myers. Not only did he take what I had to say in good part, but in fact felt vindicated by my paper. During the course of his Middle Eastern visit he had been forbidden to return to Greece, partly because civil war had broken out between the communist controlled resistance army ELAS and the much smaller EDES, and it was held that for him to return would imply approval of ELAS' hegemonistic behaviour. My paper indicated the depth of Leeper's prejudice against him and demonstrated that the decision to prevent his return was politically motivated. After all, Myers' military record in Greece had been formidable. It was he who had commanded the Harling party, which had, with the assistance of contingents from both ELAS and EDES, wrought the destruction of the Gorgopotamos viaduct carrying the railway line between Thessaloniki and Athens in November 1942, one of the most spectacular of SOE operations in occupied Europe during the entire war.

The Cumberland Lodge conference proceedings were published two years later, in 1975, by Macmillan as *British Policy towards Wartime Resistance in Yugoslavia and Greece*, after a hair-raising episode in which the completed manuscript was lost for six weeks by the Post Office. It aroused much interest in Greece where, within the space of six months, it was pirated by two newspapers, a fine example of the Greek practice of *klopiright*, the right to steal. The volume was edited by Phyllis Auty and myself, and was the first volume to be published in a series published by Macmillan in conjunction with SSEES: Studies in Russian and East European History. This was my first experience of editing verbatim discussion. This was not an easy task. Many of the speakers, myself included, muttered, rambled and repeated themselves. A striking exception to this general rule was Monty Woodhouse, who spoke extempore not merely in complete sentences but in complete paragraphs.

The Cumberland Lodge conference was a very enjoyable experience and reinforced a developing interest that I had in SOE's controversial role in Greece. It enabled me to make some useful contacts with surviving veterans of the organisation and led to useful caches of SOE material falling into my hands. These were particularly valuable given that the SOE archive itself had remained closed, guarded by the Cerberus-like figure of an old SOE hand, Eddie Boxshall, apparently at that time the oldest employee in government service. He was a fierce guardian of the archives, which had been placed in the custody of the Secret Intelligence Service, with which its relations had been poor, when SOE was wound up early in 1946.

One person with whom I came into contact was Colonel D.T. (Bill) Hudson. He had been the first member of SOE to make contact with both Tito and Draža Mihailović as early as the autumn of 1941, although his initial experiences in Yugoslavia had proved to be harrowing. Hudson after the war lived in South Africa, but when in London stayed in a charming service flat in St James' Street in Mayfair, where Phyllis Auty and I paid him a visit. Although he had not been at the Cumberland Lodge conference we were anxious to include a note of his experiences in the book, for he had never published an account for public consumption of his extraordinary experiences in Yugoslavia. In the summer of 1974 I sent him the note which Phyllis and I had prepared with a request for any alterations or corrections that he might wish to make. His response was unusual. He returned the letter with a pencilled note on it. This read 'Open letter to professors of history. Sirs. In the Battle for the World we lose our records. Where do we find one of you?' Over the next few days, I received, delivered by hand at the college, a series of hand-written notes, imprinted with what appears to be his signet ring in sealing wax and bearing much the same message, but sometimes with obscure references to *The Times*.

What these messages portended I have not the slightest idea, but we never did receive his approval for the publication of our note. The fact that he had never written an account for public consumption (although he appears to have embarked on such a project) may well have had some connection with the recent revelation that, during his time in Yugoslavia, he had contrived to bury caches of some of the gold sovereigns that he had been supplied with by SOE. After the war he got an accomplice to unearth one of these and ship it to Romania where he was then stationed. Hudson subsequently confessed to what he had done and the matter was hushed up by a Foreign Office fearful of the embarrassment that would ensue if his activities became public. A similar case was recorded by Michael Ward in his excellent memoir, *Greek Assignments: SOE 1943–1948 UNSCOB* (1992). When he left Greece in 1943 he was accompanied by another British liaison officer, whom he pseudonymously identifies as 'Eric Butler', who travelled with a personal 'reserve of funds' consisting of 250 sovereigns stuffed into a jockstrap. I calculate that his hoard would have weighed some 2 kg. It is not difficult to work out who 'Eric Butler' was. It is small wonder that picaresque activities of this kind led to SOE acquiring a bad name in some quarters.

One of those attending the Cumberland Lodge conference was Professor W.J.M. Mackenzie, the author of the official history of SOE, completed in 1947 but not published until 2000, and then unofficially. He had kept a copy for himself and he kindly allowed me to consult it in his office in the University of Glasgow. Another of those present who had a particular interest in Greek affairs was Bickham Sweet-Escott, who had been a senior member of the SOE hierarchy and was the author of one of the earliest, and still the best, books on

SOE, *Baker Street Irregular* (1965). He subsequently invited Mary Jo and me to a celebration of his libel victory over the playright Rolf Hochhuth, who in *Der Spiegel* had sought to implicate him in contriving, at Churchill's behest, the plane crash in which General Wladyslaw Sikorski, the prime minister of the Polish government-in-exile, was killed in Gibraltar in July 1943.

In the early 1980s, access to the SOE archive was granted to a former civil servant, Charles Cruickshank, to write a history of SOE in the Far East (1983). This he did with exemplary despatch and followed it up with a history of SOE in Scandinavia (1986). But SOE's activities in the Balkans remained a closed book and its activities in the region had come in for particular criticism. In a *Spectator* review of the wartime memoir, *Approach March* (1973), of the SOE operative Julian Amery, who had served in Albania, Hugh Fraser, himself a former member of SOE and like Amery a Conservative MP on the right of the party, harshly criticised the organisation from a right-wing perspective. 'At the best of times,' Fraser claimed, 'SOE was a bad organisation frequently lacking a strong or political or even honourable direction.' SOE, he added, was 'particularly inane in the Balkans, positively assisting the adventurer Enver Hodja to seize impregnable Albania for communism, and had it not been for Churchill and Macmillan's personal intervention, permitting a communist takeover in Greece'. A diametrically opposed view was advanced in the *Times Literary Supplement* from the left by an anonymous reviewer (Basil Davidson). Davidson, who had been at the Cumberland Lodge conference, maintained that the 'nabobs of SOE London', for the most part bankers or businessmen, suppressed intelligence of partisan activity in Yugoslavia 'in the interests of restoring the status quo ante bellum'.

At the end of 1980 *The Times* diary reported that Cruickshank had been given access to the SOE archive, but claimed that the record of SOE in the Balkans was so unsavoury that it could not be written until the surviving participants were 'well and truly dead'. This was a grotesque and manifestly unfair comment, so I wrote to the paper (in a letter that was published on Christmas Eve) to protest that this was less than fair to the reputation and memory of the courageous and resourceful men and women involved in SOE's operations in the Balkans. I conceded that SOE had its share of skeletons in the cupboard but argued that its overall record was a very creditable one. Thirty-five years on there could be few objections on security grounds to the release of SOE's Balkan records, and none that could not be overcome without compromising the integrity of an official history. I argued that the time had surely come for a sober and documented attempt to clear away the obfuscation, sometimes officially inspired, that continued to surround SOE's role in the Balkans. The professional jealousies, interdepartmental rivalries and personal antagonisms of which SOE had been the object a generation ago should, I urged, no longer be allowed to obscure a remarkable record.

The letter sparked off a considerable correspondence. M.R.D. Foot, the author of *SOE in France* (1966), the only published official history undertaken before the Cruickshank volumes, and the leading authority on the history of the organisation, wrote in support. He urged that unless something was done quickly 'a vital page of history – from which Great Britain will emerge on balance with enormous credit' would never get written. He mentioned Bill Deakin, Hugh Seton-Watson, Nick Hammond and Monty Woodhouse among historians who had worked for SOE in the Balkans. 'If none of them can tackle the project', he continued, 'may it be handed promptly to someone younger – such as Dr [sic] Clogg – who can consult them and their surviving colleagues.' This may have looked like a put-up job, but Foot had not consulted me before writing his letter, nor I him before writing mine. Others who weighed in included Sir Peter Wilkinson who had been active in Slovenia on behalf of SOE. He wrote that 'unless something is done soon, history will be utterly confused by the myths of the media and the partial judgements of certain of those who worked for (or against) SOE in the Balkans'.

Lt-Colonel Ronald Prentice, who had commanded the Allied military mission in west (Greek) Macedonia, wrote that 'it is to refute for good the charge of "unsavouriness" and to establish the facts based on records of the time that members of SOE request publication'. If the records of SOE's Far Eastern operations could be released, 'then why not also those of Greece, one of our closest allies with whom the British people have had ties of strong friendship and so much in common over many generations – and not least during the years 1942–44'. Eddie Myers, the commander of the British military mission in Greece, likewise wrote in to suggest that perhaps the real reason for the Government's refusal hitherto (to allow access to SOE's Balkan records) was the Foreign Office's 'wish to avoid giving further publicity to the unfortunate mistakes of some of their predecessors in senior positions during World War II'. He clearly had in mind here my contribution to the Auty/Clogg volume which, as I have suggested, he had seen as a vindication of his own activities. He made a welcome reference to the book in his letter. Another correspondent, Lt-Colonel Philip Worrall, a veteran of SOE's Greek operations, also wrote in. He referred to his extraordinary but harrowing experiences in seeking to look after an Italian force of 7,000 in the aftermath of the Italian surrender in September 1943, and urged that an official history of SOE in the Balkans be written.

The sole dissenting view was expressed by Major Fergus Chalmers-Wright, who had been infiltrated into France on behalf of the Political Warfare

Executive and subsequently by SOE. He began by saying that the writer of the letter published in *The Times* on Christmas Eve (i.e. me) had pleaded that 'common decency' required that a record of SOE's activities in the Balkans should be written without 'waiting for the *dramatis personae* to die' had emerged as M.R.D. Foot's nominee as 'playwright'. 'What common decency requires', he wrote, 'is that surviving former SOE agents who have neither publicized themselves nor sought publicity for their individual war services should be officially protected against unwanted pryings into those services by historical writers aspiring to gain access to SOE archives.' He then protested that SOE agents sent into France had not been asked whether they had been willing to have their secret wartime services publicly revealed by Professor Foot. Where SOE agents had not survived, Foot had been 'free to laud or disparage them according to his lights', which had on the whole been illuminating because he had a record of active military service which enabled him to appraise what he had found in the archives, although 'younger writers would have no such background', presumably a thrust directed at me.

The correspondence was seen by Neil Cameron, the principal of King's and, as a Marshal of the RAF and a former Chief of the Defence Staff, someone well connected in Whitehall. Here he pulled strings on my behalf to try to get me appointed as an official historian of SOE in Greece. This was a rather onerous procedure which entailed positive vetting. This involved not only an in-depth investigation of my own life but some inquiry into Mary Jo's. I was asked to supply a list of all the addresses at which she had lived in the US. This was not easy, as they included the Snyder Ranger Station on the Olympic peninsula in Washington State, which had consisted of only five houses and, by the 1980s, had been virtually abandoned. Another of the places in which she had lived had been a couple of converted railway carriages in the middle of a forest near Gilchrist in Oregon, which had housed her family while her father, on behalf of the US Forest Service, had supervised logging activities. This was one of the very last of the railroad logging camps which were once common in the US west. The railway siding had long ago been removed and the site had returned to wilderness. I was also required to sign the Official Secrets Act. I was not particularly happy about this, but it was the price I had to pay for access to the SOE archive.

I have been working on this project so long that, before my manuscript was completed, I was able, thanks to a former student who unearthed the material in the Public Record Office, to see some of the official correspondence about the decision to allow me access to the SOE files relating to Greece which had hitherto remained firmly closed. A member of the Southern European Department was deputed to consider whether there might be problems in Greece resulting from the release of the papers. Although he considered that there might be certain events which would have to be handled with care, he found no compelling reasons that would prevent such a history being published. He was also asked to consider whether my earlier writings on Greek history indicated whether I could be entrusted with such a work. He found my *Short History of Modern Greece*, which was the Southern Department's recommended text, to be very readable. He correctly noted that much of my writing up to the time of his 1982 minute related to the period of the Colonels' dictatorship. During this period it was apparent that my contacts and sympathies were mainly with the opposition 'probably because the dead hand of the junta forced the best academics into opposition'. This had led me to accept some myths about the resistance too uncritically and to give EAM/ELAS a better press than it deserved.

The member of the Southern European Department referred to the paper that I had contributed to the Cumberland Lodge conference in 1973 – '"Pearls from swine": the Foreign Office papers, S.O.E. and the Greek Resistance'. This, he wrote, demonstrated not just 'a healthy scepticism about officialdom, but some sympathy for the men in the F[oreign]) C([and Commonwealth] O(ffice] and SOE who were taking awkward decisions at a difficult time'. 'It is,' he concluded, 'by no means a biased account of events.' He could see nothing to suggest that I should not write the history of SOE 'on grounds of prejudice'. I might be slightly 'out of sympathy' with British attempts 'to focus Greek minds on fighting the Germans', but overall he thought that I would present the facts objectively and would not 'seek to distort them to suit a predetermined thesis'. The head of the Southern Department added that the FCO would not know what 'ugly worms might come out of the woodwork until the full research on the papers has been completed'.

By the 1980s, it would appear that the authorities were not so much concerned with possible breaches of security as by fear of the libel actions of the kind that had greeted Foot's pioneering official history of *SOE in France* when it had been published in 1966. As this was an official history, the government had had to pay the damages that had arisen from out-of-court settlements with SOE operatives who maintained that they had been libelled when their wartime activities had come in for criticism or been downplayed. These amounted to some £10,000 in damages, and £5,000 in legal costs, a very large sum at the time. These libel actions had resulted in a second edition, 'with amendments', which was published in 1968. A comparison of the first edition and the 'amended' one makes for fascinating and instructive reading. Cruickshank's *SOE in the Far East* had also attracted an action for libel. I was therefore required to assume myself responsibility for any possible libel actions arising from my own study. Eventually, just before Christmas 1981, Margaret Thatcher, as prime minister, signed the authorisation and I have been working on the official history of SOE in Greece ever since.

On starting to work on the project, one of the first things I did was to consult the papers of Bickham Sweet-Escott held at Balliol College, Oxford. These include the fascinating correspondence that surrounded the publication of his insider's view of SOE, *Baker Street Irregular*, in 1965, a book that he had actually completed in 1954, although he had to wait ten years before receiving permission to publish it. There was one item, a box file, which was withheld and I was told that I would not be able to consult the papers it contained without special permission. I was naturally intrigued by this latter-day Joanna Southcott's Box and, as I was now an official historian, I was able to secure the requisite permission. I went back to Balliol agog to see what dark secrets might lay within. On opening it, however, I was to be sadly disappointed, for what it contained was a copy of a report on SOE's early activities in Greece, compiled by Ian Pirie (who had occasioned something of a scandal by marrying a 17-year-old cabaret singer in Athens before he (and she) were evacuated with other SOE operatives as the Germans advanced on Athens). The report was indeed a most valuable one, but it was a copy of a document that had come into my possession after the Cumberland Lodge conference and which I myself had lent to Sweet-Escott, who had had it copied. So much for the tantalising prospect of access to a box of highly sensitive and hitherto unknown papers.

The reasons for my dilatoriness in completing the SOE history are several, but all are inadequate. The most significant is the sheer bulk of the material, there being approximately ten times as many files pertaining to Greece as to Yugoslavia. SOE's surviving papers have had a chequered history, which included a fire in the archive in the early postwar period. Some have suggested that the 'fire' was a convenient device for withholding access, although I did once see some files which showed signs of having been singed. The real problem was that I could only work on the papers in Whitehall, which became something of a problem after I moved to St Antony's. Moreover, it was some time before I had access to a word processor. I had already been required to lock up my typewriter ribbon every evening lest the notes I had taken fell into the wrong hands by someone nicking the ribbon. When I offered to bring my own rudimentary apparatus based on a BBC micro I was told that this would not be secure. My argument, that if a couple of KGB men were sitting all day in a white van outside the office in Whitehall where I was working and trying to make sense of what I was writing, then this would be an excellent way of wasting their time. This suggestion fell on deaf ears.

During my time at SSEES and King's I had some dealings with TV producers, mainly in connection with documentaries on wartime Greece. My experiences led me to the rather depressing general conclusion that the imperatives of 'good television' and academic history can seldom be reconciled in a satisfactory manner. During the Colonels' dictatorship I had acted as consultant to a programme on the junta in the influential Granada TV World in Action series. Besides advising on the general background, I helped shepherd the producer and camera crew to interview dissidents in Athens, a more difficult task then than it would be now as the filming and recording equipment at that time was much more cumbersome. The programme was excellently crafted by Barry Cox, who was subsequently to become a big wheel in London Weekend Television, while the camera crew took some striking shots of the traditional display of military might on Greek Independence Day, 25 March. This included a unit of frogmen who waddled along in ungainly fashion, wearing flippers.

By far the most contentious series of programmes with which I had a connection was the TV South series for Channel Four, *Greece – The Hidden War*. Long before the three hour-long programmes (a generous allocation of time by the standards of the TV industry) were transmitted in 1986, I had had serious doubts about the direction they were taking, and was thankful that, unlike a number of SOE friends and acquaintances, I declined to be involved in them. When broadcast they gave rise to an intense public row about the ethics of TV journalism and the difficulties inherent in portraying complex historical events through the medium of television.

The programmes were long in gestation. In April 1981, I had been telephoned by a budding TV producer, Jane Gabriel, who told me she was planning a series of documentaries about the wartime resistance in Greece and the ensuing civil war, a period in which, of course, I had a particular interest, and she invited me to lunch to discuss the project. We got on well and I promised to send her a copy of a proposal that I had submitted in 1973, via Barry Cox, to Jeremy Wallington, a leading light at the time in Granada Television. My 1973 proposal was for a programme pegged to the thirtieth anniversary of the December 1944 'Battle of Athens', when British troops became involved in bitter fighting with communist-led ELAS insurgents, at a time when the war in Europe had not yet been won. Wallington had been very enthusiastic about the project, saying that 'of all the retrospective ideas I have seen over the last two or three years this is by far the most interesting and ought to be made'. I had had the misfortune, however, to submit the proposal at much the same time that Jeremy Isaacs' 26-episode blockbuster on World War II, *The World at War*, a series which rightly met with much acclaim, was to be screened by Thames Television, and the project fell by the wayside.

In May 1983, some two years after our first meeting, Gabriel wrote to thank me for being helpful when we had met, and enclosed her formal proposal for a three-part series entitled, at that stage, '*Kapetanios* (the Greek resistance fighters)'. This was currently being considered by two television companies, TV South and Yorkshire TV. I was somewhat irritated to see that the synopsis for the first programme, 'The battle of Athens, December 1944', closely followed mine of some ten years earlier which I had lent her.

Some 18 months later, in October 1984, Gabriel wrote to say that the production was at last 'on the rails', and it was to be a TV South production commissioned by Channel Four. She asked whether I was still interested in the project. I replied wishing the enterprise well, but that I was extremely busy trying to finish two books. By this stage, I had a gut feeling that there was something odd about the whole enterprise. For one thing, Gabriel, despite being married to a Greek academic, appeared to have little understanding of the political complexities of Greece in the 1940s. Journalists are given to claiming that they are the first to throw light on events which are in fact quite well known, and often not merely to specialists. Gabriel was no exception. Speaking on the BBC's Greek Service, she stated that it was only through talking to Greek friends that she had become aware that there had even been a civil war in the country. She must have led a sheltered life.

Although I knew that a number of British friends who had been involved in wartime Greece, and whom I had got to know through my interest in SOE, were taking part in the programme, my doubts were not sure enough to share with them and thus possibly jeopardise what was clearly going to be a substantial element in the production, namely interviews with surviving British participants. With hindsight, this was a mistake. I must have subsequently agreed to give some further advice for I made an arrangement to meet with a researcher on the programme in March 1985, although this meeting was cancelled by Gabriel the day before it was due to take place. I was somewhat irritated by this so I decided to ask for the modest consultancy fee that I had been promised for my initial help and thereafter had no further dealings with her.

My growing doubts about the enterprise were to be fully justified when the programmes came to be shown on Channel Four in January 1986. Few British television documentaries can have caused such a stir as *Greece – The Hidden War*. For the best part of six months a ferocious controversy raged in the columns of the *Daily Telegraph*, the *Guardian* and in sections of the Greek press. Polemics were one thing but, sadly, as we shall see, the furore may well have cost the then controller of Channel Four, Jeremy Isaacs, the director-generalship of the BBC at a critical time in the Corporation's history. Isaacs was blackballed, quite unreasonably, for broadcasting when he was in charge of Channel Four what were deemed to be communist lies and propaganda. The BBC governors thus missed the chance of appointing one of the most creative figures in British television to what is undoubtedly the most important post in British broadcasting.

After the row died down, I wrote a long critique of the programmes in *Encounter*. This was probably an unwise choice of vehicle for the article, given the widely publicised revelations about CIA funding of the magazine that had surfaced some years previously, for it would only have served to reinforce the view of apologists for the programmes that the criticism heaped on them was part of an anti-communist, establishment conspiracy. But I could not think of any other journal that might have published a piece of the length and nature that I had in mind, and which would have reached the audience that I intended. The programmes raised important issues with regard to the television treatment of contemporary history; the ethics of documentary journalism; and the role of the Independent Broadcasting Authority, whose task it was to regulate independent television. It seemed to me that these deserved detailed consideration. I entitled my piece 'Camera Obscura: Channel Four's film on Greece's civil war'. But the editor, that redoubtable Cold War warrior, Mel Lasky, a one-time Trotskyist, unfortunately and pointlessly retitled it 'A case study in bias and distortion: Channel Four's film on Greece's civil war'. I thought my title much preferable, not least because it did not appear to prejudge the general tenor of the article.

I had no problem at all with Jane Gabriel's idea of looking at the turbulent decade of the 1940s in Greece through the eyes of the vanquished in the civil war. This was a perfectly legitimate, indeed an imaginative, idea. The programmes in the main comprised interviews with communist refugees who had returned to Greece after years of often difficult exile in the Eastern Bloc countries. These were often interesting, sometimes revealing and at times moving. But the programme's makers were not content with allowing these neglected voices to be heard. Instead they were accompanied by a tendentious and all-too-often inaccurate commentary. It appeared to be trying to demonstrate that the only effective resistance in occupied Greece was communist-inspired and that, in effect, the prime architects of the country's travails during a decade of invasion, occupation and civil war were not so much the Germans (together with their Italian and Bulgarian allies) as the British and, latterly, the Americans. The tripartite occupation of Greece had been extremely harsh. Innocent civilians had been subject to savage reprisals, villages were razed to the ground, and the German occupiers had presided over one of the worst famines in the modern history of Europe. Yet the occupiers were portrayed as more or less innocent bystanders in a titanic clash between, on the one hand, British and American 'imperialists', together with their reactionary Greek puppets, and, on the other, the forces of progress in Greece, represented by EAM, the communist-controlled National Liberation Front, and its military arm, ELAS, the Greek People's Liberation Army. Against this background, the Russians are portrayed as cynically turning a blind eye to the fate of the Greek left.

Tendentious as *Greece – The Hidden War* was, it was not as objectionable as a documentary shown on the state-controlled ERT channel in Greece in October 1982, not long after Andreas Papandreou's Panhellenic Socialist Movement (PASOK) came to power. I had the misfortune to take part in this farrago, entitled *Mnimi '40* (Memory 1940), broadcast to mark the anniversary of Greece's heroic defiance of Mussolini's short-lived invasion of Greece in October 1940. My involvement in this demented programme had made me all the more cautious about getting involved with *Greece –The Hidden War*. The underlying theme of *Mnimi '40* was that, in 1940-1, Greece's principal enemy was not Italy or Germany, but Britain, and her only friend the Soviet Union. Britain was portrayed as cynically using Greece as a bait to lure Nazi Germany and the USSR into a struggle to the death, which would leave open the way for Britain's plans for world domination, masterminded by, of all people, Neville Chamberlain. It was even strongly hinted that the dictator General Metaxas, who had courageously stood up to Italian bullying and who died in January 1941, a matter of weeks before the German invasion, had been killed by a doctored bottle of oxygen supplied by the British. When the British Embassy in Athens protested about this ridiculous programme, the PASOK government replied that it had not represented an official view, although the novelist, Vasilis Vasilikos, a political appointee and deputy director of the state-controlled ERT, called it his pride.

The PASOK government would have found *Greece – The Hidden War* very much to its taste. For the programmes in effect served to legitimise one of its cherished claims, namely that PASOK in the 1980s was the heir and natural successor to EAM in the 1940s, albeit an EAM purged of its Stalinist leadership, and that it stood for the ideals of social justice and freedom from foreign domination of which EAM had put itself forward as the champion. It is noteworthy that the two interviewees most likely to be known to non-Greek audiences, Manolis Glezos, who, with a companion, had torn down the Nazi flag from the Acropolis soon after the beginning of the occupation, and Markos Vafiadis, the leader of the communist Democratic Army in the post-occupation civil war before being purged by the Stalinist party leadership, had both climbed aboard the PASOK bandwagon. Those who had remained faithful to the KKE, the Communist Party of Greece, which had founded and from the outset controlled EAM, were largely ignored. The KKE leadership, indeed, was bitterly critical of the programmes, and I found myself in the unusual position of standing shoulder-to-shoulder with unreconstructed Stalinists in attacking the programmes for their distortion of the historical record.

PASOK certainly deserves plaudits for the long overdue official recognition of the wartime resistance. It also deserves credit for giving permission for the return of the remaining political refugees who had fled Greece following the defeat of the Democratic Army should they have wanted to do so. But, and this was a point that was ignored by the programme makers, the process of repatriation from the Eastern Bloc had already been under way, albeit on a small scale, as early as the 1950s. By the late 1970s, before PASOK came to power, some 80 per cent of those who had applied to return had been given permission to do so. Even more importantly, the programmes made no mention of the critical fact that the Slav-Macedonians, who comprised as much as a half of the fighting strength of the Democratic Army in the later stages of the civil war, were excluded from PASOK's offer of repatriation. One of those caught up in the controversy over the programmes was the left-inclined journalist Neil Ascherson. But when I pointed out to him the existence of this ban, he could not see its relevance, although, in a British context, it would be as though the Scots or the Welsh had been excluded *en masse* from permission to return. The programmes were fulsome in their praise for PASOK's commitment to national reconciliation, but made no mention of the disgraceful attempt by elements in the rank-and-file of PASOK to tar with the brush of collaboration Konstantinos Mitsotakis, the leader of the conservative opposition party. Mitsotakis was one of the few prominent postwar politicians in Greece to have a record of active involvement in the anti-Nazi resistance.

Greece - The Hidden War abounded with simple factual errors. The second battle of El Alamein, for instance, was placed at the beginning of 1943, while it was claimed that Britain's right-wing client governments had by the summer of 1945 incarcerated 80,000 'former ELAS partisans'. Certainly, large numbers of leftists, real or imagined, were rounded up and harshly treated, but even General Stephanos Saraphis, the military commander of ELAS, never claimed a *total* strength of more than 50,000. Highly debatable statements were presented as undisputed fact. A case in point is the bald assertion that the British, bent on using Napoleon Zervas, the leader of the non-communist resistance group EDES, as a counterweight to EAM/ELAS, blackmailed him into taking to the mountains by threatening to denounce him to the Gestapo. But whatever may have been the case in 1943, and still more in 1944, it is absurd to envisage such a role for Zervas in the autumn of 1942, when the various British agencies had only the haziest understanding of political realities in Greece under occupation.

Leaving aside the inherent improbability of the British placing such heavy reliance on someone who had to be press-ganged into resisting, what is the evidence for this purported British blackmail of Zervas? The programme makers relied on a passage in a Special Operations Executive report on its activities in Greece which is based on a claim made by Captain Koutsoyannopoulos, who operated an SOE transmitter in Athens. Koutsoyannopoulos, had a low opinion of Zervas and his own politics were very much on the left. It seems a flimsy base on which to make such an allegation. Gabriel attached particular credence to this report in the belief that it had been compiled by Monty Woodhouse, Brigadier Myers' successor as commander of the British military mission. But the style in which the report was written indicates that it could not have been compiled by Woodhouse, who was a master of the English language.

Predictably, the programme made no mention of the Greek communist party's ideological somersaults during the winter and spring of 1940-1, when World War II metamorphosed from being a clash between 'rival imperialisms' (British and German) into the great patriotic war for the defence of the Soviet motherland. The violence which EAM/ELAS did not hesitate to use in order to consolidate its power was very much played down. A number of British liaison officers with the resistance, almost all in their 20, had 'pinkish' views. But many of them were shocked by EAM/ELAS' willingness to resort to terror against those deemed to stand in its way. It was this, and events such as the murder in April 1944 by an ELAS unit of Colonel Dimitrios Psarros, leader of EKKA, and the forcible dissolution of his small non-communist resistance group, that provoked Churchill, in a state of near nervous collapse at this stage of the war, as his personal doctor, Lord Moran, records, to fulminate about ELAS as 'the most treacherous, filthy beasts I have read of in official papers'.

In the making of TV documentaries the availability of visual material tends to determine the content of the programmes. Indeed, I was told by someone with knowledge of the programmes that the commentary was written *after* the film material was put together, which, if this was the case, must have greatly cramped the scriptwriter's style. It is true that *The Hidden War* mercifully eschewed the reconstructions that are now the norm in historical documentaries, but which frequently carry no warning to the unwary. But the use of some of the visual material was questionable. A grainy clip of ox-drawn wagons purportedly lumbering towards the Albanian frontier during the civil war seemed either to be a scene from the exodus of Greek refugees from Asia Minor or, more likely, eastern Thrace in the wake of the Greek defeat at the hands of the Turkish nationalists in 1922. A picture of a British air drop of supplies was shown in a context which led the viewer to assume that they were being parachuted to Zervas' EDES. In fact, the photograph shows a daylight drop to ELAS on Mount Vermion in October 1944, long after the British had developed grave suspicions as to the long-term political objectives of EAM/ELAS. If the British were indeed bent on a systematic policy of provoking conflict with the left-wing resistance, then it seems odd that they should have continued to send in supplies, including weapons, at such a late date to forces that were effectively under communist control.

The most serious objections to the Channel Four programmes as television were voiced by a number of the British participants who complained that they had not been made aware of the editorial stance of the programmes, and that their contributions had been selectively edited to fit in with this editorial line. Channel Four, following its own investigation, partially upheld this complaint. One of the most disagreeable features of the controversy that followed the transmission of the programmes was the degree of animus that was manifested against British participants in the Greek resistance, and particularly against Woodhouse, who commanded the British military mission in late 1943 and 1944. Woodhouse was dismissed not only as a 'self-styled historian' but accused of being afraid of attending conferences on resistance history for fear of being confronted with uncomfortable evidence of Britain's wartime machinations. This was demonstrably untrue. It was the case that Woodhouse, the only British person with experience of wartime Greece to be invited, did not attend one particular conference on the resistance held in Athens in 1984. But what had he been asked to talk about? It was 'Contacts between the resistance organisations and the Germans', the best known and documented of which involved Zervas. Unless the organisers of the conference believed (although this can scarcely have been the case) both that Zervas' contacts with the Germans had been authorised by the British and that Woodhouse had been privy to them, it made no sense to ask a former British officer to talk on such a subject.

A German officer who had served in occupied Greece and had been directly privy to the contacts, or an historian who had worked extensively on the German archives might have been able to deliver a useful paper on such a topic. But Woodhouse had not worked on the German archives. One is left with the uncomfortable impression that this topic had been chosen to cause embarrassment to Woodhouse and his former comrades-in-arms in EDES (most of whom, likewise, had no knowledge of these contacts at the time they were made) by putting him in the awkward position of publicly categorising Zervas as a collaborator. The kind of reception that Woodhouse might have received had he attended the 1984 conference in Athens is indicated by the fact that, when part of the private letter that he had sent to the organiser of the conference was read out, there was jeering from a section of the audience. This would seem to have retrospectively justified his caution. Another Greek protagonist in the controversy over *The Hidden War* could not resist a swipe 'at the bile flowing from the pen of Richard Clogg'. It was dispiriting to see that, such were the passions still aroused by the events of the 1940s, 40 years later they could not be discussed without resort to personal abuse of this kind, coming mainly from individuals who had taken no part in the events themselves. But then we are fortunate in Britain not to have lived through a civil war within living memory.

Another of those involved with the making of *The Hidden War*, Marion Sarafis, the English widow of General Stephanos Sarafis, the military commander of ELAS, likewise displayed a disturbing animus against Woodhouse, accusing him of manifesting a colonial mentality; of refusing to come to terms with British responsibility for civil strife; and of participating in a despairing struggle to save 'the official Anglo-American interpretation'. Woodhouse had certainly not shied away from defending his view of the complexities of the occupation either in Britain or, indeed, in Greece. He was always more than willing to talk about his wartime experiences at seminars which I organised at King's College, and these usually attracted large numbers of Greek students keen to set eyes on someone who had played such a key role in shaping as well as recording their history.

More to the point, in March 1978 Woodhouse and I took part in a public discussion in Athens of the wartime period, organised by the BBC Greek Service, with which I was closely associated at the time. So far as I know, this was the first such gathering to have taken place in Greece that had included a politically representative cross-section of participants in the resistance. Moreover, it should be noted that it took place during the conservative premiership of Constantine Karamanlis. Among those taking part were Manolis Glezos, a prominent figure in the communist-controlled EAM; Komninos Pyromaglou, Zervas' deputy as leader of the largest non-communist resistance organisation, EDES; and Lefteris Apostolou, the first secretary general of EAM. Apostolou's successor as secretary general, Thanasis Khatzis, was in the audience. At that time the BBC Greek Service was probably the only organisation that could have organised such a gathering involving participants from across the political spectrum. It was a rather dramatic as well as an historic occasion for it began with the evacuation of the building as the result of a bomb scare. It was noteworthy, however, that representatives of 'official' Britain, in the shape of the British embassy and the British Council, were conspicuous by their absence. They were otherwise occupied, attending a madrigal recital by The Clerkes of Oxenford in the Catholic cathedral of St Dionysius the Areopagite, given under the auspices of the British Council.

Marion Sarafis, in an article in *Index on Censorship*, made the odd claim that in Britain 'self-censorship takes place by "osmosis"' and that the row over *The Hidden War* had developed because the establishment-manipulated system of covert censorship had broken down, thus allowing the 'servants', to pursue her analogy with the *Lady Chatterley's Lover* trial, to learn for the first time what had been done in their name in Greece. In an article in the Greek newspaper *Vima* she had warned, in language worthy of Chairman Mao, that 'the colonialist dragon, now trapped, will lash out its tail in all directions'. I tried to counter some of this nonsense in a curiously entitled (not by me) article 'The "Black Hole" revisited', likewise published in *Index on Censorship*.

Following the barrage of complaints about the *Hidden War* programmes, the Independent Broadcasting Authority (IBA) insisted that Channel Four broadcast a corrective programme in the shape of a panel discussion. An attempt was made to persuade me to take part, but this I was reluctant to do as it was clear that I was being set up to fill the 'right-wing historian' slot. The discussion, like the programmes, generated more heat than light. At the same time the IBA placed a ban on the export of the programmes. This I thought was a pity as it reinforced the view that critics were bent on silencing rather than rebutting the programmes. This ban meant that the film could not be shown in Greece. Some 20 years later, however, ERT, the state-run national broadcasting authority, showed *Greece – The Hidden War*, after claiming to have located the last surviving copy. This was a rather ridiculous claim as many people, myself included, had recorded the series at the time. The programme was accompanied by a commentary, parts of which were again tendentious. The canard about Zervas having to be blackmailed by the British was again repeated. Those making the version for showing on Greek television approached me to take part. Again I declined. As I had taken no part in the original Channel Four broadcasts there seemed to be little point in participating in the Greek version.

A basic lesson of *Greece – The Hidden War* is that historians and TV producers approach history in different ways, and that historians are ill-advised to lend their names to such undertakings unless they are given a degree of editorial control. This is most unlikely to be granted, so historians who value their reputations should steer clear of acting as historical consultants unless they have absolute confidence in the programme makers. When the BBC in 1984 broadcast a series of programmes about the Special Operations Executive, I did agree to act as consultant to the programme on SOE in Greece. This was produced by Chris Riley, who was prepared to take my advice seriously, and, in only one case was this rejected. Marion Sarafis, who, as we have seen, had been an outspoken champion of *Greece – The Hidden War*, wrote approvingly of this BBC programme. She objected to the treatment of only one particular episode, which was precisely the same episode about which I myself had made known my objections to Riley. In a letter to the programme makers she also recorded that she had been surprised, and gratified, by the criticism of Churchill's policy in Greece. 'I have always sensed,' she continued, 'a "veto" (practically amounting to censorship) on any criticism of Churchill.' But there has, of course, been a great deal of criticism of Churchill over the years.

To the outside observer it must have appeared that the controversy over *Greece – The Hidden War* was unnecessarily heated, and few, even among many of the protagonists in the controversy, would have fully appreciated all the issues involved. Towards the end, I think that pretty well everybody involved was thoroughly fed up with the whole business. But for Jeremy Isaacs, the chief executive of Channel Four, the row was to have serious consequences not only for himself but for British public life more generally. He had behaved entirely creditably throughout the whole crisis, at a time of great personal sadness when his wife was dying of cancer.

No sooner had my article criticising *The Hidden War* appeared in the February 1987 issue of *Encounter* than I received a letter from Nora Beloff, the former political correspondent of the *Observer*, and someone with whom I had had no previous contact, apart from a glimpse in the course of her famous libel action against *Private Eye*, which dubbed her Nora Ballsoff. One of the advantages of teaching at King's College was its proximity to the High Court which meant that it was possible to attend high-profile libel actions. Among these was the case of the Greek newspaper *Ethnos* versus *The Economist* in which *Ethnos* advanced, *inter alia*, the view that the CIA had developed a strain of killer mosquitoes with which to target Soviet troops in Afghanistan. It was not explained how the mosquitos were to distinguish between Soviet soldiers and the mujahideen. The proceedings involved a lot of Greek, so I took a history class from King's to listen to the proceedings and check on the accuracy of the translations.

Beloff had, with considerable reason, become a critic of the hyperbolic cult of Tito, particularly on the right, that had developed in postwar Britain. In *Tito's Flawed Legacy. Yugoslavia and the West: 1939–84* (1985), for instance, she had pointed to the fact that a Conservative MP, Sir Fitzroy Maclean, the wartime head of the military mission to Tito's partisans, had received from Tito a seventeenth-century Renaissance villa on the island of Korčula. Maclean was apparently the only foreigner allowed to acquire real estate in communist Yugoslavia. In 1998, I was able to engineer a tour of this desirable residence, about which uncomfortable questions have been asked as to the circumstances in which it had been acquired from its previous owners. The apogee of the Tito cult occurred when, shortly before coming to power in 1979, Margaret Thatcher, then the Conservative party leader, returned from a trip to Yugoslavia, where she had been shepherded around by Maclean, and declared that, in many ways, Tito's Yugoslavia was less of a socialist country than Britain.

Beloff in her note hastened to congratulate me on what she termed an excellent article in *Encounter*, and enclosed a copy of a long, ranting and ill-typed letter that she had sent to Marmaduke Hussey, the chairman of the BBC's board of governors. The board at the time was considering candidates for the director-generalship of the BBC, the most sought-after, and undoubtedly the most influential, position in British broadcasting. Beloff had shamelessly used my *Encounter* article as a stick with which to beat Isaacs, who was widely considered to be one of the frontrunners, if not *the* frontrunner, for the post. She urged Hussey and his colleagues to read my article and learn how Channel Four had transmitted three hours of what she described as 'almost undiluted' communist propaganda. This, together with the treatment of the British ex-officers who were interviewed, had, in her view, cast 'the gravest doubts' on 'Mr. Isaac's [sic] political judgement and sophistication'.

While Beloff did not doubt Isaacs' 'nose for what is artistically and intellectually fashionable', he seemed to lack 'the wisdom and sense of fairness indispensable' for the director-generalship. When *Tito's Flawed Legacy* had appeared, she had written to him suggesting that her challenge to the received wisdom over Yugoslavia would make a good TV documentary. But Isaacs had replied that Channel Four had already broadcast too much on Eastern Europe. After the transmission of *The Hidden War* programmes, she had again written to suggest that Channel Four might give attention to the vanquished of the Yugoslav civil war who, unlike their Greek counterparts, had never been allowed to return to their homeland. Isaacs had apparently replied that this was not the time to be talking about Yugoslavia. She did concede that it was Channel Four that had transmitted a Yorkshire TV programme in which Robert Kee had interviewed her and a British witness of 'chetnik [the followers of the anti-communist resistance leader Draža Mihailović] loyalty' on the occasion of the publication of her book. Nonetheless, shortly afterwards, Channel Four had transmitted a Yugoslav communist-sponsored film, with American actors taking the role of Tito and his fellow partisans. This, she wrote, had depicted the chetniks as 'unmitigated villains'. Her friend, Kingsley Amis, the novelist, had thought it shocking that such 'manifest communist propaganda' should have been given air time. Beloff denied having a grudge against Isaacs, but nonetheless felt it right that Hussey should know of this aspect of Isaacs' record before a final judgement was made.

On receiving her rant, I hastened myself to write to Hussey to say that I was appalled by Beloff's letter, and wished entirely to dissociate myself from her efforts to enlist my article in her attempt to blackball Isaacs from consideration for the director-generalship. I wrote that, although I thought the Channel Four series was seriously flawed, I could not see how Isaacs could be held personally responsible for the débâcle. Given the inordinate pressure that appears to exist on broadcasting executives to stand by their programme makers, Isaacs appeared to have reacted in a responsible fashion to the criticisms that had been made. His behaviour had certainly been a great deal more creditable than that of the IBA. I concluded by saying that, while it was none of my business, I considered Isaacs a very strong candidate for the director-generalship. He appeared to me to have the stature and tough-mindedness needed to stand up to government attempts to bully the BBC, which would be essential qualities in whoever filled the post.

This elicited by way of reply a somewhat curt note from the Secretary of the BBC, Patricia Hodgson, saying that Hussey had asked her to thank me for my letter. At the same time, I copied my letter to Hussey to Beloff. She replied that she had sent an additional 'PS' to Hussey containing a letter from Monty Woodhouse, prompted by my *Encounter* article and due to be published in the next issue of the magazine, in which he described the programmes as the longest party political transmission in broadcasting history. Woodhouse, like me, placed more blame on the IBA than on Isaacs, but Beloff disagreed with this. She believed that the IBA had reacted predictably, covering for the programme makers, whereas 'the man responsible for allocating time for the programme and for refusing time for Yugoslavia was Isaacs and I think this disqualifies him from heading the BBC'. She irritated me by adding that 'you may argue that this was only a tiny crumb in relation to his entire responsibility and it is precisely for this reason that I commended your article: as the case was so minor that it may well have escaped the notice of the BBC governors'. She concluded by saying that, on Yugoslavia, I obviously thought her prejudiced.

I replied that there was nothing in my letter to Hussey that could give rise to such a perception. I had not only read, but had enjoyed reading, *Tito's Flawed Legacy*, although I believed that she had somewhat overstated her case. I went on to point out that she had misunderstood a fundamental point in my *Encounter* article. This was that the programmes were not communist propaganda, for the Greek communist party had been fiercely critical of the series. The problem was that the programmes were in effect propaganda for the current PASOK socialist (populist) government in Greece. I concluded that, in an ideal world, someone at Channel Four should have been able to see this, although it was unreasonable to expect Isaacs personally to vet every individual programme.

Some months later, after Isaacs had been turned down for the director-generalship, I read in the *Evening Standard* that he was contemplating writing his memoirs. I therefore sent him copies of the Beloff/Hussey/Clogg correspondence and received in reply a letter thanking me for letting him see 'so fascinating a correspondence'. When his account of his time at Channel Four was published, it was clear that the row over *Greece – The Hidden War* had indeed played a by no means negligible part in his not being appointed director-general. On being interviewed for the post in early 1987 Isaacs found the BBC governors to be much exercised by the need to obviate programme cock-ups. In *Storm Over 4: A Personal Account* (1989), he records that, when he suggested a means by which this might be achieved, Daphne Park (aka Baroness Park of Monmouth), one of the BBC governors, principal of Somerville College, Oxford, and formerly a big wheel in the Secret Intelligence Service (MI6), had pointedly asked him, 'How can we believe that you could prevent such things? [...] You broadcast those lies on Greece.' The series had been disgracefully one-sided, she insisted. Isaacs felt that he did not know enough to challenge Park's barbed comments.

In the event, the appointment of a BBC accountant, Michael Checkland, as director-general signified the ascendancy of the suits over creative talent of the kind so effectively epitomised by Isaacs. This ushered in an era of uninspiring leadership reflected in the subsequent director-generalship of John Birt, whose principal legacy was a peculiarly managerialist manner of speaking, dubbed 'Birtspeak' by *Private Eye*, and who, characteristically, endeared himself to Tony Blair, to whom he became an adviser on 'blue skies thinking'.

When, in 1981, Greece entered what was then the EEC, I organised a small conference to mark this significant step in the country's history by producing an anatomy of Greece in the 1980s. I asked Donald Nicol, as the head of our small department of Byzantine and Modern Greek Studies, to say a few words to open the conference, and he ruffled some feathers, as I recall, by words to the effect that turning from Byzantium to modern Greece was akin to going from the sublime to the ridiculous. No doubt he meant his remark jocularly, but this kind of ironic remark did not go down well. Greece's accession to the Common Market prompted a fundraising endeavour on my part to reinforce the department's coverage of contemporary Greek affairs. A (virtual) Centre of Contemporary Greek Studies was established and a small committee was established to raise funds. Besides myself and Donald Nicol, this consisted of Monty Woodhouse, Peter Calvocoressi and Philip Nind, who had been a British liaison officer in wartime Greece. George Jellicoe, at that time chairman of the Council of King's, was also loosely involved with the project. Although we came nowhere near to raising the ambitious sum that we sought, enough money was raised to give a significant boost to library expenditure and to cover the cost of a number of academic conferences and lectures devoted to modern Greek matters, both in London, and after I subsequently moved to St Antony's in Oxford. Besides *Greece in the 1980s* (1983), which included the papers given at the 1981 conference, an anatomy of Pasok's first decade in power was published as *Greece, 1981-1989: The Populist Decade* (1993). Other such collective publications were *The Greek Diaspora in the Twentieth Century* (1999) (translated into Greek in 2004); *Minorities in Greece: Aspects of a Plural Society* (2002) and *Bearing Gifts to Greeks: Humanitarian Aid to Greece in the 1940s* (2008).

My connection with SSEES and my years as secretary/treasurer of the British National Committee of the Association Internationale d'Études du Sud-est Européen, which was chaired by Sir Steven Runciman, gave me a particular interest in Romanian history. I was one of those who felt it important to maintain contact with Romanian historians, many of whom clearly found life under the Ceauşescu regime intolerable and welcomed the occasional contact with Western colleagues. I took part in a number of Anglo-Romanian historical colloquia, some held in the UK, some in Romania. Those in the British delegation were well aware that some of the Romanian participants would be informants for the loathsome Securitate and that our conversations would be bugged. It was no surprise therefore to read, after the downfall of the regime, of the steps taken to spy on us at one such gathering in the Transylvanian city of Cluj in September 1987, a time when the situation in Romania was at its grimmest. The Securitate reported 'operational intelligence measures' such as bugs in hotel rooms and at dining tables and reliance on sources code-named Florina, Costea and Apulum. Employing historical arguments, both secular and religious, these sources, so the Securitate files maintained, had emphasised the continuity of the Romanian people, positively influencing the delegation. I myself was reported as saying that our visit to the thirteenth-century church at Densuş was worth 100 articles making the case for Romanian continuity. It is unlikely that I made such a remark as it would have sat ill with my scepticism about the obsession with historical continuity in Romanian (and, for that matter, Greek) official historiography.

My relatively frequent visits to the country had given me an insight into the grim realities of life in communist Romania, which had become particularly gruesome during the twilight years of the Ceauşescu era, so I was particularly gripped by the astonishing collapse of this singularly nasty dictatorship at Christmas 1989. Although it is difficult to shed too many tears at the fate of the Ceauşescus, the end I would have chosen for them would have been not summary execution but rather to deprive them of their life of obscene luxury and oblige them to spend the rest of their lives in the abject misery in which they compelled almost all Romanians (the communist *nomenklatura* naturally excepted) to exist in the late 1980s, i.e. with very little food, obtainable only after hours of queuing, virtually no heating, power cuts and a single 40 watt bulb per household for lighting, with the sole 'entertainment' being two hours of television a day of an unbelievably obsequious banality centred on the heroic doings of the 'Giant of the Carpathians' and his megalomaniac spouse.

The Queen's stripping of Ceauşescu's honorary knighthood that had scandalously been bestowed on him ten years previously injected a note of surrealism into the Romanian drama that was worthy of a play by Eugène Ionesco. This had occurred more or less as he was being lifted by helicopter from the roof of the central committee building in Bucharest in a doomed attempt to flee the wrath of his enslaved subjects. The ludicrous decision to honour this latter-day Caligula with the Knight Grand Cross of the Order of the Bath had apparently been taken by David Owen when Foreign Secretary, in part at least at the urging of the right-wing Tory MP Julian Amery. Both, seemingly oblivious of his appalling human rights record, had deluded themselves that Ceauşescu could, like some latter-day Tito, be weaned away from the Warsaw Pact, while the Callaghan government was hoping to conclude a lucrative deal on behalf of British Aerospace and Rolls-Royce. The Queen, in return, was decorated with the Order of Socialist Romania (First Class). This scarcely seemed a fair exchange.

There seems to have been cross-party support for his being knighted. David Steel, the Liberal MP, following a shooting trip as the guest of the tyrant, presented him as a thank you one of his own labrador's puppies, a solicitous gesture which was the source of some subsequent embarrassment after Ceauşescu had been toppled. Like the Ceauşescus themselves, the dog apparently had its own food taster. The unfortunate Romanian ambassador in London had been expected to buy dog food at Sainsbury's (one version I heard was that the dog food had to came from Harrods) for the animal out of his miserable US$300 a month salary. One of these ambassadors, incidentally, was so hard up that his wife had been caught shoplifting a pair of scissors.

Ceaușescu's KGCB was awarded in the course of his 1978 state visit when the couple enjoyed the singular honour of actually staying at Buckingham Palace, an unprecedented gesture for an Eastern Bloc head of state. The Queen did, however, draw the line at the Romanian couple being accompanied by their food taster, while their suite narrowly escaped having its wallpaper stripped in the search for bugs by the over-zealous thugs of the Securitate. In November 1973, Ceaușescu was poised to become the first European head of state to visit the Colonels' Greece, but the visit was called off in the wake of the brutal repression in that month of the student occupation of the Polytechnic. I well remember Eleni Vlachou's scorn when it was revealed that the advance guard of Securitate heavies wanted empty column bases on the Acropolis, the obligatory port of call for any official visitor to Greece, to be filled in lest they be used to secrete bombs.

Ceaușescu, of course, was not the only dubious recipient of an honorary knighthood. Some of the others make a questionable crew. They include Caspar Weinberger, the former US secretary of defense, pardoned by President George Bush just as he was about to be tried for his alleged complicity in the Iran Contra scandal, and Eduard Shevardnadze, who had a nasty reputation as party boss in Georgia before becoming Soviet foreign minister. As president of an independent Georgia, he had personally witnessed the summary execution of alleged looters, and was finally driven from office amid a welter of accusations of corruption. When Shevardnadze was awarded his gong at Buckingham Palace, the effect was rather spoiled by the fact that the flunkey who was charged with handing the Queen the regalia to present to the Georgian tyrant had gone off to the pub for lunch. He was apparently not, as I should prefer to think, inspired by revulsion at honouring such an unworthy figure. The weight which Ceaușescu himself attached to his royal honour was demonstrated by the placing of his KGCB regalia in close proximity to the certificate recording his honorary citizenship of Disneyland in the museum in Bucharest devoted exclusively to hymning the praises of the dynamic duo.

The hacks duly picked up on the story of Ceaușescu's honorary knighthood, but the obsequious toadying to Elena on account of her supposed scientific genius by British academics who should have known better was largely ignored. I therefore enjoyed exposing in an article in the *New Scientist* the antics of members of the UK academic chemical establishment in pandering to the absurdly inflated ego of the self-appointed tsarina of Romanian science, Academician Doctor Engineer Elena Ceaușescu. Elena herself, before the London visit in 1978, had set her sights on an honorary fellowship of the Royal Society. But despite the despatch of an emissary from the Romanian Academy of Sciences to plead her cause, the Royal Society would not play ball, nor would Oxford or London come up with an honorary degree despite the pleas of the Foreign Office, not to mention those of an increasingly frantic Romanian ambassador whose job was on the line. But the Royal Institute of Chemistry and the Polytechnic of Central London came to the rescue with offers of a fellowship and an honorary professorship respectively.

The most cursory inquiry of a Romanian scientist or of anyone with more than a passing knowledge of the country would have revealed that a very serious question mark hung over Elena's supposed academic credentials. A graduate of the Universitatea Muncitorească (Workers' University), an institution aimed at workers with few or no educational qualifications, her doctoral thesis for the Bucharest Polytechnic, which was by all accounts excellent, had been written for her by her professors. There was none of the thanks to supervisor(s) normally to be found in the prefaces to theses. The thesis was subsequently published in English, appropriately enough by another con artist, Robert Maxwell. It had also been, or was being, published in Italy, Greece, Switzerland, China and the Soviet Union. In her preface to the book which emerged from the thesis, *The Stereospecific Polymerization of Isoprene* (1983), the Nobel prize-winning and left-leaning chemist Dorothy Hodgkin conceded that, although she did not know much about the subject addressed by Comrade Elena, she was nonetheless sure that it was an excellent piece of work. Hodgkin gushed at the reference made to 635 scientific papers from all over the world that had been cited and marvelled at the way in which Elena, wife of the 'dynamic' Nicolae, had managed to combine the roles of First Vice-Prime Minister of the Romanian Government, President of the National Council for Science and Technology, Chairwoman of the Scientific Council of the Central Institute of Chemistry and 'not the least important' President of the Romanian National Committee 'Scientists and Peace'. In this role she had demonstrated 'outstanding' scientific research and the nurturing of the 'young, very intelligent scientists growing up under her guidance'.

Neither the Royal Institute of Chemistry nor the Polytechnic of Central London displayed the slightest doubt as to Elena's standing in the world of science. They laid on the full red carpet treatment for a world-class chemist, and the Foreign Office, of course, had no interest in disabusing the naive academics involved that Elena's academic pretensions were fraudulent. At the Royal Institute of Chemistry, with a picture of Nicolae Ceaușescu hanging on the wall and in the presence of such chemical luminaries as Dorothy

Hodgkin and Sir Frank Hartley (at the time vice-chancellor of the University of London and subsequently, in advanced retirement and seemingly somewhat deaf, to preside over my interview ten years later for the Koraes professorship), the president of the Institute, Professor Sir Richard Norman, lauded Elena's achievements as a 'distinguished scientist' and contributor to macro-molecular experimental chemistry. He sang the praises in particular of her contributions on 'the stereospecific polymerisation of isoprene, on the stabilisation of synthetic rubbers, and on copolymerisation'. In addition to the certificate testifying to her honorary fellowship, she was presented with a scroll lauding her achievement as a 'distinguished chemist'.

From the Royal Institute of Chemistry, Elena proceeded to the Polytechnic of Central London, now the University of Westminster, where she was made a professor *honoris causa*, the first such distinction bestowed by the polytechnic on a foreign scientist. Here, after the playing of the Romanian National Anthem, even more egregious flattery was heaped on her. The Senior Pro-Rector, Professor Terence Burlin, hailed her as one of the most distinguished graduates of the Bucharest Polytechnic and as a researcher of great distinction in the difficult field of polymer chemistry. He went on to praise her for steering her children into scientific careers. Her son Nicu, until the downfall of his parents the heir apparent of the dynasty, had likewise been trumpeted in the tightly regimented Romanian press as a scientist of international reputation and the author of treatises on nuclear physics. The second child, Elena Zoe, was head of the mathematical section of the National Institute for Scientific Creativity. The third child, Valentin, had graduated from Imperial College in London with an undistinguished degree in physics, and, despite the best efforts of the Foreign Office, Imperial had declined to accept him for a postgraduate degree. This did not prevent him from becoming scientific secretary of the Bucharest Institute for Physics and Nuclear Energy. Burlin concluded his eulogy by listing some of the honours, more than 100 in all, that had been heaped on Elena by academic institutions world-wide. Not for nothing did Romanians joke that this was a case not of socialism in one country but socialism in one family.

On returning to Romania, the Ceaușescus were showered with the oriental obsequy which attended their every activity and which, already by 1978, should have been bizarre and hyperbolic enough to give their Western apologists serious pause for thought. Institutions ranging from the Romanian Academy of Sciences to the Satu Mare Women's Committee deluged Elena with telegrams hailing the 'homage' paid by prestigious scientific institutions in Britain to her 'brilliant scientific merits', her 'prodigious activity' and her distinction as a 'world famous scientist', which had now received international recognition.

My *New Scientist* article, published in January 1990, exposing the absurd affair provoked a rather lame reply from the registrar of the Royal Society of Chemistry, into which the Royal Institute had metamorphosed, to the effect that her fellowship application had been supported by a long list of papers published over the period 1961 to 1972, of whose authorship the Society had no reason to be suspicious, and that the fellowship had been presented at a ceremony 'no grander than would have been arranged for any other spouse of a head of state'. This immediately begs the question as to how many other spouses of heads of state had ever been offered a fellowship by the Society. He went on to say that the Society's disciplinary machinery had been set in motion to remove Elena's name from the register of members two days before the removal of Nicolae's honorary knighthood but had been overtaken by events. Readers of *New Scientist* were clearly unused to mischievous articles of this kind, and the features editor asked me if I had any similar pieces up my sleeve. Alas, I am irredeemably innumerate and with no scientific background whatsoever (at school, as I vaguely remember, I had only one year of science in which I managed to come top of the form in physics and bottom in chemistry). So I could only respond that my piece on Elena was my one and only contribution to scientific knowledge. This was a pity because *New Scientist*, as I remember, paid rather well, by academic standards at least.

On Christmas Day 1989, Nicolae and Elena Ceaușescu were summarily tried in a drum-head court martial which was immediately followed by their execution by firing squad, while fighting by die-hard loyalists continued in Bucharest. One of the buildings that caught fire in the city during this fighting was the Central University Library. Dramatic images of the blazing building, which held many rare items, were shown on British television. Dick Crampton, Stevan Pavlowitch and Dennis Deletant, three fellow Balkanist colleagues, and I quickly hatched a plan to launch an appeal for academic books for the stricken library. Letters in the *Times Higher Education Supplement* and the *Guardian* met with an astonishing response. Private individuals, academic institutions, learned societies and publishers contributed enormous quantities of books, very few of which proved unsuitable for despatch to Romania. Dr Alex Comfort, the author, *inter alia*, of a world bestseller, *The Joy of Sex*, donated what must have been a substantial portion of his library. There were similar appeals in Scotland and elsewhere and within the space of three months what must have been getting on for half a million books were amassed. These were then despatched to Bucharest in 8 juggernauts.

Prince Charles issued a warm endorsement of the project and Roy Jenkins agreed to preside over the formal handing over of the books in the course of a lightning visit to Bucharest in early May 1990. Unfortunately, he was under the impression that the books were a donation from the University of Oxford of which he was vice-chancellor, and Romanian newspapers published accounts of the donation under headings such as 'Thank you, Oxford.' None of the four of us at that time had any connection with Oxford. Mary Jo, as a librarian, gave us a salutary warning that a donation on this scale had serious implications for Romanian librarians who would face major problems in accessioning such an enormous mass of books.

During my time at SSEES and King's, and subsequently at Oxford, I supervised some 20 PhD/DPhil theses and encouraged my students, who were for the most part Greeks wanting to work on their own history, to explore topics which placed Greek history in its Ottoman context, given that, for 400 years, much of the Greek world had come under Ottoman rule. Although these PhD students were almost all from Greece, I did once receive an application from a Japanese student. She seemed well qualified and wanted to work on a Greek topic and so I accepted her. As the beginning of the autumn term grew near, I received a number of increasingly agitated telephone calls in which she requested the status not of a postgraduate student, which her academic qualifications suggested was appropriate, but of a member of the faculty. I felt that to concede this status would be unfair to my other postgraduates, whose qualifications were in no way inferior to hers. When she turned up, she continued to insist on such a status which, apart from any other consideration, I was in no position to grant. She was clearly upset by my seeming obduracy but Donald Nicol, the head of department, came up with an imaginative solution to the problem. This was to give her a key yielding access to the women's academic staff lavatories. This appeared to do the trick. Some weeks later I invited her to dinner with some of my other postgraduates. Just as we were finishing our pre-prandial drinks and were about to file in for dinner, the doorbell rang and the virtually monoglot driver of a large Japanese embassy car made it clear that he had come to collect the status-conscious student and, without a word of explanation, away she went. Apparently at this time, in the early 1980s, the embassy expected attractive young female students to help entertain visiting Japanese businessmen, rather in the manner of geisha girls. Although Nicol's imaginative ploy seemed to have resolved the vexed matter of status she did not stay long at King's and moved to Oxford. Whether Oxford granted her wish for faculty status I do not know.

I combined academic writing with reviewing, writing obituaries, principally of Greek politicians and former SOE operatives, and the odd foray into journalism. Occasionally, I would find that something I had published in English had appeared in Greece without any kind of acknowledgement. Of course I did not mind my effusions appearing in Greek, but I did rather take exception to their appearing without any recognition of their authorship. A case in point was my review of a memoir of his wartime experiences in Greece by Nigel Clive, who subsequently became a good friend. We still know relatively little about the Secret Intelligence Service (MI6)'s wartime activities in Greece and Clive's is a rare and valuable memoir by a SIS operative. The review was published at the end of May 1985 in the *Times Literary Supplement*. A week or so later virtually the entire piece, dressed up as an anonymous despatch from London, appeared in a prominent Athenian newspaper *To Vima*. One or two passages caused the anonymous translator-cum-plagiarist some difficulty, e.g. a reference to a New Zealand liaison officer with the Greek resistance, who deemed acquiring some knowledge of the Greek language as a manifestation of 'arse-crawling', but overall the translation was more or less verbatim. There was, however, one significant alteration to my original text. Where I had written that the British embassy in 1944-5 had tried to encourage the emergence of a moderate centre in the political spectrum, which was undoubtedly the case, the plagiarist inserted the word *legetai*, 'so it is said' or 'supposedly'. The next time I was in Athens I called on Charalambos Bousbourellis, the senior man in the *Vima* editorial hierarchy. He received Mary Jo and me graciously, offered us a cup of coffee, and immediately confessed that this was manifestly an instance of the age-old Greek practice of *klopiright*, a pun on the Greek word *klopi* or theft. Without more ado, he reached into a drawer, pulled out a 5,000 drachma note and we parted on the best of terms. This was enough to buy me a useful pair of shoes in a shop which adjoined the *Vima* offices.

One of my trials at King's was entirely of my own making. This was the 'Armenian visit' of Marion Sarafis to our department. In Greece (and also in Romania and Bulgaria) overstaying your welcome is deemed to be an 'Armenian visit', which seems a little hard on the Armenians. But what should by rights have been a visit of some six months turned out to be one lasting several years, so that Mrs Sarafis came to be an almost permanent fixture in the department in the late 1970s and early 1980s. In the 1930s, Marion Pascoe, as she then was, after reading classics at Oxford, had been a Student at the British School at Athens where, as we have seen, she recorded that most of those at the School had greeted the imposition of the Metaxas dictatorship in 1936 with indifference. In 1938, her researches took her to the island of Milos where she met Colonel (subsequently General) Stephanos Sarafis. In the early 1930s he had been Greek military attaché in Paris, and had ended up a political exile on account of his involvement in the abortive Venizelist coup of 1935. This had resulted in his being cashiered in humiliating circumstances and narrowly avoiding a death sentence.

Aged 24, Marion had been immediately attracted to Sarafis, who was exactly twice her age. But it was only in 1952 that they were able to marry after Sarafis had been released from harsh postwar internment as the erstwhile military commander of ELAS, the military arm of the communist-controlled resistance movement EAM, a position that he had assumed in circumstances that remain ambiguous. At this time he had also secretly joined the Communist Party. Following release from internment, Sarafis had been elected in 1956 as a deputy for EDA, a party which drew its support from the far left, as the Communist Party of Greece remained a banned organisation until 1974. Marion's marriage was tragically cut short when, in 1957, General Sarafis was killed in Athens by a car driven by a US serviceman. Marion was herself knocked unconscious and her leg broken, with the result that she always walked with a pronounced limp. She, and many others in Greece, did not believe this to be an accident and she strongly suspected CIA involvement.

Thereafter, Marion was tirelessly devoted to the memory of her husband and to defending the cause of the Greek left. She was instrumental in bringing out an English translation of Sarafis' wartime memoir, *ELAS: Greek Resistance Army* (1980). I gave it a rather favourable review in the *Observer*, but, unfortunately, the distribution of the relevant issue was severely limited by a strike, to Marion's chagrin. I had first got to know her during the Colonels' dictatorship when, together with Diana Pym, she worked indefatigably on behalf of the League for Democracy in Greece. Essentially a communist front organisation, the League had been founded soon after the war to champion the cause of the Greek left and, through its offshoot, the Greek Relief Fund, to raise funds for the support of political prisoners in Greece. It is odd to record that its first president was Compton Mackenzie who, by his own account, was the man Mansfield Cumming, the first head of MI6, had wanted to succeed him in the early 1920s.

I did not have a great deal to do with the League, which had been given a new lease of life by the Colonels' dictatorship. In fact, I was mildly irritated that, when I once turned down an invitation to speak at an anti-Colonel meeting that it had organised, my polite refusal metamorphosed into a message of solidarity. However, Marion and I were on perfectly friendly terms. After the downfall of the Colonels and the subsequent legalisation of the Communist Party of Greece, I learned that the League *for* Democracy in Greece was in effect being wound down and its name changed to the Friends *of* Democracy in Greece. I asked Marion what was going to happen to the League's archive, and told her that the department at King's would be glad to give the archive a permanent home. Together with a few of my postgraduate students, we loaded the numerous boxes of files onto a large trolley which we then trundled down Kingsway to the college. Among those who helped with the move was Dimitris Loules. He was himself the son of a prominent member of the Communist Party of Greece, and sadly died a few years later in a car accident.

Although in a somewhat disorganised state, the archive proved to be extensive and was clearly a valuable source for the modern history of Greece, which has been used by a number of scholars. Marion kindly volunteered to put the papers in order, an undertaking which I, naively, thought would take six months or so. She duly came to the department one afternoon a week and set to work in the large cupboard in which the archive was housed before being moved to the college archive. What I had not realised, however, was that she had no telephone in her Woking flat, so a good part of her time was spent in the departmental office on the secretary's telephone, taking mainly incoming calls. Not surprisingly, successive secretaries were not best pleased by this arrangement. In effect, the cupboard became her central London *liméri*, or lair, where she received those wanting to pick her, admittedly very well-stocked, brain about the wartime resistance and such-like matters.

This went on for several years, and just as she appeared at last to be coming to the end of her labours, she declared she would need further time to number each of the documents consecutively. When I asked her why, she replied that she was concerned lest the CIA or MI6 might clandestinely insert forged documents into the archive in an effort to discredit the work of the League. I would certainly not put dirty tricks beyond the CIA or MI6 (I discuss one instance of dirty tricks, seemingly practised by MI6, in Chapter 7), but found it difficult to believe that either organisation would be concerned in the 1980s to refight a battle fought, and, indeed won, in the 1940s, when the Communist Party of Greece was effectively destroyed as a political force. The only part of the Greek world in which the far left has remained a significant force is Cyprus, and this, paradoxically, has been one of the consequences of British colonial rule. But Marion herself was obsessed with fighting old battles. At this stage I began gently to exert pressure on her to wrap up her work, which she eventually did. As I remember, the numbering of the papers had not taken place.

As well as working on SOE while at King's I wrote, *inter alia*, two histories of Greece. The first was entitled *A Short History of Modern Greece* (1979; 2nd ed. 1986), published by Cambridge University Press, and the second *A Concise History of Greece* (1992; 2nd ed. 2002; 3rd ed. 2013), also published by Cambridge University Press, in their series of *Concise Histories* of many of the countries of the world. Although the chronological range of the *Concise History* was in fact shorter than that of the *Short History*, I deliberately dispensed with the epithet 'modern'. Over the years I have been fighting a lonely, and wholly unsuccessful, battle to dispense with 'modern' when talking about Greece in recent times. Greece is the only country which we routinely call 'modern', whose inhabitants we designate as 'modern' Greeks, and whose language we invariably call 'modern' Greek. My contention is that we should reclaim the word Greece to describe the modern country and oblige the Byzantinists to refer to Byzantine or medieval Greece and the classicists to speak of ancient or classical Greece. It is absurd that a book entitled *The Greeks Overseas* (1964), as is one of the books of an erstwhile Oxford colleague John Boardman, should have as its subject the Greek colonies of the ancient world rather than the worldwide Greek diaspora in modern times. It would be nonsensical to call a book on the latter subject *The Modern Greeks Overseas*.

The futility of my campaign was strikingly illustrated when the A.G. Leventis Professorship of Greek Culture was established in 2008 at Cambridge, with a £2.3 million endowment. 'Greek', for its purposes, was taken to refer to the periods before the foundation of Constantinople in AD 330. Another setback was the absurd decision of the Universities Funding Council (subsequently the Higher Education Funding Council for England) to lump 'modern' Greek studies, despite the protests of their practioners, with Byzantine studies, classics and ancient history for the purposes of the fatuous Research Assessment Exercise (RAE), on which the disbursement of research funding critically depended. 'Modern' Greek studies were similarly lumped together with classics and Byzantine studies in the Research Excellence Framework (REF), the successor to the RAE. Needless to say, Italian studies were not similarly grouped together with classics, despite the fact that the Italians, like the Greeks, are heirs to a likewise 'glorious' past in antiquity. In the 2001 RAE the panel of assessors in classics, ancient history, Byzantine and modern Greek studies consisted of 15 members. I had heard of four out of the 15 and was familiar with the work of only one. I rather doubt whether many, or even any, of the 15 were familiar with my own work.

I was tempted in this memoir to place 'modern' in relation to Greece in quotation marks to register a feeble protest against the way the classicists have annexed 'Greece' for their own purposes, but good sense prevailed. I might add that not only is the epithet 'modern' prefixed to Greece, Greeks or Greek problematic, but so is the very word Greek. The official English title of the Greek state is 'The Hellenic Republic', while the English title of the *Symvoulio Apodimou Ellinismou* (SAE), the body established in 1995 to represent the interests of the world-wide Greek diaspora, is World Council of Hellenes Abroad. Incidentally, the Greek Works website, which appears no longer to exist and which reflected a progressive Greek–American viewpoint, describes the 'magniloquently named but pathetically inept' SAE as 'utterly useless'. As we shall see, in the 1990s the London School of Economics established an

'Hellenic Observatory', to encompass the work of what it initially intended to call the Venizelos Chair of Contemporary *Hellenic* Studies, until wiser counsels, conceivably including my own, prevailed and the chair was entitled a chair of Contemporary *Greek* Studies.

The use of Greek and not Hellenic clearly rankled in some Greek quarters and, in the 1990s, a 'National Society Ellas' was created to propagandise for the substitution in English of Hellas and Hellenes for Greece and Greeks. Nothing much seems to have emerged from its activities, but its stated objectives are worthy of record. Hellas is hailed for its 'beauty and musicality', whereas Greece is pronounced in the same way as grease. It was pointed out that the Oxford English Dictionary defines a Greek as, *inter alia*, a 'cunning or wily person; a cheat, a card-sharper', while a 'merry Greek' apparently designates a roisterer, usages quite unknown to me. Some of the opprobious uses of 'grec' in French were also emphasised. The continued use of 'the unfortunate and erroneous name' Greece and Greek could only result in reinforcing 'the subconscious belief of the foreign nations that "Greeks" [...] have no relationship with their past which has shown achievements unique in the history'. Whether the society, which claimed to enjoy the support of the Nobel prize-winning poet Odysseus Elytis, still survives is not clear.

Although my two histories covered more or less the same ground, and, indeed, had the same publisher, I obviously tried to make them as different as possible. For instance, the *Concise History*, in contrast to the *Short History*, is well illustrated, with the illustrations accompanied by long captions which can be read as miniature essays in their own right. This proved to be a winning formula, for the book has not only sold well in English but has been translated into a dozen or so languages, including all the languages of the Balkans, Turkish not excepted. Among these languages are Japanese and Chinese, and it must be one of the first books on the modern history of Greece to be published in Chinese. The Chinese translation that appeared in Taiwan was given a new and rather cumbersome title and one that was certainly not of my choosing: *The State that Missed Out on Progress: The Road to Modernization in Greece*. I was rather alarmed to learn that one of the puffs on the cover of the English original had been translated as being a history 'written from a humorous perspective', when the review in English from which it had been excerpted had read that the book was a 'vigorous, well-written, somewhat opinionated and occasionally humorous view of Greek history since 1770'. Some years later a translation of the third edition is to be published in Beijing. In an interesting insight into the consequences of globalisation, the book was also reprinted in China in English in 2006 by the Shanghai Foreign Language Education Press, but with a bilingual English/Chinese cover. In the past such a book might possibly have been pirated in China, but not now.

I thoroughly enjoyed selecting the 60 or so illustrations for the *Concise History*, and soon came to the conclusion that a carefully chosen photograph, accompanied by a fairly detailed exegesis, can be worth many pages of text. No picture researcher, however competent, can substitute for personal selection, unless (s)he shares with the author a really good understanding of the subject matter. The hunt for telling illustrations was assisted by the generosity of those institutions in Greece with photographic archives and the readiness with which they granted permission to reproduce the illustrations in their custody, much more often than not without charging a reproduction fee. Some years after the *Concise History* was published, browsing in the Oxfam bookshop in Malvern, I came across Tom Stone's *Greece: an illustrated history*, published in New York in 2000 by Hippocrene Books. Every illustration relating to the modern period was taken, without acknowledgement, from the *Concise History*. Picture research is not always an easy task and it must be helpful when another author does it for you.

One of the photographs in the second and third edition of the *Concise History* shows Prince Charles and Evangelos Venizelos, the minister of culture, on the steps of the Parthenon in late 1998. Venizelos expressed the hope that the prince's visit would prove to be a symbolic first step towards the return of the Elgin Marbles in the British Museum to Athens, a demand which had become ever more insistent after Melina Mercouri had been made minister of culture by Andreas Papandreou in the early 1980s. I initially wanted to give the Charles/Venizelos picture the caption 'We've lost our marbles', but toned this down to 'Give us back our marbles', which, even so, could be interpreted by the maliciously inclined in more than one way. Incidentally, the Trustees of the British Museum on 5 December 2014 expressed their 'delight' in announcing the decision to lend the Russian State Hermitage Museum, on the 250th anniversary of its foundation, the sculpture of the river god Ilissos from the West pediment of the Parthenon. This was the first time one of the Parthenon marbles had been loaned since their acquisition by the Museum from the 7th Earl of Elgin in 1816. Whatever view is taken of the appropriate site to display the Parthenon marbles, whether in London or in Athens, it was surely tactless of Neil MacGregor, the director of the British Museum, not to have notified, let alone consulted, the Greek government about a loan which, unsurprisingly, prompted a fiercely hostile reaction in Greece. Moreover, the announcement by the Museum trustees coincided precisely with the 70th anniversary of the beginning of one of the darkest episodes in the modern history of Greece, namely the outbreak of fighting between British forces, in support of the Greek government, and their former allies in ELAS, the military wing of the National Liberation Front (EAM). This tragic confrontation was probably the only occasion during World War II when former allies ended up fighting each other. This anniversary was likely to prove the last major occasion on which a few of those involved in the events were still living. The importance of this turning point in the country's recent history was demonstrated by the fact that there were no fewer than three academic conferences devoted to the December 1944 events in Greece, in which Britain was very heavily involved. The timing of the British Museum Trustees' decision, thoughtless though it may have been, was unlikely to have been a deliberate attempt to add insult to injury. It was more likely to have been due to ignorance of the modern history of Greece on the part of the classical scholars at the Museum with their vast expertise about the ancient world.

One of the most moving photographs in the *Concise History* was taken by Dimitris Kaloumenos, the photographer to the Ecumenical Patriarchate, in the aftermath of the highly destructive anti-Greek riots of 1955 in Istanbul, known in Greek as the Septemvriana, the September events, and in Turkish as the Altı-Yedi Eylül Olayları, the 6/7 September events. This violent rampage effectively spelled the end of the once flourishing Greek minority in the city. Kaloumenos' photograph depicts the Ecumenical Patriarch, Athinagoras, seen through the bars covering a window in the church of the Panagia Veligradiou. The Patriarch is seen walking bareheaded in the church, which had been burned out and was a total ruin (see Plate 22). One of the most significant and instructive illustrations in the second edition of the book relates to the same event. This was a photograph which I took myself in 2000 in İstiklâl Caddesi (the old Grande Rue de Péra, once the most fashionable shopping street in Istanbul, run down in recent years, slowly recovering, but still with a long way to go). This showed a poster which formed part of an exhibition, sponsored by the Yapı ve Kredi Bankası, marking the 130th anniversary of the foundation of the municipality of Beyoğlu (Pera). To my surprise, the poster showed a tank positioned in İstiklâl Caddesi to maintain order in the aftermath of the 1955 riots, a classic instance of closing the stable door after the horse has bolted, for while the pillage was in full swing the police and army were noticeable for their absence (see Plate 23).

Over the years, the Turkish authorities have scarcely sought to draw attention to such depredations so it was not only surprising but, in the circumstances, encouraging to find such a poster on public display and accompanied by a caption detailing the devastation wreaked on the *Rum vatandaşlarımız*, our Greek compatriots. The first time I saw it I did not have a camera with me. But when, the following day, I returned with one I was initially mildly put out to see a small scrum obstructing part of the poster. However, this turned out to be a party of Turkish schoolchildren, boys and girls, with their schoolmaster who was explaining the significance of the poster. This made for a much better shot and the group was unaware of being photographed. Had the photograph been taken by anybody else I might have suspected that it had been shot for propaganda purposes. A minor puzzle is that, standing at the edge of a group, is a woman wearing a headscarf and seemingly listening intently to what the schoolmaster had to say. I had assumed that she, likewise, was a teacher, but a Turkish friend pointed out that, at that time, it would have been out of the question for a woman teacher to wear a headscarf while on duty. Some time later I told an elderly Greek diplomat who had been working at the Greek consulate-general at the time of the 1955 riots of my pleasant surprise at this attempt to come to terms with a difficult past in respect of the treatment of minorities in Republican Turkey (there was another poster on İstiklâl Caddesi about the Varlık Vergisi, the discriminatory wealth tax introduced in 1942 and aimed primarily at the country's non-Muslim minorities). He sagely observed that Pera is not Turkey.

Perhaps my favourite illustration in the *Concise History* is that of the wedding in 1921 in Salt Lake City of a young Greek couple, Anna Marcellas, born in Piraeus, and Nicholas Mouskondis, born in Aghia Marina, Crete. At the time the Greek community in the city had no church so the wedding had taken place in the Paradise Café (*Kapheneion o Paradeisos*) (see Plate 24). Helen Papanikolas, who had done so much to rescue the memory of the Greeks of the inter-mountain West from oblivion, had secured the photograph for me from the Utah Historical Society. When I visited her in Salt Lake City in the early 1990s, I went with her to the Greek church one Sunday morning when she introduced me to a daughter of the marriage. In characteristic fashion, the young groom in the photograph had prospered mightily in the new world.

Another of my favourite illustrations showed the Australian prime minister, Bob Hawke, a determined proponent of multi-culturalism and, like any streetwise Labour politician, anxious to drum up support among ethnic minorities, attending the Greek Festival in the heavily Greek suburb of Coburg in Melbourne in 1988, the Australian Bicentennial Year (see Plate 25). Also visible are Bishop Ezekiel of Melbourne and two Greek parliamentary deputies, Stelios Papathemelis, PASOK's Minister for Northern Greece, and Nikolaos Martis, his New Democracy predecessor and counterpart, both prominent latterday *Makedonomakhoi*, or 'Macedonian warriors', who took the lead in promoting the Greek nationalist cause when the Macedonian issue became a *kafto thema*, or burning issue, in the early 1990s. As part of the bicentennial celebrations, James Jupp had been commissioned to edit an encyclopaedia of Australian ethnic groups, modelled on a similar volume commissioned for the American bicentennial in 1976. The article on Macedonians had caused grave offence in Greek nationalist circles. A prominent member of the huge Melbourne Greek community got wind of the fact that Papathemelis and Martis were planning to lobby the prime minister about the article in the Jupp volume and tipped him off. Hawke's reply was characteristically forthright: 'Go tell them to fuck themselves.' In the photograph Hawke has his arms around two small boys dressed in traditional Greek dress, *foustanella* and all. When, in 1999, I gave a lecture at Monash University in Melbourne I was pleased to meet one of the boys, by that time a student at the university.

When in Melbourne for the 25 March Greek Independence Day celebrations in the same year, 1999, I, together with a group of visiting Greek *episimoi* or dignitaries, including a different pair of parliamentary deputies, attended the Greek Orthodox cathedral on Palm Sunday, only for us to be publicly admonished by the bishop for having been seen eating meat in Lonsdale Street, home to a number of Greek restaurants, the previous evening and thus breaking the Lenten fast. A year or two earlier, non-Greek television viewers in Melbourne had been bemused by the repeated replaying of a clip of a curious incident at the same cathedral. This had shown the Greek consul-general in the city being manhandled down the steps by Orthodox clerics. His offence had been to pay a visit to an Old Calendarist Church in Melbourne, home to Orthodox hardliners who refuse to accept Greece's adoption of the Gregorian calendar in 1924. It was during this same visit to Australia that I got an early insight into the way in which Greek public opinion would incline during the Kosovo conflict. When the prime minister, John Howard, a strong supporter of intervention on behalf of the Kosovars, turned up at the Greek Independence Day celebrations on 25 March in Sydney he was roundly booed, not only by the Greeks but also by the Macedonians, who normally turned up to do battle with the Greeks.

To my surprise and pleasure (and indeed modest profit) both my short/concise histories have been adopted as textbooks in a number of Greek universities. The *Short History* has been used in the University of Athens for over 30 years. In the Greek translation various corrections to my text have been apparently incorporated, but I have regrettably never had the energy to go through the English and Greek texts line by line. I never envisaged that either book would end up being used in this way when I was writing them. I was writing for an English-speaking audience for whom the modern history of Greece would be very much *terra incognita*. If I had any potential reader in mind then it was a 'virtual' third or fourth generation 18-year-old Greek of the diaspora, a native speaker of English whose Greek was not up to reading a history in the language but who wished to know more about his/her roots. Interestingly, I have come across in real time a number of such individuals who have told me that they had found the book a useful introduction in this respect.

Although the British constitute one of the largest cohorts of foreign visitors to Greece, most of them are holidaymakers interested only in the four s's: sun, sea, sand and sex. Even the often highly educated members of the groups which I shepherded around Greece and Turkey for Wings in the 1960s, while in many cases very knowledgeable about the Greek lands in antiquity, had little understanding of the modern country. Some may have remembered that Byron had dreamed that Greece might yet be free and had subsequently died in Greece during the Greek war of independence; or that Turkey in the nineteenth century had been dubbed the 'sick man of Europe'; or be familiar with Melina Mercouri in *Never on Sunday* and her campaign for the return of the Elgin Marbles when minister of culture. Some might have been aware of Greece's heroic resistance to the Italians and Germans in the 1940s, although most of this knowledge would have been mediated through films such as *Ill Met by Moonlight* and the perennial Christmas-time TV favourite, the *Guns of Navarone*. But, by and large, there is little knowledge, let alone understanding, of Greece's turbulent history in modern times. This meant that, in writing my books, I could not take any prior knowledge for granted, any more than a Greek author writing a short history of Britain for a Greek audience could take even a basic knowledge of British history for granted. This has led to some criticism in Greece that my books were not really suitable for Greek students. I would tend to agree. But the remedy would seem to lie in the hands of these Greek critics themselves. They should write such books, knowing what could and could not be taken as read, although among Greek historians there seems to be something of an aversion to writing books of synthesis aimed at that elusive figure, the educated 'general reader'.

The degree of ignorance in Britain of the recent history of Greece on the part of those who should know better was strikingly demonstrated by a long article that appeared in the *Observer* magazine at the end of November 2014. This was timed to coincide with the 70th anniversary of one of the unhappiest events in the modern history of Greece, the shooting of left-wing demonstrators in Syntagma Square in the centre of Athens on 3 December 1944. The article, entitled 'Athens 1944: Britain's dirty secret', was written by two *Observer/Guardian* journalists, Ed Vulliamy and Helena Smith.

This was a tendentious piece which sought to trace the origins of most of the ills that have afflicted Greece in the period since the end of World War II to the effects of British policies towards the country during the 1940s. These disasters included the Colonels' regime that misruled Greece between 1967 and 1974, and the rise of the thuggish ultra-right-wing Golden Dawn party that emerged towards the end of the twentieth and the beginning of the twenty-first century.

The article prompted a spirited, cogent and wholly justified rebuttal by seven distinguished Greek historians. I was asked to sign their collective démarche but I thought it preferable if the signatories were all Greek, otherwise it might be thought that I was simply defending British policy at this fraught stage in relations between the two countries, although I had been critical of aspects of British policy during this period in a number of my publications.

The seven sent their lengthy critique to the *Observer* but this was clearly too long to be published in the paper. Their démarche, however, was published in English in the *Athens Review of Books* on 27 December 2014. The seven made telling criticisms of what happens when efforts are made to shoehorn the past into the present. The first of their criticisms, about which there could be no argument about its inaccuracy, was that it was not, as Vulliamy and Smith maintained, the British army but the Greek police that fired on the civilian demonstrators, killing some 15 (the precise figure is disputed) and wounding many more. British history is marked by a number of horrors, the Amritsar massacre of 1919 among them, but the shooting in Syntagma square is not one of them.

The *Observer*'s response to their critique was woefully inadequate. The paper's readers' editor, Stephen Pritchard, wrote to the seven historians that their criticisms had been shown to an 'independent historian' who had found 'many inconsistencies' in their claims. In later correspondence he declined to specify that nature of these 'inconsistencies' (not, it should be noted, errors). At the same time he gave the text of the short, and woefully misleading, correction by the *Observer* to the claim that it was British troops who had opened fire. This was published in the paper at the end of December 2014. This purported correction continued to maintain that British troops were involved in the shooting but added that 'firing could also have come from the Greek police'.

At this stage I decided to intervene in the controversy, pointing out in a letter to Pritchard that almost 40 years earlier, Dr Lars Baerentzen, the Danish historian of Greece, had analysed in great detail in *Scandinavian Studies in Modern Greek*, an article of which Vulliamy and Smith were clearly unaware, the various sources for the tragic events of 3 December 1944 (official documents, journalistic despatches, eye-witness accounts and books). This established beyond doubt that British troops did not fire on the demonstrators. The journalists seem to have based their erroneous version of events on a chronology of events in Greek history compiled by a Danish littérateur to accompany the Danish translation of the memoir of Mikis Theodorakis, the composer.

It took a further two months for Pritchard, two-term president of the Organization of News Ombudsmen, to concede that the initial correction was 'plainly inadequate'. This he did in an unusual fashion. Corrections in the *Observer* and most newspapers are short records of factual error. Pritchard chose further to obscure the issue by publishing an article in which he advanced the absurd view that the *Observer*'s error was caused by reliance on the mistaken recollections of men now late in life of a reality 'filtered through perceptions clouded by a day filled with violence and considerable confusion'. In fact, the offending article quotes the recollection of a single, still living, witness to the events of that day 70 years earlier, that of Titos Patrikios, the poet, sociologist and lawyer. Patrikios is quoted at the beginning of the article as saying 'I can still see it very clearly, I have not forgotten [...] the Athens police firing on the crowd [...] in Syntagma Square.' He made no allegation that it was British troops that had opened fire.

The publication of the Greek translation of the *Concise History* prompted a discussion in the newspaper *To Vima* as to why there are so few introductory histories of this kind aimed at a non-specialist audience in Greece and written by Greek historians. One such was published in 1953 by Nikos Svoronos, one of the great panjandrums of the historical profession in Greece. Originally published in France for a French audience in the *Que sais-je?* series as *Histoire de la Grèce moderne*, it subsequently appeared in Greek translation in 1976, accompanied by a very substantial bibliographical guide. This slim volume, akin to a lengthy encyclopaedia article and offering a Marxist interpretation of the modern history of Greece, continues to be reverentially regarded by Greek historians on the left. Appearing as it did just a few years after the victory of the right following a viciously fought civil war, the book led to Svoronos being stripped of his Greek citizenship.

In seeking to explain the rarity of such endeavours, Philip Carabott, my successor in teaching the modern history of Greece at King's College, picked up on this point, stressing that Greeks tended immediately to locate their own historians in a specific political–ideological space, with half the Greeks being deemed traitors and the other half heroes or vice versa. Moreover, in countries with an imperial past such as Britain, there was a tradition of writing about the history of other nations, while in Greece there was no such tradition.

A single word in the *Concise History* led to my being unwittingly, albeit peripherally, caught up in a furious controversy that raged in Greece over a school textbook published in 2006 for sixth-year primary school pupils. All school textbooks in Greece are published for the Ministry of Education and are used throughout the school system. In the early years of the twenty-first century the ministry commissioned a new history textbook for these 11- to 12-year-olds. This was produced by a small four-person team led by Maria Repousi, a professor of education at the University of Thessaloniki (and subsequently a member of parliament on the Democratic Left ticket). This was an excellent piece of work, a far cry from the dull textbooks of my own schooldays. It made particularly imaginative use of illustrations, of which there were more than 300. *Inter alia*, the book sought to offer a corrective to the traditional view that the centuries of Ottoman rule in Greece had been unremittingly negative. It eschewed popular myths that had been the staple of earlier such primers. One of these was the legend of the *krypho skholeio*, or secret school, whereby Greek letters had supposedly been kept alive during the dark years of Turkish tyranny by the clergy, who had taught Greek children by candlelight after dark. This was a scene immortalised in a painting by Nikolaos Gyzis, one of the most renowned of nineteenth-century Greek painters. No evidence, however, has emerged of the existence of such clandestine schools, and indeed the Ottomans placed no serious obstacles in the way of schools for the Empire's numerous minorities. The teaching of the Turkish language in such schools, for instance, only became mandatory as late as 1894.

The Orthodox Church, in the guise of Archbishop Christodoulos of Athens, emerged as one of the fiercest critics of the Repousi book. He denounced it as a work of impure history, aiming at the enslavement of young Greeks. Most of the criticism came from conservative nationalists. In 2007, the ultra-right-wing Golden Dawn party burned copies in Constitution Square on the Greek national day, 25 March, the supposed date of the beginning of the Greek war of independence, when Bishop Germanos of Old Patras is held to have blessed the Greek flag at the monastery of Agia Lavra in the Peloponnese. This scene was immortalised in another well-known painting of 1865 by Theodoros Vryzakis. But the Repousi book also came under fire at the other end of the political spectrum, with the Communist Party of Greece numbered among its critics. There were claims that the publication had been subsidised by foreigners (the European Union had given a grant for its preparation), and that it had been influenced in part by 'earthquake diplomacy', the, albeit partial, rapprochement between Greece and Turkey that emerged after both countries had been struck by serious earthquakes at the end of the twentieth century. The book sold an amazing 175,000 copies and demands for its withdrawal became ever more insistent.

A good part of the controversy centred on a single word in the text. This stated that, following the sacking of Smyrna in September 1922 by Turkish forces, thousands of Greeks had 'crowded' on the waterfront seeking to scramble on to boats and flee to Greece. The textbook contained a well-known photograph of the scene, an image that I had used myself ten years or so earlier in my *Concise History of Greece*. It was pointed out that I had used the same word 'crowded' in describing the scene, although I went on in the caption to brand the killing of some 30,000 Christians and the hacking to death of the Archbishop of Smyrna, Chrysostomos, that had followed the arrival of the Turkish army, as a bloodbath. The authors conceded that the word on its own was an inadequate description of the horrors attendant on the Turkish re-conquest of the city but an amendment to the text was not enough to save the book from being withdrawn. The alarming manner in which the furore as to the book's veracity and its appropriateness as a school textbook developed was a disturbing indication of the way in which the remarkable transformation which had characterised the writing of the country's history in academic circles in the decades following the *metapolitefsi* of 1974, the return of democracy after the grim years of the Colonels' dictatorship, had not met with much understanding at a popular level.

While at King's I also wrote a book about the foundation of our department of Byzantine and Modern Greek Studies at the end of World War I and of the ructions which had quickly ensued. But this is an intriguing story with consequences that I did not anticipate and which deserves a chapter to itself. As we shall see, writing this book, *Politics and the Academy: Arnold Toynbee and the Koraes Chair* (1986), impinged on my career in ways that I did not, but perhaps should have, foreseen.

4

Knitting a sock for my head: on washing dirty academic linen in public

'And some may perhaps consider me as writing in a hostile vein; it being my duty to cover up all the faults of the Greeks […] in a chronicler of public affairs in no wise is anything other than the truth acceptable'.
—Polybius, *Histories*, Book XXXVIII/4[1]

'At the supreme crisis in the fate of the Greek nation – probably without exaggeration the most decisive since Xerxes – […] [Toynbee] plunged into a violent propagandist campaign in favour of the Turks […] it was wholly incorrect to agitate against the nation to which the foundation of his own post was due'.
—Professor R.W. Seton-Watson, King's College (1924)

The Turkish language has some pungent sayings. Some are of universal application: 'the public purse is a great trough, he that does not sup of it is a pig'. Some are of more local relevance: 'a Greek can no more be a brother to an Armenian than you can make a prayer mat out of the skin of a dog'. Some are macabre: when people are plotting against you, they are said to be knitting a sock for your head. Although I did not realise it at the time, when I wrote my book on how Arnold Toynbee was hounded out of King's College in the 1920s, I was in effect knitting a sock for my own head. If the events of 1988, which are the subject of the next chapter, are to be properly understood, the circumstances under which I came to write about the Toynbee affair; the aspects of the book that gave offence to some self-styled leaders of the Greek community in London; and the reaction to its publication must be placed in context.

The writing of the book, *Politics and the Academy: Arnold Toynbee and the Koraes Chair*, was a factor, although a minor one and only one among several, that militated against my being appointed to the chair of which Toynbee was the first incumbent when it fell vacant in 1988. There would be a pleasing symmetry if I could plausibly claim that it was the writing of a book about Toynbee's 'involuntary resignation', as he put it, from the Koraes chair that had led to my own uncovenanted departure from the college. But matters, as we shall see, were considerably more complicated than that. Nonetheless, the book did afford ammunition to those who found it expedient to claim that I had a propensity to upset 'the Greeks' and, more particularly, those wealthy London Greeks who continued to look upon the Koraes chair as 'their' chair and were, in turn, looked upon as potential sources of funding by a college which, at the end of the 1980s, was in dire financial straits.

Writing about Greece and its modern history can sometimes prove harmful to one's academic health. For Greek nationalists (and the Greeks are of course by no means alone in this) are acutely sensitive to the country's image, and it is not difficult to cause offence by writing, in a hopefully objective fashion, about the country's fascinating, if troubled, history. It is not for me to judge the degree of my own impartiality, but the fact that my *A Concise History of Greece* has been translated into all the languages of the Balkans (including Turkish) and that the Greek translation is used as a textbook in Greek universities must afford some indication that I try to be even-handed in writing about Greece and its relations with its neighbours. Another testimonial to my at least relative impartiality was the invitation to contribute to a volume of a Greek encyclopaedia (Malliaris-Paideia), published in the early 1980s. I was the only non-Greek out of some 70 contributors, and my task was to write on the history of Greece between 1941 and 1981, a period covering the occupation, the civil war and the Colonels' dictatorship, truly a *kafto thema* or 'hot potato' if ever there was one. Relatively new states, and the final borders of Greece, it should be remembered, were only established in 1947, and states that view themselves as in some sense threatened by their neighbours, as many Greeks do, tend to be more than usually sensitive about their image in the outside world. I was fortunate in that I did not incur serious Greek wrath for the best part of 20 years after my appointment to a lectureship in the modern history of Greece, the first of its kind in Britain. But what precipitated my, perhaps inevitable, fall from grace was the very long article (subsequently published as a book in 1986) about the foundation in 1919 of the Koraes Chair of Modern Greek and Byzantine History, Language and Literature at King's College, London, and its subsequent rapid implosion, when the young Arnold Toynbee was appointed to it.

I had heard vague rumours about the Toynbee imbroglio of the early 1920s when, in the mid-1960s, I was a postgraduate student at King's. At the time I spent a morning in the office of a member of the college secretariat who acted as invigilator while I read through a small cache of papers relating to the fracas, although these gave only a sketchy indication of the nature of the controversy. These papers were at that time still kept locked up in the college secretary's office so sensitive did they continue to be regarded, although they related to events that had occurred 40 years previously. Some time later I was also able to see the small collection of papers which Peter Calvocoressi, a prominent Anglo-Greek and the last secretary of the Koraes chair subscribers' committee, which represented the interests of those who had donated to the foundation of the chair, had handed to the then principal of King's, Sir Peter Noble, in the early 1960s, receiving in return a cup of tea and a pink cake.

The selection of papers which I saw was too small to get the whole picture, but my appetite was duly whetted to find out more about what was clearly an intriguing episode in the college's history, and in the mid-1970s I began to be seriously interested in the affair. Through the agency of Robert Browning, professor of Classics and Ancient History at Birkbeck College, I lent Toynbee, whom unfortunately I never actually met, a few books about the Greek independence period, together with one or two of my own articles. These he used in writing his last book, *The Greeks and their Heritages*, which was published posthumously in 1981, although it had basically been completed in 1974. This connection prompted me to write to Toynbee, then aged 85, to ask whether he had any papers relating to his time at King's.

In a letter of 27 July 1974, which must be one of the last that he wrote, he replied that he did indeed have a cache of papers relating to the chair, some of which turned out to be helpfully annotated. He said that he would be happy to lend these to me, adding that 'there is nothing confidential about them, as far as I am concerned, but, though they are now ancient history for me, they do have a permanent interest because of their bearing on the perennial question of academic freedom'. He had said as much in a letter written 50 years earlier, in January 1924, to Professor R.W. Seton-Watson, who had emerged as his main critic in the college: 'personally, I have always wished that full public light should be thrown upon the whole history of the chair and of my tenure of it'. There was clearly never any question but that Toynbee wanted the whole extraordinary story to be in the public domain, and I likewise was now determined to ensure that, sooner or later, it was. In his letter to me of 27 July, Toynbee suggested a meeting at Ganthorpe to which he had recently moved, a process which appears to have placed a great physical strain on him. Ganthorpe is near Castle Howard in Yorkshire, the palatial family home of the mother of his first wife, Rosalind. At Ganthorpe, we would be able to talk over the Koraes chair fracas and I would have been able to pick up his papers relating to it. But to my regret, this meeting, scheduled for the morning of 17 August, never took place.

On the night of 3-4 August, Toynbee sadly suffered a devastating stroke from which he did not recover before his death in October of the following year, 1975. He was unable to communicate, but Browning told me that from time to time he would write something down in Greek characters but that what he wrote was unintelligible. Some part of his brain, so deeply penetrated from an early age by Greek, seems to have continued to function. As Toynbee himself put it, between 1899 and 1911 he had received a 'Byzantine-like' education. He had been taught not only to read the Greek authors but also to imitate their various dialects, vocabularies, styles and metres: 'the drilling in Hellenic Greek that I received from English classical scholars was, I should guess, as thorough and as correct as the instruction given in the second century by Dio Chrysostom or in the fourth century by Libanius'.

It was to be some time after Toynbee's death before I wrote to his widow, his second wife, Veronica (Boulter), to ask whether I might consult her husband's papers relating to his time at King's. It turned out that Toynbee's archive, by then held in the Bodleian Library, was closed pending its use by Toynbee's authorised biographer, the historian W.H. McNeill. But, as her husband had already given me permission to look at his papers relating to the controversy at King's, Toynbee's widow was prepared to make an exception and allow me to consult these. I was very grateful for this permission, and I looked at the relevant files in the early 1980s.

At about the same time, at a conference at Anatolia College in Salonica in 1981, I was told by Professor Joachim Joachim of the University of Cyprus of a cache of papers relating to the affair in the Gennadeios Library of the American School of Classical Studies in Athens. This was, on reflection, an obvious place to look, for the library was based on the huge collection amassed by Joannes Gennadius, a compulsive bibliophile who, for many years, had been Greek minister in London. Not only did the library house his enormous library but also his papers. These were of particular interest to me as he had been a leading protagonist in the Toynbee controversy and was Toynbee's most vociferous critic in the Greek community in Britain.

It now became apparent that there would probably be enough material for an article on the subject. The King's archivist located a number of relevant papers in the college archive which I was able to look at, although with the proviso that the permission of the college secretary would be needed if I were to quote from them. As London University is a federal institution it was likely that material might also be found in Senate House. And, indeed, it turned out that the principal of the university, William Taylor, had access to a cache of papers (these appear have been kept outside the main university archive) and, after looking through them, he kindly allowed me to borrow them, subject again to the university retaining the right to give permission for quotation.

I thus came to have access, in one way or another, to the papers of all the major protagonists in the controversy: those of Toynbee himself; of King's College; of the University of London; of the subscribers' committee, which brought together the principal Greek donors; and finally to those of R.W. Seton-Watson, Toynbee's principal antagonist at the college. Access to this last archive was thanks to my friend and colleague at SSEES, Hugh Seton-Watson, and of his brother Christopher, the historian sons of R.W. The one exception appeared to be Burrows' own personal archive. This had apparently been given by his widow, Una, to the Greek legation in London. Efforts to locate the papers in the somewhat chaotic archive of the Greek Foreign Ministry in Athens proved fruitless, so I wrote to Professor Dimitri Kitsikis of the University of Ottowa, the author of a valuable study on the propaganda activities of the Greek government at the time of the Versailles peace conference, to see whether he could throw light on their whereabouts. He had had access to the papers in the early 1960s when they were still housed in what had by then become the Greek embassy in London. He replied, rather oddly, that he had photocopied 'the related dossiers' in London and offered to prepare a separate article to be published as an appendix to my own publication. This was an unusual suggestion which had no great appeal, and there the matter rested. At least part of the Burrows archive, however, namely the papers relating to the establishment of the chair, which were of particular interest to me, had ended up in the college archive, thanks to Principal Burrows' widow. To these, of course, I had access.

In 1984, I gave a talk on the Toynbee affair at a seminar organised by Professor Elie Kedourie of the London School of Economics. Kedourie, an observant Jew, was, to put it mildly, no fan of Toynbee, who had regarded post-Biblical Jewish history as no more than a 'fossil'. After the seminar, he asked me whether I would be interested in writing up the affair for *Middle Eastern Studies*, the journal of which he was editor. I was pleased to say yes, for I had always been grateful to Kedourie, a profound student of nationalism with a considerable interest in its Greek manifestations. In 1969, when I was starting on my career and was thus very much an unknown quantity, he had published one of my first articles, an annotated translation of a late eighteenth-century anti-Western tract by the Patriarch Anthimos of Jerusalem, in *Middle Eastern Studies*. When I subsequently wrote to him that my article on the Toynbee affair was getting longer and longer and might have to appear in instalments, he replied that this was no problem, as I could have an entire issue of the journal for my piece, to be published on the occasion of the 21st anniversary of its foundation, a very generous allocation of space indeed. Published originally as a 117-page article, 'Politics and the Academy: Arnold Toynbee and the Koraes Chair' did not quite fill the whole of Volume XXI of *Middle Eastern Studies* (October 1985). Interestingly, in a lecture delivered shortly before his death in 1992, Kedourie made reference to the Toynbee affair and to Toynbee's conclusion that 'Greeks were no better than the Turks'. For Kedourie, Greece was 'from its inception an unstable and intrigue-ridden Near Eastern backwater'. The title of his lecture, which was published posthumously in 1992 in the US journal *Commentary*, was *Politics and the Academy*, the title which Kedourie had given to my lengthy article and short book. In this article he included a summary of the Toynbee affair at King's.

I was now able to set to work compiling as detailed an account of the affair as I could, with effectively no constraints of space. The first point to strike me was that this was an episode in the history of the college of which King's College, for understandable reasons, scarcely seemed to be proud. There had been no greater scandal in its history since the Christian socialist F.D. Maurice's enforced resignation in 1853 from his chair of theology for denying the notion of the eternal punishment of the wicked. As already noted, Gordon Huelin makes no mention of the Toynbee episode in his sesquicentennial history of the college published in 1978. The centennial history (1928), written by F.J.C. Hearnshaw, an historian who had been a member of the board that had appointed Toynbee and thus had firsthand knowledge of the affair, did not refer to Toynbee by name. Hearnshaw made clear, however, his distaste for the pioneering academic entrepreneurialism of the principal of the college at the time of Toynbee's appointment, Ronald Burrows. 'The fact', he wrote,

> that governments and politicians were interested in these modern linguistic [*sic*] chairs had advantages in securing money and promises of money for their inauguration and maintenance – although the actual payment of foreign government grants proved to be liable to frequent interruption by revolution or change of administration. It carried with it, however, that grave disadvantage that the holder of these subsidized seats found his academic freedom compromised. He was expected to teach what was agreeable to his patrons.

The first holder of the Koraes chair, he went on, 'became embroiled on political grounds with the Greek government and the Greek committee in London,

1. The author's introduction to *I kath'imas Anatoli* (The Greek East) when, in the summer of 1960, he assisted in the uncovering of the thirteenth-century wall paintings in the Church of Hagia Sophia (Divine Wisdom), Trebizond. David Winfield (wearing hat) was in charge of the restoration. The author stands in the front row. In 1960 the church served as a mosque. It subsequently became a museum and, in 2013, reverted to being a mosque, and the laboriously uncovered wall paintings were screened off.

2. A partially uncovered thirteenth-century wall painting depicting the miracle of The Feeding of the Five Thousand in the narthex of the Church of Hagia Sophia in Trebizond. Photographed in 1960.

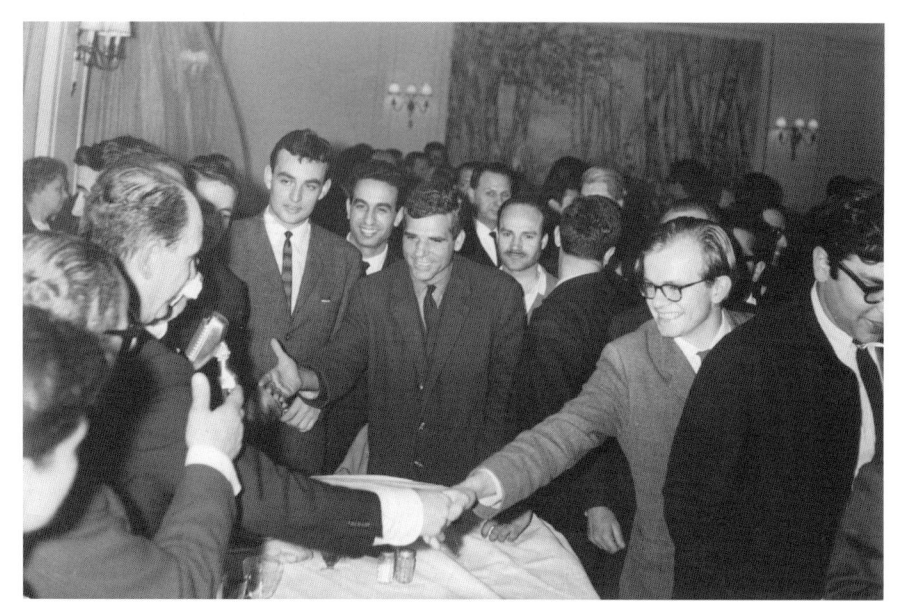

3. The author shaking hands with Andreas Papandreou at a meeting in Athens of the Cretan Students Association shortly before the military coup of 21 April 1967. George Frangos is just visible on the right.

4. Constructing socialism in Albania, 1975. The author earning a 'Young Pioneer' scarf by working for a few minutes on the construction of the Pogradeci-Prrenjas railway.

5. Singing the praises of Enver Hoxha with a group of Dutch Marxist–Leninists in 1975: a few bemused Albanian student 'volunteers' (not sporting 'Young Pioneer' scarves) can be seen in the background.

6. Remembering the past: a round table discussion of the wartime resistance organised in Athens by the BBC Greek Service in 1978. From right: Komninos Pyromaglou (deputy leader of EDES); Paul Nathanail (Greek Service Programme Organiser); Monty Woodhouse (commander of the Allied Military Mission to the Greek Resistance); Manolis Glezos (who, with Apostolos Santas, tore down the Nazi flag from the Acropolis in May 1941); and the author. Not included in the photograph is Lefteris Apostolou, the first secretary-general of EAM. The audience included Thanasis Hatzis, Apostolou's successor.

7. 'The People united will never be defeated': some of the foreign critics of the Colonels' regime at the King George II hotel in November 1983 on the tenth anniversary of the Athens Polytechnic uprising. Main table, right to left: Monty Woodhouse, Sir Hugh Greene, Lady Amalia Fleming, Peter Thompson, Benedict Birnberg (with spectacles), the author and Anthony Marreco. Behind, to the left of Peter Thompson, is Melina Mercouri.

8. Nathan on the hydrofoil from Rhodes to Patmos, August 1989.

9. Left to right: Dick Crampton; Stevan Pavlowitch; William Waldegrave, Minister of State at the Foreign Office; the author; and Dennis Deletant at the despatch from Westminister Bridge of eight juggernaut loads of books for the Biblioteca Centrală Universitară. This caught fire during the December 1989 fighting in Bucharest that accompanied the overthrow of Nicolae Ceaușescu.

10. France Pavlowitch, Dick Crampton and the author taking the waters in Bucharest in 1990.

11. 'A Night on the Bare Mountain': Mary Jo and Rachel in the mountains above Krasnaya Polyana in August 1992.

12. Rachel and Nathan in the mountains above Krasnaya Polyana in August 1992.

13. The author with Odysseus Dimitriadis on board the *Odysseus* during the 'Cruise of the Philhellenes' organised by the Foundation for Hellenic Culture in June 1993. Dimitriadis, whose parents had migrated from Trebizond to Batumi in Georgia, had been the musical director of the Greek theatre in Sukhum in the 1930s. He subsequently became a prominent conductor in the Soviet Union.

14. The author discussing Caucasian affairs with John le Carré at George Hewitt's inaugural lecture as Professor of Caucasian Studies at the School of Oriental and African Studies (1996).

15. The author sharing a joke with Margaret Thatcher and William St Clair at the publication of Noel Malcolm's *Kosovo* (1998).

16. The author, with the Russian Monastery of St Panteleimon, Mount Athos, in the background, 1998.

17. The author with Gough Whitlam and Christos Tsirkas at the Greek Community Centre in Melbourne, March 1999. Whitlam studied Greek under Enoch Powell at the University of Sydney before World War II.

18. Mary Jo and the author at St Antony's in 2002.

19. The author and Rachel as Fellow and Max Hayward Visiting Fellow of St Antony's, 2002.

20. Archbishop Gregorios of Thyateira conducts a service of blessing of the tombstone of the Ecumenical Patriarch Meletios II (1768–1769) in the Methodist Church in Muswell Hill, London before its return to his *patrida* or homeland (May 2013).

21. Anglo-Greek Relations: Byron and his dog, Lion, at Missolonghi in 1824.

22. The Ecumenical Patriarch Athinagoras in the burnt-out ruins of an Orthodox church, the Panagia Veligradiou, in Istanbul, 1955.

23. Coming to terms with the past: Istanbul, 2000.

24. A Greek–American wedding in Salt Lake City, Utah in 1921.

25. Ethnic politics in Australia: Bob Hawke at a Greek community festival in Melbourne, 1988.

and his position became an intolerable one'. When a successor was elected the conditions of tenure had to be radically amended, although, he might have added, they were not amended radically enough.

Christine Kenyon Jones' recent history of the college was published in 2004 on the occasion of its 175th anniversary, many years, of course, after my book had appeared. But the author makes no reference to Toynbee, let alone to the Toynbee affair or to my book, one of a handful of books relating to the college's history. Her lavishly illustrated and handsomely produced volume would appear to have been written in the hope, *inter alia*, of appealing to benefactors, so any mention of furious rows between donors and the college might have struck a jarring and unhelpful note. She does allude to the Frederick Denison Maurice imbroglio, but this occurred safely in the distant mid-nineteenth century. Room is found to mention such worthies as Ivison Macadam, the first president of the National Union of Students, and John Yudkin, the nutritionist, but not Arnold Toynbee, by any reckoning one of the most distinguished figures ever to have taught at King's. Perhaps when a history is published to mark the 200th anniversary of the foundation in 1828 of King's, as it doubtless will be, appropriate attention will at last be paid to the Toynbee affair, which was clearly one of the most extraordinary, divisive and public episodes in the life of the college. But I would not count on it.

The moving spirit behind the establishment of the Koraes chair was Ronald Burrows, principal (and the first layman to hold the office although his father was a clergyman, his wife the daughter of a bishop and his cousin a bishop) of the college between 1913 and his premature death in 1920. A classicist by training, his first academic post had been as an assistant to Gilbert Murray, who had been appointed at the age of 23 to the chair of Greek at the University of Glasgow. This was a connection that was to have important consequences in the filling of the chair. Murray was what one might call a militant philhellene. When one of his students, H.N. Brailsford, announced that he was going as a volunteer to fight alongside the Greeks in the war of 1897 against the Ottoman Empire, Murray entrusted him with his pistol. Unusually for a classicist, Burrows was fascinated by the modern country of Greece and was impressed by the vigour of its politics, which contrasted with the apathy that characterised municipal politics in Glasgow. After his time in Glasgow, Burrows was successively professor of Greek at Cardiff and Manchester before moving to King's in 1913.

During his time in Manchester, Burrows maintained good relations with the Greek community (whose prosperity at the time is reflected in the fine neo-classical Orthodox church in the city) and had hoped, vainly as it turned out, to persuade the Manchester Greeks to fund a lectureship in modern

Greek. Modern Greek was seemingly first taught at a British university in the 1890s in the University of St Andrews and the teacher, Antonios Jannaris, during his cold and fogbound exile north of the border, not surprisingly pined for the warmth of his native Crete. The Manchester community would have been overwhelmingly supporters of Eleftherios Venizelos, the Greek politician by whose charismatic personality Burrows, like so many of his British contemporaries, was bowled over. Venizelos was undoubtedly a charismatic figure. I have never seen a poor photograph of him, and it increasingly strikes me that being photogenic is one of the essential attributes of political charisma. Burrows' passionate Venizelism was reflected in a poem that he published in 1913, in the wake of Greece's astonishing successes in the Balkan wars, which led to a massive increase in its territory. In this he called on Venizelos to show forth his master power:

> 'Lord of all Hellenic men,
> Make our country great again'.

Burrows' move to London and the fact that his principalship of King's College coincided with the Great War, afforded him the opportunity to give more practical expression to a naive and trusting phihellenism. In 1913 he was involved with some in the Greek community in Britain in the foundation of the Anglo-Hellenic League. One of these, D.J. Cassavetti, was among those keen to transplant the ethos of the 'muscular Christianity' of the British public (that curious British circumlocution for private) school to Greece. He was convinced that what the Greeks needed above all was 'the physical and moral education of the Public School'. To his regret, it was 'the excitable coffee-house politician' who had come to be regarded as the representative Hellene, whereas it was the *evzone*, the kilted Greek soldier, 'with his manliness and his jolly but courteous ways', who was the true counterpart of the English public schoolboy. Whenever attempts have been made to introduce such schools to Greece, however, they have proved a failure, sometimes hilariously so, as Kenneth Matthews, a teacher in the 1930s at one such school, the Anargyreios School on the island of Spetses, demonstrated in his novel *Greek Salad* (1935). Another of those involved in the League, William Pember Reeves, the director of the London School of Economics, was, like Burrows, in thrall to Venizelos, whom he did 'most utterly and completely trust'. Like Burrows, he was a poetaster, being the author of 'Greek Fire, a Byzantine Ballad'. A New Zealander, he apparently never tired of 'drawing parallels [...] between ancient Greece and modern New Zealand'.

The Anglo-Hellenic League, which still survives, albeit with difficulty, now emphasises that it is 'strictly non-political'. It found little difficulty, however, in peaceful coexistence with the Colonels' regime that misruled Greece between 1967 and 1974, with the Greek ambassador, General Ioannis Sorokos, a junta appointee, holding high office in the League. This, of course, was a political stance, which is one reason why I have never become a member, particularly after a good friend, Stavros Papastavrou, the Lewis-Gibson lecturer in modern Greek at Cambridge, had resigned in protest at the League's pusillanimous attitude towards the junta. The difficulty in sustaining a strictly non-political stance in times of political turbulence is demonstrated by Lady Katherine Brandram's resignation as chief patron and president of the League during the era of the Colonels. This was one of the more dramatic events in the normally placid life of the League. Lady Brandram was the daughter of King Constantine I and the last surviving great-granddaughter of Queen Victoria. Her resignation had been prompted by the Colonels' treatment of her nephew, the former King Constantine II.

I did once give a lecture for the League in the 1980s, for which members were charged a not negligible sum to attend. Clearly, sales of the tickets had not gone well, for I was rung up a few days before I was due to speak by the secretary of the League, Nan White-Gaze, and told that my students could attend the lecture for half-price. I had to inform her that my students, alas, were reluctant to hear me pontificate even when they did not have to pay for the privilege. On another occasion I was invited to a League gathering whose purpose was to interest younger people in membership, but I imagine that many would-be recruits were put off by the fact that membership was only for the well-heeled. Tickets for the League's 90th anniversary dinner in 2003 cost £100.

There was, however, no pretence of being above politics in the Anglo-Hellenic League's early years, when it adopted a highly political stance and put itself forward as the unabashed champion of a Venizelist 'Greater Greece'. Venizelos, who was prime minister on the outbreak of the war, was strongly pro-Entente and, from the outset, tried to bring Greece into the war but met with such resistance from King Constantine, who advocated neutrality, that in the autumn of 1916 he established his own provisional government in northern Greece. In 1917 Venizelos was installed in the premiership in Athens by the Entente Powers and promptly aligned Greece with them.

Throughout his time at King's, Burrows proved a tireless publicist on behalf of Venizelist Greece. Newspaper and periodical articles poured from his pen in justification of Greece's territorial claims in general and of Venizelos' policies in particular. In a speech to the Historical Association in 1919 Burrows maintained that there was more in common between Britain and Greece than with most of Britain's allies. 'We are both', he wrote, '"a nation of shopkeepers", and yet we have not been found wanting in the day of battle. We are both [...] a nation of sailors. At our best we turn out something of the same type of man'.

The war gave Burrows the chance of not merely propagandising on behalf of Venizelist Greece but the opportunity of helping to shape its history. In the autumn of 1915, after Bulgaria had thrown in its lot with the Central Powers, he, along with R.W. Seton-Watson, crafted a scheme for the *enosis*, or union, of Cyprus with Greece, then under British rule, in return for Greek assistance to the embattled Serbs. This was probably the most opportune of such proposals between the British occupation of Cyprus in 1878 and the granting of a qualified independence to the island in 1960 but, unfortunately, it did not succeed. So closely was Burrows identified with the Venizelist cause that the Greek statesman, shortly after he had established his provisional government in Salonica, asked Burrows to act as his 'semi-official representative' in London. This proposal was not followed up because the Greek minister in London, Joannes Gennadius, subsequently a leading player in the Toynbee affair, had resigned from the service of the royalist government and was thus able to represent the Venizelist 'Government of National Defence' in Britain. In fine, Burrows had many opportunities to display what the crusty Admiral Sir John de Robeck, the British High Commissioner in Constantinople in 1920, dismissively termed his 'ingenious enthusiasm' in promoting the Greek cause, opportunities which the indefatigable Burrows seldom failed to take.

Once World War I had broken out, Burrows responded with alacrity to R.W. Seton-Watson's proposal to establish a School of Slavonic Studies (subsequently SSEES). This became a powerhouse of propaganda in favour of the self-determination of the peoples of Eastern Europe, most of whom, conveniently, were under the rule of Britain's enemies, the Central Powers. It was against this background of academic entrepreneurialism and political activism that Burrows developed his project of establishing a post in modern Greek studies. In 1915 he learned that Venizelos was prepared to make available £300 annually from government funds for such a post. Burrows requested an intermediary to ask William Miller, a sympathetic and acute observer of things Greek both as journalist and historian, whether he might be interested in the position. But Miller was unwilling to accept a chair if the endowment were to be provided directly or indirectly by a foreign government. If it were, he prophetically wrote, 'then I may at once decline all further consideration of the matter'.

Burrows now turned to the idea of raising funds for the chair from the well-established, prosperous and very largely Venizelist community in

Britain. At one stage he had hoped to secure the endowment in one fell swoop from the frumpish, but hugely rich, Helena Schilizzi, soon to become Venizelos' second wife. Burrows also set his sights on the likewise enormously wealthy Sir Basil Zaharoff, a Constantinopolitan Greek and enigmatic arms dealer known in the popular press as the Pedlar of Death. He even figures, as Basil Bazarov, in one of the Tintin books. But Zaharoff declined as he had already given £25,000 to endow a chair of aviation at Imperial College London, and was to endow similar chairs at the Sorbonne and at the University of Petrograd. He was also to endow the improbably named Field Marshal Earl Haig Chair of English Literature at the Sorbonne and the no less oddly named Marshal Foch Chair of French Literature at Oxford, for which it was proposed by the university that he should be one of the electors. Of the five chairs that Zaharoff founded, only those at Oxford and, vestigially, at Imperial College survive.

In his approach to Helena Schilizzi, Burrows made clear that he envisaged the appointment of 'an English Phil-Hellene of high standing'. He believed that 'the great potential force of the English public school [Burrows had himself been at Charterhouse] and University man', nurtured on ancient Greek language and literature, had yet to be tapped. The person appointed, Burrows maintained, would have very little routine work and would thus be able to give 'practically his full time to the general promotion of the cause', the cause being that of a Venizelist 'Greater Greece'. For some reason, the English expression for the Greek *Megali Ellas* is not 'Great Greece' but 'Greater Greece', which has more of an irredentist nuance. Burrows envisaged that the holder of the chair would have the opportunity of giving 'public lectures on propagandist subjects'. Helena Schilizzi did not, as Burrows had hoped, come up with the entire sum required, although she did make one of the largest individual contributions.

Burrows now had to look to the wider Greek community to raise the rest of the endowment. He was greatly helped in this endeavour by Nicholas Eumorfopoulos, a fellow of University College London, where he was known by his nickname 'Eumo', taught physics and was active in college affairs for over 50 years. In a letter circulated to potential subscribers, Burrows stressed the importance to Greece of establishing such a chair in the heart of the British Empire. There were teachers of ancient Greek by the score, whereas teachers of the modern language, where they existed at all, were 'untrained journalists, or language masters without salary, standing or dignity'. Stretching a point somewhat, he argued that education in ancient Greek literature is 'immeasurably deeper and wider-spread' in England than in any other country in Europe. The project of establishing a chair was 'a vital, practical matter affecting the political and business interests' of the Greek kingdom. Some £12,200 was raised and it was agreed that the salary would be £600 per annum, the minimum professorial salary decreed by the University of London as far back as 1900 and substantially below the normal minimum salary of £800 at the time at the college. Until the 1960s, the salary of the holder of the Koraes chair appears to have been lower than that of other professorships within the college.

Burrows, possibly influenced by Miller's negative response, realised that the donors might try to retain some kind of control over the chair. It would not, he warned potential benefactors, be possible to include one of their number on the appointments board. In the event, however, the overbearing Joannes Gennadius, by now restored to the post of Greek minister in London, was included in the board of advisers for the chair. Burrows, most unwisely as it transpired, was also prepared to concede that the trustees of the fund could retain control of the endowment, until the professor resigned, reached the retiring age of 65, or died. Burrows was quick to exploit Venizelos' visit to London in November 1917, when the prime minister attended a huge meeting in solidarity with Greece at the Mansion House, to solicit contributions, and his efforts were helped by the Greek government now having voted the subsidy of £300 for the new department. The Greek subscribers, who invariably corresponded with each other in English, agreed to drop their original insistence that the holder of the chair should be either a British or a Greek national: someone of British or Greek descent whose 'national sympathies' were British or Greek would be acceptable. They left it to the good sense of the university not to appoint a Turk.

A process described by the principal of the university, Sir Edwin Cooper Perry, as 'the oral examination of a gifted horse', now got under way. But unfortunately it did not extend to two further concessions made to the subscribers, which were to be the source of much subsequent friction. The subscribers were to be sent the scheme of work to be undertaken by the department at the beginning of each session, while every three years they were to receive a report on its activities, with a request for criticisms and suggestions. But the university's misgivings about the degree of the subscribers' control of the endowment were broadly assuaged, and the college was now free to commence the search for a professor for the chair.

A proposal to call the chair after Venizelos himself was rejected on the ground that it was unwise to name it after a living person, although Burrows had been prepared to name the chair after Zaharoff had he come up with a large enough donation. (There is now a Greek-funded Venizelos chair at the London School of Economics, but that is another complicated story about which more in Chapter 6.) Instead, it was named after Adamantios Korais, a classical scholar of genius and the 'intellectual father', as Burrows put it, of the Greek national movement in the early nineteenth century. Korais, although born in Smyrna, had been passionately devoted to the progress of the island of Chios, which was also the *patrida*, the ancestral home, of many members of the subscribers' committee, the *Englezochiotes* or Anglo-Chiots. There is a certain irony in naming a chair that included within its purview the history, language and literature of Byzantium after Korais, for he had a Gibbonian contempt for the monkishness and obscurantism characteristic of Byzantine civilisation: he once wrote that reading so much as a page of a Byzantine text was enough to bring on an attack of gout.

The search for the Koraes professor now began in earnest. The range of the chair, embracing as it did the history, language and literature of modern and medieval Greece over a period extending to some 1,500 years, was very wide, but it is clear that both Burrows and the subscribers envisaged that the chair would go to a modern historian. Burrows had still not abandoned the hope of attracting William Miller and wrote, misleadingly, to reassure him that there would be no control by the Greek government and that he would be free to develop what he termed the 'propaganda work' on foreign affairs on which he was engaged. But once again Miller was not to be tempted. He insisted that he remained a 'solitary *Privatgelehrter*', who knew nothing of colleges save for 'the dim reminiscences' of his undergraduate days. As a second choice, Burrows favoured F.W. Hasluck, an authority on arcane aspects of the history of the Levant but with little discernible interest in the contemporary affairs that were of such concern to the principal. This would have been an excellent and imaginative choice, but Hasluck was already in the advanced stages of the illness, tuberculosis, that was soon to lead to his early death in a Swiss sanatorium.

With his first and second choices not available, Burrows now began to take soundings among British, Greek and French scholars both as to who might fill the chair, and also the lectureship in modern Greek which was to be established concurrently and which was to be held by a native speaker of the language. In the case of the lectureship this was not as straightforward a matter as it seemed, given the importance in Greece of the 'language question'. This was the perennial, frequently bitter, and at times violent, controversy over which form of the language should be written and taught, the *katharevousa*, or 'purifying' form, closer to the ancient language, or the *dimotiki*, based on the everyday spoken language. Burrows appears to have been open minded on the issue. But he had something of a problem, for Gennadius was a committed champion of the *katharevousa*.

Professor N.G. Politis, the great folklorist, proposed his son for the lectureship. More seriously, A.J.B. Wace, the director of the British School at Athens, suggested the distinguished academic proponent of the *dimotiki*, Manolis Triandaphyllidis. Leon Maccas, a Greek diplomat, put forward the name of a Greek man of letters 'de l'école d'Alexandrie [...] qui est un esprit remarquable', a certain Monsieur Cavafis. Burrows clearly had not heard of Constantine Cavafy, and, indeed, it would at this juncture have been odd if he had. There was never any serious possibility that the poet would move from Alexandria to London, but it is interesting to speculate how the newly established department might have fared if he had, and what effect such a move might have had on the poet. Another person considered for the lectureship was John Mavrogordato, whom Burrows considered to be an example of 'the best type of the Anglo-Greek colony', whose natural indolence, combined with a private income, meant that he had only got a second-class degree although he was a first-rate scholar. Subsequently Mavrogordato, as we shall see in Chapter 6, became, in rather odd circumstances, the Bywater and Sotheby Professor of Byzantine and Modern Greek Language and Literature at Oxford, a chair first filled almost concurrently with the Koraes chair. Burrows was a great admirer of the Sorbonne school of Byzantine and Modern Greek Studies, and in the end the lectureship went to Lysimachos Oeconomos, who had studied in Paris under Hubert Pernot.

Burrows consulted widely about filling the chair, including his old mentor Gilbert Murray, by now Regius Professor of Greek at Oxford. Murray mentioned the chair to his son-in-law and former student, Arnold Toynbee. Until 1915, Toynbee had been a tutorial fellow in ancient history at Balliol College but his work for the Foreign Office during the war had given him a taste for the modern history and politics of the Near East. Toynbee duly contacted Burrows about the chair, but decided not to apply, writing to the principal to say that, among other considerations, he thought the chair should go to someone who was 'more of an active Philhellene' than he felt himself to be, a phrase whose resonance will become apparent later. At much the same time, he had written to his father-in-law, Murray, that 'one might be in a false position towards the London Greeks if one isn't particularly Philhellene'. Another of those approached, R.M. Dawkins, the great authority on the modern Greek dialects of Asia Minor and a previous director of the British School at Athens, ruled himself out. He was much keener on a post at Cambridge, or the Bywater and Sotheby chair at Oxford, to which he was duly appointed in 1920. A famously shy individual, he dreaded having to keep in touch with the Anglo-Greek community. As he wrote to Hasluck, 'most awful of all the professor [...] must keep in touch with the Greek community in London and then there is the Anglo hell league [*sic*] and as a principal ramping Ronald [Burrows] a great light in the same league; so altogether thanking God for my private means I think no thank you'.[2]

Towards the end of October 1918, the board of advisers met to consider the applications of those who had put in for the chair. Burrows always thought that it would best be filled by an Englishman, a view with which the subscribers seemingly concurred, but he had essentially drawn a blank with those 'Englishmen' who had formally applied, while he dismissed the Greek applicants as hopeless. Early in the new year, 1919, he feared that Gennadius, who had recently retired, at the age of 73, after many years as Greek minister in London, might formally apply for the chair. Burrows wrote 'quite between ourselves' to Pember Reeves, 'G[ennadius] has been hinting that he would like to be our professor'. Moreover, as he wrote to George Macmillan, the publisher, although Gennadius was a 'wonderful man', he had become increasingly difficult to work with and had clashed with many of his colleagues. What was more, he was 'a purist of the Purists on the language question', as well as having a strong aversion to the use of the typewriter. Eumorfopoulos, the secretary of the subscribers' committee, put it more bluntly, describing Gennadius as behaving like a 'perfect boor' at meetings of the subscribers' committee. Fortunately, Burrows was saved from possible embarrassment by the university's retirement age, which was 65.

At the time that Burrows was considering how to see off Gennadius without causing offence, no easy task, he received in January 1919 another letter from Toynbee asking if the chair were still vacant. Burrows replied that it was. Toynbee made clear to Burrows that, if elected, he would hope to keep in touch with the 'political intelligence' side, and might wish to travel in the region on behalf of the Foreign Office. Shortly afterwards, Gilbert Murray sent Burrows a testimonial on behalf of his son-in-law, Toynbee. Despite the hesitation caused by the fact that he was writing on behalf of someone to whom he was related by marriage, the testimonial was nonetheless fulsome enough:

> as an historian he stands in the very front rank of the younger historians produced by Oxford [...] There can be no doubt of his being a man of striking and unusual powers of mind [...] I think his combination of knowledge, linguistic and historical, past and present, with political insight and originality of mind is of a kind very rarely met with.

In the event, Toynbee was unanimously appointed to the chair. When he had expressed doubts as to his capacity to teach the modern language, Burrows had set his mind at rest, saying that it was only important that he be able to understand his Greek students speaking 'on difficult subjects beyond that range of the vocabulary one uses with a peasant'. He was able also to reassure Toynbee over a rumour that had reached him that the donors were unhappy with his appointment and would have preferred someone who specialised in modern literature. Toynbee was due to take up the chair in October 1919.

Even before he had arrived at the college, Toynbee had asked Burrows if he could miss the autumn term to continue to work on behalf of the Foreign Office. Burrows, however, was not keen on the idea. In May, Toynbee had written to Burrows to say that he had suffered a minor breakdown, but he recovered in time to take up the chair in the autumn. It was about this time, and possibly connected with his breakdown, that he had the most grandiose of the mystical experiences that he underwent at various junctures in his life. Walking along Buckingham Palace Road, he had found himself

> in communion, not just with this or that episode in History, but with all that had been, and was, and was to come. In that instant, he was directly aware of the passage of History gently flowing through him in a mighty current, and of his own life welling like a wave in the flow of this vast tide.

It is difficult to know quite what to make of such an extraordinary vision and likewise of a dream in which Toynbee had been warned of the intellectually stultifying consequences of becoming a university don.

Shortly before Toynbee told Burrows of this breakdown, Greek forces had landed in Smyrna, with the blessing of Britain, France and the United States. The ostensible pretext for this occupation was the protection of the Christian, and more particularly Greek, populations of western Asia Minor, pending the settlement with the Ottoman Empire at the Paris peace conference. It was also intended to pre-empt any Italian move northward from the region of Antalya, where Italy harboured territorial ambitions of its own. Burrows' initial delight at the news of the Greek landing was tempered by reports of the violence that had ensued, demonstrating that there were limits even to his philhellenism. Over 100 Turks had been killed and irreparable harm had been done to Greece's self-proclaimed 'civilising mission' in Asia Minor. Burrows wrote to Venizelos to express his alarm at what had happened, and the Greek prime minister had replied that the first he had heard of the shooting of Turkish prisoners by their Greek captors had come from Burrows himself.

Toynbee was fully recovered from his breakdown by the beginning of the autumn term of 1919 and duly delivered his inaugural lecture on 'The place of medieval and modern Greece in history'. The chair was taken by Gennadius who began the proceedings with an effusive tribute to Venizelos, who was present in the audience:

> our beloved and trusted great Leader, who has transformed our secular dreams into realities, who has raised Greece from ignominy to honour, and who has won for himself and for Greece, the appreciation, the respect, and the confidence of the civilized world.

He went on to take a swipe at the Catholic Church, arguing that the Byzantine Empire had saved 'the world from universal submission to the Papacy'. Toynbee was somewhat taken aback by the length of Gennadius' preamble, just as Burrows was rather perturbed by the density of Toynbee's argument in the inaugural. He feared that this might pass over the heads of his students at King's. In an interesting anticipation of one of the issues that were to concern him during his brief tenure of the Koraes chair, Toynbee observed that 'Greek statesmen will be exercised by the problem – which Turkey never attempted to solve – of enabling Europeans and Moslems to live together, not only as peaceful neighbours but as members of the same democracy'.

Of all his many academic initiatives at the college, which included the establishment of the School of Slavonic Studies, the Cervantes chair of Spanish and the Camoens chair of Portuguese, the founding of the Koraes chair was undoubtedly the most dear to Burrows. He must have been greatly pleased that the Koraes chair had not only been established but had been filled by such an outstanding a scholar as Toynbee. But soon after Toynbee's inaugural, Burrows underwent two operations for cancer. Within six months he was dead. Throughout this period his thoughts were very much with Greece. When, in May 1920, he learned that his cancer was inoperable he wrote an extraordinarily moving farewell letter to Venizelos. In this, he quoted in Greek from the *Nunc Dimittis* 'in all joy and solemnness'. He was delighted that the terms of the Treaty of Sèvres, of which he had just heard, had been agreed and that Venizelos was taking 'the good news in triumph back to Greece'. Venizelos had recreated 'a united Hellas' and Burrows had no doubt that he would sweep the polls at the forthcoming election (due to be held in November 1920), an expectation in which not only he but so many others were to be mistaken.

The Treaty of Sèvres envisaged the creation of what Venizelos' supporters optimistically proclaimed as the Greece of the 'two continents and the five seas' (Europe and Asia, and the Ionian, Aegean, Mediterranean, Marmara and Black seas). But the treaty was, from the outset, to prove a dead letter, for its acceptance by the supine government of the Sultan was repudiated by the Turkish nationalists. For the latter, under the leadership of Mustafa Kemal (subsequently Atatürk, the 'Father' of the Turks), the Greek occupation of western Asia Minor was to serve as a catalyst. Burrows' valedictory message to Venizelos continued: 'you are thank God, young and strong, and you can do such mighty things these next ten years if you have the whole nation behind you'. Burrows concluded by repeating his 'unbounded faith in you, my Pericles' and his love for 'Hellas as a whole': 'Goodbye, φίλε μου [my friend], and may you and Ελλάς sometimes think of me'. Just over a week later he was dead.

Universally esteemed within and outwith the college, Burrows' death was premature. But at least he died in the belief, albeit mistaken, that the 'Greater Greece' of which he and Venizelos had dreamed was about to be realised, and unaware of the fact that, within the space of a few years, his beloved Koraes chair would be in serious jeopardy. In 1928 a fitting memorial was established to him in the shape of the Burrows Library at King's College. The nucleus was formed by his own library and it remained a separate entity until the early 1990s, when it was merged with the main college library. It is the largest collection devoted to the study of the modern Greek world in a British university library. One happy consequence of my book about the Toynbee episode was that I was invited to write the entry on Burrows for the *Dictionary of National Biography*. In this I was pleased to pay tribute to an enthusiastic and entrepreneurial progenitor in the British university system of what subsequently became known as 'area studies', although I also pointed out that his naive philhellenism was to plunge the college into turmoil.

It is clear that Toynbee was not going to be overburdened with work as Koraes professor. Indeed, within less than a year of taking up the chair, he was to apply for study leave, hoping to see at firsthand 'how Greece is handling her Moslem minority'. In October 1920 he was granted leave by the Senate of the university to travel to Greece, there to establish connections 'with professors, officials and publishers in order to strengthen the bonds between Greece and the Department of Modern Greek in the College'. No reference appears to have been made to the fact that he was to act as a special correspondent of the *Manchester Guardian*. Always careful in money matters, Toynbee subsequently calculated that, between 7 January 1921 when he left London, and 20 September, when he returned, he had made a profit of £5 17s 4½d through his journalistic endeavours. When he submitted his final accounts to the *Guardian* in September 1921, the paper's accountant congratulated him on his 'beautifully rendered' expenses claims.

Toynbee duly arrived in Athens in mid-January 1921, just a few weeks after Venizelos' defeat in the elections of November 1920. He stayed at the British School. The strictures about Students of the School, as they are known, commenting publicly on current Greek politics, which I encountered at the time of the Colonels' dictatorship in the late 1960s and early 1970s, were either in abeyance or were not enforced in the 1920s, for Toynbee was soon off to investigate the situation on the ground in the territories administered by Greece in Asia Minor. He received telegrams from the *Manchester Guardian* addressed to him at the School, while at the same time he was also careful to acquire, as a Student of the School, the useful perk of a free pass to museums and archaeological sites.

By the end of January, Toynbee was in Smyrna, from where over the next three months he made three forays into the hinterland to see how well Greece was administering an ethnically mixed population. It was while visiting Ephesus in February 1921 that he had another of his baffling visions. In the ancient theatre he saw two 'dishevelled figures' who, he wrote, must have been Gaius and Aristarchus, and an 'ineffectual-looking creature' who must have been Alexander:

> but at the moment when the cries of 'Great is Diana' are dying down [...] the life flickers out of the scene as the spectator is carried up again instantaneously to the current surface of the Time-stream from an abyss, 19 centuries deep into which the impact of the sight of the theatre at Ephesus had plunged him.

Although conscious of the pattern of reprisal and counter reprisal that followed from the violence that had accompanied the Greek landings in Smyrna, Toynbee believed that, on the Greek side at least, this had only become organised in late March or early April of 1921, in the wake of the battle of İnönü, in which the Turks had put up fierce resistance to a Greek offensive which had eventually failed. By this time, Toynbee had moved from Smyrna to Constantinople and had been joined by his wife, Rosalind. From Constantinople they were able to make a number of forays into areas where Greeks and Turks had clashed on the southern shores of the sea of Marmara. Here, in the Yalova-Gemlik region, they were confronted with firsthand evidence of Greek atrocities.

In later life, Toynbee recalled how, in his view, the Greek case was receiving more favourable publicity in Britain than the Turkish. Obedient to the precept *audi alteram partem* (listen to the other side), he had therefore been determined to get an insight into the conflict from the Turkish viewpoint. But he had run up against a wall of suspicion and hostility from the Turks. It was known that in his wartime capacity as a government propagandist Toynbee had been harnessed to the British government's 'The Turk must go' campaign, directed by the novelist John Buchan, author of *The Thirty-Nine Steps* and *Greenmantle*. Toynbee was the author of propaganda tracts with lurid titles such as *The Murderous Tyranny of the Turks* (1917). Moreover, he had compiled the government Blue Book on Turkish maltreatment of the Armenians (1916) on behalf of Lord Bryce, a Gladstonian figure if ever there was one. Moreover, Toynbee was now a professor of modern Greek studies and, furthermore, a correspondent for that most Gladstonian of newspapers, the *Manchester Guardian*. It is clear that, a century later, Toynbee's work on the Armenian atrocities, which has frequently been used to help sustain the view that the terrible events of 1915 amounted to genocide, still rankles with the Turkish establishment. As recently as 2005, the Turkish Grand National Assembly, in a letter to the British parliament, called on Westminster to dissociate itself from Bryce and Toynbee's Blue Book, while in 2000 an Armenian-American institute reprinted the original, redacted version of the Blue Book with the addition, *inter alia*, of the names of hitherto anonymous informants where these are now available.

After a number of unprofitable interviews with Hamid Bey, the director of the Red Crescent in Constantinople, Toynbee was challenged at short notice to sail to Yalova on a Red Crescent ship. On his return, he showed Hamid Bey the text of a telegram he was about to send to the *Manchester Guardian*. Hamid was overjoyed that the Turkish case was at last being heard. He was even more delighted when, some days later, Toynbee was able to show Hamid a copy of the newspaper containing his despatch. Almost 50 years later, Toynbee recalled in *Acquaintances* the scene in the Red Crescent offices: 'big Hamid Bey with the English newspaper in his hands, and his colleagues crowding round, with radiant faces. Their case was being put in Britain at last'. An example of the kind of despatch that proved so gratifying to Hamid Bey and his colleagues appeared in the *Manchester Guardian* on 21 May 1921. In this, Toynbee warned that, in the Yalova district, the entire Muslim population was being 'terrorised and in daily danger of death'. The 'malignity and inhumanity' of the local Greek military authorities was undisguised: 'if Greece values her status as a civilised nation her government must stop the atrocities, dismiss the officers implicated, and facilitate the alleviation of the pitiable conditions of the victims'.

Toynbee's wife, Rosalind, was, if anything, even more outraged than her husband by what she had witnessed. She wrote a long account, sending it to her mother for circulation in the influential circles in which she moved. The Cretan captain in charge of the Greek forces at Yalova was, Rosalind wrote, 'more like a stage brigand than I could have believed possible – a face so full of undisguised and uncontrolled malignity I have never seen'. She described a crowd of Turkish women surrounded by a mob of 'diabolical "Christians" threatening and jeering'. She was bitterly critical of British policy which, she believed, was 'quite evidently to shield the Greeks in every possible way [...] partly from the confused idea that they must be better really than the Turks'. To her father, Gilbert Murray, Rosalind wrote that the representative of the International Red Cross had been 'absolutely overwhelmed by what he had seen – the methodical and diabolical system of extermination of the whole Moslem population'. She wrote that not only the Greek military and the *chetis* (bands of, in this case Greek, irregulars) but 'all the Christian population, Greeks and Armenians alike, had somehow become semi-human. They had ghastly bestial faces as though they had been drinking blood: the whole crowd often seemed demoniac'. It was a scene out of Conrad: 'as though all men were gradually changing back into wild beasts that were obscene and unnatural, and beyond belief'.

Toynbee saw himself as not merely as a historian-cum-journalist, recording the scenes that he had observed for posterity. He did what he could personally to alleviate the suffering that he had witnessed, which led T.S. Eliot sneeringly to dismiss him as 'a noxious humanitarian'. For instance, he sent a telegram to the Greek commander-in-chief and secured his express order for the evacuation of three villages, claiming to his mother that he had 'personally saved 700 people'. He saw himself, moreover, as someone who was uniquely placed to help broker peace between the warring armies. As he wrote in June 1921 to his mother, he was

> now about the only Englishman who is both in the confidence of the Turks and in touch with the F[oreign] O[ffice], and peace between London and Angora is the key to general peace out here, and to the end of this massacre, devastation and economic ruin.

'If I can do the slightest bit towards bringing this about,' he added, 'it is up to me to put everything else aside – as in fact I am doing'. In May 1921, he wrote, probably to a former colleague in the Foreign Office, that it was

> literally true that millions worth of economic loss is being suffered, thousands of people are dying, and hundreds of thousands being made acutely miserable in the Near East because half-a-dozen people in London and Paris quite genuinely cannot spare half-a-dozen hours to discuss the Near Eastern question.

He was determined to do his best to ensure that they should, outlining his own ideas for such a settlement in the *Manchester Guardian*.

He relished trying to make, as well as comment on, history, as when he spent an evening, in April 1923, with a Mustafa Kemal (Atatürk) well lubricated with whisky. Toynbee appears to have found Kemal as magnetic a personality as Burrows had found Venizelos. Kemal, as he wrote to Rosalind, was 'undoubtedly a great man'. He gave the impression of being 'different from the rest', a quality that he believed to be a 'sure outward sign of being genuinely something beyond the ordinary'. In appearance, he added, you would swear that he was an Austrian or German, which he seems to have regarded as a compliment. Toynbee was well aware that atrocities were also being committed on the Turkish side, but the fact that he did not personally witness these seems to have diminished their impact on him. As he conceded in correspondence with John Mavrogordato, a scholar and prominent member of the Anglo-Greek community, he had considerably less information about what was happening on the Turkish side of the front. Moreover, he believed that the Greeks had begun the cycle of atrocity and counter-atrocity. He believed that a new chapter 'much more systematic and official' had begun in April 1921 when the Greeks had failed in their initial attempt to capture Eskişehir, whereas, from what he had heard from American relief workers who had been in Nationalist territory, similar atrocities had begun on the Nationalist side only in July. 'I hope you don't feel that I have simply turned from a "pro-Greek" into a "pro-Turk". I was never pro-Greek in "my country, right or wrong" sense, and I don't think I am a pro-Turk in that sense now'. Having helped to expose atrocities committed by the Turks during the course of the First War, he felt in honour bound to do the same when the Turks themselves had become victims. He was taking the line that he did because he believed that Greece was currently in the wrong: 'when the Cyprus question comes up, you will find me taking up the cudgels for Greece'. This he was indeed to do, demonstrating sympathy for the *enosist* aspirations of the islanders, as in a long article in the Chatham House *Survey of International Affairs* for 1931.

He told Mavrogordato that he was intending to turn a series of public lectures that he had been giving at King's College into a book. Written at tremendous speed, this, *The Western Question in Greece and Turkey: A Study in the Contact of Civilizations* (1922), was what some (myself included) consider to be the best book in his vast oeuvre. In it he sought to demonstrate the corrosive effects of nationalism, a European construct, on traditional societies such as the Ottoman Empire. One point he tried to get across was that it would be a serious error to assume that the Turks were more unrighteous than the Greeks. In support of his argument he deployed a rather curious calculus. It was true, he conceded, that the Turks had committed more atrocities against the Greeks than had the Greeks against the Turks. But this was because, between 1461 (the date of the fall of the Empire of Trebizond) and 1821, the beginning of the Greek war of independence, almost all Greeks had been under Ottoman rule, whereas the Greeks had held sway over sizeable numbers of Turks only since 1912. To those who would dispute his argument, he suggested that the total number of atrocities inflicted by Greeks and Turks against each other be divided by the number of opportunities to inflict them, the result to be weighted, if possible, by the strength of the stimulus in each case.

One of the fundamental points that Toynbee sought to get across in *The Western Question* was that the Greeks were no more capable of administering Asia Minor well than the Turks had been in administering Macedonia well after 1878. Greece had proved as incapable as Turkey, or indeed any Western country, of the good government of 'a mixed population containing an alien majority and a minority of her own nationality'. Toynbee was fully aware that his journalistic despatches from the Asia Minor front, together with the more academic strictures about Greek policies contained in *The Western Question*, were likely to provoke fierce controversy and profoundly upset those who had contributed to the establishment of his chair. In fact, he had offered his resignation to Ernest Barker, Burrows' successor as principal of King's, by the same post in May 1921 in which he had first reported on Greek atrocities to the *Manchester Guardian*. He repeated the offer a year later, when *The Western Question* was published, while pointing out that such a resignation would constitute 'a considerable disaster' for him personally as he had a young family to support. On neither occasion did Barker, a resolute champion of Toynbee's academic freedom, remotely consider the possibility of his resignation. Toynbee had submitted the preface to *The Western Question* to Barker in advance of publication for his comments, some of which he accepted, some of which he did not. He took Barker's point that it was important not to give the impression that he had been given leave of absence by the college and university specifically to study the crisis in Asia Minor.

When Toynbee had first broached the issue of leave of absence, in August of 1920, less than a year after he had taken up the chair, he had anticipated that Venizelos would stay in power for the foreseeable future and had not expected to be a witness to Greek atrocities. Although Barker was unwavering in his support for Toynbee's freedom of speech, there were nonetheless signs of nervousness on his part. In April 1922, he had suggested to Toynbee, not '*ex cathedra, sed tanquam amicus*' (not in my official capacity but rather as a friend), that he should sign letters to newspapers, but, not 'unless you feel you must', newspaper or magazine articles. But, he insisted, he was not concerned about the views of the Greek government. He knew that Toynbee was simply concerned to tell the truth and he was more than content with whatever action he took in achieving this end.

In the revised preface, Toynbee sought to anticipate some of the criticisms that he knew would be made of *The Western Question*. He accepted that the fact that he was neither a Greek nor a Turk created no presumption of his being fair-minded for, as he pertinently observed, 'Western partisans of non-Western peoples are often more fanatical than their favourites'. He went on to maintain that, while it might be painful to Greeks and philhellenes that material unfavourable to Greece should have been published by the first holder of the Koraes chair, nonetheless 'from an academic point of view' that was less unfortunate than if his findings on Greek behaviour in Asia Minor had been favourable to Greece and unfavourable to Turkey. At least this precluded any 'suspicion that an endowment of learning in a British University has been used for propaganda on behalf of the country with which it is concerned'.

Toynbee's book was published in the early summer of 1922. This was only a few months before the rout of the Greek armies in Asia Minor, the burning of much of 'Gâvur İzmir', or 'Infidel Smyrna', and the subsequent uprooting, in the exchange of populations, of the many Greek communities, some of which had been settled in Asia Minor for thousands of years. Many Armenians likewise fell victim to the Turks. The book's topicality ensured that it was widely reviewed and the reviews were almost universally favourable. The anonymous reviewer (in fact Harry Pirie-Gordon, scholar and spy) in the *Times Literary Supplement*, for instance, wrote that Toynbee proceeds 'to demolish the theories of the Philhellenes, who affect to maintain that the sons of Pericles can do no wrong, no less than those of the equally stubborn adherents of the dogma that the Turk is a gentleman'. Both sides would be able to quarry what they wanted from the book.

In Greek circles, however, unsurprisingly it was not well received. One hastily composed tract, by Major G. Melas, formerly a secretary to ex-king Constantine I, and published in the unlikely town of Hove in the same year as *The Western Question*, was a swingeing attack on Toynbee and his 'unsatiated hatred' of the Greeks. He insinuated that this 'blind disciple' of Jakob Philipp Fallmerayer, the Austrian hellenist who had maintained that not a drop of pure (ancient) Greek blood flowed in the veins of the modern Greeks, had been bought by the Turks. Toynbee did not help matters by initially suggesting that it was the Greeks rather than the Turks that had set fire to Smyrna, although he was subsequently to back down on this claim.

The first hint that trouble lay ahead for Toynbee in the college came when the Greek subscribers held, in January 1923, what appears to have been their first meeting since the establishment of the chair. Clearly aware that a frontal assault on Toynbee's views on the Asia Minor catastrophe, in many of which he had been proved right, might prove difficult to sustain, the subscribers instead concentrated their fire on Toynbee's failure to provide the committee with either the annual scheme of work of the department or the triennial report 'with a request for criticism and suggestions' that had been a condition of the endowment. The four subscribers present, who included Gennadius and Eumorfopoulos, resolved to request the two documents. This was not only the first intimation that Toynbee had of the conditions attaching to the chair but it was also Principal Barker's. When Barker received the committee's request, he wrote to Toynbee that he could count on him absolutely to back his espousal of views unpalatable to the donors, for he valued academic freedom more than most things. That freedom it seemed to him 'to have been entirely sacrificed at the time of the foundation of the Chair which you hold'. He believed that the position he and Toynbee found themselves in to be nothing short of tragic. Nonetheless, he wrote, invoking words of Lady Macbeth, 'what *is* done is done' and they had no option but to comply with the request. Toynbee, advised by Murray, promptly agreed to submit the required material, while both he and Barker insisted that they had been quite unaware of the subscribers' stipulation.

Others have noted that Toynbee was highly sensitive to criticism, but he lost no time in preparing a substantial document of some ten typewritten pages. In this he gave details of his various academic activities since his appointment to the chair and, as had been originally requested by the Subscribers' Committee, invited suggestions and criticisms. Somewhat disingenuously, Toynbee wrote of his time in Asia Minor, which had given rise to the ensuing furore, that, thanks to the leave of absence that he had been granted during the second and third terms of the 1920/1 session, he had been able to increase his knowledge of the Greek lands 'by travelling in and around Smyrna and Constantinople', which he had never before visited. He did not mention that he was contracted as a journalist to the *Manchester Guardian* during the period in question, although he made no secret of the fact in the preface to *The Western Question*, pointing out that the status of special correspondent had opened doors that would otherwise have been closed.

In deciding how to confront King's College, a furious row now broke out among the subscribers. A draft of a letter among Gennadius' papers was bitterly critical of Toynbee, referring to his 'unmeasured abuse' of the Greeks, and saying that even in the United States he was known as the 'unofficial advocate' of the Kemalists. He had employed 'every device known to professional propagandists in decrying, defaming and damaging the cause of the Greek people'. He had suppressed the fact that the acts that he denounced were 'really the reprisals of a people goaded to desperation by centuries of unrelenting oppression'. While enjoying emoluments from a Greek foundation he had accused the Greeks of themselves burning Smyrna. Moreover, he had been unwilling to jeopardise his position as a mediator by drawing attention to atrocities, and there were many, committed by the Turks. In short, Gennadius' draft letter continued, Toynbee had shown 'blatant contempt' for the 'unwritten law governing the conduct of gentlemen'.

Eumorfopoulos, who had been in contact by letter with Toynbee during the growing crisis in a reasoned and non-confrontational fashion, reported to the subscribers' committee that William Pember Reeves of the LSE had recommended toning down Gennadius' draft letter and proposed an alternative draft which closely followed Pember Reeves' critique of Toynbee's report to the subscribers. In this version, the subscribers declared themselves to be 'somewhat embarrassed in endeavouring to understand a mentality which finds it possible to consider the political activities' to which they had adverted as compatible with holding the Koraes chair. The subscribers did not dispute the professor's right to his political views. Nonetheless, 'the persistent purpose of injuring national causes dear to the heart of all Greeks and of promoting the interests of her enemies [...] has caused bitter exasperation among Greeks and their friends'.

Gennadius emphatically did not agree with Eumorfopoulos' toned-down letter and complained that the revised draft had emasculated his original version 'to such a degree as to suppress all reference to the grave charge broadcast against us Greeks that it was we who set fire to Smyrna'. Gennadius argued against any delay in sending a reply so as not to give Toynbee any 'respite for the staging of his new impersonation as an ardent Philhellene', a reference to Toynbee's calling for Cyprus and the Dodecanese to be incorporated in the Greek kingdom. Eumorfopoulos' response was to offer to resign from the subscriber's committee, while Gennadius, in his turn, himself threatened to storm off in a huff. In the end, both remained on the committee. It was Eumorfopoulos' view that eventually prevailed, and the committee placed much emphasis on what it considered to be Toynbee's neglect of his academic duties. But Toynbee's political views were by no means ignored. Toynbee, the subscribers maintained, had demonstrated a 'pronounced hostility' towards Greece and his attitude had amounted to an 'unequivocal advocacy of the enemies of Greece in the Middle East'. He had emerged as one the 'bitterest critics' of the Greeks, scarcely to be distinguished from the 'professional advocates' of Turkey. They reproached him for maintaining that it was the Greeks who had burned Smyrna, 'the native town of Koraes himself', and for his failure to comment on the uprooting of 'a million and a half souls in circumstances of unexampled barbarity', a reference to those caught up in the exchange of populations between Greece and Turkey. The Koraes endowment had proved during Toynbee's tenure of the chair to be 'a prolific source of injury to Greece'. Although Toynbee was subsequently to change his mind on the burning of Smyrna, by then the damage had been done, while his critics accused him of failure to react appropriately to the enormity of the human consequences of the 'catastrophe', the Greek débâcle in Asia Minor.

Consulted by Toynbee, Murray counselled that the subscribers' letter was intended to make him resign. Therefore, he should think twice before making the natural riposte which would be 'take your damned chair and give it to a Greek propagandist'. To Barker, however, Murray wrote that he had been having doubts as to whether Toynbee should remain as Koraes professor: 'though his intellectual judgement is, I think, remarkably impartial, his emotional sympathies are with the Turks rather than with the Greeks'. It was, he believed, quite natural for the donors to 'feel hurt or ill-treated'. Even his mother, herself a highly educated woman, reproached him that he might be 'a little obsessed with your Turks'.

Barker now consulted with the Delegacy (the governing body) of King's College and with the Senate of the university. Cooper Perry, the principal of the university, in replying to the subscribers, made it clear that that it was against the 'spirit and tradition' of university life to interfere with the political opinions of professors. Nonetheless, Toynbee had offered to place his resignation at the Senate's disposal. It would now be open to the subscribers either to withdraw the endowment from the university or to change the conditions attaching to the chair. Barker meanwhile sent the subscribers a spirited defence of Toynbee's academic work. After a delay occasioned by the summer holidays, the subscribers wrote to Cooper Perry to say that they entertained the confident hope that Toynbee's resignation had been accepted. Toynbee now had little alternative but to go ahead with his resignation, although he reserved the right to make public his reasons for doing so.

At this time, Barker was coming under pressure from a group within the college, led by R.W. Seton-Watson, to try to salvage the chair and not to return the endowment if Toynbee resigned, as Barker had originally agreed with Toynbee and Murray. Seton-Watson acted in part out of loyalty to the memory of Burrows, with whom the foundation of the chair had been so closely associated. It had been, in the words of Burrows' biographer, George Glasgow, Burrows' 'pet creation'. Less creditably, Seton-Watson and his supporters feared lest the dispute with the Greek subscribers should threaten the edifice of subsidy by foreign governments on which the School of Slavonic Studies at King's was in part based. The Czech government, for instance, besides its support for Seton-Watson's own Masaryk chair, provided funding for a lectureship in Czech and Slovak. The newly created Kingdom of the Serbs, Croats and Slovenes, before long to metamorphose into Yugoslavia, had funded the lectureship in Serbo-Croat, while the Polish government had underwritten a post in Polish. Remarkably, at the height of the Toynbee controversy, Barker and Seton-Watson were negotiating with the Romanian government for a subsidy to support a lectureship in the history of Romania and the Near East, together with a part-time lectureship in Romanian.

Seton-Watson in fact regarded the conditions attached to the Koraes chair by the subscribers as not unreasonable, and sought a way of repairing what he deemed to be Toynbee's deplorable blunder. 'The very idea that the University or College,' he wrote, 'could repudiate its obligations towards Greece, simply because the candidate it appointed conducted an active political campaign against Greece and so found himself in an untenable position is one which I do not like to contemplate'. He felt 'exceedingly sorry' for Toynbee, but did not think that he had a leg to stand on. Barker, in turn, told Toynbee that he was torn between two conflicting emotions. On the one hand there was 'the desire to vindicate you and the principles for which you have stood (even though, as I must frankly confess, I think you have carried it a long way)'. On the other, there was 'the desire to maintain a chair, *provided it is a free chair*, which deals with Byzantine and Modern Greek History and Literature'. At the same time, the Delegacy discussed the future of the chair, and considered whether, if the endowment were returned to the donors, it might be used to fund a position in language and literature, thus eschewing the explosive potential of history.

In searching for a compromise, Principal Barker met with the subscribers, but they maintained a hard line in their unwillingness to drop the 'obnoxious conditions' attaching to the chair. When Burrows' widow, Una, met with Gennadius, and, in her anxiety to ensure the continuance of the chair, suggested that the subscribers make some concessions, Gennadius was unmoved. Toynbee could not, he said, be allowed to resign 'with colours flying'. He was all for some kind of condign condemnation of Toynbee: an 'unchequed [sic], vitious [sic] and malevolent attack is not liberty but abuse of speech'. The onus of a 'just and satisfactory' solution rested squarely with the university authorities. The 'savage, perfidious and dishonourable propaganda' directed against the Greek people by a man 'who first became known on his appointment to a Greek chair and on his receiving a Greek salary' must first 'be settled on its own merits'. Quite what Gennadius had in mind here was not clear, but he was manifestly after some sort of public reprimand for Toynbee or his dismissal.

Toynbee duly submitted his resignation to the university. His next step was to publicise this decision through a letter to *The Times*. This was published on 3 January 1924 alongside a letter from Barker to Toynbee. In his letter, Toynbee recorded that during the course of a visit to the Near East in 1921 he had felt it his duty to comment publicly 'in a strongly unfavourable sense' on the behaviour of the Greek authorities in Asia Minor, although he barely touched on his role as a special correspondent of the *Manchester Guardian*. He had since given free public expression to his opinions as the situation had developed, believing this to be his right as a professor in a British university. It had been clear to him, however, that such action might affect the interests of the college and university. For this reason, by the same post which contained his first despatches unfavourable to Greece, he had offered his resignation, making it clear that he would resign at any time if the situation became too embarrassing. He had not known that the donors retained some legal control over the endowment, and had learned of the stipulations they had attached to it only in the fourth year of his tenure of the Koraes chair. Had he learned of these conditions at the time of his appointment he would have followed another career. Had he learned of them at Yalova on 24 May 1921 then he would have done 'precisely what I have done since then'. He concluded with a passage in Greek by Polybius, 'a very much more eminent historian' than himself and written more than 2,000 years ago, to the effect that it was the duty of the chronicler of public affairs to tell the truth and not to cover up the faults of the Greeks. *The Times* did not publish this quotation. Barker in his letter of 26 December 1923, printed alongside Toynbee's, confirmed that ever since Toynbee had begun to write about events in Asia Minor he had always been prepared to offer his resignation.

Once Toynbee's resignation, to take effect from July 1924, had been announced it was inevitable that public controversy should ensue. George Glasgow, Burrows' biographer, who was later to marry Burrows' widow, Una, was quick off the mark with a letter criticising Toynbee in *The Times*. Toynbee, Glasgow wrote, had every right to attack Greece at any time, but he should surely have resigned the moment he started to do so. The following passage, so Gennadius was informed, had been omitted from Glasgow's letter: 'Mr Toynbee actively contributed to a Greek disaster, one of the most tragic in Greek history, and was able to do so precisely because of the prestige he derived from holding the Greek chair'. But much of the press comment on the affair was sympathetic to Toynbee. E.N. Bennett, sometime Fellow of Hertford College, Oxford, was scathing in the *Observer* about the university for granting to 'a body of foreigners' the virtual right to dismiss a professor because of his 'private opinions on political or international questions', while the *Yorkshire Post* denounced the University of London as 'a stronghold of Grecophilism'.

An anonymous editorial in *The Nation and the Athenaeum* came out strongly in support of Toynbee. This, not entirely accurately, maintained that Toynbee had initially declined to apply for the chair in part because in chairs 'founded by the natives of particular countries for the study of those countries there was sure to be an element of propaganda, which would be incompatible with the necessary freedom of the Professor's teaching'. Toynbee was 'an historian and scholar of unusual brilliance', whom it would be utterly unfair to describe as anti-Greek. Since being appointed, he had written in favour of the *enosis*, or union, of Cyprus and the Italian-occupied Dodecanese with Greece; he had been active in seeking help for the Greek refugees from Asia Minor; and he had supported Greece when Mussolini had bombarded and briefly occupied Corfu in 1923. Nonetheless, 'on the one great question about which all the emotions of Greece were aroused', the Koraes professor 'had pronounced against the beliefs and wishes of Greek patriots'. The anonymous author went on to say that it was an 'invariable and almost sacred rule in all self-respecting Universities that, when once money is given to the University for scientific purposes, it belongs absolutely to the University and the donor retains no control or power of interference'. The force of this editorial was somewhat diminished by the fact that it had been written by Gilbert Murray, who, of course, was Toynbee's father-in-law. Toynbee's mother was rather disappointed to learn this, as she hoped it had been written by an outsider and dispassionate critic: 'of course we will be secret: it would be injurious if it leaked out'.

If Toynbee thought that his critics within the college had been stilled for the remaining months before his resignation took effect then he was mistaken. Seton-Watson, on seeing Toynbee's letter in *The Times*, wrote to Barker to say that he had not expected the principal to have been treated with such a lack of consideration and common decency. He regarded the writing of such a letter as 'quite abominable'. Those with whom he had discussed the matter in the college were likewise appalled by Toynbee's behaviour. These had included Bernard Pares, the Professor of Russian History, and A.P. Newton, the Rhodes Professor of Imperial History. To this Barker responded by saying that he had not regretted either his action or inaction in the past:

> if I had put pressure on Toynbee, I should have done worse than I did by not putting pressure on him. I was in a dilemma, and I chose the less of two wrongs – the wrong of interfering with a professor, and the wrong of letting the holder of a Greek chair continue to attack the Greek cause.

Seton-Watson also wrote to Toynbee to say that he regarded his letter in *The Times* as 'an open declaration of war'. In a draft of this letter he wrote that in his opinion Toynbee had shown 'an utter disregard for [the] interests of [the] University and College and [of] your own chair and have cruelly compromised Barker'.

In January 1924, a meeting, which verged on a kangaroo court, was held in the college in connection with the row. At one stage it was proposed that no discussion be allowed. Glasgow, who had been supplying Seton-Watson with 'ammunition' for the onslaught on Toynbee, suggested that his critics should turn up at the meeting and ask whether comments were to be allowed. If not, they should ceremoniously walk out before Toynbee made his statement: 'won't this be more effective than simply staying away? This is just a suggestion which I quite see may appear brutal, but my blood is up'.

Murray tried to take the heat out of the situation by having a meeting with two of Toynbee's severest critics on the British side, Glasgow and Seton-Watson. The latter, in agreeing to a meeting with Murray, repeated his view that Toynbee's behaviour had been 'altogether scandalous and unjustifiable […] at the supreme crisis in the fate of the Greek nation – probably without exaggeration the most decisive since Xerxes'. Toynbee 'had plunged into a violent propagandist campaign in favour of the Turks'. It had been wholly wrong to agitate against the nation which had created his post. He believed that because the dispute involved a small country and 'a minor subject of study', the university had failed to act against him. Had, say, Spanish or Italian chairs been involved, their respective ambassadors or, so he alarmingly believed, the Foreign Office, would have intervened. At the same time, Murray had correspondence with Burrows' widow, who held that Toynbee's behaviour was tantamount to 'hitting below the belt – which is not done'. At a meeting of the Senate of the university in December 1923, Sir Wilmot Herringham, a distinguished, albeit blimpish, physician and a former vice-chancellor of the university, had made an angry riposte to a speech in defence of Toynbee. This began 'if the freedom of a professor means the liberty to be a cad'. Another of Toynbee's critics on the Senate, Canon J.A. Douglas of the Crusade for the Redemption of Saint Sophia, which agitated for the restoration of the Emperor Justinian's great church in Constantinople to Christian worship, denounced Toynbee in print as a 'fugelman', or mouthpiece, for the Kemalists.

The subscribers, with Gennadius in the lead, still wanted some kind of formal censure of Toynbee. At a meeting of the University Senate at the end of January 1924, the anti-Toynbee faction succeeded, by a majority of 16 to 12, in passing a resolution, after what was clearly an acrimonious debate, to the effect that it recognised that 'having regard to the conditions attached to the foundation of the Chair' the subscribers were 'fully justified in deploring the circumstances which have imperilled the continuance of the Koraes chair'. In sending Gennadius a copy of the Senate's formal reply to the subscribers' committee, which included the implicit censure of Toynbee, Cooper Perry, who was clearly anxious to save the chair, made his own feelings in the matter clear by telling Gennadius that he had been 'very badly treated and "wounded in the house of your friends"'.

When the Greek government, in protest at Toynbee's behaviour, withdrew its subsidy for the lectureship in modern Greek, Oeconomos lost his post. Toynbee made an effort to get another position for him, writing on his behalf to the president of Robert College (now Boğaziçi University) in Istanbul. The modern language does not appear to have been taught again in the University of London until the early 1970s, when, following agitation by Philip Sherrard and myself, a lectureship was created in modern Greek language and literature. This, like Sherrard's and my post, was a joint lectureship between the SSEES and King's College. The first holder of the new post was Peter Mackridge.

Many of the more virulent attacks on Toynbee came from members of the Greek community in England. This was scarcely surprising as the funding for the chair came from the community and its members were understandably angered by Toynbee's stance. One prominent Anglo-Greek, however, with whom Toynbee remained in contact throughout the crisis was John Mavrogordato, an alumnus of Eton and Oxford and later the Bywater and Sotheby professor at Oxford. Writing to Toynbee in September 1922, he wrote that, while he disagreed with a number of points that Toynbee had made in *The Western Question*, he nonetheless congratulated him on 'a remarkable and masterly performance – the best book yet written on the Near East'. While he greatly disagreed with some of it, nonetheless so strongly did he agree with Toynbee's general conclusions and with his 'moral of toleration and charity' that his chief feeling was one of gratitude. Moreover, he shared Toynbee's belief that 'if a holder of the Koraes chair is to touch politics at all it is preferable that he should NOT wear the uniform of a philhellene'. Nonetheless, he believed that Toynbee had often been 'very unjust to the Greeks'.

It is in correspondence between Toynbee and Mavrogordato that we get the fullest explanation of Toynbee's own view of the controversy. Peter Mackridge drew my attention to this exchange in the Mavrogordato archive now housed, like Toynbee's papers, in the Bodleian Library in Oxford. In May of 1923, soon after a meeting at which Toynbee had come under heavy criticism, Mavrogordato wrote to him to say that 'in effect but not in intention' he regarded Toynbee as 'definitely anti-Greek, sometimes quite outrageously unfair to the Greek point of view'. 'But', he added,

> I have always thought and always shall that the flagrant honesty of your intentions and the [word illegible ... quality?] of your historical work should be quite enough to secure a friendly reception for you in any civilised and learned society.

Mavrogordato continued that Toynbee's tenure of the chair was open to criticism, not because the professor should act as a paid Greek propagandist or in any way be inhibited from proclaiming the truth as he saw it, but rather because the Greek community was only persuaded *'with great difficulty'* (Mavrogordato's emphasis) to set up the chair instead of spending their money on political propaganda. He could not help fearing that never again would 'an English university get an endowment of any sort out of the Greek community', although he was only guessing that this would be the case. No subscriber to the Koraes chair fund had actually said as much to him.

Mavrogordato could not help feeling that the literary and philological side was to some degree being neglected in favour of international affairs and that the professor might do well by confining his attention to academic subjects, rather in the way that A.M. Andreades (the economic historian and the author of a history of the Bank of England) had done during the First War, pleading that he was a university professor. He was said to be 'the only man in Athens who was neither a Constantinist [a supporter of King Constantine I] nor a Venizelist'. But such criticisms were not enough, in Mavrogordato's opinion, to justify any change in the Koraes professorship. For some years, in writing of Balkan affairs, Mavrogordato had made a practice of writing in favour of Greece without casting aspersions on other nations. As a consequence he had never made any kind of accusations, and had avoided altogether 'the subjects of massacres and atrocities'. Just the previous week he had invited the Balkan Committee to join him in such a self-denying ordinance.

Toynbee replied that he had tried to act on the principle of causing

> the least possible embarrassment to the University, firstly by not sitting tight if they wanted me to go, but secondly [...] by not forcing upon them, by creating a precedent, the principle that the professor of a modern study can only hold his chair so long as he speaks and writes in favour of the nation with which that study is connected.

If he had resigned against their judgement he would be affecting the position of colleagues as well as his own: 'so, while taking any odium upon myself, I shall continue to be guided by their judgement as regards my tenure of the chair'. The question of neglecting literary and philological issues in favour of historical and political ones was simpler to answer because he had had the matter out with Burrows at the outset. When the chair had originally been established he had decided not to stand as his training and interests covered only part of the field, although Burrows had urged him to reconsider and several months later he had decided to stand but on the condition, accepted by Burrows, that he would be allowed to specialise in history and politics. On the day of his interview, he felt that this principle had not been clearly established so he had offered to withdraw but Burrows had reaffirmed that such a specialisation would be acceptable. On this point, Toynbee believed himself to be 'absolutely clear', although he could not make it public for he could not bring himself to drag in 'poor Burrows'. There was the additional, practical point that while there was little demand in the university for language and literature there was a genuine demand for history ('interpreted broadly, so as to take in the whole Near East') and in this area he had been 'slowly but steadily gaining ground'.

If the Greek community, Toynbee continued, had wanted to derive political profit from their endowment ('which was of course a perfectly proper and legitimate aim') they were unwise to donate to a British university, given that academic freedom was a long-standing convention. His correspondence had been conducted 'entirely with Burrows, and to this day [he had] no notion whom the subscribers' committee consists of or what the circumstances were which led to the foundation of the Chair'. He did blame Burrows: 'for it was his business to make sure that both the subscribers and I knew exactly how we stood – they, in giving their money, and I in applying for the chair'. He did not know how Burrows had represented the chair to the subscribers (he had, as we have seen, offered them what was, in effect, a chair of propaganda) but, so far as Toynbee was concerned, he had told Burrows that he 'was neither Philhellene nor anti-Greek [a questionable assertion, as we shall see], but deeply interested in Near Eastern history and politics'. Moreover, when, after the election, he had heard an unpleasant rumour that the subscribers had been unhappy with the outcome, Burrows had assured him that they had nothing to do with what was purely a university matter. Neither the university's official announcement of the chair nor Burrows' letters to him had given any hint that the chair was 'technically or morally on a different footing from any other chair in the University'.

Toynbee in the early summer of 1923 could not foretell whether he would be able to remain in the chair, but he hoped that he would, as he felt that he could do useful work both inside and outside the university on near eastern history and politics, for these were going to be vitally important for England during his and Mavrogordato's lifetime. On the whole he expected his personal position to become easier, for he considered that the end of a chapter had been reached and 'when the next opens, the relationships of the characters may all be reversed!': 'indeed, I don't despair if I have time, of justifying my tenure, on the balance, even from the Greek community's point of view. But of course I may not have time'. What had really disturbed Toynbee had been Mavrogordato's feeling that he had failed, though unintentionally, to be fair to the Greek point of view: 'that is really alarming, for bona fide prejudice is the disease that devastates all Near Eastern Studies, and if once one catches it, one had better go on the scrap heap at once – which I don't at all want to do'. The beleaguered Toynbee concluded with more thanks for Mavrogordato's letter than he could express.

During the early 1920s, and particularly while Toynbee was in Asia Minor, one can see the genesis of his monumental 12-volume work, *A Study of History*, published between 1934 and 1961. As he wrote to his mother from Constantinople in June 1921, 'in these few months I have learnt things about life which illuminate the whole history of the N[ear] and M[iddle] East'. In May of the same year he had been able to give a short course of lectures at Robert College in Constantinople, in which he was able to develop his 'stunt' 'about civilisations being the smallest intelligible historical units'. While observing the current crisis in Asia Minor he was aware that it represented 'a historical problem throwing light on other historical problems back to 4000BC'. In his autobiographical *Experiences* (1969) he recorded that, on the Orient Express on his way back from Turkey to the United Kingdom in the autumn of 1921, he had sketched out on half a sheet of paper 'a dozen headings which turned out to be the subjects of the principal divisions' of the as yet unwritten *A Study of History*.

With Toynbee's resignation, an involuntary one as he was himself subsequently to describe it, the story ends. Later in 1924, however, there was a renewed flurry of interest in the controversy. When rumours had begun to circulate that Toynbee had accepted a post at the University of Istanbul, he sought to clear these up in another letter to *The Times*. What had happened is revealed in correspondence with Yusuf Kemal, the minister in London of the newly founded Turkish Republic. The latter had written to Toynbee in March to say that the Minister of Public Instruction was anxious to engage the services of foreign scholars. Toynbee was a natural choice, Yusuf Kemal wrote, for he was unanimously loved and esteemed in Turkey both for his services to the Turkish cause and on account of the *éclat* of his teaching in British universities. Toynbee had replied that he had been both touched and greatly honoured by the minister's letter. He much appreciated the invitation on account of his own feelings towards Turkey and the Turkish people. He was currently doing some work for the British (subsequently Royal) Institute of International Affairs (Chatham House). This might result in his being offered a permanent position, but, if not, then 'the attraction which I feel in any case for the Ministry's generous offer would remain'. He therefore asked that the offer be held open for a year. He was contemplating asking for a salary of £1,200 per annum, tax free, twice what he had been receiving at King's College. In the end, however, alternative employment opened up for him at Chatham House. Interestingly, Muallim Cevdet, a prominent Turkish teacher and educationist, writing in the mid-1920s, drew attention to the way in which rich Greeks had managed to extend their sway over foreign universities. They funded individuals who served the cultural, commercial and political interests of the Greeks; 'in the universities and colleges of London, Paris and Vienna there are chairs and research centres subsidised with Greek money'. He mentioned the case of Toynbee, whose chair had been founded with benefactions by rich Greeks, but who, when he began to speak up for the Turks, had been forced to resign.

Such, in outline, is the story of the establishment and rapid implosion of the Koraes chair. In the event, the subscribers did not withdraw their funding and the chair survived, if only narrowly. There is, however, a curious sequel to the story of Toynbee's tenure. In 1989, four years after the appearance of my study, William H. McNeill published his impressive authorised biography of Toynbee, *Arnold Toynbee: A Life*. As has been seen, pending the completion of this book I had been restricted in my access to those of Toynbee's papers relating directly to the controversy at King's College. But the closed files now became freely available and they revealed a facet of his character of which I had been unaware when I wrote my study, and one which gave a different complexion to the subsequent imbroglio. It was only on reading this material that I came to realise the full import of Toynbee's initial hesitation in applying for the Koraes chair. He had written, as I already knew, to Principal Burrows in September 1918 that he felt that the holder of the chair should be 'more of an active Philhellene' than he felt himself to be. To put it mildly, this turned out to be a serious understatement.

These further files throw revealing light on Toynbee's attitude to Greeks. If 'mishellenes' (Greek-haters) or 'anthellenes' (anti-Greeks) do indeed exist, then Toynbee, to judge by his letters to his mother written during his *Wanderjahr* in 1911-12, was one such. On graduating from Oxford he had been awarded a Craven scholarship and had spent the academic year in Greece before taking up the tutorial fellowship in ancient history to which he had been elected at a precociously young age, even before sitting his final examinations, by his old Oxford college, Balliol. On the evidence of these letters, he clearly should not have applied for the chair, so deeply was he out of sympathy with the aspirations of the people whose history he would be expected to profess. To have appointed a propagandist for the Greek cause, as Burrows wished, would likewise have been disastrous, but the holder of such a chair should surely have had a basic empathy for the people he studies rather than a positive dislike.

It was not merely that Toynbee was not 'particularly Philhellene'. After all, not a few nurtured on the classics before and since have shown themselves curiously resentful of the fact that the 'modern' Greeks bear little obvious resemblance to the idealised worthies of Periclean Athens whom they had been taught to revere.[3] As Toynbee himself was to write towards the end of his life, ancient Greece had been for him as a boy at Winchester 'a city of refuge from which one could keep the present-day world at bay'. But he harboured not merely a dislike of the present-day Greeks who appeared to threaten his refuge but a profound loathing.

What is especially remarkable about Toynbee's mishellenism is both the intensity of his dislike of Greeks and the extraordinary rapidity with which it developed. He had, he records, arrived in Greece in November 1911, bent on seeing 'the best' in the Greeks and determined not to succumb to the prevailing prejudice that existed among the Students of the British School [of Archaeology] at Athens. This could be summed up as 'all Levantines are "dagos" in their language, and the would-be cultured among them "black coats"'. Within days of arriving in the country, and before he had a chance to make even the most cursory acquaintance with its people, he was writing from Naxos to his mother, with all the self-assured arrogance of a precociously brilliant 22-year-old educated at Winchester and Balliol, that the Greeks were the 'hangers-on of Europe, and come to us for their models in everything – and their best is always a second rate imitation of our second best'. He had a 'rather pathetic' encounter with the local schoolmaster in Naxos, who spoke in a French a good deal better than Toynbee's own, and wore 'a European cloth cap and overcoat'. The reason he thought this to be rather pathetic was that here was a man 'trying to be educated and up-to-date in a place no European had been to for two years (why should they go there?)'. Within three weeks of reaching Greece he had come to the conclusion that the Greeks were 'dreadful'. In contrast, he found the *Arvanites*, the Orthodox Christians of Albanian descent and language who had settled in Attica, Boeotia and Argolis, to be 'white men, with fair hair and square faces – far superior to these half-baked, flabby cheeked Greeks'.

The indolence, as he saw it, of present-day Greeks was an affront to the hyperactive Toynbee, who is reckoned to have hiked some 3,000 miles during his time at, or more accurately out of, the British School, in expeditions lasting between two and 25 days. Toynbee was not amused by what he termed the 'café-loafing' of the locals: 'at 11 a.m. you will find all the men in a village sitting in front of the café doing nothing: they have been there since 5 a.m. and will stay there till their siesta, whereafter they will return for the evening'. As he wrote to his mother, barely a month after arriving, he would have liked to install 'a government of Englishmen' in the country so as to 'dragoon these café loafers (who might make more wealth even out of this stony country, if they worked)'. There was no 'meaning' (what he implied by this is not clear) in present-day Greeks as there was in England, Germany, Russia and Japan. Literacy rates might be high, but there was no corresponding tradition of education. He wrote that the Greeks were 'negatively democratic' (another expression which he did not explain). The 'black coats' were 'really abominable': 'many there be that wear black coats: but your "Black Coat" will spit on the floor, take bribes, and throw his slops into the street'.

Although Toynbee shared the contempt of many a classicist for the modern inhabitants of Greece, this did not reflect itself, as it so often did in the case of other jaundiced classicists, in an excessive adulation of the worthies of ancient Greece. He had no time for the 'intrinsic and permanent supremacy of the Greek genius': 'ancient Greek politics', he observed, 'were like modern – bribery and jobbery: and every man heard the orators, just as now every man reads the papers (orators and papers equally in someone's pay)'. He found all kinds of parallels, usually discreditable, between ancient and modern Greece. The Great Powers' dealings with the Balkans and Crete put him in mind of the Romans before they 'sat' on the Greeks in 147 BC: 'these people are quite irresponsible, and don't care how much trouble they give respectable people, over their quite childish affairs – and respectable people tolerate them, then as now, because of the glamour of Hellenism'. During one of the periodic uprisings on Crete in pursuit of *enosis*, or union, with the Kingdom of Greece, the European Powers had sent half a dozen warships to police the situation instead of 'hanging the whole population and having done with it'. 'And why not hang them?' he continued, for 'their existence is utterly pointless: you feel that they will never get any further (nor did the ancient Greeks get any further than the city-state)'. He contrasted the 'dirty, unshaven, underfed (or, if prosperous, under-exercised and double chinned)' moderns with the ancients, who were 'healthy and well set-up and did not wear heavy moustaches and a week's bristles on the rest of their face'.

His contempt for Greeks came to a head in an incident in the summer of 1912, a time of heightened tension just a few months before the outbreak of the First Balkan War. Toynbee was arrested as a suspected Turkish spy while trying to cross on foot the Asopos viaduct, which had recently been built and which carried the railway line to the north towards the contested territory of Macedonia – at that time, although not for much longer, an Ottoman province. Toynbee, then aged 22 it should be remembered, was furious when he was interrogated by no fewer than 11 people in turn, with the local gendarmerie chief emptying his pockets and counting out his money. He was further humiliated by being marched through the streets at gunpoint and detained for nine hours. He maintained that throughout he had been able to keep his temper: 'contempt for the dago has a wonderfully calming effect'.

On his return to Athens, he had hastened to the British legation to register a formal complaint with the minister, Sir Francis Elliot. Toynbee assured his mother that his captors and inquisitors, and more particularly the gendarmerie chief, would all receive heavy punishment. He recorded that 'one little man' had remarked that '"he is only a schoolmaster, he is not anything: it does not matter what we do"'. But when the time came for punishment to be meted out to his captors they would say '"Ah, he was a great *lordhos* after all."' It was beyond the comprehension of the 'dago' that, although Toynbee was truly 'not anything', it nonetheless mattered how they behaved. The rule of law, applying equally to all, was as strange a concept as a fixed price: 'it is the struggle for existence uncurbed – the man with power uses his power to crush the man without it'. He reassured his mother that 'these little men' at Lamia would be dropped on heavily enough so that they would be deterred from 'playing the fool' with the next archaeologist they came across.

In his autobiographical work *Experiences* (1969), published towards the end of his long and extraordinarily productive life, Toynbee showed a commendable sense of contrition for his youthful hot-headedness and suggested that the British minister had had the good sense to let the matter rest. Not surprisingly, after getting on for 60 years, his memory of the event was somewhat shaky, but it is clear that not merely Toynbee but the British School, and, indeed, the British minister were affronted by the attitude taken by the Greek authorities. For in February 1913, several months after the incident, A.J.B. Wace, soon to become director of the British School, enquired of J. ff. Baker-Penoyre, the London secretary of the School, whether any satisfaction had been given by the Greek government in connection with Toynbee's arrest and detention. Wace's enquiry was made when Greece was in the throes of the First Balkan War and when it would seem that the Greek government had other things on its mind. One can see how the tunnel vision of many of those at the British School, seeing most things that happened in the country in terms of their consequences for archaeology and archaeologists, did not always make it popular with the Greek authorities.

Just before leaving Greece at the end of July 1912, in what seems to have been the last letter to his mother from the School during the course of his *Wanderjahr*, Toynbee invoked 'all blessings on this country, and all curses on its inhabitants'. He was clearly overwhelmed by the natural beauty of Greece, which penetrated him 'more and more, I never before knew what beauty was'. But his time in Greece had confirmed in him the 'soundness of race prejudice, and the meaninglessness of the "Rights of Man"'. He was returning to Britain to engage in studying 'the dago deeply': 'unlike the barbarian, he is a parasite – he can only grow under the shadow of a vigorous civilisation – his nature is unsuccessful imitation'. He did not think that Greeks had become dagos until they came into contact with Europe at the time of the war for independence in the 1820s: 'even now the remoter villages, and all the shepherds in the mountains are not dagos yet, but white-skinned savages: the savage picks the vermin from his body, while the dago fidgets and pretends they are not there'. He intended on his return to Britain 'religiously' to preach 'mishellenism to any philhellene I come across'. He found support for his views in the 'consensus of dislike for the Greeks among Europeans who have lived and worked for many years in the country'. Even Greek hospitality drove him almost to desperation.

His profound distaste for Greek 'dagos' was in marked contrast to his enthusiasm for the Muslim Turks. Muslims could not be dagos: 'there is something primitive and independent in their religion which saves them from imitativeness'. An encounter with the Greek-speaking Muslims of Crete confirmed him in this view. Unlike Greeks, these were 'delightful people – not inquisitive and rude', although Toynbee was mildly put out when a Muslim inn-keeper where he was lunching one day took off his turban to wipe Toynbee's fork.

I have dwelt at some length on Toynbee's mishellenic spleen to demonstrate that his outbursts were not isolated manifestations of frustration when people of a different culture do not behave quite in the way one would expect or would wish. Rather they reflect a degree of loathing that was of an astonishing intensity. It speaks to Toynbee's integrity as an historian that he appears to have made no effort to weed his voluminous papers of remarks that sound profoundly offensive to the modern ear. It should be borne in mind, however, that the kinds of disparaging remarks about 'dagos' and 'the lesser breeds without the Law' that I have quoted were commonplace in Britain at the time he was writing in the early years of the twentieth century when the Empire was at its zenith.

It is tempting to dismiss Toynbee's broadsides as the immature post-adolescent rantings of someone from a privileged background when encountering, for the first time, a culture so markedly different from his own. But during his year in Greece, Toynbee felt that he had grown up to manhood: 'anyhow I am feeling quite ready to take up man's work at Balliol', a reference to the tutorial fellowship in ancient history that he was soon to take up, one of the most prestigious posts in the British university system. He had already shown himself to be a prodigy, publishing while still an undergraduate a highly erudite note on Herodotus in the *Classical Review* in 1910.

It is, of course, possible that the views of Toynbee, in 1921 and by now Koraes professor, on encountering Greeks again in large numbers at the age of 32, might have been very different from the views of the 22-year-old in 1911. Indeed, he did perceive a change in the Greek character, possibly occasioned by the fact that large numbers of Greeks were now subject to military discipline. In some ways he thought them to be 'rather different from what they were nine years ago – not nearly so Levantine', although one might question how many military men he would have met with as a 22-year-old Student at the British School. He supposed that military culture was 'the opposite of Levantinism'. Be that as it may, he had been, as he wrote to his wife, Rosalind, 'bowled over' by the Greek officers whom he had encountered in the early

1920s; 'they are something quite different from my impression of G[ree]k officers nine years ago. These men are well shaved, lean and smart'. In fact you might take the dark ones for Frenchmen or the fair ones for Englishmen or Germans, which he presumably deemed a compliment. He could not meet more charming soldiers in any country and was particularly impressed by the Venizelist officers. Two generals whom he encountered had 'very good, reserved (non-Greek) manners', and were capable of conversing on all kinds of politics and not merely those of their own country, and of taking a real interest in the fate of Asia Minor. He believed them to be 'enormously influenced' by the years spent on the Macedonian front in the Great War alongside French and British troops. He thought it was possible to detect Anglo-Saxon influences externally in the way they clipped their moustaches and brushed their hair. The fighting divisions at the front in Asia Minor were all Venizelist and 'I must say that they are an advertisement for Venizelos'. Venizelist politicians, by contrast, were, by all accounts, 'awful blighters'.

Despite his enthusiasm for Greeks under military discipline, Toynbee seems to have retained his youthful prejudices about the artificiality and shallowness of Western civilisation when transplanted to the Levant. Moreover, he remained charmed, 'as everybody is', by the Turks. Just as in 1911, when he had witnessed a review of the Greek fleet at Salamis, which had him 'laughing inside all the time' at its diminutive scale, so, in 1921, Smyrna made him 'laugh from the first moment I saw it'. An encounter with a Levantine family returning to the city, who conversed in English with a Greek accent, enabled him to catch 'the smell of Smyrna' which was 'neither a G[ree]k nor a Moslem smell'. The contrast between Athens and Smyrna he deemed to be 'an advertisement for the Greeks, or at any rate for their success in taking the Western inoculation'. But, he added, 'I mustn't let myself be Philhellene'.

This last remark, it should be remembered, was made when he was already Koraes professor. He may have been impressed by Venizelist army officers but there is no evidence that he had significantly changed the strongly negative views he had formed of Greek 'black coats' in 1911-12. It was clearly wrong of Principal Burrows to have held out to the Greek community the prospect of establishing a chair whose incumbent could act as a more or less full-time propagandist for a Venizelist 'Greater Greece'. At the same time it is difficult to see how Toynbee could appropriately have accepted such a chair, given not merely his lack of empathy for Greeks, but his profound antipathy towards them, or at least those educated 'black coats' he would inevitably encounter as Koraes professor. The combination of Burrows' naive philhellenism and Toynbee's deep-seated mishellenism was not merely an unhappy one. It was a recipe for disaster. The parting of the ways between King's College and Toynbee was, as we have seen, not long in coming.

On reading McNeill's biography and looking at some of Toynbee's papers that I had not been able to consult when writing *Politics and the Academy*, I thought it important publicly to set the record straight by giving some account of Toynbee's youthful mishellenism, for this went no little way towards explaining the virulence of the subsequent clash between Toynbee and the donors. I decided to do this by means of an article 'Beware the Greeks: how Toynbee became a mishellene' in the *Times Literary Supplement* (17 March 2000), the periodical in which I had first discussed the Toynbee affair in a lengthy piece in 1986. Mary Jo cautioned me against this, saying that whatever I wrote would be bound to be misconstrued by some Greeks, particularly those who had been critical of *Politics and the Academy*. I dismissed her misgivings as unduly alarmist but, inevitably, she was proven right and, for my pains, I was branded in print as an institutionalised mishellene by Constantine Buhayer, in the London Greek newspaper *Paroikiaki*.

Buhayer's article appeared under the peculiar title: 'Stop the torture, we are humans, not milk chocolates'. My piece in the *TLS*, he maintained, gave the initial impression that blatant racism against the Greeks had been uncovered and, by implication, condemned. He interpreted 'mishellene' for his readers as meaning 'racist against Greeks', although a more accurate and less anachronistic expression would be 'hater of Greeks', for the term racism entered the English language only in the middle of the twentieth century. 'In fact', he continued, 'by sprinkling his article with humorous, Anglo-Saxon quips that seem to wink at the reader that Toynbee was just being a bit of a chap, Clogg, at best, gently reprimands Arnold Toynbee'. Buhayer accused me of depicting the King's College fracas as 'some kind of moral pistols-at-dawn', with Toynbee, the 'lonely human rights activist' on one side, and manipulative Greeks, 'bent on killing Turks' and funding the Koraes chair to promote a positive image of their homeland, on the other. He accused me of failing to explain the context in which the chair had emerged. This included what he terms the genocide of the Pontic Greeks. Did my quoting of Toynbee's various anti-Greek outbursts, Buhayer asked, imply that I condemned them or should readers infer that I myself am a mishellene? He took me to task for using the word prejudice to describe Toynbee's mishellenic streak. 'So there you have it', he continued, 'if someone like Toynbee hates you, abuses you for being a dago, non-white Greek, and then maliciously condemns worldwide your people, this has nothing to do with racism'. The stamp of Toynbee, Buhayer maintained, continued until the present to loom over the department of Byzantine and Modern Greek Studies at King's College, London.

After *Politics and the Academy* appeared in 1985 as virtually the entire 21st anniversary issue of *Middle East Studies*, I was pleased when Frank Cass suggested publication in book form. Unfortunately, misprints in the original could not be corrected. This meant that the few words of Greek appeared accentless and somewhat garbled and the principal of the University of London, Sir Cooper Perry, metamorphosed into Copper Perry. I decided to forego my modest royalty and donate the profit from the in-house sale of the book, some £700, for the purchase of books for the Burrows Library at King's College in memory of the protagonists in the controversy, for all of them, in their different ways, were deeply committed to the promotion of Byzantine and modern Greek studies. This sum was not quite as modest as might appear and more or less equated to the annual book purchase grant at the time for the Burrows Library, which was home to a fine collection of books on modern Greece. This eirenic gesture, which was intended to demonstrate that I had some sympathy with the viewpoints of all those caught up in the imbroglio of the Koraes chair, however, did little to still the brewing controversy provoked by my raking over the embers of the Toynbee scandal.

One consequence of the article's re-publication as a book was that a few copies were sent out to reviewers. Professor Cem Çakmak, of the Middle East Technical University in Ankara, in a substantial review-cum-précis of the story in the *Mülkiyeliler Birliği Dergisi*, pleased me by saying that I had written up the fracas 'with the craftsmanship of a novelist'. One or two readers indeed told me that once they had picked up the book they had carried on reading it straight through to the end, a view shared by another reviewer, Richard Harrison, who wrote that, once started, it was a difficult book to put down. It was certainly short enough to be read at a single sitting. Matthew Anderson wrote in the *Times Higher Education Supplement* that I had written what must be one of the fullest accounts in print of the making of any British university appointment. In a review in *Albion*, a journal of British studies, Kirk Willis wrote that

> academic politics possess a curious fascination. To the uninitiated beyond the walls of the university, they too often seem trivial and inexplicable, fought over issues unworthy of attention. To those within the academic community, by contrast, such politics seem both major matters of principle and sad testimony that ours too is a fallen world. Virtually irresistible, therefore, is an academic controversy – such as that here recounted by Richard Clogg – which unites both academic intrigue and lay involvement.

Willis concluded that *Politics and the Academy* was 'a sad, edifying, and well-told tale'.

Some saw a positive side to the imbroglio. Professor M.E. Yapp, for instance, wrote in the *Bulletin of the School of Oriental and African Studies* that if Burrows had not taken risks then

> British scholarship in general and the University of London [where Yapp taught at SOAS] in particular would have been a good deal poorer. That one of his creations went sour for a while was a small price to pay for his successes.

The same point was also made by Professor Theophanis Stavrou of the University of Minnesota. He wrote in the *Modern Greek Studies Yearbook* that, while academic freedom should be safeguarded at all costs, nonetheless he could not help but 'reflect on the scholarly results in Near Eastern, Byzantine and modern Greek studies which accumulated because of the establishment and activities of the Koraes Chair'. Despite the 'temporary controversy' of the 1920s it remained to this day 'one of the most productive centers of modern Greek studies'.

In a lengthy review in the American *Chronicle of Higher Education*, Irving Spitzberg, a former General Secretary of the American Association of University Professors, stressed the contemporary message of this study of what he aptly termed 'the political economy of academic freedom'. This 'sad chapter' in the history of the University of London was the equivalent of an AAUP Committee A case, where the Association investigates alleged infringements of its 1940 Statement of Principles on Academic Freedom and Tenure. 'The scandal of the Koraes chair,' he wrote, 'is waiting to happen on many campuses in contemporary America'. My own cursory researches into the subject indicate that they already had occurred, not only in the United States but throughout the English-speaking world. Such scandals, Spitzberg wrote, could only be prevented by 'caution, prophylactic action, and publicity'. Despite its tedious detail, the book, he declared, should be required reading by 'scholars, faculty leaders, presidents, and especially vice presidents for development'. (Another reviewer, Katherine Fleming, described it as 'meticulously – indeed, obsessively – documented'.)

Spitzberg's advice was indeed sound, but the only university president who, to my certain knowledge, has read the book is John Brademas. Brademas, of Greek descent (albeit a Methodist) and sometime Democratic majority whip in the US House of Representatives, later became president of New York University. Somewhat to my surprise, he told me that he had read the book when I had lunch in 1987 with him and Duncan Rice, the Scottish Dean of Arts and Science. I was being looked over, in a distinctly half-hearted fashion, for the directorship of the Onassis Center for Hellenic Studies at NYU, which had been funded with a massive endowment from the Onassis Foundation. Brademas signally failed to imbibe the implicit message of the book, and within a few years the Onassis Center was, like the Koraes chair, to implode, amid much recrimination, a story that is touched upon in Chapter 6.

As I have mentioned I gave a copy of the book to Ralf Dahrendorf, the warden of St Antony's, Oxford, when I levanted there in 1990 in the aftermath of another Greek-related fracas at King's which is the subject of Chapter 5. He read what he termed my 'thriller' with apparent enjoyment, and was struck by the rather discreditable role of William Pember Reeves, who, when director of the London School of Economics, had acted as a behind the scenes adviser to the subscribers' committee. At the time, Dahrendorf, himself a former director of the LSE, was writing its history. I think that the story of Toynbee's time of troubles may have given him an inkling of the nature of my own troubles at King's. I also lent the book to Dahrendorf's successor as warden, Sir Marrack Goulding, an important figure in the UN before coming to the college, but some months later he returned it to me, unread, saying that the print was uncomfortably small.

Most of the reviewers noted the fact that I did not take sides in the controversy but rather let the facts speak for themselves. But, if pressed, I would incline to the view of Arthur Engel who reviewed the book in the *American Historical Review*. He considered that only two participants emerged from the story with enhanced reputations: William Miller, the scholar-journalist who declined to put himself forward when he learned of the source of the funding of the chair, and Ernest Barker, Burrows' successor as principal of King's College. While Toynbee had 'the letter of academic freedom on his side' there was evidence of bad faith on his part. His pro-Turkish views should have led him to decline the chair, since he knew the source of the endowment even if he did not know the detail of the subscribers' powers. The Greek subscribers and the professoriate at King's were, Engel held, bent only on protecting their own interests, while Burrows himself bore a large measure of blame for the ensuing fiasco. 'Perhaps the greatest blame, however,' he wrote,

> must be allotted to the council [i.e. Senate] of the university. Even after the Toynbee débâcle, their desire to keep the endowment was so intense that they permitted the continuance of powers for the subscribers that were contrary to academic autonomy and that they already knew could easily lead to scandal.

The electors seem to have learned only one lesson from the affair: subsequent professors were appointed in fields 'safely removed from modern politics'. All in all, J.S.F. Parker, in a review in the *English Historical Review*, considered the book to have been an 'illuminating and poignant footnote to an unhappy phase of Anglo-Hellenic relations'.

One reviewer, Andrew Mango, sought in *Cahiers d'Études sur la Méditerranée Orientale et le Monde Turco-Iranien* to make an overt connection between my writing about Toynbee's departure from King's in the 1920s and my own departure in the 1990s. Mango wrote that one of my objectives in writing the book had been to draw attention to the consequences of pursuing rich benefactors forced on British universities by the policies of Margaret Thatcher. Two years after writing the book, I was among the candidates for the Koraes chair when its holder retired. But, Mango wrote, I came up against the opposition of Greek nationalists. Although the subscribers' committee no longer existed,

> Clogg's opponents found allies in King's College. The unity of Greek culture from antiquity until the present is the basic credo of Greek nationalists. Clogg did not appear to subscribe to it, insisting more on the Levantine character of modern Greece.

Did, Mango asked, the argument that it would have been unwise to appoint as Koraes professor someone whom Greek nationalists distrusted play a role in my non-appointment? Proof was lacking, but the authorities at King's had given me the title of professor of Balkan history, which carried no obligation to teach and enabled me to carry out research at St Antony's. There remained some suspicion, Mango wrote, that my researches into the Toynbee affair had a certain connection with the Clogg affair in the 1980s.

There was a curious sequel to the publication of the book. In 1985, the Anglo-Hellenic League established the Runciman Prize for a literary work 'wholly, or mainly about Greece'. This was named after Sir Steven Runciman, the Byzantinist, at that time still alive at an advanced age. The money for the prize, £1,000, was put up by the Onassis Foundation. Initially, the organisation of the prize was handed over by the Anglo-Hellenic League to the Book Trust. Characteristically, 'works of a polemically political nature' would not be eligible, a fatuous condition as one person's statement of the obvious is another's polemics. In the Anglo-Hellenic League's case a book critical of the Colonels' dictatorship that misruled Greece between 1967 and 1974 would presumably be deemed to be 'polemically political'.

It could perhaps be argued be that *Politics and the Academy* was a book more about the mores of academic life in Britain than about Greece, but it appeared to me worth a try and I put in for the prize. My publisher, Frank Cass, submitted the requisite four copies to the Book Trust. The judges (Claire Tomalin, Peter Levi and Colin Thubron) duly deliberated and issued a press release saying that they had determined that 'none of the entries came up to the standard required'. I found this irritating. There was a possible case for rejecting the book on the ground that it did not really relate to Greece, but not, I like to think, on the ground of quality. After all, Malcolm Yapp of SOAS and someone rather better qualified to pronounce on the book's merits than the Book Trust's judges, had described it as

> a beautifully crafted little book, the narrative elegantly constructed mainly from the letters of those involved in the controversy, the issues allowed to appear by themselves without being forced upon the reader and the conflicting views presented with sympathy and understanding.

When I sought from the Book Trust details of the other books submitted alongside mine in that year I met with refusal, so it is difficult to know what the 'standard required' might have been been. It seems a fair supposition, however, that my book was rejected as 'anthellenic', anti-Greek, possibly even as 'polemically political', and likely to upset some Greek readers, not to mention the sponsors of the prize, the Anglo-Hellenic League and the Onassis Foundation that had put up the money for it.

Besides Mango's review there were other indications that writing the book was scarcely a smart career move on my part. Perhaps the most significant of these came in the form of a lengthy letter from Stanford Shaw, professor of Turkish and Near Eastern History at the University of California at Los Angeles. In March 1986, after reading the article in *Middle Eastern Studies*, which preceded the publication of the book, he wrote to offer 'most sincere congratulations' on what he, somewhat ominously, termed my 'courageous and enlightening' study. I had not previously thought of the book as being in any sense courageous, but had rather looked on it as simply an attempt to disentangle a curious and fascinating tale of academic and political intrigue. Subsequent events, however, led me to see what he meant.

Shaw enumerated a number of cases in which ethnic communities or foreign governments had endowed chairs which they hoped would give support to the political aspirations of the donors. A case in point was the Armenian community of Boston which had given $250,000 to endow a chair of Armenian studies at Harvard in the mistaken expectation that this would go to Avedis Sanjian. But Harvard was 'strong enough to take the money and avoid the propaganda'. When the Greek government had endowed the George Seferis Chair of Modern Greek Studies at Harvard (housed, inevitably, in the classics department), the expectation, again mistaken, was that it would go to Speros Vryonis, whom Shaw described as 'a very strong Greek nationalist'.

He wrote that the Armenian community in the US had endowed two chairs at UCLA, one for Armenian language and literature, the other for modern Armenian history on the 'clear understanding' that they would go to scholars who would disseminate Armenian nationalist propaganda and 'spread anti-Turkish propaganda as well and to do everything possible to destroy our Turkish program'. He expressed the hope that my study of the Koraes chair would 'open the gate to other, even less savory, situations of the same sort'.

Shaw concluded his letter on an alarming note. He had been under attack by his Armenian–American and Greek–American colleagues, 'who brought thousands of Armenians onto the UCLA campus to demand my dismissal from the University and suppression of my books'. In the course of this agitation, his house had been bombed while he, his wife and daughter were asleep inside. What was more, his life had been threatened on several occasions by Armenian terrorist organisations, threats serious enough for the FBI twice to advise that he leave the country with his family. That these threats had to be taken seriously was demonstrated by the assassination in 1982 of the Turkish consul-general in Los Angeles. This had followed the killing in Santa Barbara in 1973 by Armenian terrorists of the then Turkish consul-general and a member of his staff.

As it happens, I already knew about the bombing because, by an odd coincidence, I had given a lecture at UCLA on the day that it had happened in October 1977. The lecture had been arranged by Professor Speros Vryonis, a Byzantinist and the author of a 126-page philippic directed at the *History of the Ottoman Empire and Modern Turkey* (1976) written by Shaw and his wife. He turned out not to be at the university on the day agreed and my academic host was Professor Bariša Krekić. He asked whether there was anyone I should like to meet while at UCLA. I replied Stanford Shaw, and he looked rather aghast. When it was clear that I had no idea why, for I had flown down in the morning from Seattle and had not seen any Californian papers, he told me that Professor Shaw was at home clearing up after the bombing of his home in the early hours of that morning. I duly bought a copy of the *Los Angeles Times* (I still have the yellowing clipping) which contained photographs of Shaw and a Los Angeles Police Department detective examining his bomb-damaged house. Shaw was quoted by police sources as saying that he had been threatened by Armenian and Greek students at various times over the previous two years.

There were other indications that, as the Irving Berlin song has it, 'there may be trouble ahead'. It was soon clear that I had upset some elements in the Greek community in London. Donald Nicol, my head of department at King's, told me that he had been to a dinner in London at which, during talk about the Toynbee book, a prominent member of the community in London had said that I had completely misunderstood Toynbee, although Nicol did not specify in what way. At a party given by Matti and Nicholas Egon, who was shortly to become a patron of the department at King's, Professor Takis Vatikiotis, a Palestinian-born Greek teaching at SOAS, told me he had been asked by members of the Greek community, why, as a member of the editorial board of *Middle Eastern Studies*, he had 'allowed' such an anthellenic work as mine to be published. He had sought to disarm criticism by drawing attention to the fact that I had pointed out that the Turks had sought to buy up Toynbee with the offer of a chair at the University of Istanbul. I rather doubt, in fact, whether Elie Kedourie took advice from Vatikiotis as to whether or not to publish the article. At the same gathering, Dr Victoria Solomonidis, a former student and cultural counsellor to the Greek Embassy, took me aback when she told Mary Jo and me that the book had given her a sleepless night. When I asked her why, she replied that she was sure that the Turks would use the book in their propaganda. I did subsequently hear that my book was being held up in the Middle East Technical University in Ankara as an illustration of Greek duplicity.

After writing *Politics and the Academy*, and in the process publicly airing a prodigious amount of dirty academic linen, it was not difficult for a handful of self-proclaimed community leaders to put it about that I was *persona non grata* with the London Greeks or even with Greeks in general. Thus, when, two years later, in 1988, the Koraes chair fell vacant, the perception existed in some quarters in the college that I had a tendency to upset 'the Greeks' and that this would render it difficult touching them for money, an increasingly important desideratum for universities in Thatcher's Britain. Writing frankly about a skeleton in the cupboard of the institution that employs you may not, as I was to find out, be a smart career move. We shall see, however, that writing the book was but one small factor in my downfall.

Arthur Engel in his review in *The American Historical Review* noted that the Koraes professors appointed after the Toynbee débâcle were specialists in fields safely removed from modern politics. This is perfectly true, although one may question his use of the word 'safely'. The first four professors after Toynbee were all Byzantinists, and the most recent is a specialist in modern literature. But if the university authorities thought that they were playing for safety in eschewing modern history, they were to be sadly mistaken.

A.J.B. Wace, a classical archaeologist who had been director of the British School at Athens was quick to state a claim to succeed Toynbee in the Koraes chair. In addition to his interests in the Greek lands in antiquity he had written on the ethnography of the Vlachs in Greece and had expertise in the field of Greek island embroideries. A month after the publication of Toynbee's letter of resignation in *The Times* a curious notice, presumably inspired by Wace himself, appeared in the *Observer* in early February 1924. This, incorporating a swipe at Toynbee, stated that

> it is now known that Mr A. J. B. Wace would accept the post if offered to him, and the general feeling is that so distinguished an occupant would go far towards redeeming the Chair from the hectic atmosphere which has enveloped it so far, and would be able to develop the school of Modern Greek on more academic lines.

In the event, however, the first appointee after Toynbee was F.H. Marshall. Like Wace, Marshall was a classical scholar with interests in ancient jewellery and archaeology. He had also worked on the literature of the seventeenth-century Cretan Renaissance. As a teacher in the University of London he would have witnessed the Toynbee fracas at firsthand and no doubt as a consequence strove to maintain a low profile, an endeavour in which he succeeded. In 1926, Marshall, gave his inaugural lecture anodynely entitled 'Some debts to Byzantinism'. It was introduced by the Greek minister in London, Dimitrios Caclamanos, who, diplomatically, referred to Principal Barker's efforts in 'overcoming some difficulties' with regard to the Koraes chair, and, a mere four years after Greece's crushing defeat in Asia Minor, hailed Greece as 'a modern nation, which by its efforts and struggles strenuously works for the accomplishment of its national, historical and civilising mission in the East'. Marshall ended his bland inaugural on an upbeat note, declaring that 'all periods of history have their inspiring qualities, and that if Professorships have any value they should be directed in the main to showing that the epochs and peoples with whom they are concerned have accomplished things calculated to inspire rather than to depress'.

Marshall had published a number of works of interest to the classicist, including, *inter alia*, a 1920 survey of archaeological discoveries in the Greek lands during the previous 50 years. In 1929 he published translations of three plays of the seventeenth-century Cretan Renaissance, which made these works available to an English-speaking readership. An introduction was contributed by John Mavrogordato. Marshall certainly seems to have imbibed one of the key lessons of the Toynbee era: namely that a Koraes professor seeking a quiet life should steer well clear of modern history. In July 1931 he wrote to John Mavrogordato that he had read the manuscript of Mavrogordato's *Modern Greece: a Chronicle and a Survey 1800–1931* (1931) with enjoyment and admiration for the way he had covered a very complicated subject. He added that no doubt Mavrogordato would be prepared 'for a good deal of violent criticism, which no one who treats largely contemporary questions in the frank way you have done can hope to avoid'. As well as steering clear of contemporary politics, the modern literature of Greece does not seem to have struck much of a chord with Marshall. Certainly he was dismissive of Cavafy, the Alexandrian poet, writing that 'personally, I could dispense with about two-thirds of Cavafy's poems, though I recognise that he was an artist in words'.

The first two of Marshall's successors, the Byzantinists, Romilly Jenkins and Cyril Mango (the third was Donald Nicol) managed to incur varying degrees of opprobrium from Greek chauvinists. This was a point noted by Averil Cameron in her second (1990) inaugural at King's, this time as professor of Late Antique and Byzantine Studies, when she remarked on what she termed the 'curious hostility' towards Byzantine civilisation that she detected even on the part of modern practitioners of Byzantine studies. John Koliopoulos, in an intriguing, if all too short, contribution to the Festschrift for the anthropologist-cum-historian, John Campbell has written that

> from George Finlay [a first-rate historian with firsthand experience of the Greek war of independence] to Toynbee and from Toynbee to Romilly Jenkins and Cyril Mango, the Greeks have been measured up against constructs of the past and found wanting in qualities associated with either classical Greece or Byzantium.

Is it mere coincidence that three out of these four were holders of the Koraes chair, while the fourth, Finlay, had died almost 50 years before the chair was even founded? It is curious to note that in her second inaugural, Cameron, far from eulogising her predecessors, as is the norm on such occasions, sought to distance herself from Jenkins and Mango. She nonetheless had fulsome words of praise for Stewart Sutherland, the then principal of King's, and for one of his predecessors, General Sir John Hackett. The latter, so we are assured, was not only a philhellene and a patron of the classics but kept a copy of Thucydides at his bedside.

Romilly Jenkins, who had succeeded Marshall in the Koraes chair, upset some Greeks in his *Byzantium and Byzantinism*, the printed version of his lectures in memory of Louise Taft Semple at the University of Cincinnati (1963). In this, he maintained that the claim of many, indeed most, Greeks in the nineteenth century to racial continuity with the ancients scarcely lay 'in the realm of sober, historical fact'. The vociferous Greek critics of Jakob Philipp Fallmerayer, the Austrian hellenist, who had poured scorn on his contention that 'not a single drop of pure Hellenic blood flows in the veins of the Christian population of modern Greece', were, so Jenkins maintained, more 'animated by spleen than by scholarship'. Fallmerayer, he wrote, had been 'nearly a century in advance of his time in distilling the essence of Byzantinism: its theocratic and monolithic structure, its divinely sanctioned claim to world domination, its instinctive hatred and mistrust of the heretical West'. Elsewhere, Jenkins had written of the lives of the saints, which are a staple of Byzantine literature, that it is a 'painful reflection that, during a thousand years, so much time should have been given to the writing and reading of what was almost always absurd and very frequently disgusting'. These kinds of remarks sparked off a vigorous debate, with the Byzantinist Speros Vryonis leading the charge. Vryonis, who in an interview for the BBC Greek service had attributed to Jenkins a 'fearful loathing not only of Byzantium but above all of modern Greece', accused the erstwhile Koraes professor of espousing racist views.

Although Jenkins' academic reputation principally rests on his formidable expertise as a historian of Byzantium, he did make some forays into the modern literature and history of Greece. In *The Dilessi Murders*, for instance, Jenkins wrote about the kidnapping in 1870 of a party of aristocrats (three British and one Italian) on a day excursion from the Greek capital to Marathon, and their subsequent murder by brigands who had hoped to ransom their well-connected captives. Some have seen the book as prompted by the crisis in Anglo-Greek relations arising from the violent anti-British campaign in the 1950s for the *enosis*, or union, of Cyprus with Greece, although it was not in fact published until 1961, when the Cyprus crisis, for the time being at least, appeared to be over. In writing of the symbiotic relationship between brigandage and the Greek *politikos kosmos*, or political world, Jenkins' book, rather like my own *Politics and the Academy*, was not well received in some Greek circles. The chapter on 'Truth and "Ethnic" Truth', in which Jenkins sought to draw a distinction between observed truth and an 'upper level of ideal truth', which bore no relation to reality, but was the version of the 'truth' which Greeks sought to proclaim to the outside world, caused particular offence. One can see why. Jenkins maintained that the entire system of government in nineteenth-century Greece was 'radically vicious'. No party, he maintained, had the slightest interest in reform or development, while 'the dislike of foreigners was in fact universal: they were unpleasant necessities, to be spied upon, flattered or defamed as occasion offered'.

Jenkins quoted with enthusiasm King George I of Greece's reported remarks to the Sir Henry Elliot, the British ambassador to the Ottoman Porte, that elections in his adopted country were 'mere delusions, and managed both by intrigue and the actual intimidation of brigands'. Jenkins' critics seldom drew attention to the fact that he was scarcely less scathing about the shortcomings in the British version of parliamentary democracy just a few decades before the period about which he was writing in *The Dilessi Murders*. He readily conceded that among British members of parliament there were many as unscrupulous as Alexandros Koumoundouros and as corrupt as Theodoros Deliyannis. It is characteristic that the one venture up to that time by a Koraes professor into the minefield of the modern history of Greece since Toynbee's tenure of the chair should have occasioned such upset among some Greek readers.

Cyril Mango, who succeeded Jenkins in the Koraes chair in 1961, in his inaugural lecture, *Byzantinism and Romantic Hellenism* (1965) understandably skated over the Toynbee affair. Content to leave the 'ghost of racial continuity' in the hands of Jenkins, who had eloquently said all that could be said on the topic, he dwelt on the issue of intellectual continuity and, in particular, on Byzantine eschatology. Among Mango's pronouncements was that 'Byzantinism [...] was much more Biblical than Greek' and that 'the Byzantines in general did not evince the slightest interest in what we understand by classical Greece'. The Great Idea, he argued, was 'nothing else than messianic Byzantinism in a new dress'. Furthermore 'Hellenism, both romantic and national, was not of indigenous growth; it was implanted from abroad, and in being so implanted, out of its natural context, it produced a break in continuity'.

When Mango's inaugural was published in Greek translation in the periodical *Epokhes* early in 1967, it provoked a series of articles by the philosopher E.P. Papanoutsos in the newspaper *To Vima* on the eve of the Colonels' coup. Papanoutsos, not surprisingly, took issue with the questioning of cherished notions of Greek continuity by Jenkins and Mango, the latter of whom he referred to as a British historian. Philip Sherrard had subsequently written to Papanoutsos to say that Mango was a Greek from Constantinople. Although Greek by origin, the family had British citizenship, but Papanoutsos clearly subscribed to the widely held view in Greece that once a Greek always a Greek. It was a tragic irony, Papanoutsos believed, that such heretical views should have been espoused by someone whose background lay in 'unredeemed Hellenism', in a Greek community that had never been liberated from the Turkish yoke. The fact that here was a Constantinopolitan Greek speaking of Byzantium and 'Hellenism' (a vague and ambiguous concept that I myself prefer to avoid) in his inaugural lecture, while holding a chair which had been founded on the initiative, and with the money, of the Greeks in England, had a significance that he could not leave without comment.

Had the young professor reached his conclusions on his own, Papanoutsos asked, or had he unthinkingly adopted the views of his teacher, Romilly Jenkins? Jenkins had scored a considerable success in having his Greek student named as his successor at King's College. (Mango had not, in fact, been a pupil of Jenkins.) This would ensure continuation of the tradition established by the first holder of the chair, Arnold Toynbee, a tradition that went back to Gibbon, a scholar notably unsympathetic to Byzantium. As a result, the ideas of this particular school of thought would now be proclaimed not by a British but by a Greek scholar, or better still, by a Byzantine Greek voice. Let the Byzantinists and neo-hellenists of 'little Greece whose inhabitants' minds are muddied by ancestor worship' dare to hold them to account. The example of Mango, Papanoutsos maintained, demonstrated how difficult it was to keep as philhellenes young Greeks, who, from a tender age, go abroad to sit at the feet of foreign scholars, above all those in the field of humanistic studies. If, perchance, their university professors have their own ideas about 'Hellenism', then they adopt them, even if they are not at all favourable to the nation and national traditions, and they consider it their duty to sustain such notions with even more rigour than their teachers, so as to show that they are elevated above the common herd.

Such has been what Professor Antonis Liakos has described as the 'blood-stained' history of the Koraes chair. In 1988, three years after the publication of my study of the Toynbee débâcle, Donald Nicol retired, and somewhat surprisingly, in view of the dire financial situation at King's, it was decided that it would be filled. I put in an application. The curious and unedifying story of the election is the subject of the next chapter.

5

The sock knitted

'If one tells the truth, one is sure, sooner or later, to be found out'.
—Oscar Wilde

'Ουδέν απιθανότερον της απλής αληθείας'
—Alexandros Papadiamantis

From the mid-1980s (and for all I know earlier), as Donald Nicol's retirement from the Koraes chair at King's College in 1988 loomed on the horizon, the serried ranks of Byzantinists began to mobilise to retain their hold on the chair, if (and this was a big if in the Thatcher years) and when it should be filled. As we have seen, ever since the Toynbee débâcle in the early 1920s, the university and college had timorously appointed only Byzantinists in the, albeit forlorn, hope of avoiding unwelcome controversy. When Cyril Mango had arrived at the college in the early 1960s as the new Koraes professor, he asked the principal, Professor Peter Noble, what he should do. Noble replied that the most important thing was to keep his name out of the papers.

Over the century or so since its foundation, Byzantinists had come to believe that, as a consequence of the college's self-denying ordinance, they had acquired squatters' rights to the chair: that, as the Greeks might say, it was their *tsifliki* or, as one might (very) loosely translate it, their turf. Nonetheless, after 20 years at the college helping to establish the department of Byzantine and Modern Greek Studies as one of the leading such departments (not that there are many of these) in the English-speaking world, I aspired to succeed Nicol. It soon became apparent that I faced an uphill task as the Byzantinists began to manoeuvre, in characteristically 'byzantine' fashion, to maintain their grip on the chair.

In 1985, the British National Byzantine Committee (BNBC), the Byzantinists' trade union, charged its chair, Averil Cameron, to make representations about the present state of Byzantine studies to the University Grants Committee (UGC), which was looking into future provision in the humanities. Cameron was professor of ancient history at King's, with interests at the time in the late antique period. In this connection, Anthony Bryer, a Byzantinist at the University of Birmingham and the secretary of the BNBC, wrote to her about what he termed the phenomenal growth of Byzantine studies in the UK over the previous decade. The UGC had previously recommended that Birmingham should go ahead with its Byzantine centre on the grounds that 'London does not want it; Oxford is inert'. Since then, however, Bryer wrote, the situation in London and Oxford had totally changed.

If London were to be a 'recognised centre', he argued, then there should be a recognised coordinator. In an apparent swipe at Nicol, the Koraes professor, Bryer wrote that Cameron appeared *de facto* to be that coordinator, although 'logically it ought to be the duty of the Koraes chair'. But he was dismayed that there was talk of its demise on Nicol's retirement. He urged that the chair be maintained 'with the duty of co-ordinating London byzantine activities'. 'Lest I be misunderstood', he rather pompously added, 'I have no intention of applying for the post'. Cameron enclosed Bryer's letter with her submission to the UGC. In this, she declared that, when Nicol retired, leadership would be 'absolutely vital' and, crucially, that this should be supplied by 'a strong Byzantine historian'.

Alongside Bryer's letter, she enclosed a memorandum she had drawn up with Nicol on Byzantine studies at King's. This again stressed the need for vigorous leadership, which needed to be given by the holder of the Koraes chair. If the chair were not to be filled then the recently appointed 'new blood' lecturer in Byzantine language and literature at the college would be left in isolation. This particular appointment had given rise to controversy at the time. Complaints were made that the person appointed was over the age limit (35) stipulated for such posts, which were intended to bring new and relatively young blood into the university system. This seemed rather hard on those who were a few years over the limit but who had not applied because they believed that the college would apply the rule strictly. This had provoked letters of complaint to the then minister of education and to the chairman of the UGC. My own view was that such posts should more accurately be termed 'bad blood' posts.

By 1987 Nicol's retirement was imminent. A vigorous campaign was launched by the Byzantine lobby (which was given to complaining that there were 'only' 18 Byzantinists in post in British universities) to ensure that the only two established chairs in the field, the Koraes chair at King's College and the Bywater and Sotheby Chair of Medieval and Modern Greek Language and Literature at Oxford, should continue to be held by Byzantinists. This was despite the fact that both chairs, as their titles indicate, were intended to cover both the medieval and modern periods. This lobbying took the form of letters and articles in the British and Greek press by, and about, Byzantinist panjandrums and how brilliant they all were and how hardly they were done by. One of these puffs advanced the somewhat unlikely claim that undergraduates in the field were of such exceptional ability that they were not only capable of, but indeed likely to, carry out genuinely original research. Another was an interview in a Greek newspaper, conducted by one of Nicol's former students, with Sir Steven Runciman, who was hailed as 'the most distinguished byzantinist of our time', a judgement with which not all would agree. One of the points Runciman made was that any idea of abolishing the Koraes chair would provoke an outcry from the Greek community in Britain, which had pointed out that the chair had been originally endowed by Greeks. This seems to have been the first explicit and public mention of interest in the future of the chair on the part of the London Greeks, some of whom had maintained a kind of proprietorial attitutide to it ever since its foundation. Runciman's remark appeared to confirm what Nicol told me in the early summer of 1988, namely that a committee had been established by London Greeks to monitor the fate of the Koraes chair.

The rather unsettling news about the future of the chair gave rise to touching letters by Greeks offering part of their pensions to save the chairs, sometimes the motivation being to counter the Turkish government's lavish support for Turkish studies. Melina Mercouri, the larger-than-life film star and minister of culture in Andreas Papandreou's populist PASOK government, also weighed into the campaign, and was reported to be deeply shocked to learn that the two chairs were under threat. Mercouri, presumably with some prompting, made the point that at Oxford, which was threatening to axe the Bywater and Sotheby chair, there were no fewer than 31 teachers of French. (Incidentally, when I was at St Antony's, there were some 23 historians of ancient Greece and Rome at Oxford and one (myself) of modern Greece. Moreover, while I held a college fellowship, I had no university post.) Stewart Sutherland, the principal of King's, responded to these scare stories by saying that the college had made no proposal to abolish the Koraes chair.

The campaign by the Byzantinists to create a head of steam both for the maintenance of the two chairs and for branding them as the hereditary preserve of Byzantine scholars was clearly effective. Moreover, in the early spring of 1988, there was a development which was to have serious implications for anyone whose interests lay in the post-Byzantine Greek world and who might wish to put in for the chair. This was a monumental falling out between Cyril Mango, the Bywater and Sotheby (and former Koraes) professor and Cameron. This had been brought about by a bitter argument over the location of a project, lavishly funded by the British Academy, to create a prosopography of the Byzantine Empire, covering the period between AD 641 and AD 1261, an undertaking which some cynics likened to the compilation of a Byzantine telephone directory.

As the initiator of the project, it was scarcely surprising that Mango intended to oversee it. He was the obvious chairman of the British Academy's prosopography planning group, for the project covered a period of Byzantine history on which he was an acknowledged authority. Certainly no one in the UK had greater knowledge of this period. He naturally wished it to be based in Oxford. Cameron, however, wanted it to be housed at King's. In this, she was supported by Sutherland, who, in February 1988, wrote to the Academy to reaffirm Cameron's earlier assurance that the college would be willing to accommodate the project. Cameron's enthusiasm is difficult to fathom as the prosopography covered the middle Byzantine period, whereas her own area of expertise was in the late antique period, i.e. before AD 641, the starting point for the project. Moreover, in her representations to the UGC, she had emphasised that, after Nicol's retirement, leadership in the Byzantine field at the college would be absolutely vital, although she herself had 'neither the time nor the expertise to take this on fully'.

Matters came to a head at what was clearly a stormy meeting at the British Academy of the prosopography planning group at the end of March 1988. The odds were heavily stacked against Mango, for two of the four academic members of the group, Cameron and Nicol, were at King's, while the prospective prosopographer, John Martindale, not himself a Byzantinist, had a personal preference for King's. It would clearly be more convenient for him to travel to and from King's from his home near Cambridge than to undertake the wearying cross country journey to Oxford. Two papers, setting out the case for Oxford and London respectively, were considered at the meeting.

Cameron had a problem in claiming the project for King's, as, in theory at least, there was no certainty that Nicol's successor would be a Byzantine historian, capable of supervising the project. This did not stop her maintaining at the Academy meeting that the prosopographer would be able to call on the daily help of 'the next holder of the Koraes chair which is shortly to be advertised'. This was despite the fact that the chair might go to a modern historian, linguist or specialist in modern literature, none of whom were likely to be of much help in offering guidance to the project. Nor did Nicol, then in his last few months as Koraes professor, appear to have pointed to this rather basic fact. It would appear that both Cameron and Nicol envisaged a leading role in supervising the project for the next Koraes professor, a role that could only be filled by a Byzantine historian.

Mango insisted that there was no one at King's, or in London University more generally, qualified to oversee what was a very costly project. Nonetheless, he was predictably outvoted and, at the end of April 1988, the prosopography was formally adopted as a British Academy research project to be located at King's. This decision was taken by a small Academy committee, none of whom, true to the tradition of British amateurism, had the least connection with Byzantine studies. One of these was Professor J.B. Trapp, a specialist in renaissance English literature, whom we shall encounter later in this dispiriting tale of academic intrigue. The others were Egyptologists, classicists, historians of Tudor England and of the industrial revolution, with no knowledge of the subject and its inherent problems.

Mango unsuccessfully called for the Academy to review the whole matter and, despite the urgings of his fellow academicians, declined to have anything further to do with what had been his pet project. Of all these, in every sense of the word, 'byzantine' machinations, I heard nothing from the principal of the college, Sutherland, or from Cameron and Nicol. Indeed, I must have spoken with Cameron scarcely half a dozen times during the almost 20 years that we were colleagues. On the other hand, I saw Nicol, the head of our minuscule department, regularly and frequently lunched with him in the rather grim college refectory. That he had serious prosopographical interests is apparent from his obituary in the *Daily Telegraph* and the much longer obituary in the *Bibliographical Memoirs of Fellows of the British Academy*, where he is described as a 'godfather' of the Academy-supported prosopography and active in bringing the project to King's. But he had breathed not a word to me about the project, let alone the unedifying row to which it had given rise. Given that the project, which would cost the British taxpayer £1 million or more, a huge sum for a research project in the humanities, had been awarded to King's College, it would necessarily have major implications for our very small department. This was, to put it mildly, disturbing. After all, there were only two departments in the country whose title included the word Byzantine, one of which was ours. This consisted, besides Nicol, of two members, myself as reader in modern Greek history and Roderick Beaton, as lecturer in modern Greek language and literature, or two and a half, if the 'new blood' lecturer in Byzantine language and literature, who was mainly based in the classics department, was included. Given that the college's financial situation was dire, and certainly precluded any thought of establishing a new post, whom did

Cameron, Nicol and Sutherland envisage as supervising the prosopography project now that it was definitely coming to the college?

When, much later, I sought information from King's under the Freedom of Information Act about the negotiations between the college and the British Academy before the prosopography project got under way at King's in the autumn of 1988, I was informed that not a single document relating to such a contested and hugely expensive project either before or after it came to the college has been preserved. The disappearance of these papers may not be unconnected with the subsequent embarrassing realisation that the King's proposal was duplicating a better resourced research project already under way in Germany and of which the proponents of the Academy scheme were unaware.

A few weeks after the row at the Academy, I did learn something of what was going on but, needless to say, not from anyone at the college. I told an old friend and former BBC colleague a little of these manoeuvrings. He told me that a rather disquieting Turkish saying came to mind: 'they're knitting a sock for your head'. The feeling that this indeed was the case was reinforced when I learned that Mango had written to Sutherland to complain, *inter alia*, that, despite having been invited to be a member of the appointment board established for the Koraes chair, he had subsequently been bumped off. This deselection, one may surmise, was at least in part a result of the perceived awkwardness of having both Mango and Cameron, at daggers drawn over the prosopography project, on the same board.

Further unease was occasioned by sight of an internal college document, which was not circulated to me. This related to a proposed conference on William of Ockham, the medieval scholastic philosopher. It was a measure of the college's desperate financial plight that it was hoped to attract funding for this from the Sainsbury supermarket group on the somewhat tenuous grounds that its headquarters were in Southwark, where Ockham's career had begun in the early fourteenth century. The document noted, *inter alia*, that 'whether we like it or not, it will depend on whom we appoint to the Koraes chair which Greeks, if any, will donate'. I found this worrying because of the perception that existed in some Greek quarters that I was an anthellene, or anti-Greek, and that, as a consequence, I might be an obstacle to fundraising by the financially hard-pressed college.

There were also the rumours, as we have seen, that members of the London Greek community had established a committee to monitor the fate of the Koraes chair. It is not difficult for a foreigner immersing him or herself in the history and politics of modern Greece to acquire a reputation as an anthellene or even to be viewed as a *praktoras*, a spy, whose historical interests are a cover for darker arts. Amalia Fleming, the Greek widow of the discoverer of penicillin, Sir Alexander Fleming, and a doughty opponent of the Greek Colonels, certainly thought that I was such a *praktoras*, engaged in infiltrating the anti-Colonel movement on behalf of the 'Intelligence Service'. My book on the Toynbee imbroglio, in particular, had also, as we have seen, ruffled some, although of course by no means all, Greek feathers. It was clear that there was a view in the college that my writings had a tendency to upset 'the Greeks'.

The feeling that fundraising considerations loomed large in the minds of the powers that be in the college was reinforced by a proposal on which Sutherland and Cameron were very keen, namely the establishment of a Centre for Hellenic Studies. Their inspiration was the very recently established such centre at New York University, for the directorship of which I had recently, if perfunctorily, been interviewed (see Chapter 6). The proposed centre at King's, which was to be given the same title as the New York University venture, would embrace in a single department all activities in the college that could be deemed to have 'Hellenic' connotations. The Onassis Center for Hellenic Studies at New York University had been lavishly funded by the Onassis Foundation to the tune of $15 million, and it was clear that Sutherland and Cameron saw in the establishment of a similar centre a funding opportunity.

I did not share their enthusiasm for the idea. It seemed to me likely that modern Greek studies, traditionally the poor relation of classical and Byzantine studies, would be in danger of being swamped by the classicists and Byzantinists, who could be pretty ruthless in pursuing their own objectives. In particular, my own interests in the modern history and politics of Greece would no doubt be forced to take a back seat. It would manifestly be a nonsense for the modern history and politics of Italy to be included in a centre 'melding' classics with medieval and modern Italian studies. What is so different about the modern history and politics of Greece? I certainly made no secret of my conviction that the recent history of Greece should be treated in exactly the manner of that of other European countries.

Moreover, the very notion of a Centre for Hellenic Studies covering the whole sweep of Greek studies, from 'Plato to NATO' as the saying goes, or as I prefer it, from 'Aspasia to Mimi',[1] seemed to me a questionable one. Such a centre appeared to legitimise in advance a, or rather the, key element in the traditional Greek construct of the past, namely that there is an unbroken continuity, not merely linguistic (which is manifestly the case), but also 'racial' and cultural, in the sense that the present-day inhabitants of Greece are the direct descendants of the worthies of ancient Greece and the true custodians of the classical tradition. Attempts have even been made to determine whether there is any genetic underpinning in support of theories of 'Hellenic' continuity but these have proved inconclusive in the absence of data on the 'genetic polymorphisms' of the ancient Greeks.

This claim to unbroken continuity, as we have seen, was a debatable one that had been famously challenged in provocative fashion by Jakob Philipp Fallmerayer, when, in the 1830s, he had argued that the modern Greeks were essentially hellenised Slavs. The mere mention of the name of Fallmerayer, as that acute observer of mid-nineteenth-century Greece, the American minister in Athens, Charles Tuckerman, once noted, was enough to reduce an Athenian professor to apoplexy. Perhaps significantly, Averil Cameron, in her inaugural lecture as Professor of Late Antique and Byzantine Studies at King's in 1990, before a heavily Greek audience, took a swipe at 'Fallmereyer' [sic] as not only putting the case against ethnic continuity but also as an anti-clerical and supporter of Ottoman Turkey to boot.

This cherished notion of continuity between the ancient and modern Greeks had, as we have seen, been questioned by previous Koraes professors, notably by Jenkins and Mango. It remains very much a live issue. In 1998, the Runciman prize (named after the Byzantinist) for the best book on an 'Hellenic' topic published during the previous year was awarded by the Anglo-Hellenic League to M.L. West, the Oxford classicist, for his *The East Face of Helicon: West Asiatic Elements in Greek Poetry and Myth* (1997). West's investigation of the parallels between Greek poetry in antiquity and the literatures of the ancient Near East called into question the uniqueness of ancient Greek culture. In so doing, he incurred the wrath of Stelios Papadimitriou, the chairman of the Onassis Foundation, which supported the prize with a generous subvention. So angry was Papadimitriou with West's questioning of the uniquely 'Hellenic' nature of ancient Greek poetry that he pulled the plug on the Runciman prize. It was only saved when the National Bank of Greece stepped into the breach with its own subvention.

The degree to which the world view of some, but of course by no means all, Greeks is conditioned by reference to the heritage of the ancient Greek past is strikingly demonstrated in remarks by Melina Mercouri:

> the Europeans have an obligation towards us. It is to us that they owe their very name – Europe. They have a duty to behave towards us in a manner which is rational, fair and ethical – ethical being a concept they have again derived from us. We are justified in reprimanding Europe for its forgetfulness and ingratitude. Europe has borrowed from our cultural heritage in order to achieve decency and dignity and to develop itself. Decency and dignity require that they should repay their obligations.

The notion that the west owes a debt of obligation to the Greeks as the *fons et origo* of Western culture has often been reinforced by Westerners. For instance, Ian Gilmour, at the time minister of state at the Foreign Office, in moving in the House of Commons in 1980 the ratification of Greece's treaty of accession as the tenth member of the then European Economic Community, intoned that Greek entry could be seen as a 'fitting repayment by the Europe of today of the cultural and political debt that we all owe to a Greek heritage almost 3000 years old'. In similar vein, the French president, Valéry Giscard d'Estaing, arriving in Athens to sign the treaty, declared, amid much acclaim, that France as 'the daughter of classical Greece' should now act as the sister of the modern country.

The subsuming of every branch of study that was concerned with the Greek world, past or present, in a single 'hellenic' centre in the college seemed to me, in effect, to foreclose debate on the continuity issue. Establishing such a centre would be to pander to the *progonoplexia*, ancestor fixation, and the *arkhaiolatreia*, the excessive, even obsessive, reverence for antiquity which has been so characteristic a feature of the cultural life of the independent Greek state and, in the process, has deflected attention from the modern country that is Greece. In making my reservations known to Sutherland, I remember using the old saw that 'good fences make good neighbours' *à propos* the proposed merger of our small department with the much larger department of classics. This was clearly a tactical mistake, as I was thus identified as someone who might stand in the way of a project on which he and Cameron were very keen, and which might bring money to the college.

Also disquieting was a meeting which Sutherland convened in January 1988 with Cameron, Professor Norma Rinsler, the dean of the Faculty of Arts, and myself. At this the idea of a Centre for Hellenic Studies, about which I was not enthusiastic, was discussed. Sutherland appeared somewhat agitated and it was clear that Cameron had again been pushing the importance of the Koraes chair for Byzantine Studies. After the meeting, in the course of a brief conversation, she said, 'Richard, you must hate me'. I replied that she was fighting her corner while I was fighting mine. This may have been a gentlemanly response but it was a singularly inapposite one. For this was not a boxing match in which we would meet in the ring but rather a bout of which she was one of the judges and, so the evidence indicated, a judge with strong views as to the desirable outcome.

When I learned of the composition of the appointment board I became even more alarmed. Everyone in academic life knows that such boards can be constructed so as to secure a particular outcome and this was demonstrably the case with the board proposed by the college. Given the federal structure of the University of London, the choice was theoretically made by the university, but this was the case only in a technical sense.

As we have seen, the vast, even intimidating, scope of the Koraes chair covered six discrete fields, modern Greek and Byzantine history, language and literature over the best part of two millennia. Yet the two external advisers stipulated by university regulations were both Byzantine historians, although Byzantine history was only one of the six fields. Both of them would have been aware, even if all the other members of the board were not, that the prosopography was now going to be located at King's and that the college would have a pressing need for a byzantine historian capable of supervising it. Indeed, one of the external advisers, Bryer, had actually voted for the prosopography to go to King's and had sent Sutherland a copy of his 1985 letter in which he had urged that that the Koraes chair be filled by someone capable of coordinating 'London Byzantine activities'.

The other external adviser was Dimitri Obolensky, the retired Professor of Russian and Balkan History at Oxford. Obolensky was a distinguished Byzantinist but, at the age of 70, he was over the age limit of 66 stipulated in university regulations. This condition could be waived in 'special circumstances', but when I subsequently asked the university registrar what these might have been, she lamely replied that the committee that had appointed him was aware that he was an emeritus professor, which scarcely qualified as a special circumstance. As we have seen, Mango, aged 59 and well within the prescribed age limit, and no less distinguished a scholar than Obolensky, was willing and able to act but he had been bumped off the board without explanation.

University regulations specified that the internal adviser be drawn from the university but not the college and should be well acquainted with the subject as a whole, and with the promise and achievement of other scholars in it. But the person appointed, J.B. Trapp, Professor of the History of the Classical Tradition and director of the Warburg Institute, was without question a distinguished scholar but his speciality was the reception of classical literature in England during the Renaissance. He had no expertise, or, indeed, any discernible interest in, any of the fields embraced by the Koraes chair. But, as a member of the small committee of non-Byzantinists that had ratified the adoption of the prosopography as a British Academy research project, he would have been aware of the college's pressing need for a Byzantine historian to replace Nicol. At least one who fitted the bill did apply. The person concerned had been a research fellow at the Warburg Institute during Trapp's directorship. This individual's PhD supervisor, Bryer, was one of the external experts. They had subsequently published an edited book together. Likewise, the applicant had published a book with Cameron. Whether Trapp, Bryer or Cameron acted as referees for this particular Byzantine historian is not clear, but it is worth noting that the college's guidance to heads of department in making academic appointments stipulates that applicants should avoid proposing as referees supervisors or co-authors. Incidentally, Cameron at the time of the appointment was a member of the Warburg's management committee.

The committee which established the board acknowledged that Bryer, Obolensky and Trapp were not experts in modern Greek but suggested that, if the nature of the applications indicated, the opinion of two American scholars should be sought. This was worrying for me as it implied that applications from specialists in the modern Greek field were not really expected. The two Americans were Professors John Petropulos and Edmund Keeley. Petropulos was an excellent historian, but his career had been spent at Amherst, a liberal arts college with no graduate school (whereas a significant part of my work at King's was given over to the supervision of graduate students) and had no experience of the British university system. Mike Keeley, professor of English and Creative Writing at Princeton, was another fine scholar with an excellent knowledge of matters modern Greek, and who did have a good knowledge of the British educational system, but, in the event, he received no request for comment on any of the applicants. The college thus did not abide even by its own inadequate procedures. Such was the slovenliness of the college and university that they did not even bother to inform Keeley, let alone seek his agreement, before assigning him the role of adviser in relation to possible modernist applicants.

Sutherland subsequently declared that, when drawing up the appointment board, there had been 'no names of specialists in modern Greek studies in the UK available to the college'. One can only hope that the college puts greater effort into finding relevant specialists when filling chairs in the medical faculty. John Campbell, a fellow of St Antony's, was a mere 50 miles away in Oxford and, unlike Obolensky, was not over the stipulated age. A distinguished anthropologist and historian, he was the author of a seminal study of the Sarakatsani, the transhumant shepherds of northern Greece and the co-author of an excellent history of modern Greece. He was of course familiar with the British university system and, moreover, he had had a large number of graduate students working on modern Greek historical and anthropological topics. Apart from Douglas Dakin of Birkbeck College, who had retired in 1974, Campbell and I for many years were the only university historians of modern Greece in the country.

The manifestly unbalanced nature of the board soon became known in our small field. I protested to Sutherland that the playing field was demonstrably an uneven one, and given that there was no one on the board with knowledge of my own work, he agreed that I could submit additional testimonials. But he soon gave up reading these. He thanked at least two of those who had protested at the unbalanced make-up of the board for their comments on my work, although neither had so much as mentioned my name. Eventually, in the light of these complaints, Petropulos was added to the board as 'an additional nominee' of King's and was flown over, at considerable expense, for the interviews. Whether university regulations provided for such additions to a board once it had been established is not clear.

The chair was advertised in the middle of May. The further particulars sent to intending applicants made no mention of the imminent arrival in the college of the Byzantine prosopography project. These further particulars were sketchy in the extreme, scarcely half a page, in contrast with the 15 pages for the Bywater and Sotheby chair when it was advertised in 2006. Interviews were held towards the end of July 1988. Shortly before, a mysterious dinner took place for some of those interested in the outcome. Those present included Sutherland, Nicol, the retiring Koraes professor, Lord Flowers, the vice-chancellor, and Nicholas Egon, the painter husband of a Greek shipping heiress. What his *locus standi* was in the whole business is not clear, and is just one more of the many anomalies surrounding the appointment. Another member of the London Greek community had been to see Sutherland before the appointment was made to discuss the future of the chair. He was a member of the Society for the Promotion of Byzantine Studies and, indeed, soon afterwards he was to join its executive committee.

When the board met on 22 July, neither the vice-chancellor nor the principal of the university, who were technically members, were present, but this was by no means unusual. Instead, the board was chaired by a 77-year-old, long-retired pharmaceutical chemist and former vice-chancellor, Sir Frank Hartley. (He had taken part in the farce of awarding Elena Ceaușescu a fellowship of the Royal Institute of Chemistry in 1978.) Sutherland assured those who subsequently complained about the way in which the appointment had been made that it was a university rather than a college appointment, and one which had been conducted in a thoroughly professional manner under the distinguished chairmanship of Hartley. But during my interview at least, Hartley, who seemed to be somewhat deaf, was inert and took no part the proceedings.

Besides Trapp, Obolensky and Bryer, there were five nominees of King's: Sutherland; Cameron; Peter Marshall, professor of Imperial History; Norma Rinsler, professor of French and dean of the Faculty of Arts; and Petropulos as the 'additional nominee'. In a committee of nine, three were Byzantinists, all three of them historians and all three members of the executive committee of the Society for the Promotion of Byzantine Studies (including its chair and its secretary), two of whom had voted in the British Academy prosopography planning group for the project to be located at King's. At least four (Sutherland, Cameron, Bryer and Trapp) and probably five (Obolensky) were aware of the imminent arrival of the prosopography project and of the need for somebody capable of supervising it. Whether the other members of the board were told of the project is not clear. Applicants for the chair were not notified, although it can be assumed that the fierce struggle over the location of the project would have been known to at least some of the Byzantinist applicants.

The interviews were held in the morning. Discussion continued in the afternoon, when Obolensky had to leave, apparently for a dentist's appointment. It was then agreed that the other external adviser, namely Bryer, could also leave. By that stage, I had already been knocked out. Two names were still in contention, the Byzantine historian who would have been able to oversee the prosopography project and was at this stage the favourite, and Roderick Beaton, the lecturer in modern Greek language and literature in the department. Finally, the Byzantine historian having been eliminated, the puff of white smoke went up and Beaton emerged as the new Koraes professor.

Paradoxically, Beaton's field, modern Greek literature, was one of the two fields, the literature and language of modern Greece, in which there was no expertise among any of the members of the board. Sutherland later informed me that the board had been impressed by the range of Beaton's interests. This was presumably a reference to an as yet unpublished study of the medieval Greek romance. But when this was published a year later it was the subject of a harsh, book-length critique by two specialists in the field, a volume which for many years was not to be found in the college library.

Kenneth Dover in his idiosyncratic, at times scandalous but always entertaining memoir, *Marginal Comment*, has written that confidentiality at Oxford is seldom respected and that his turning down of the Regius Chair of Greek immediately became known. Nor, he added, was the maintenance of confidentiality an outstanding characteristic of electors to chairs at Cambridge. Thus when, in the early 1970s, he failed to be appointed to the Regius Professorship of Greek he had soon been able to 'reconstruct the views and arguments of all those involved'. Alas, I have been able to glean very little of what had gone on in the interviews and the subsequent discussion before the appointment was made.

An odd feature of the appointment was that members of the board were required to leave their papers for destruction at the conclusion of the interviews. When, after the Freedom of Information Act had come into force,

I enquired about papers relating to the appointment in the college archive, I was told that only a single document survived. That only a single document out of the mountain of paperwork generated by an appointment that, as Sutherland himself put it, had provoked an inordinate degree of interest, should have survived in the archive is puzzling. Any future historian seeking to delve into what happened in 1988 would confront slim pickings.

The contrast with the large amount of material still in the college archive relating to the appointment of Toynbee in 1919, material which included the original references for the candidates, and of which I had made extensive use in *Politics and the Academy*, could scarcely have been starker. What possible reason could there have been for such secrecy? It is noteworthy that the references and testimonials submitted by the pioneering woman Hellenist, Jane Harrison, in connection with her unsuccessful applications in 1888, exactly a century before the 1988 election at King's, and in 1896 for the Yates Professorship of Archaeology at University College, London still survive, together with the report of the electors, and make for interesting reading.

Beaton's emergence as the new Koraes professor must have come as a shock to those hoping for a Byzantine historian. It also clearly presented a problem for the college which, having manoeuvred to house such a large-scale research project as the Byzantine prosopography, now had no one in place to supervise it. This particular difficulty was overcome by the simple, and, most important, cost-free, expedient of rapidly rebranding Averil Cameron, hitherto professor of ancient history, as professor of late antique and Byzantine studies, although she had earlier declared herself to be lacking expertise in the Byzantine field.

I was not formally informed of the outcome until the end of August. A few days before, I received, in what was clearly a not very subtle attempt to sugar the pill, notification that I been appointed to a personal chair in modern Greek history. The sting in the tail of this conferment of title was that the Thatcher government had recently abolished tenure for those accepting promotion. It seemed to me in the circumstances more than risky to accept this offer when the result would have been a department consisting of two professors and half a lecturer, bringing to mind the old music hall joke about a South American army: all generals and no privates. To give up tenure when the college was on its uppers, with a deficit of £6 million and about to implement a 'restructuring' plan involving the loss of more than 200 posts seemed unwise. Clearly, 'senior management' would have cast a beady eye on such a ludicrously top-heavy (and expensive) department in which demand for undergraduate places had always been low. So I felt unable to accept the personal chair until the situation became clearer. When, following the rebranding of Cameron as a Byzantinist, it was decreed that that her new post would be shared between our department and classics, the situation became even more anomalous, with an unheard of ratio of two and a half professors to half a lecturer.

My fears as to what might happen if I gave up tenure were by no means unfounded. When in 2010 the 'credit crunch' began to affect the universities, it was reported that all members of the arts faculty at King's would be required to reapply for their jobs. This was at a time when the college was spending £20 million acquiring the east wing of Somerset House, which is adjacent to the Strand campus. Byzantine and modern Greek studies were included among the subjects in which the administration wanted to 'disinvest', and what had been my post in the 'dangerous' field of the modern history of Greece disappeared. Such were the protests provoked by these 'disinvestment' proposals that an odd quasi-solution was stitched up. This involved shunting the Koraes professor into the Centre for Hellenic Studies, cannibalising the department and establishing a new MA in Greek Tradition. The champions of Hellenic continuity had finally prevailed.

The nearest to an explanation as to why I had fallen by the wayside at an early stage came from the horse's mouth so to speak, in a letter from Sutherland to Philip Nind, a friend of mine who had served as a liaison officer to the resistance in occupied Greece. In this, Sutherland insisted that the board had included specialists representing the range indicated in the title of the chair, which was demonstrably not the case. The board contained no expert at all in modern Greek language and literature, precisely the fields in which the appointment had nonetheless been made. What was of particular interest in Sutherland's letter, however, was his insistence that the criteria for appointment to an established chair such as the Koraes chair, carrying with it the headship of a department, are somewhat different to those for appointment to a personal chair, such as I had now been offered. He wrote that for appointment to a personal chair the procedure was extremely rigorous and was focused on a 'rather narrower set of concerns largely weighted towards research, than the concerns which more broadly must be taken into account when appointing to an established chair and *de facto* to a headship of department'. What could have Sutherland have meant by this oracular statement? I had, after all, been acting head of our minuscule department not long before and the heavens had not fallen in.

Once Beaton had been appointed and Cameron had been rebranded as a Byzantinist, the way was clear for the creation of a Centre for Hellenic Studies, after the pattern established at New York University, through the fusion of the classics department with our department. Beaton, too, enthusiastically espoused the idea, although he did not bother to discuss its implications with me, the only full-time member of his department. Nor did Cameron discuss the idea with the Classics department before a joint meeting of the two departments was held, the purpose of which was to ratify the merger. I was not present, as I was laid up with flu, but I should certainly have enjoyed it, for the scheme was blown out of the water by the united opposition of the classicists, who manifestly did not relish the idea of linking their fate with ours. It is clear that Cameron had seen the purpose of the meeting as being simply to ratify a *fait accompli*. Her department, however, had other ideas and rejected the scheme out of hand, despite the pleas of Cameron, Beaton and the 'new blood' Byzantinist.

It is clear that fundraising loomed large in the eyes of those advocating the scheme. Cameron observed that Sutherland had arrived at the notion of a Centre for Hellenic Studies with a view to attracting 'a certain sort of funding'. Could she have meant funding from enthusiasts for the notion of hellenic continuity? That this may have been the case is suggested by the fact that when, after the merger of the two departments had been torpedoed, and Cameron pressed ahead with a less formal grouping (still with the same title), the college gave it a dowry with which to purchase books specifically on the continuity of Greek culture. This added confirmation to my fears about at least one of the academic purposes of the enterprise. It was clearly intended to legitimise notions of hellenic continuity questioned by previous holders of the Koraes chair, but which were thought to be dear to many potential Greek benefactors, although these in practice subsequently proved to be thin on the ground.

In 2015 it was announced that to secure the future of the Koraes chair an appeal for almost £3,400,000 was to be launched. Later this amount was reduced to £1,640,000. Most of those approached for funding would have been Greek institutions or wealthy Greek individuals. With Greece in the throes of an appalling economic crisis and beset by a seemingly uncontrollable tide of refugees resulting from the wars in Syria and Iraq, this scarcely seemed to be an appropriate time for the launch of such an appeal. To imply that without such a lavish new endowment the Koraes chair would disappear essentially amounted to little more than blackmail. It is one thing to appeal for funds to establish a new chair but another to suggest that if funds were not forthcoming an existing chair might be abolished. Potential donors would be well advised to insist on cast iron guarantees that any donation be ring fenced to support the Koraes chair, in case the college should undergo one of the recurrent financial crises that have afflicted it in recent years.

Not only did Beaton not trouble to consult me about the proposed merger with classics, he failed to consult about other important (and less important) matters, including the creation of a new lectureship in the department. Despite the fact that its remit included modern Greek history, I was not asked to sit on the appointment board. Nor was I invited to have any input into the planning of a new BA degree in 'Hellenic' studies. There were other rather childish slights, such as the failure to invite me to a lunch for the Greek ambassador, whom I actually knew. Despite the college's parlous financial condition, money was frittered away on costly paid inserts recording this momentous occasion in the court and social pages of *The Times*, the *Daily Telegraph* and the *Independent*.

Some years afterwards, in 1992, Beaton wrote a letter to Sutherland's successor as principal, which I learned of many years later when I acquired a copy of my personnel file at the college. In this, he maintained that I had done the bare minimum of teaching and research during the 1988/9 and 1989/90 sessions. He added that I had made numerous allegations against the college and individual members of staff. These had had, he maintained, a damaging effect on relations between the department and outside bodies with which the department had common interests. These included the Foreign Office, foreign universities, the Greek community in London, unspecified officials and, again unspecified, potential donors. He made no effort to substantiate these damaging claims. Those concerned with Greek studies were necessarily interested in the fate of the Koraes chair, and I certainly did not subject myself to a self-denying ordinance in speaking about it. Some rather alarming rumours, indeed, were circulating as to why I did not get the job. I certainly did not level any allegations against Beaton himself. Indeed, I remember more than once, in discussing the fracas, pointing out that, after all, he had not appointed himself.

Beaton ended his letter on a bathetic note. The department had already had to pay a high price for what he, in the best Churchillian manner, termed appeasement. This, he continued, should not be allowed to jeopardise the academic integrity of those such as he who had worked hard to establish a leading international position for Byzantine and modern Greek studies at King's. The department's high reputation had in fact been established by Donald Nicol, Philip Sherrard, Peter Mackridge and myself before Beaton's arrival at the college in 1981.

Improperly, Beaton's letter had been placed in my personnel file without my knowledge and without the opportunity to rebut his allegations, which could easily have been done. The main research project, for instance, on which I had been working during the academic years in which Beaton claimed I was doing the bare minimum of teaching and research, was my *Concise History of Greece*, published by Cambridge University Press. This had been published in 1992 *before* Beaton wrote the offending letter. Now in its third edition, the *Concise History* (a not so concise 321 pages long) has been translated into

13 languages, and has sold over 40,000 copies in the English edition. The claim that I had neglected my teaching was likewise demonstrably inaccurate. A student who had attended one of my courses during the relevant period had written to thank me for a course that she had found 'incredibly interesting'.

In a university system where tenure had been abolished, my position would indeed have been precarious should the college authorities have chosen to take seriously Beaton's demonstrably untrue allegations of serial professional negligence on my part. I duly appointed myself head of the escape committee and set about engineering my departure from King's. In this campaign I was fortunate to have the support of a number of good friends who had protested to Sutherland and to the vice-chancellor about what had happened. The vice-chancellor, Lord Flowers, told one of his deputies that he had never received such a volume of complaints about a single appointment. I myself had a singularly unprofitable meeting with him, at which he disquietingly maintained that it was perfectly reasonable to constitute an appointment board with a particular candidate in mind. Moreover, he could see nothing objectionable in the creating of a Centre for Hellenic Studies and in its shaping to accord with the perceived wishes of potential donors if that was the only way of ensuring the continuation of a particular field in hard economic times.

The cumulative protests of my claque of supporters began to have their effect. I was indeed very grateful to people such as Lars Baerentzen, John Campbell, Nigel Clive, Peter Mackridge, Philip Nind and Monty Woodhouse. They and others had immediately seen that my position at King's was impossible and had done what was within their power to help extricate me from the mess. Another tower of strength was Sheila Ford, the secretary of our department, who was always ready to provide a sympathetic ear. One particularly effective intervention was that of Monty Woodhouse, who had resigned his visiting professorship in the department in protest at what had happened. As the wartime head of the Allied Military Mission to the Greek Resistance, a former Conservative MP for Oxford, and a prolific author of erudite books on post-classical Greece, his was clearly a voice which carried weight. Woodhouse's letter to the vice-chancellor was forthright: 'I have a strong feeling that those responsible for making the appointment failed to appreciate the potential damage to the department by their selection'. But this, he said, was past history, and he urged my transfer to St Antony's, whose warden, Ralf Dahrendorf, would warmly welcome me there. He concluded by saying that such a step would further weaken the department at King's, but he feared in any case that 'it would take a very long time to repair the damage that has already been done'.

By a very fortunate coincidence, John Campbell reached retirement age in 1990, two years after the appointment to the Koraes chair had been made. He had many years earlier given up his lectureship in modern Balkan history at Oxford, but as a fellow of St Antony's he had kept the Greek flag flying in the fields of the anthropology and modern history. If transferred, I could at least strive to maintain the fine tradition that he had established in the study of the modern history of Greece, although scarcely in anthropology.

Woodhouse's letter, coming on top of the other complaints that had been made to Flowers, seems to have made a significant contribution to breaking the logjam at King's. Flowers' reply was emollient. He concluded by saying that he was 'grateful' (an odd word in the context of his earlier reactions) to Woodhouse for writing and that he was taking the liberty of forwarding a copy of his letter to Sutherland so that he would be aware of Woodhouse's concerns. From this time onwards, the college began to show encouraging signs of a willingness to find a way out of the impasse that had arisen.

At a meeting in the early summer of 1989 the outline of an acceptable means of resolving the mess began to emerge. Sutherland proposed that I be granted a five-year leave of absence. This would commence in October 1990 and would be funded in part by the college and in part by outside sources. This prolonged sabbatical leave, presumably one of the longest on record, would be spent at St Antony's, Oxford. The deal was sealed when I was awarded a three-year research grant by the Leverhulme Trust to enable me to work on the history of the Greek people since the fall of Constantinople, which would incorporate the history of *I kath'imas Anatoli*, the Greek presence in the Near East, and of the Greek diaspora proper, with the history of the Greek state.

This was as good a deal as I was likely to get and I was pleased to depart in the autumn of 1990 for pastures new in Oxford. The arrangement provided that if, after the five-year period, St Antony's were not in a position to assume responsibility for my salary, then I should have the option of returning to King's. This was not exactly an enticing prospect and, finding St Antony's a very congenial refuge, I later managed to engineer an advantageous early retirement deal which would enable me to remain at Oxford. It was clear that my pension would be significantly increased if I were to accept the personal chair that had been on offer since 1988. I agreed to accept this, as my apprehensions about loss of tenure would no longer be relevant, although, anxious to put some distance between myself and the Centre for Hellenic Studies, I wished to change the title from professor of modern Greek history to professor of modern Balkan history. This proposal prompted another wearying saga. When Cameron had been rebranded as a Byzantinist her new title was quickly agreed by the university. In my case, although I was every bit as much of a Balkanist as she was a Byzantinist, I had to undergo once again the whole rigmarole of consulting internal and external experts.

One of these remained the same, Professor M.L. West of All Souls College, Oxford, a highly distinguished classical scholar but someone with no obvious knowledge of, or discernible interest in, the subjects which are of concern to me. This was yet another instance of the marginalisation of modern Greek studies, which still tend to be looked on as the poor relation of classics. It can safely be assumed that I would never be called upon to pronounce on the scholarly credentials of a classicist. Why should the reverse be the case?

The real problem, however, arose with those initially nominated as external experts in connection with my wish to adopt the title of professor of modern Balkan history: Richard Crampton, formerly professor of east European history at the University of Kent and by this time time a colleague at Oxford, and Stevan Pavlowitch, reader in Balkan history at the University of Southampton. These were the obvious assessors in the UK, but they were held not to be appropriate. I have no idea what the objections to the choice of such external experts might have been. One member of the University of London committee responsible for pronouncing on my eligibility was opposed even to the proposed title, professor of modern Balkan history. However, things were eventually smoothed over and I received the title, although I was never asked to deliver an inaugural lecture.

Everything was now set for my retirement from King's in 1995. By a bizarre coincidence, on the very morning of the meeting at which a final settlement with the college was thrashed out, Mary Jo had suffered a broken toe when a chunk of the lavatory wall dropped on it at the City of London School for Girls, where she was librarian. It had been agreed that she could attend as a kind of 'McKenzie friend'. Gamely, she hobbled into the meeting on crutches.

By this time Sutherland had ceased to be principal of King's and had himself moved on to pastures new. Firstly, he became vice-chancellor of the University of London, a job he combined with being Chief Inspector of Schools. He then became principal of the University of Edinburgh. But the process of returning to his Scottish roots turned out to be rather fraught, and one that I observed with a degree of *Schadenfreude*. The row that broke out was provoked by a series of anonymous letters circulated by a disgruntled member of the medical faculty and revolved around the creation of a new part-time senior lectureship in virology to which Sutherland's wife was appointed after she had come close to being the only candidate. The acting principal temporarily suspended the selection procedure pending investigation by the university rector, a post in Scotland elected by the student body.

The rector and his assessors had concerns that communication had been 'suboptimal', but were reassured to learn that a field of two was not uncommonly small for such a position. While the actions of Sutherland and his wife were found to be beyond reproach, the rector recommended that the university lay down clear and explicit rules should such a situation arise in the future. The University Court subsequently ruled that in such cases the terms of the advertisement and the job specification should be drawn sufficiently widely that they could not be said to correspond with the qualifications and experience of a particular applicant.

Looking back on the 1988 fracas I realise that I should not have been too surprised by what had transpired. There were other problematic appointments at King's. A case in point was the appointment of the professor of palaeography at much the same time as the Koraes chair was filled. At an advanced stage in the proceedings, it was announced that Albinia de la Mare was prepared to stand, although she had made neither a formal application nor solicited references. Her appointment was subsequently settled by correspondence, to the disquiet of the external experts. Partial confirmation as to what happened is afforded by my recollection of de la Mare's appointment being announced at a meeting of the academic board at King's, subject to her references proving satisfactory. All became clear in the obituary of de la Mare in *The Independent* and the revelation that her predecessor as professor of palaeography at King's, Julian Brown, had decreed on his deathbed that Tilly de la Mare and no one else should succeed him. If the circumstances surrounding de la Mare's appointment were indeed thus, then my own complaints were nothing out of the ordinary.

6

Greeks bearing chairs: chairs bearing Greeks

'As we all know, the history of academic posts in Byzantine and Modern Greek in British universities has not been an easy one'.
—Averil Cameron

It scarcely needs to be said that the field of Byzantine and modern Greek studies is a somewhat recondite one. Both disciplines, and particularly modern Greek studies, have suffered from being regarded as the poor relations of the classics. Indeed, until relatively recently, what little was published about the modern country that is Greece was often the work of classicists, few of whom have been able to bring themselves to view the modern Greek world save through the distorting prism of the ancient. This chapter looks at some of the posts established in these fields in Britain, at some of those that have held them and at the controversies to which these appointments have not infrequently given rise. Many of those in the field would agree with Averil Cameron that the history of academic posts in Byzantine and modern Greek studies in British universities has indeed not been an easy one. I also have something to say about the Onassis Center for Hellenic Studies at New York University, as I was a kind of placebo in the university's patently threadbare attempt to demonstrate that it had run a proper search for its first director.

I have already had more than enough to say about the Koraes chair at King's College. Although it was in fact established after the Bywater and Sotheby chair at Oxford, the first Koraes professor, Arnold Toynbee, had been appointed in 1919, a year before the first Bywater and Sotheby professor, R.M. Dawkins. Dawkins came to modern Greek studies rather late. He had initially trained at King's College London as an electrical engineer, a profession which he found unappealing. He entered Emmanuel College, Cambridge as a student at the age of 26, subsequently becoming a fellow. He was a Student at the British School at Athens in 1902, oversaw excavations in Crete and at Sparta, and, in 1906, was appointed director of the School. His interests were wide and ranged from the study of Greek dialects to island embroideries and folk tales. One of Dawkins' greatest contributions to scholarship was his monumental *Modern Greek in Asia Minor* (1916), a study of the Greek dialects of Cappadocia, where the language in the nineteenth and early twentieth centuries was fighting a losing battle with Turkish in many communities. His timing (he carried out his research between 1909 and 1911) was fortunate, for after World War I, the Greeks of Asia Minor were swept up in the exchange of populations between Greece and Turkey, and the distinctive dialects of the region gradually died out among the displaced refugees. After war service in Greece, he was appointed to the Oxford chair. He had been an obvious contender for the Koraes chair when it was first established but, a famously shy individual, he dreaded having to keep in touch with the Anglo-Greek community. He was a productive and original scholar in both the Byzantine and modern Greek fields although, as he records in an unpublished memoir, during his time at Oxford he had only three students. He retired in 1939. His shyness was combined with eccentricity. Osbert Lancaster records an unlikely encounter with him, when cackling laughter had revealed Dawkins perched up a tree at Exeter College, of which he was a fellow and where the Bywater and Sotheby professorship was, and continues to be, based.

Little appears to be known of the circumstances of Dawkins' appointment in 1920. However, thanks to the existence of a small bundle of letters, entitled 'How to become a professor', preserved among the papers of his successor, John Mavrogordato, in the Bodleian Library at Oxford, we know quite a lot about how Mavrogordato came to be appointed as Dawkins' successor in 1939. The papers reveal an all too familiar tale of the backstage intrigue characteristic of academic appointments. When the chair had fallen vacant, Mavrogordato had felt diffident about applying. He had written some well-regarded works, including an admirable short history of Greece in modern times, but he had not held an academic post. Moreover, he was aged 57. Besides, as an Anglo-Chiot of private means, he had no pressing need of the £600 a year salary that was on offer in return for four month's residence in Oxford and a scarcely onerous teaching load of two lectures a week for two eight-week terms.

Despite these hesitations, two of his friends had strongly urged him to apply. These were John Johnson, a papyrologist and Printer to the University, and Philip Argenti, who, like Mavrogordato, was a member of a prominent and well-to-do Anglo-Chiot family. Johnson was a fellow of Exeter College, where he had been an undergraduate at the same time as Mavrogordato in the early years of the twentieth century, and was to assume the role of Mavrogordato's principal promoter and campaign manager. Three of the electors, conveniently, were, like Johnson, fellows of Exeter, with whom he would be able to have a 'discreet word […] without putting it formally on paper'. Argenti, himself a scholar and bibliophile, as he put it took on the role of a 'well-intentioned pimp' in the electoral process. He was particularly anxious to scupper the chances of the Russian linguistic scholar then at the University of Birmingham, Nicholas Bachtin, whom he thought certain to be an 'intreaguer' [sic]. Mavrogordato, incidentally, thought Argenti himself to be 'excessively conspiratorial'. In Argenti's view, 'Mavro' would be the ideal candidate as he would combine 'the English and Greek points of view', whereas Bachtin would do neither.

Mavrogordato, however, continued to have doubts about applying, and consulted Romilly Jenkins, at the time Lewis-Gibson lecturer in modern Greek at Cambridge and who, after World War II, was to be appointed to the Koraes chair. If Jenkins were himself to stand then Mavrogordato would not. Nor would he do so unless he had some indication that Dawkins, the retiring professor, would look favourably on his candidature. His friendship with Dawkins precluded the possibility of putting him in a position where he would be obliged 'to tell me that he likes me personally but thinks me a very unsatisfactory scholar and sadly ignorant of Greek grammar of all periods'. Jenkins was able to reassure him that he would not himself be applying but warned him it would be quite impossible for Dawkins to provide a testimonial for someone who might be his successor.

While Mavrogordato demonstrated a decent hesitation, Johnson showed no such scruples as he set about lobbying on Mavrogordato's behalf. To E.A. Barber, one of the electors, a classicist, and, like Johnson, a fellow of Exeter, he wrote that 'we all loved Mavro when we were young, and we who remain love him and respect him now'. He wrote, too, to Norman Baynes, honorary professor of Byzantine history at University College London, to ask him for a testimonial, for Mavrogordato was 'too shy and nice' to write himself: 'as I love you and as you love me and we both love Mavro will you be willing to write a commendation, if I send you the factual gear?' At the suggestion of Mavrogordato, Johnson also approached Sir Stephen Gaselee, Librarian of the Foreign Office and a fellow of Magdalene College, Cambridge, to suggest changes in the testimonial which Gaselee had agreed to write. It would be helpful if Gaselee could say that Mavrogordato's short history of modern Greece was the standard work, while the deletion of any reference to his activities during the Great War, when, for a time, Mavrogordato had worked for the Greek legation in London, would avoid any suggestion of 'secret service'. Johnson also suggested that it would be tactful if Gaselee removed any reference to 'young men' in his testimonial as Dawkins had never had any students, which was not quite the case.

Johnson's greatest concern was that Gaselee should emphasise that Mavrogordato was, in the Oxfordian sense, *salonfähig*, someone capable of behaving graciously and appropriately in fashionable, not to say snobbish, society: 'We all of us know who know Mavro, how lovable he is, how great an acquisition he would be to any Common Room with his gracious and artistic sense. I know no one who would be more suited to lend grace to Common Room life in Oxford'. While this might be thought obvious to Exeter men, it was not necessarily the case, for only one present fellow, R.R. Marett, the anthropologist, remembered 'Mavro' from his undergraduate days. Even the Exeter dons among the electors would not be aware of his social graces. Gaselee did as he was asked, albeit with a degree of reluctance. In Cambridge, so he wrote to Johnson, it would never do to recommend a man for a professorship on the ground that he would be a valuable acquisition to a Combination Room. Indeed, to do so would actually harm his chances, 'but I appreciate that things are different at Oxford'.

Johnson also appears to have been instrumental in persuading Mavrogordato to get Sir Edward Boyle, the former chairman of the Balkan Committee, to lobby on his behalf. Boyle duly undertook to approach two of the electors whom he knew personally, Arnold Toynbee, then at the Royal Institute of International Affairs and the London School of Economics, and G.S. Gordon, the president of Magdalen College, Oxford, a former Merton Professor of English Literature and a man who, in Johnson's estimation, was readily swayed by great men and titles. When Boyle asked what he should say to the two, Mavrogordato suggested that he should write to both to the effect that, while not competent to pass judgement on Mavrogordato's work on medieval Greek, he did feel qualified to say that his short history was admirable in both judgement and impartiality ('you hope Toynbee agrees with you here') and in style ('you hope Gordon agrees with you here'). In each case he should slightly flatter them, especially Gordon. Boyle duly did as he was asked and sent his letters in the first instance to Mavrogordato, for forwarding if he approved of their tone, or destruction if he did not. Mavrogordato also approached Dimitrios Caclamanos, a former Greek minister in London, who undertook to do what he could to help. Caclamanos made no secret of his obvious delight that Dawkins was about to depart, complaining that his incumbency had reduced the chair to a 'mere fiction'. All he had done was to publish some pamphlets on dead Greek dialects in which no one had the slightest interest.

Mavrogordato duly submitted a formal application, together with testimonials from Baynes, Gaselee, F.H. Marshall (the Koraes professor) and Jenkins. Jenkins wrote glowingly of Mavrogordato's 'lucidity, breadth of education and sanity of judgement'. 'By antecedent a Greek, by residence and education an Englishman, Mr Mavrogordato is bi-lingual and "bi-national" in a degree which would render him exceptionally well equipped to interpret the one nation to the other'. No interviews seem to have been held and, concurrently with receiving a letter from Marett announcing his unanimous election, Mavrogordato read in *The Times* that he was to be the new professor. The following day he received a letter from the university registry asking for a schedule of lectures. The appointment of the at once clubbable and scholarly Mavrogordato as the Bywater and Sotheby professor ensured that the challenge from Nicholas Bachtin was seen off. Whether or not in the event he added grace to the Exeter senior common room, his portrait by Mark Gertler continues to adorn it. Shortly after the appointment, Mavrogordato bumped into Sir Sydney Waterlow during a visit to his old school, Eton. The recently retired British minister in Athens tackled him 'resentfully and reproachfully' as he had seemingly been running the novelist Nikos Kazantzakis for the chair, arguing that this was an opportunity to appoint 'a really distinguished foreigner'. Waterlow subsequently tried, unsuccessfully, to get a readership for Kazantzakis at the University of London.

Mavrogordato held the chair until 1947 when he was succeeded by Constantine Trypanis, a German-trained classicist. Besides being a productive scholar, Trypanis had a reputation as a poet, writing in English and admired, *inter alia*, by W.H. Auden. Following the downfall of the Colonels' regime, he served as Minister of Culture in Greece. Trypanis was briefly succeeded as Bywater and Sotheby professor by one of his former students, Karolos Mitsakis. Mitsakis, who had previously been professor of comparative literature at the University of Maryland, was appointed to the chair in 1968, shortly after the Colonels' seizure of power. When it was learned that Mitsakis had also been appointed to a chair in the University of Thessaloniki and was commuting between Oxford and Thessaloniki, he was told that he should make up his mind between the two. He chose Thessaloniki.

As well as the Bywater and Sotheby chair, a lectureship in modern Greek was established in Oxford after World War II. The first holder was Robin Fletcher, whose acquaintance with the modern Greek world had begun when he was a member of the Levant Schooner Flotilla in the Aegean during World War II. When in 1979 Fletcher exchanged his lectureship for the wardenship of Rhodes House it was to be expected that, as a graduate of Oxford, Peter Mackridge, who had been at King's College as lecturer in modern

Greek language and literature for some seven years would put in for the job. Mackridge was an obvious candidate to succeed Fletcher, but in the end he got it only by the skin of his teeth. One of my students at King's happened to be visiting the Greek embassy a day or two before the appointment was made and heard someone say over the phone it was important that Mackridge be kept out of the job, on quite what grounds is not clear.

I was able to tip Mackridge off about this particular plot, but otherwise there was little I could do to help. It was clear that, on this occasion, the object of the *kombina*, or intrigue, as the Greeks would say, was to appoint Peter Levi. Levi was an ex-Jesuit, a classicist cum literary scholar and an accomplished poet who subscribed to the unusual view that the poet cum diplomat, Giorgos Seferis, had practically invented the modern Greek language. He had dabbled in modern Greek literature but had published nothing of substance in the field. Levi already had a lectureship in classics at Christ Church (a junior post rather different from a lectureship at other universities) and was the clear favourite for the job, for a majority of members of the appointment board were from Christ Church and college loyalties tend to be very strong. One member of the board, however, was supplied with evidence of Levi's inadequate knowledge of the modern language and, despite the determined attempts that were made to railroad his appointment at the meeting of the board, Mackridge got the job.

At Oxford, Mackridge put in many years of sterling service, with an excellent and wide-ranging record of publication stretching back to the Byzantine period, and this despite the punishing demands of teaching a whole degree course more or less single-handed, with assistance only from a language instructor. As Cyril Mango approached retirement in 1995 from the Bywater and Sotheby chair, Mackridge was as strong a candidate for the chair as he had been for the lectureship in 1980. But, once again, the Byzantinists proved to be a well-organised and ruthless lobby and were able to appoint one of their own, someone who had not even applied for the job. With the Byzantinists having lost their grip on the Koraes chair in 1988, there had been no realistic chance of a modernist being appointed to the Bywater and Sotheby chair. The original *kombina*, moreover, had envisaged the appointment of a Byzantine historian, although the chair was restricted to language and literature, and had demonstrably been intended as such by the person who endowed it, Charlotte Bywater. She was the wealthy wife, successively, of Hans Sotheby and of Ingram Bywater. Both were classics dons and both had been fellows of Exeter College, with which the Bywater and Sotheby chair has always subsequently been associated. Bywater, on Gladstone's nomination, was to become Regius Professor of Greek. A considerable scholar, he never once set foot on

Greek soil. His imagined vision of the Academy and the Lyceum, we are told, caused him to shrink 'from the desecrated temples and the spurious pretensions of modern Athens'. He was by no means the only classicist who felt that way. Quite what was the nature of Charlotte Bywater's interest in the modern Greek world is not clear.

There were early signs that all was not as it should have been in the process of filling of the Bywater and Sotheby chair in 1995. A head of steam was clearly building up for an appointment in the Byzantine field, as had been the case with the Koraes chair in 1988. As we have seen, the Society for the Promotion of Byzantine Studies in the 1980s had greedily laid claim to both chairs. In 1992, the Committee for Byzantine Studies at Oxford held a special meeting to consider the future of Byzantine studies in the university. It concluded that a chair devoted to Byzantine studies should be established at Oxford and that the 'present definition' of the Bywater and Sotheby professorship was no longer 'sustainable in terms of contemporary scholarship', for no one person could seriously cover the two fields. The committee called for the chair to be redefined as a chair of either Byzantine or modern Greek language and literature, and, not surprisingly in view of its composition, plumped for the former.

A year later, in 1993, the Literae Humaniores (i.e. classics) Faculty Board expressed its concern at the prospect of a major reduction in provision for 'an area of growing scholarly interest', namely Byzantine studies. While the Modern History Faculty Board saw the (unexplained) 'pragmatic argument' for modern Greek, it wished 'ideally' that the chair be devoted to Byzantine studies. These attempts to appropriate the Bywater and Sotheby chair for Byzantium reflected the aspiration to create a single centre within the university for classical and Byzantine studies, an ambition achieved with the opening in 2007 of the Stelios Ioannou School for Research in Classical and Byzantine Studies. The way in which the resources devoted to the study of the modern country, language and culture of Greece are dwarfed by those devoted to the classics and Byzantine studies is illustrated by figures issued by the Oxford Faculty of Classics, the largest in the world. In 2003, 500 undergraduate and over 100 graduate students were being taught or supervised by 80 established scholars in the various branches of the subject.

The Modern Languages Board, obedient to the wishes of the Charlotte Bywater, declared its support for a chair of language and literature, and, accepting that one person could not cover the entire field, was prepared to leave the particular field of expertise, whether medieval or modern, to the discretion of the electors. The views of the Faculty of Theology are not, so far as I know, on record. The General Board of the Faculties (the University of Oxford at that time had a structure that, while essentially democratic, could only be described, in the modern English usage of the term, as 'byzantine') deemed that the 'combined weight' of the views expressed by interested parties suggested that, given the existence of a lectureship in modern Greek, held by Mackridge, 'the electors might be informed that, other considerations being equal, it would be desirable to appoint someone whose special interests lie in the byzantine period'.

The Literae Humaniores and History Faculty Boards had in their submissions both stated a preference for an appointment in Byzantine 'studies', and not language and literature. Those of a suspicious nature, which included most of those in the field, myself not excepted, were alarmed (although some were of course gratified) to see that the chair in the 1990s began to be referred to in official university publications as the Bywater and Sotheby Professorship of Byzantine and Modern Greek *Studies* or, what was worse, as the Bywater and Sotheby Chair in *Byzantine* Studies rather than the title which was given when it was endowed, namely medieval and modern Greek language and literature. This was attributed by the university authorities to what was, astonishingly, claimed as 'poor copy-editing'. This may conceivably have been the case, but the use of the term *studies*, had it gone unchallenged, would have opened up the chair to applications by historians, and more particularly by Byzantine historians, as well as by linguists and literary scholars, clearly contrary to Charlotte Bywater's wishes. Would-be donors to Oxford should take note that attempts may be made surreptiously to override their wishes in like manner.

One of those who applied for the chair wrote to A.P. Weale, the Secretary of Faculties, with copies to the vice-chancellor and Sir Anthony Kenny, the chairman of the electoral board, that it was beginning to look as though this was not simply a case of clerical error. Rather, the letter continued, it appeared to be 'the result of a concerted effort to create a *fait accompli* in which the professorship is perceived no longer to be on the establishment of the faculty of medieval and modern languages but on the establishment of modern history'. Weale replied with the assurance that this was a simple mistake and not the result of a conspiracy. Just as in 1988 I had had to complain, when the process of filling the Koraes chair was already under way, about the appointment of two Byzantine historians as the external assessors, so this particular applicant had to complain about what may have been an attempt to manipulate the title in order to secure a particular appointment. In both cases, we were placed in the invidious position of complaining while the process of appointment was already under way. This can hardly have helped our respective causes.

The Bywater and Sotheby Chair of Byzantine and Modern Greek Language and Literature had been reprieved by the university only after individual

Greeks and the Greek government had contributed substantial funds to boost the endowment when the professorship was threatened with abolition by the university. This was 'on the understanding that Modern Greek language and literature would fall within its purview'. The fundraising process to save the chair in essence had differed little from blackmail since would-be donors were told that unless they stumped up the necessary funds it would be abolished. It is one thing to seek an endowment for a new chair, which potential donors can endow or not as they see fit, and quite another to say to that, without financial help, an existing, and indeed endowed, chair will be allowed to fall into abeyance.

Not only was momentum building up for an appointment in the Byzantine field, but it appeared that the board of electors had been constituted with such an end specifically in view, as had been the case with the Koraes chair in 1988. The board was chaired by Sir Anthony Kenny, a philosopher and warden of Rhodes House, who, in accordance with sensible Oxford convention, had been chosen from outwith the field and was thus not identified with either the 'ancients' or the 'moderns'. There were two representatives of Exeter College. The nominee of the Theology Board was Bishop Kallistos of Diokleia (formerly known as Timothy Ware). The nominee of the Literae Humaniores Board was Professor Averil Cameron, the warden of Keble College and now professor of late antique and Byzantine history in the university and, as we have seen, formerly at King's College London. The nominee of the History Faculty Board was James Howard-Johnston, university lecturer in Byzantine studies. There were two nominees of the Modern Languages Board, Christopher Robinson, university lecturer in French but also a specialist in modern Greek language and literature, and Professor Roderick Beaton of King's College. The external expert was Ihor Ševčenko, Dumbarton Oaks Professor of Byzantine History and Literature at Harvard.

There was thus a discernible bias towards the Byzantine field, and indeed towards byzantine history, in the composition of the electoral board. Moreover, the General Board had already, of course, determined that, 'other considerations being equal' it would be desirable to appoint someone with special interests in the Byzantine period. By coincidence, a working party that had been set up at Oxford at much the same time to review the process of appointments to statutory posts, of which the Bywater and Sotheby professorship was one. The working party expressed its concern that electoral boards could be tailored with a particular outcome in mind. This had been the case with the Koraes chair in 1988.

At the time of the election Ševčenko was 73. The university's statutes at the time provided that no one over 70 could be appointed a member of any university body, and that no one 75 or over could continue in office on any university body. However, it was open to the university council to suspend these provisions in individual cases, which it duly did in the case of Ševčenko. As far as the age limit goes, there appears to be no upper limit on the age at which people can serve as external experts on electoral boards at Oxford, provided that the university suspends the relevant statutes. This also appears to be the case at the University of London. Barring people from boards of electors when they are past the normal retirement age would seem sensible. It gave me some pleasure to point out a couple of years later, in a letter to the *Oxford Magazine,* that the very same council which had suspended the statutes to enable the 73-year-old Ševčenko to sit on the board of electors, was seeking to deprive retired members of the university of membership of congregation, the university's 'parliament', on the ground that those over 65 are 'inevitably less in touch with the central activities of the university than when they were in post'.

At the same time, I also drew attention to the even more anomalous case of Lord Weidenfeld, the publisher. Not only were the statutes suspended to allow him to serve, at the age of 74, on an electoral board, but this board was established to elect the Weidenfeld Visiting Professor in Comparative Literature, a post which he had himself funded. This was but one example of the way in which donors are gradually being given a say, or at least a veto, in appointment to posts which they have founded. When Wafic Said, the Syrian-born businessman, in the mid-1990s gave £20 million to help fund a new school of management at Oxford, the gift contained an unusual and pernicious provision. This was that the election of the director would be subject to the approval of the trustees of the Wafic Said Foundation, a body external to the university. Such approval, we were assured, was not to be *unreasonably* withheld, but no insight was offered into what *reasonable* grounds might be invoked to withhold approval. What was particularly objectionable about this arrangement, which was scheduled to last for 200 years, was that the university would be likely to apply a self-denying ordinance and not appoint someone to the directorship who was known, or even worse was thought, to be unacceptable to the Wafic Said Foundation trustees. Oxford University is always banging on about its world-class status, but would Harvard, Yale or Princeton concede such a right of veto to outsiders in the making of an academic appointment?

A short list was drawn up from those who had applied for the Bywater and Sotheby chair. As well as Peter Mackridge and others in the field this included Paul Magdalino of the University of St Andrews. Magdalino is an excellent Byzantine scholar, but is demonstrably an historian and not a specialist in either Byzantine or modern Greek language and literature. Moreover, he appears not initially to have applied for the chair, no doubt because he was not a 'lang and lit' person, but nonetheless had been invited to apply. This invitation seems to have come from Ševčenko, who had been telling all and sundry in the United States that the next Bywater and Sotheby professor would be Magdalino, long before any appointment had actually been made. It was also clear that Ševčenko was not the only member of the board pushing hard for the appointment of Magdalino.

In November 1994, the Greek ambassador in London, Elias Gounaris, had drafted a letter about the future of the chair. Judging by its content he may also have heard of the *kombina*, although on this occasion, unlike in the 1980 election of a lecturer in modern Greek language and literature at Oxford, the Greek embassy seems to have favoured the appointment of Mackridge. The letter was clearly intended to be helpful to Mackridge's cause, but whether an intervention by the embassy would ultimately have been helpful is not obvious. Gounaris made the point that it would be unrealistic to expect any one person to cover the whole sweep of scholarship from Romanos the Melodist in the sixth century AD to Takis Sinopoulos in the twentieth. He continued that 'as far as we Greeks are concerned, we would like the emphasis of the professorship to be shifted, if possible, towards modern Greek literature and language'. In the event, the ambassador did not send his letter. At the time I thought this was a sensible decision, but, in retrospect, so heavily were the cards stacked against Mackridge, that I cannot see that it would have done any harm. It might conceivably have done some good.

In an effort to help Mackridge, which proved to be unavailing, I wrote in December 1994 to the chairman of the board of electors, Sir Anthony Kenny, to say that I was surprised to learn that at least one Byzantine historian had been short-listed, given that the further particulars for the post had specified that the professor would be 'required to lecture and give instruction in byzantine and modern Greek language and literature'. I made the point that scholars of world-class reputation with interests in the specified field had applied for the chair and that there could be no grounds for appointment outside the field of language and literature unless the post were to be re-advertised, making it clear that historians as well as linguists and specialists in literature were eligible to apply. I also made the point that had I realised that historians were to be considered for the chair then I should myself have put in an application.

I concluded by asking Kenny for an assurance that an appointment would be made in the fields specified both in the advertisement for the chair and in the further particulars. I fully expected him, at best, to ignore my letter or, at worst, to refer me, in effect if not in so many words, to the precedent established by *Private Eye*'s lawyers in the now famous case of Arkell v. Pressdram, i.e. a bald injunction to 'fuck off'. In the event I was gratified to receive a prompt and courteous reply from Kenny, who wrote to assure me that the appointment would be made in the advertised field. He added that my letter would be placed before the electors to the Bywater and Sotheby chair. I was pleasantly surprised by Kenny's reply, although it was perhaps a little remiss of him to bring my letter to the notice of the electors without first seeking my permission, but he may have feared that I would not agree to his making use of it. However, had he asked, I certainly would have agreed. Kenny's hand was strengthened to a much greater extent when one of the electors threatened to resign from the electoral board if an historian were to be appointed. That really would have set the cat among the pigeons.

From the outset, Ševčenko and his allies on the board were determined that Mackridge should not be appointed, and, with Magdalino now out of the running, none of the other short-listed candidates were deemed suitable. Eventually, after several meetings, the chair was offered to Elizabeth Jeffreys. At the time of her appointment she was a senior research fellow in the department of Modern Greek at the University of Sydney, and had apparently not applied for the Bywater chair. On her appointment, *The Oxford University Gazette* referred to her as being 'the driving force of a project on the early Byzantine chronicler, John Malalas, which led to two books: *The Chronicle of John Malalas: a translation* (1986) and *Studies in John Malalas* (1990)'.

I must confess to having felt a slight tinge of regret that Magdalino had not been appointed. I would then have had no hesitation in suing the university on the grounds that the electoral board had acted *ultra vires* and that I would myself have applied had I known that the chair would go to a historian. With luck, and a good lawyer, I might have hoped to secure a generous settlement, thus confirming that it is possible to make quite a comfortable living from not being appointed to chairs in the field of Byzantine and modern Greek studies.

With hindsight one can see that Mackridge, despite his obvious qualifications for the chair, never had a realistic chance of being appointed by an electoral board stuffed with Byzantinists determined to protect their own turf. Having lost control of the Koraes chair the Byzantinists were desperate to hang on to the Bywater and Sotheby chair. Indeed, shortly after the appointment was made, Ševčenko, at a dinner at Wolfson College, told another of the guests that 'we have defended the field'.

On learning of the result, I wrote to the vice-chancellor of Oxford, Dr Peter North. I basically made two procedural points. I drew his attention to the fact that, although university regulations stipulated an upper age limit for members of electoral boards, the university can and does suspend these regulations in particular cases, on this occasion placing Ševčenko on the board. I then asked whether, if an exception could be made in the case of the 73-year-old Ševčenko, why not in the case of the 81-year-old Robert Browning, emeritus professor of classics and ancient history in the University of London, who had an encyclopaedic knowledge of the Greek language at all stages of its evolution. If there was in effect no upper age limit, then why not give consideration to appointing the 92-year-old Sir Steven Runciman to the electoral board? I pointed out that most people would regard the prospect of a nonagenarian member of an electoral board as a self-evident absurdity. But at what precise age between 73 and 92 did age become an insuperable bar to appointment?

I asked whether it would not make better sense for the university to make the then university retirement age, at 65 or 67 depending on the conditions of appointment, the upper age limit for electors, a limit which could not be breached in any circumstances. I pointed out that it was difficult to think of any other walk of life in which individuals long past retiring age were able to have a determining say in appointments. I might usefully have pointed out that even that bastion of gerontocracy, the Vatican, has an upper age limit, 80, above which cardinals are barred from voting in a conclave to elect a new pope (although not, curiously, from being elected pontiff), whereas no such limits appear to apply at Oxford. The second point in my letter concerned the way in which Byzantinists dominated the electoral board so that they were able to outvote the faculty nominees on the electoral board. Should not the faculty concerned be sovereign in the matter of appointment to its statutory chairs? I concluded by urging that Mackridge be given a personal chair in modern Greek language and literature.

To this letter the vice-chancellor replied defending the fact that non-members of the faculty had such influence over the appointment. He did not think it right for an electoral board to be 'dominated', as he curiously put it, by members of any one faculty. One shudders to think what might be the consequences if the faculty of medicine, for instance, yielded sovereignty over those it appoints to members of other faculties. As for a chair for Mackridge, that, he said, would 'have to take its place in the long list of priorities for new posts in an era of reduced funding'. Mackridge was awarded the title of professor of modern Greek in 1997, but this was what I term a 'Potemkin' chair, i.e. the title without the emoluments of a professor. The scheme, introduced in the 1990s, was a wonderful scam introduced by the university to help deal with the problem of uncompetitive pay. The intention was that within a few years most of those teaching at Oxford would have the title of professor, but without a professorial salary. When the matter was being debated in congregation, the university 'parliament', one champion of

'Potemkin' professorships argued that when attending conferences, particularly in the United States, if you did not have the title of professor you would be unlikely to be given a room with a view in the conference hotel.

Elizabeth Jeffrey's term as Bywater and Sotheby professor came to an end in 2006. There were early indications of potential trouble ahead. The *University Gazette* recorded that the composition of the electoral board for the Bywater and Sotheby chair had been amended. It would now contain only one nominee of the Faculty of Medieval and Modern Languages, while at much the same time the board for the professorship of ancient philosophy contained three nominees of the Philosophy Faculty. The explanation given, that more than one faculty shared 'sovereignty' over the Bywater and Sotheby chair, made no sense. Nor could the university authorities indicate when the chair was supposed to have become a chair shared by several faculties. How could a chair that was demonstrably in the field of medieval and modern language and literature fall under the jurisdiction of any other faculty than the Faculty of Medieval and Modern Languages?

It was encouraging to note, however, that the two external members of the board established for the Bywater and Sotheby chair had interests primarily in the early modern and modern periods. The board could not be described, as had been the case in 1995, as being weighted in favour of Byzantinists. There was, however, an anomaly in its composition: the chair was Averil Cameron. There is a long-standing Oxford convention that chairs of electoral boards are drawn from those with no connection to the field of study involved, thus standing above the fray in elections that are frequently hotly contested. It clearly makes sense when making appointments to have a neutral chair person, and this seems to be the practice in most British universities. But Cameron, who had moved to Oxford in 1994 on becoming the warden of Keble College, had subsequently become a pro-vice-chancellor, and, additionally, professor of late antique and Byzantine history, and was demonstrably not above the fray in the small field of Byzantine studies. It is worth noting that she was concurrently chair of the electoral board for the Wykeham professorship of physics. A chair of physics is about as far from medieval and modern Greek language and literature as it is possible to imagine. When the Bywater and Sotheby chair had last been advertised in 1995 the chair of the electoral board had been Sir Anthony Kenny, a philosopher and someone demonstrably removed from the field.

A protest to the vice-chancellor, Dr John Hood, against this breach of a long-standing and eminently sensible convention elicited the reply that there had been a number of these electoral boards in the recent past for which the chairman had had 'an intimate knowledge of, or is indeed a practitioner in the field. I have no evidence that this handicapped them from acting in a wholly impartial manner'. The vice-chancellor, however, was unable to provide examples of such electoral boards. Cameron remained chair of the board. In the event, Professor Marc Lauxtermann of the University of Amsterdam became the seventh Bywater and Sotheby professor. It is true that he was principally a specialist in Byzantine language and literature but he had demonstrable and serious interests in the modern literature of Greece. So honour was satisfied.

Hood, a New Zealander, was the 293rd vice-chancellor in the university's history and the first to be appointed from outside the Oxford academic community. He arrived on a mission to 'reform' Oxford's admittedly somewhat cumbersome but nonetheless manifestly democratic system of governance. This was clearly anathema to a thrusting businessman and academic administrator. His proposals included measures to address 'under-performance' on the part of the dons; to overturn the university's system of self-government, whose roots went back centuries; and to hand considerable powers, on the American model, to a council containing a majority of businessmen from outside the university. These would no doubt have included a number of prominent bankers, or 'banksters' as Harold Macmillan was wont to call them, a number of whom were to demonstrate themselves to be greedy and/or recklessly incompetent in the financial tsunami of 2008.

These efforts to institute reforms came in for scathing criticism. The warden of New College, Alan Ryan, for instance, was quoted in *The Independent* as saying that watching people

> wrecking Oxford is disagreeable. You stick a businessman in charge of a university and it's all a complete cock-up. He doesn't know what the job is about and he doesn't know what the place is for. His first act is always to get into a fight and piss everyone off.

In a nice donnish touch, Ryan, a political theorist, counselled Hood to read the section in Machiavelli's *The Prince* on the 'difficulties of reducing free states to subservience'. As a pro-vice-chancellor, Averil Cameron was very much in the vice-chancellor's camp. In one of the debates on the proposed 'reforms' in Congregation, Cameron, in coming to the aid of the beleaguered Hood, was reported as saying that she detected 'a whiff of conspiracy, with academic freedom being used a slogan to rally the troops'. This intervention was not well received.

One of the earliest and most productive centres in the field of modern Greek language and literature has been the University of Birmingham. This was in large measure due to the efforts of George Thomson, who became professor of Greek there in 1936, the year in which he joined the Communist Party of Great Britain. He was a pioneer in the Marxist interpretation of ancient Greek drama and a hard-line communist who, in 1951, had been the only member of the party's executive committee to vote against the party programme, *The British Road to Socialism*, because it omitted mention of the dictatorship of the proletariat. He subsequently became an apologist for the Maoist variant of communism. A remarkable linguist (he had translated the Odyssey and the Book of Common Prayer into Irish), Thomson had a considerable interest in modern Greek, for the teaching of which he compiled a manual (1966), published by an appropriately left-wing publisher, Collet's. He established what was in effect the first department of modern Greek in a British university. In this, Thomson's daughter, Margaret, was appointed a lecturer in the modern language. The family connection was reinforced by the addition of Christos Alexiou, Margaret's husband, to the department.

Margaret Alexiou subsequently moved to the Seferis Chair of Modern Greek Studies at Harvard, a chair founded with a subvention by the Greek government. The president of Greece at the time of the chair's establishment was Konstantinos Tsatsos, whose wife was the poet Seferis' sister, which no doubt had something to do with the title given to the chair. Because of her left-wing heritage, her husband, Christos, having been on the 'wrong' side during the Greece civil war, Alexiou was required to make what Eric Hobsbawm, writing of a scholar with a 'dangerous' political past, has termed a 'formal abjuration of past sin'. A public statement of right-wing (American) political orthodoxy was made a condition of receiving the necessary visa to enable her to take up the Seferis chair. This took the form of a letter to *The Economist* shortly before the 1985 Greek elections in which she warned that the prospect of a narrow victory by Andreas Papandreou's PASOK, 'with the balance of power held by the Soviet-dominated Communist party of the Exterior', might constitute a threat to the free world and to democracy in Greece itself. The letter seems to have done trick.

In a *New Yorker* profile of Anthony Giddens, at that time director of the London School of Economics, Professor the Lord Meghnad Desai of St Clement Danes is on record as saying that whereas dons at Oxford and Cambridge are snobbish about wine and food 'at LSE we are snobs only about intellect'. One might reasonably expect, therefore, a degree of transparency in the procedures whereby members of the academic staff are appointed at so august an institution, and one, moreover, as Professor Giddens, a champion of the Blair's 'third way', declared, in true Blairite fashion, that was destined to become once again 'an intellectual beacon'.

The regulations of the LSE and of the University of London, of which the LSE is part, stipulated the presence of experts, external to the college and the university, on boards making appointments to established chairs. Yet it required repeated letters to an oddly defensive Giddens to elicit the identity of the external experts involved in the first appointment in 1997 to the Venizelos Chair of Contemporary Greek Studies at LSE, which is combined with the directorship of the oddly named Hellenic Observatory. While there is arguably a case for withholding the identity of the external experts, or, indeed, of the other members of a board while an election is in process for fear of 'jury nobbling', there can be no conceivable reason for not disclosing this information once an appointment has been made.

It is worth noting, incidentally, that Oxford routinely publishes in the *Oxford University Gazette* the names of members of the electoral boards for established chairs at the outset of the electoral process. This is not the case in London. 'Jury nobbling' does of course go on, but, for obvious reasons we do not hear much about it. Isaiah Berlin, whose letters throw an unattractive light on the seamier aspect of academic politics at Oxford and reveal a distasteful propensity to snobbish gossip, recorded the intrigues surrounding the appointment of E.R. Dodds to the Regius Chair of (Ancient) Greek at Oxford in 1936. Gilbert Murray, the retiring Regius professor, advised Stanley Baldwin, the prime minister in whose patronage the appointment lay, that his successor should be Dodds, in itself a breach of the sensible convention that an academic should have no role in the appointment of his successor. Maurice Bowra, another aspirant, got wind of this intervention, and Berlin came under pressure from Bowra to be 'bold, bloody and resolute' in an (unsuccessful) approach on his behalf to the warden of New College, H.A.L. Fisher.

In one letter Giddens asked what my interest in the chair of contemporary Greek studies was, and, unprompted, said that he had no reason to suppose that proper procedures had not been observed. I replied that, as one of fewer than a handful of academic specialists in Greek history and politics at the time in Britain it would be unusual if I did *not* have an interest in who was appointed Venizelos professor. I added that I had written an entire book on the establishment, and subsequent implosion, as a consequence of the meddling of donors, of the first chair in Byzantine and modern Greek studies to be established at a British university, the Koraes chair, a chair which, like the Venizelos chair, had been established with Greek money. Thirdly, I pointed out that I was currently writing a book about what I termed 'ethnic' chairs and the 'privatisation of knowledge' in the English-speaking world. This was true at the time, although that particular project has since metamorphosed into this memoir. Lastly, I wrote that I had been concerned for some time about the inadequacies of the procedures for appointment to established chairs in the University of London.

That such a chair should have been established at the LSE certainly made a good deal of sense. There is a long tradition of Greek students studying at the LSE, and a significant number of the country's politicians, businessmen and technocrats, not to mention academics, are LSE-trained. In the 1990s there were some 20 researchers and teachers of Greek origin at the School. LSE alumni include George Papandreou who, as a member of his father Andreas Papandreou's PASOK government, played an important role in the campaign to establish the chair. Part of the funding came from the budget of the Greek ministry of education but most appears to have come from Greek banks where the LSE 'mafia' is particularly well entrenched. Andreas Papandreou's successor as prime minister, Costas Simitis, who became leader of PASOK in 1996, had himself studied at the LSE.

It was George Papandreou who, in October 1995, when alternate minister of foreign affairs, inaugurated the Hellenic Observatory, which was established in conjunction with the chair. The function of the Observatory is stated as improving 'knowledge and understanding of Greece today among international decision-makers and opinion leaders', i.e. to engage in what the Greeks term *provoli*, the boosting of the country's image. The puzzling appellation 'Hellenic Observatory' appears to have been a sop to those among the donors who had initially wished to use the title 'chair of contemporary Hellenic Studies'. This would have sounded strange to the British ear, for 'Hellenic' has strong connotations of Greek antiquity. I may, indeed, have had something to do with changing the title when I pointed this out to one of the prime movers in its establishment. But there is undoubtedly sensitivity in some Greek circles about the purportedly pejorative meaning of the words 'Greek' and 'Greece'.

In the event, a compromise appears to have been reached whereby the chair became 'Greek' but the 'observatory', confusingly, remained 'Hellenic'. Incidentally, one of the stated objectives of the Hellenic Observatory is to develop close links with the 'wider Greek community' in London, estimated to number some 16,000. But this statistic ignores the presence in London of tens of thousands of Greek-speaking Cypriots. For all the public rhetoric about the common fate of 'Hellenism', it is clear that many Greeks do not in their heart of hearts deem the Greek Cypriots to be part of the *omogeneia*, or kith and kin, although such attitudes, for obvious reasons, are seldom explicitly articulated. I sent a copy of the brochure containing this figure of 16,000 to a friend at the Cyprus High Commission, who agreed that it demonstrated an all too common attitude among *Elladites,* mainland Greeks, remarkably few of whom have ever visited Cyprus despite the public professions of undying support for their 'Hellenic' brethren.

The involvement of the Greek government and of the banks in the funding of the chair, coupled with the high degree of politicisation of public life in Greece, inevitably led the more cynically minded (myself included) to speculate that the donors would wish the chair to go, if not to *o dikos mas anthropos*, one of our own (politically), as the expressive Greek phrase has it, then at least to somebody who is not deemed to be antithetical to 'new PASOK'. Be this as it may, there were a number of unusual features about the chair and the electoral process.

If an 'ethnic chair' is a post established with subventions from a foreign government, ethnic community or an individual with the implicit (and not infrequently explicit) aim of promoting a favourable image of the country involved,[1] then the donors and/or those responsible for setting up the chair at the LSE (which purports to be an 'Equal Opportunities' employer) seem to have wanted to add an additional, although unspoken, condition, namely that the holder should actually be a Greek. How else are we to interpret the stipulation in the further particulars that the holder of the chair be 'totally fluent in English since he/she will teach and supervise in that language, although fluency in Greek, is, of course, also necessary'? Since when has there ever been any suggestion that the language of instruction at the LSE should be anything other than English?

As it happens, the only applicants short-listed were Greek, and indeed the appointment of Loukas Tsoukalis as the Venizelos professor was reported in the Greek press several months before it was formally announced in Britain. In the same article it was announced that a committee would exercise oversight over the chair. This was to include Dr Nikos Garganas, the deputy-governor (and subsequently governor) of the Bank of Greece, an LSE graduate and one of the prime movers in the fundraising effort for the establishment of the chair. When I last looked into the matter, all the members of the advisory board, with the exception of the current Venizelos professor, were Greek.

An odd feature of the Venizelos chair when it was advertised in late 1996 was that it was open to those in the fields of politics, economics, business studies, public policy, international relations or political economy, but not history, whether contemporary or otherwise. The distinction between contemporary history and politics, as the latter is often professed in the UK, is a fine one. In this particular instance the omission of history had the unfortunate consequence of ruling out of consideration, one trusts unintentionally, one or two outstanding British scholars in the field of modern and contemporary Greek history.

This omission of contemporary history seems all the more strange given that one of the external experts on the board of advisers, as I was eventually able to establish from Giddens, was himself a modern historian. This was Professor Martin Blinkhorn, a distinguished historian of modern Spain and Italy to be sure, but not someone with any specialised knowledge of Greek matters. A further anomaly was that, according to university regulations, such external experts were to be chosen from among those 'expert in the discipline concerned', whereas, of course, history had been specifically excluded from the remit of the chair. The other external expert, Professor Alasdair Smith of the University of Sussex, is certainly a distinguished political economist, but again, to judge by his publications, he had no particular expertise in matters Greek. The third expert, external to the college but internal to the university as stipulated by university regulations, was Professor Roderick Beaton of King's College, a specialist in modern Greek literature. It cannot often transpire that someone who specialises in, say, medieval and modern German literature helps to fill positions in the University of London devoted to German politics, but I can see that LSE would have been in some difficulty in finding someone with appropriate expertise in the university. All the more reason then, one might have thought, for the authorities to take reasonable steps to find at least one external expert whose major expertise lay in modern and contemporary, non-literary Greek studies. As far as I have been able to determine, Beaton would have been the only member of the board able to read any of the applicants' publications in Greek. Such a state of affairs would surely never be tolerated in a chair devoted to, say, German or Spanish studies, and is yet another unfortunate example of Greek exceptionalism.

If the begetters of the chair did indeed want it to go to a Greek they must have been pleased to learn that the shortlist for the first appointment was an all Greek one. Moreover, it could scarcely have been shorter, consisting as it did, of just two names. Given that applications were invited in no fewer than six fields in the social sciences this was odd. For just as Greece has, historically, been an exporter of manpower, so, more recently, it has been a major exporter of academic manpower, particularly in the social sciences. One such academic export, of course, was Andreas Papandreou, a distinguished economist who rose to become chairman of the economics department at Berkeley before returning to Greece to assume a highly successful, if controversial, career in politics. His career, moreover, gave the lie to the naive presumption of some academics that if only more of their ilk were to become practising politicians then political life would somehow be conducted on a more rational basis.

Not having been involved in the selection process it is, of course, difficult to say how many serious applicants (Greek and non-Greek) there were, but it can be said with some certainty that there would have been significantly more than two. It can also be said with some confidence that more than two of these would have been electable. One of those who did apply for the chair but was not short-listed, was Professor George Mavrogordatos of the department of political science of the University of Athens and the author of one of a handful of truly path-breaking books on Greek politics. His absence from the short-list was puzzling, the more so as one of the external experts, Professor Blinkhorn, had recommended that he be included on it.

The two names on the short list were those of Loukas Tsoukalis of the department of political science in the University of Athens, and of Theodoros Georgakopoulos of the Athens University of Economics. Both enjoyed international reputations in the fields of European integration and economics respectively. At a very late stage, it seems to have dawned on Giddens that a short list of two did not look very good for a chair at the 'intellectual beacon' that was the LSE, and that the net should be cast rather wider. This resulted in Paschalis Kitromilides, likewise a professor in the department of political science of the University of Athens, being invited, indeed pressed, to apply. He had not done so in the first instance as he felt that his interests were too historical and insufficiently focused on contemporary Greece. An invitation to apply for a chair at LSE, however, is not something to be lightly turned down and he duly submitted an application. His *curriculum vitae* only reached the LSE a matter of days, if not hours, before the interviews were held. This was scarcely satisfactory if members of the electoral board were to have the opportunity to read, as they surely should, at least some of his voluminous publications.

Kitromilides and Tsoukalis were duly interviewed in mid-June but, puzzlingly, one of the external experts, Professor Blinkhorn, was not present at the interviews. There is some confusion as to whether Georgakopoulos was actually interviewed, as apparently he had been ill at the time. That Blinkhorn was not present was scarcely his fault as the date of the interviews was set without consulting him and he had a pressing prior commitment which prevented him from attending. This hardly seemed a satisfactory state of affairs, although Giddens assured me that Blinkhorn had indicated that he would support whatever decision the board took.

True to form, the early history of the Venizelos chair was a troubled one and the first holder of the chair, Loukas Tsoukalis, resigned after little more than three years. On the second occasion that the chair was filled, in 2001, Greeks were kept at arms length by the LSE, seemingly quite deliberately. Professor Nikos Mouzelis, an LSE professor and a distinguished sociologist who had been involved in establishing the chair, was not involved in the electoral process. I do not know who the other applicants were on this occasion, but

Kevin Featherstone was appointed. Like his predecessor, Featherstone had published more about European integration than about Greece itself.

Another Greek-sponsored fellowship that proved controversial was the Bodossakis research fellowship at Churchill College, Cambridge. A college founded as a memorial to Winston Churchill was an unlikely home for a fellowship funded by, and named after, Prodromos Bodosakis-Athanasiadis, a hugely rich Greek of Anatolian origin who had made his fortune, *inter alia*, in the manufacture and sale of arms. On the eve of World War II, his Poudreries et Cartoucheries Helléniques, with some 12,000 employees, was the largest industrial undertaking in Greece. He is known to have sold weapons to both sides during the Spanish civil war, while in 1940 he was supplying weapons to British forces in the Middle East on highly disadvantageous terms that were deemed by the Foreign Office to be akin to blackmail. Not long after the German occupation of Greece in April 1941, Bodosakis was reported to be about to sell a substantial part of his shares in his factories to a German armaments manufacturer, which would have resulted in the harnessing of his factories to the Nazi war machine, while a year later the US Director of Naval Intelligence described Bodosakis as 'a thoroughly disreputable character, by some considered the most dangerous of all Greeks'. The British also believed that 'minute investigation' of his business affairs might reveal 'definite contact with the enemy'.

It was at the direct behest of Churchill that Bodosakis was arrested in Egypt in 1944 by the British military police and unceremoniously bundled off into exile in the Lebanon. Churchill believed Bodosakis to have been behind republican dissidents in Egypt who had been making life difficult for the Greek government-in-exile and for King George II, to whose somewhat forlorn cause the British prime minister had a perilously strong emotional attachment. Churchill looked on Bodosakis as a 'capitalist intriguer', and urged that he and his close associate 'this wild man [Byron] Karapanayiotis', be sent to 'some remote island [Mauritius, the Seychelles and South Africa were considered] and their supporters made to feel out of it for several months, if not years'. Whether Bodosakis was aware of Churchill's responsibility for his Babylonian exile is difficult to say. But if he did, then clearly he bore his memory no grudge. Neither did Churchill College appear to have troubled itself that the Bodosakis fortune may have been amassed in a rather unsavoury fashion. No doubt the college authorities were acting on the principle famously propounded by an American academic fundraiser when he said that the trouble with tainted money was that 'there t'aint enough of it'.

An insight into the curious circumstances surrounding the establishment of the Bodosakis Fellowship is contained in the splendidly name-dropping (and unintentionally revealing) memoirs of Spyros Markezinis, the Greek politician who acted as an intermediary in its establishment. Once one of the rising stars in the Greek political firmament, Markezinis by the early 1970s had become a marginal figure, and was one of the very few politicians prepared to collaborate with the Colonels' regime. In the seventh volume of his memoirs, published in Athens in 1979 (the other six seem never to have seen the light of day), he dwelt at length on his ill-starred and short-lived premiership in the summer and autumn of 1973. This came about when he agreed to participate in Colonel Papadopoulos' forlorn attempt to move towards a 'guided' democracy, over which as president he would continue to hold the whip hand, with Markezinis as prime minister.

Markezinis records that, shortly before becoming prime minister, he met with Sir William Hawthorne, the master of Churchill College, and Dr Kenneth McQuillen, the senior tutor, who had been invited to Athens by Bodosakis to discuss the endowment of a fellowship. The Cambridge party was entertained both by Markezinis and, with 'Oriental splendour', by Bodosakis himself. Markezinis subsequently appears to have asked Hawthorne to act as a consultant to the ministry of energy established for the first time in Greece – this was the year of the first oil crisis – when he became prime minister in June 1973. Markezinis published in his multi-volume illustrated history of Greece, à propos of nothing and quite out of context, a photograph of Hawthorne standing before the portrait of Bodosakis-Athanasiadis that is housed in Churchill College. In Markezinis' estimation, Hawthorne was one of 'those centre stage and behind the scenes personalities who were to be met with chiefly in the era of the British world empire'. He also records a rather pathetic scene in December 1973, a few weeks after the Markezinis government had collapsed and his patron, Colonel Papadopoulos, had himself been deposed following the army's bloody suppression of the student occupation of the Athens Polytechnic. Our man in Athens, Sir Robin Hooper, visited Markezinis to complain that he could not find a minister to whom he could hand over the plans prepared by Hawthorne.

On taking office, Markezinis had received some rather embarrassing messages of congratulation from English friends and acquaintances. These included Douglas Dakin, professor of history at Birkbeck College, with a considerable interest, and expertise, in the modern history of Greece that dated back to war service in the Middle East. He revealed that he had predicted to his friends that Markezinis would return to political office and would place his great talents at the disposal of the nation. Another who sent a laudatory telegram was Hawthorne himself. He sent his warmest congratulations and best wishes for the historic task on which Markezinis was embarked, from himself and from all Markezinis' friends at Churchill College. These were sentiments shared by few Greeks, who could see that Markezinis was simply providing a fig leaf for the perpetuation of the dictatorship.

The agreement to establish a research fellowship was negotiated in June 1973 between Bodosakis-Athanasiadis and Churchill College. It read as follows:

> The Fellowship shall be offered to a person doing research in contemporary Greek history, or British Foreign Policy in the Eastern Mediterranean, or the Eastern Question during its 19th or 20th century phases, or any other historical subject in any way connected with the writings, ideas, views or policies of the late Sir Winston Churchill associated with Greece and the above geographical area; or to a person doing research in Comparative or Common Market Law or Institutions.

Elections preferably were to alternate between the fields of Greek studies and law, while, other things being equal, preference would be given to a Greek citizen. Although one of a handful of historians in Britain at that time with an interest in Greek history, I did not learn of the existence of this fellowship until 1978, and then only by chance. But when I did, it struck me that one of my postgraduate students, a Greek–American, George Alexander, fitted the bill almost exactly. He had just completed his University of London PhD thesis on 'British Policy towards Greece 1944–47', based on extensive research in the then recently released British Foreign Office and War Office papers. Churchill had, of course, been heavily involved in the making of Britain's Greek policy during this period. That he was, indeed, almost obsessively interested in the complex political situation in Greece at this time is confirmed in the memoir by his personal doctor, Lord Moran, and by his extraordinary decision to undertake the hazardous flight to Athens on Christmas Eve 1944. Alexander's thesis had not yet been examined, but there seemed little doubt that he would sail through with flying colours.

Alexander duly submitted an application for the Bodossakis Fellowship in December 1978, but no one was appointed. I was puzzled by this. Obviously there could have been better qualified applicants, but to make no appointment at all when Alexander was demonstrably a highly competent researcher whose thesis had been heavily focused on Churchill and Greece was odd. When I raised this matter with Hawthorne, he replied that none of the candidates had reached the high standard of dissertation that was required. Nonetheless, he said that Alexander could apply when the fellowship was next advertised. This he duly did in November 1979, by which time the thesis had been examined by John Campbell of St Antony's and James Joll of the LSE. Despite being his supervisor, I was one of his examiners, in accordance with the strange practice of the University of London. I understand that this is no longer the case, although the supervisor is still permitted to sit in on the examination. It is manifestly unsatisfactory to have the thesis supervisor act as an examiner, or to be present as an observer, as, to a degree, it is the supervisor whose role is under scrutiny. It is not easy to be critical of a thesis when the person who presumably gave his blessing to its being submitted is present. In Alexander's case, however, there was never any doubt that the thesis would be well received. I duly sent Churchill College a very strong reference on his behalf together with the favourable comments of Campbell and Joll. I reinforced this with the opinions of two noted authorities on Greece during World War II, Monty Woodhouse and Elisabeth Barker. Both had read the thesis and had been much impressed. Further testimony to its excellence is the fact that it was accepted, in revised form, for publication by the Clarendon Press, the prestigious scholarly imprint of Oxford University Press, as *The Prelude to the Truman Doctrine: British Policy in Greece 1944–1947* (1982).

Alexander was again unsuccessful, although on this occasion Dr Kenneth McQuillen, the secretary to the Fellowship electors, wrote to say that he had been among the top three contenders, but in the event the fellowship had been awarded to an outstandingly brilliant lawyer. This was again puzzling news, for nothing had changed in respect of Alexander's application other than the fact that the thesis, already completed in 1978, had now been examined. Later inquiry revealed that three of the first four holders of the fellowship had been lawyers and that none had been Greek citizens. I hardly think that Bodosakis, in endowing the fellowship, would have imagined that his largesse would go to support the study of such subjects as the 'civil law practice of the Court of Admiralty in the early modern period'. Although the fellowship had been established in 1973, it was only in the 1990s that it began to be awarded to Greeks (including Greek Cypriots) studying Greek-related subjects. This heavy emphasis on law rather than on Churchill and Greece may have been due to the fact that Basil Markesinis, an academic lawyer and the son of Spyros Markezinis, was for many years involved in the election of the Bodossakis fellows. He had been a research fellow at Churchill College in the early 1970s and continued to be involved with successive elections for many years afterwards. In 1993 I was told by the college bursar that 'fortunately Professor Markesinis, who was close to the donor at the outset and who was in many ways instrumental in securing the fellowship in its present form is invariably at hand to assist in the assessment of the candidates'.

Possibly the only position in modern Greek studies at a British university to which, so far as I am aware, no whiff of controversy, let alone scandal, attaches, is the Lewis-Gibson Lectureship in Modern Greek at Cambridge.

This was established through the generosity of Scottish twins, Agnes Smith (subsequently Lewis) and Margaret Smith (subsequently Gibson). Born in Irvine, devoutly Presbyterian and seriously wealthy, they lived for many years in Cambridge. Privately educated, they travelled extensively in the Near East and developed a formidable degree of expertise in Syriac and Arabic studies and had a considerable interest in the modern history of Greece and its language. Agnes, once described as 'the most learned lady in England', wrote two books recording her impressions of the Greek world: *Glimpses of Greek Life and Scenery* (1884) and *Through Cyprus* (1887). The first holder of the Lewis-Gibson Lectureship was Romilly Jenkins, who held the post for ten years, from 1936 until 1946, with a break for war service in the Foreign Office. In 1946, he moved to the Koraes professorship at King's College. His successor was Stavros Papastavrou, who had studied at the Universities of Thessaloniki and Oxford. He held the lectureship for 32 years until his death in 1979, and was a doughty and principled opponent of the Colonels' dictatorship. Papastavrou was succeeded by David Holton, with wide interests in Cretan Renaissance literature and the modern language. But the Lewis-Gibson Lectureship has disappeared following the retirement of Professor Holton after a campaign to boost the endowment of the post was unsuccessful.

In 1991 Merton College, Oxford advertised a generous senior scholarship, funded by the Leventis Foundation, in the field of 'Greek studies, including the study of Greek culture and the civilisation of the Aegean and Eastern Mediterranean in any of their aspects from the Bronze Age up to 1453'. According to the further particulars put out by the college it was to be open to applicants from Greece or Cyprus. This seemed reasonable enough, although a modernist might regret that post-Byzantine studies were excluded, as is so often the case with such benefactions. However, the press release (in Greek) about the scholarship put out by the Leventis Foundation in Athens told a somewhat different story. It announced that for the first time ('and this has a special significance') Merton College, one of the oldest in Oxford, had agreed to establish a scholarship for those of a particular nationality. But instead of saying that applicants should be citizens of Greece or Cyprus it specified that they should be *Ellines to genos* from Greece and Cyprus, that is to say ethnic Greeks or Greeks by race or descent. *Ellines to genos* could almost be translated 'kith and kin'. The press release put out by the Leventis Foundation in Cyprus declared the scholarship to be open to Greek Cypriots and *Elladites*, that is to say mainland Greeks. The wording of the Greek language advertisements could be held to exclude Cypriot nationals of Turkish, Armenian or Maronite descent or Greek nationals of Turkish, Pomak, Slav-Macedonian, Vlach, Albanian, Armenian or Jewish descent. The matter could have been simply resolved by declaring that the scholarship was open to 'citizens' of Greece and Cyprus, as was the case with a scholarship offered in 1992 by the Goulandris Museum of Cycladic Art for which '*arkhaiologoi Ellinikis ypikootitas*' ('archaeologists of Greek citzenship') were invited to apply.

In 1987 came news of what was, potentially, the most exciting development ever in our field. This was that the Onassis Foundation, which had for years been locked in an unedifying row with Thierry Roussel, the fourth husband of Aristotle Onassis' daughter, Christina, over the future of the Onassis fortune when their daughter came of age, had endowed New York University with $15 million to establish a Center for Hellenic Studies. It was initially announced that the Center would fund six academic positions covering the whole range of 'Hellenic' studies. I had heard from an excellent source in Athens that an unspoken condition of the endowment was that Speros Vryonis, a Byzantinist at the University of California at Los Angeles, be appointed director. That this had indeed been the case would seem to be confirmed by an article in *Odyssey*, a magazine aimed at affluent members of the Greek diaspora, that appeared after Vryonis had left the Onassis Center in New York. It purported to throw light on the unhappy circumstances in which he had departed and maintained that 'at least officially' NYU and not the Onassis Foundation had appointed him director. Vryonis is an excellent, prolific and polymathic scholar but, since New York University aspired to be among the top rank of American universities, it had at least to go through the motions of holding a search for the post of director.

One afternoon in November of 1987, as I was nodding off over the SOE files which at that time were housed in Century House, the headquarters of MI6 'somewhere in the south of England', I was telephoned by the Dean of Arts and Sciences at NYU, Duncan Rice, a Scot with a disembodied mid-Atlantic accent, who must have got my number from the departmental secretary at King's. He told me that my name had come to the attention of the search committee, and it would like to invite me to New York for interview. From the outset I realised that the search committee was merely going through the motions. On the other hand, an expenses-paid trip to New York is always an agreeable prospect and, what is more, the January sales were only a few weeks away. Dean Rice seemed anxious that I should visit New York quickly, whereas I wanted to put off the visit until the sales. As we ran through various dates, I perjured myself by saying that none of these were possible, hoping eventually that we could agree on an early January date. The dean began to show mild signs of losing patience and said that I must be a very busy man, and that if I could not fairly soon make it to New York, then he would have to come to London and talk to me there. This was a disastrous suggestion to be avoided at all costs, so I quickly found a couple of days in a week or so's time when I said that I might be able to squeeze in a trip to New York.

The instructions I received were suspiciously simple. I was to take a cab from Kennedy Airport and make my way to One Park Avenue. This I duly did and found myself, late in the evening, outside an apartment building and not, as I had expected, an hotel. The porter pointed out this rather obvious fact, and as I was about to leave to find an actual hotel another porter emerged in the nick of time to tell me that an apartment had been set aside for me. It turned out that NYU had once owned the entire building but had been forced to sell it in some financial crisis. It had, however, hung on to a few apartments, one of which was assigned to me.

Over the next couple of days I had a few rather perfunctory meetings with NYU faculty. The nearest I came to a formal interview was a meeting with the dean and three or four worthies from the history and related departments. My impression that they were indeed simply going through the motions, albeit in a not disagreeable manner, was soon confirmed. As none of us was taking the process seriously, the experience was even quite enjoyable. One of the questions they put to me was how well I thought I could adjust to living and working in the United States. I thought I had the perfect answer. Mary Jo is American-born and as a result I am a frequent visitor to a country which I could claim to know better than many of my fellow countrymen. The next question followed naturally. Where was she from? Oregon, I replied, although it rapidly dawned on me that, if there ever had been a realistic chance of my being appointed, then this was the moment when I would have blown it. One could almost see the famous and much (poorly) imitated *New Yorker* cover by Saul Steinberg welling up before their eyes. This showed the view of the US and peripherally the world as seen from Ninth Avenue in Manhattan, not so far in fact from where we were sitting. In Steinberg's cartoon, a few features such as New Jersey, Utah, Nebraska and Las Vegas are scattered on a crudely drawn map of the US. Trees, lumbermen, cowboys and perhaps the endangered northern spotted owl were clearly the sum of my interlocutors' knowledge of the Beaver State. One of them drily observed that I would find New York City a rather different place than Oregon.

If they had only known where in Oregon Mary Jo had attended school then their disbelief would have been all the greater. Lakeview, at 4,800 ft the 'tallest' town in Oregon, with a population of 2,500 or so, is the seat of Lake County and stands on the fringes of the Great Basin. Lake County extends over 8,000 square miles and is more or less the same size as Wales but with a population of scarcely one person for each square mile. This, in the words of the *Lonely Planet* guide, is big, lonesome country. Lakeview appears on many maps of the US, however small scale, by virtue of the fact that there is nowhere else within 100 miles or so. The *Lonely Planet* guide rather unkindly says that it takes 'a kind of devotion, or else *extreme* carelessness, to end up out here'. Clearly, in my case it had been a kind of devotion. In a strongly Democratic state, Lake County distinguished itself by having the highest percentage of votes for Donald J. Trump in proportion to population in the 2016 presidential election.

If the denizens of Manhattan who were interviewing me had had any idea of the National Park Service ranger station on the Olympic peninsula in Washington State; one of the last mobile logging camps in the wilds of Oregon where the accommodation consisted of converted railway carriages; and the apricot orchard in California, in all of which Mary Jo had lived as a child, their incomprehension would have been all the greater. Had they known that the days, or even weeks, that I had spent driving from nowhere to nowhere along the lonely roads of the fantastically beautiful high desert of the western United States had given me a liking for country and western music, distaste would have been added to their disbelief. The country was so remote that, at best, one might hope to pick up a single station on the car radio, which would be pumping out nothing but country and western music. I learned to appreciate that these songs represented the tail end of the British ballad tradition, with many of them telling a maudlin tale. One of my favourites is Boxcar Willie's 'Divorce me C.O.D'. This contains the memorable verse 'I ain't no college professor. I ain't a got no PhD'. This speaks to my condition. Whereas I have been a college professor I have never acquired a PhD. It has always struck me as odd that while a taste for the blues, the music of dispossessed blacks, is the height of radical chic, a taste for the music of dispossessed whites is treated with disdain. As my brother-in-law, Dan, once reminded me, you only need to play a country and western record backwards to get your wife, your job and your dog back.

In the course of the NYU interview, which turned into an agreeable conversation, I made two suggestions. The first was that it would be futile for the proposed Center of Hellenic Studies to try to compete with well-endowed, prestigious and relatively nearby institutions such as Princeton, Yale and Harvard, with their well-established traditions in classical, Byzantine and, in the case of Princeton, 'modern' Greek studies, by attempting to cover the whole spectrum of Greek history and culture. Instead, the centre should seek to carve out a distinctive niche by focusing on the study of the Greek diaspora in modern times. This seemed to me to make particular sense as, surprisingly, there is no such academic institution devoted to the study of the diaspora in Greece itself. This fascinating subject at the time was under-researched, although since then the study of diasporas, transnational communities and ethnicity has become an increasingly fashionable topic in the academy. It is gratifying to note that a Centre for Greek Diaspora Studies has recently been established at Royal Holloway College of the University of London.

It would, I suggested, be particularly appropriate for such a centre of diaspora studies to be endowed with part of the Onassis fortune. For the Smyrna-born Aristotle Onassis had been forced to flee his homeland after the Asia Minor disaster and had initially settled in Argentina, a country of which he remained a citizen until the end of his life. Not only was Onassis an archetypal Greek of the diaspora, but New York, with its large community of Greek origin, situated in a country with much the largest Greek diaspora population, would have been an obvious location for a centre of this kind. This suggestion, however, went down like a lead balloon, not least because none of those round the table had much knowledge of the modern Greek world, or of the salience within it of emigration. More to the point, the Onassis Foundation had clearly decreed that the centre, as a condition of receiving a massive endowment, should bolster the notion of the unbroken continuity of Greek culture from antiquity to the present day. Courses with titles such as 'The Greeks from Homer to the present' soon appeared in the prospectus.

My second recommendation was that NYU should appoint as director not me but John Iatrides. He is a Greek-born scholar who has made his career in the United States, and was also one of those notionally being considered by the search committee. He is a first-rate historian, a member of the tiny evangelical protestant community in Greece, largely descended from Greeks in Asia Minor, who, under the influence of American missionaries, had became protestants in the nineteenth century. The evangelical community had constituted part, albeit a very small one, of the great influx of refugees that had flooded into Greece in the 1920s. It has always seemed to me that the combination of the *daimonio*, the enterpreneurial genius, of the Greek, with the Protestant work ethic is an unbeatable one. But NYU had clearly received its marching orders from the Onassis Foundation.

During my time in New York, I had lunch with the president of NYU, John Brademas, a Greek–American, and, like Iatrides, a Protestant. Brademas, who had presumably negotiated the deal with the Onassis Foundation, had been the first Greek–American to be elected to Congress, where he had become the Democratic majority whip in the House of Representatives. According to his Wikipedia entry he was awarded 47 honorary degrees, which must surely be something of a record. Brademas surprised me somewhat by saying that he had read *Politics and the Academy*, although he signally failed to imbibe its lessons, for the predictable clash between NYU and the Onassis Foundation was not long in coming. I was recently reminded by a friend that I had predicted from the outset that the Onassis/NYU venture would end in tears. Had NYU appointed Iatrides such a confrontation might well have been avoided, and a major centre for the study of the modern Greek world might have been established on a secure basis. As it was, Vryonis was duly appointed director, as I had known all along would be the case, and the farce of the search was brought to an end. After a few short years, following a bust-up between Vryonis, the Onassis Foundation and NYU, the opportunity to create a really worthwhile academic programme was lost, and large amounts of money had been spent to no great purpose.

What lay at the root of this particular 'neo-Hellenic' row is not very clear, to me at least. Vryonis complained of administrative incompetence by New York University, departmental animosities and interference by the Onassis Foundation. One source of tension was clearly the failure of the Onassis Foundation to understand the mores of American academic life. In *Odyssey* magazine, Phillip Mitsis, Vryonis's successor as director, stated somewhat enigmatically that the centre had 'quite frankly' become 'a leading voice for a certain partisan political group'. This had not played well 'with an important segment of the Greek-American public'. 'Political discussions should take place at the Center in a non-partisan atmosphere. If we're seen by the public as a grandstand for a certain political view, no one will take us seriously'. Unfortunately, Mitsis did not make clear what this certain political view was. Another factor was that the Onassis Foundation appeared to be unhappy with the amount of time that it claimed that Vryonis was devoting to the Speros Basil Vryonis Center for the Study of Hellenism in Sacramento, named after his son who had died in tragic circumstances. This led to claims by the president of the Onassis Foundation, Stelios Papademetriou, that the Onassis Center had become 'a ghost center', with Vryonis devoting only a part of his time to its development. After he had announced his departure, the Onassis Foundation issued a statement harshly critical of Vryonis, declaring that the 'monopolization of exclusivity, authority, uniqueness, competence and of being above criticism on the eve of the 21st century is unacceptable'. After Vryonis had left, a reduced Onassis programme continued at NYU. One member of the faculty in 2008 was puzzlingly listed as *Clinical* Professor of Hellenic Studies. Is this in the sense of dispassionate or diagnostic?

Vryonis, after falling out with the Onassis Foundation, went back to run the Sacramento centre. This was a curious institution, founded in 1985, and dedicated to the promotion of 'a better knowledge of Hellenic values' through the study of Hellenism. This was interpreted as containing 'the totality of the historical and cultural experience of the Greek-speaking people'. Ambitiously, it sought to model itself on Harvard University's Dumbarton Oaks Center for Byzantine Studies in Washington. Before it closed down, it consisted basically of a very large library set in a business park in Rancho Cordova on the outskirts of the Californian capital. It so happened that one of my American brothers-in-law lives only a few miles from what I called Vryonis West, on the analogy of Frank Lloyd Wright's Taliesin East and Taliesin West. I was, therefore, able to visit the centre on a couple of occasions during its relatively short life.

On my last visit, Vryonis, as we were leaving, asked me to sign the visitors' book, which I was of course happy to do. He then slightly puzzled us by asking Mary Jo to sign also. This she, too, was quite happy to do. It was only a year or two later that it dawned on me why we had both been asked to sign. The very rich Sacramento real estate developer, Angelo Tsakopoulos, who was funding Vryonis West, had apparently become rather concerned that each visitor/researcher was costing x thousand dollars, so the more names that were listed in the vistors' book the lower the overall cost of each visit. Eventually Tsakopoulos' patience finally ran out and he withdrew his support for Vryonis West. The splendid, but massively underused, library came within an ace of being donated to Yale. Instead, it went to Sacramento State University, which did not make nearly as much sense. The fate of the Speros Basil Vryonis Center was yet another instance of the expenditure of large amounts of money with little in the end to show for it.

One of the motives behind the establishment of the Onassis Center and also, to a degree, the Vryonis Center seemed to be to counter the Turkish government's efforts to promote Turkish studies in American universities. The fighting of proxy wars in the academy had become such an issue in the US that a 1987 federal law required universities to report all foreign donations of more than a quarter of a million dollars to the Department of Education. This measure reflected an attempt to monitor possible foreign influence exerted on institutions of higher education. Vryonis certainly showed himself an energetic combatant in these proxy wars. He engaged in vigorous polemics with his sometime colleague Stanford Shaw, professor of Turkish history at UCLA, while one of Vryonis' last publications was *The Mechanism of Catastrophe: The Turkish Pogrom of September 6–7, 1955, and the Destruction of the Greek Community of Istanbul* (2005), a massively detailed study of the events known in Greece as the *Septemvriana*, which sounded the death knell of a once large and prosperous community in Turkey. This I reviewed, favourably and at some length, in the *Times Literary Supplement*.

Vryonis was a bitter critic of the activities of the Institute for Turkish Studies Inc., founded in Washington in 1982 and funded by the Turkish government to the tune of $3 million as well as by US companies, particularly weapons manufacturers, doing business in Turkey. This he saw as the academic arm of a concerted attempt by the Turkish government to burnish its image in the United States. He pointed to the fact that many of the 69 signatories to full-page advertisements in the *New York Times* and the *Washington Post*, calling on the House of Representatives to exclude reference to the Armenian 'genocide' in the proposed 'National day of remembrance of man's inhumanity to man', had been in receipt of research grants in the field of Turkish studies from the Institute.

Vryonis' minute examination of the activities of the Institute for Turkish Studies was contained in a book published by the Institute of Balkan Studies in Thessaloniki: *The Turkish State and History: Clio Meets the Grey Wolf* (1991). It thus did not cover the major row that erupted when Heath Lowry, who had been the director of the Institute for Turkish Studies since its inception in 1982, was appointed in 1994 to the Atatürk Chair of Turkish Studies at Princeton, a university that takes itself very seriously. This chair, as the name would suggest, had been funded with a $1.5 million grant from the Turkish government. Lowry had been one of the academics who had signed the petition to the House of Representatives. His appointment to the Atatürk chair was criticised in some circles as a kind of reward for his services to the Turkish government in his role at the director of the Institute of Turkish Studies. What these services might have been were subsequently revealed in an article published in *Holocaust and Genocide Studies* in 1995. This offered a rare insight into some of the murkier aspects of academic life, which seldom see the light of day.

The article reprints a letter written by the then Turkish ambassador in Washington, Nuzhet Kandemir, which followed more or less to the last comma a suggested draft written by Lowry. The only difference was that the ambassador concluded his letter 'Yours sincerely', whereas Lowry had concluded his draft 'Sincerely yours'. This draft was included by mistake with the ambassador's letter which was sent to Professor Robert Jay Lifton, the author of *The Nazi Doctors: Medical Killing and the Psychology of Genocide* (1986), a book that the ambassador was unlikely to have glanced at, let alone read, without prompting. Ambassador Kandemir declared himself to be shocked by Lifton's references to what he termed 'the so-called "Armenian genocide" allegedly perpetrated by the Ottoman Turks during World War I'. To equate the fate of the Armenians in the Ottoman Empire with the holocaust was, he maintained, 'simply ludicrous'. The question that naturally arises is how Lowry's draft, prepared for Kandemir's signature, together with an even more forthright memorandum likewise penned by Lowry at the ambassador's request, came to be included with the ambassador's letter sent to Lifton. Was it simply by mistake or, as some have mischievously suggested, was their inclusion a deliberate act by someone in the Turkish embassy who had fallen out with Lowry? Alas, we shall probably never know. A petition signed by some 80 academics and writers, some of the latter well known, was circulated following these revelations. This accused the Turkish government of seeking to manipulate American academic institutions.

Clearly, what the Onassis Foundation had been looking for in the director of the Onassis Center was someone who could do effective battle with the Turks. Quite apart from any other consideration, I did not qualify as a militant defender of Greece's *ethnika zitimata* or national concerns. The dubious world of sponsored scholarship and proxy wars in the academy was highlighted by another scandal involving the Institute for Turkish Studies. This arose when Donald Quataert, an Ottoman historian, resigned as chairman of the board of governors in 2006 after writing that the fate of Armenians in the Ottoman Empire during World War I met the UN definition of genocide. Quataert resigned after the Turkish ambassador told him that his comment had angered influential figures in Ankara and had threatened the Institute's funding. The row prompted the resignation of a number of members of the board. It is clear that would-be recipients of research funding from the Institute tend to steer clear of such *kafta themata*, or burning issues, as the Armenian genocide, as many would characterise it. The incident reflects the way in which the concerns expressed by Arnold Toynbee some 90 years ago remain a live issue. It also confirms the view that when scholarship and money come into conflict it is generally money that prevails.

There is clearly a feeling in some circles, particularly in the Greek diaspora, that departments of modern Greek studies should openly espouse Greek nationalist causes, particularly at times of crisis. This is sometimes combined with the feeling, in English-speaking societies, that Anglo-Saxon scholars in the field should wear their philhellenism more openly on their sleeves and actively propagandise on behalf of Greece. Vryonis seemed to harbour an animus against Anglo-Saxon scholars, while Constantine Buhayer, who had denounced me as an institutionalised mishellene, had, after I had left King's College, sought to portray my former department as a centre of anthellenism. I was once told by an acquaintance that at a dinner party of 'philhellenes' in London my name had cropped up and I had been dismissed as the person who wrote about Greece as though it were North Vietnam. From the context this was clearly intended as an insult, but in fact I found the comment rather flattering. I think it quite appropriate to write about Greece as though it were any modern country, and not to view it through rose-tinted, or should that be blue-tinted, philhellenic spectacles, just as I would think it right to write about North Vietnam as though it were Greece.

Inevitably, such critical views tend to surface at times when Greece is perceived to be under threat. This was the background to the Toynbee fracas at King's College. A more recent, and admittedly rather extreme example of this phenomenon occurred in Australia in 1992, as the frenzy over the question of the naming of the newly independent state of Macedonia was coming to the boil. The resentment felt by some Greek–Australians about the department of modern Greek at Sydney, and in particular the ill-feeling against the British scholars in charge of the department, surfaced in the Greek–Australian paper, *Neos Kosmos*. In an interview by Giorgos Hatzivasiliou with Dr Alfred Vincent, a long-standing pillar of the department, Hatzivasiliou targeted the chair of modern Greek, founded in 1969 with a donation from Sir Nicholas Laurantus. Laurantus was the first Greek-born Australian to receive a knighthood, the owner *inter alia* of a chain of cinemas and one of the wealthiest landowners in New South Wales.

Hatzivasiliou's onslaught reflected the same sense of proprietorship with which some of the London Greeks continue to regard the Koraes chair. The Laurantus chair, so Hatzivasiliou declared, is 'the beacon of *Romiosini* [a word for which 'Greekness' is an inadequate translation], the guardian of our language and culture'. *Inter alia*, he complained that Greek history was not being correctly taught in the department, adding, curiously but revealingly, that Greeks (for which read Greek–Australians) should be taught Greek history in a different way from Americans or the French: 'Without wanting to contravene their academic freedom, I would suggest that academics teaching history take account of the patriotic sensitivities of their students'. He complained that the chair had become cut off from the Greek community; that the community's intellectuals were ignored; and that it had never organised any scholarly events in connection with 'our' national concerns and particularly with the Macedonian issue. 'If', he said,

> the English professors of modern Greek had taken a pro-Greek stand over the Macedonian issue in the English language media, propaganda emanating from Skopje [the capital of independent Macedonia] would have suffered a major defeat, because English-speaking readers would place more credence in one of their own academics than in a Greek. They have not done this, however, even as a token of solidarity with the Greek community.

Hatzivasiliou's complaints undoubtedly reflected the feeling among some in the Greek–Australian community that its efforts to retain a sense of Greek identity and resist the tide of acculturation among second and third generation Greek–Australians were failing.

7

Plus est en vous. St Antony's College

'Great and Good is the Typical Don, and of evil and wrong the foe,
Good, and Great: I'm a Don myself, and therefore I ought to know.'
—A.D. Godley (1903)

I arrived at St Antony's in 1990 in circumstances that were anomalous. As I was still employed by King's, I could not be a member of the governing body of the college, so I was made an associate fellow. However, in 1995, on taking early retirement from King's College, I became a Governing Body Fellow. The 15 years I was at St Antony's was the most rewarding and certainly the most enjoyable part of my academic career.

I had a number of graduate students at Oxford (St Antony's is an all graduate college) but no formal teaching obligations. I had some responsibilities in the college and for some years I was the general editor of the series published by Macmillan, subsequently Palgrave, and then Palgrave Macmillan. But I had plenty of time for research and to enjoy the lively intellectual climate, the unending stream of (for the most part) interesting academic visitors, and the extraordinary range of seminars on offer both at St Antony's and elsewhere at Oxford. Moreover, one happy consequence of my anomalous status is that I was never subject to appraisal, an obnoxious feature introduced into British academic life from the late 1980s onwards.

While I was delighted to have found refuge in such an agreeable milieu, like many outsiders coming to Oxford, I found the university and its workings and procedures at times baffling. Take for instance the following ruling by the vice-chancellor in 1995:

> For some time now, women members of the University have been required to wear either a square hat or a soft cap at university ceremonies, in contrast to men, who

customarily remove and carry their caps when indoors. It has been recognised that the wearing of a square cap can be inconvenient when bowing or curtsying [*sic*]. Earlier this year the Proctors canvassed opinion about a proposal to permit women to carry, rather than wear, square caps at university ceremonies. An overwhelming majority of those consulted favoured change to allow women the choice of wearing or carrying a square cap.

St Antony's was founded in 1950 with a hefty donation from Antonin Besse, a wealthy French trader who was based for many years in Aden. Part of his wealth derived from the mass slaughter of leopards for their skins (at times 1,000 a month), gazelles (2.5 million a year), antelope and cheetahs, a source of funding that would now regarded in some environmentalist circles as almost as heinous as Nazi gold. Besse was much impressed by some of the young, public school educated British men that he had encountered in the Horn of Africa and was anxious that young Frenchmen should enjoy the supposed benefits of a spartan Christian education. Besides his funding of St Antony's, he was a generous benefactor of Gordonstoun School, one of the last remaining bastions of muscular Christianity, and it was due to Besse that St Antony's and Gordonstoun share the same motto, *Plus est en vous*.

St Antony's pops up in a number of le Carré novels as a training ground for spies. Others have also made this connection, and not only in novels. One academic writer, Hugh Wilford, for instance, has written that the college 'long functioned as an interface between British academe and the secret services'. I myself saw little evidence of this supposed connection, if only because there were relatively few British students among the student body. But the conspiratorially minded would presumably argue that the large number of American students was an indication of a close link with the CIA. When the junior common room organised a college ball in 2002 that included James Bond and KGB rooms and with the overall theme of 'Spies like us', the warden, Marrack Goulding, was not amused. I thus have had the misfortune in my career to be associated with two institutions, the British School at Athens and St Antony's, which have been widely seen as nurturing spies.

Although John Campbell retired in 1990, Greek studies still had a foothold in the college through a scheme whereby academics from Greek universities were able to spend a term or two as visiting fellows. The scheme was effectively administered by the London Hellenic Foundation, the cultural arm of the Greek ship-owning community in London, although much of the funding was put up by the Leventis Foundation. It was never clear to me how the visiting fellows were selected. Essentially, the choice of visiting fellow seemed to lie with Professor P.J. Vatikiotis, the academic adviser to the Foundation and a retired specialist in Middle Eastern politics with a loose connection to the college. Those chosen were excellent scholars, and some were personal friends of mine and of John Campbell, but they were drawn exclusively from a single department in the University of Athens. There were rumblings about this and complaints that no women had been selected. I thought it important that we should try to regularise the appointments procedure, and it seemed self-evident that St Antony's should have some formal role in the appointment of the fellows. Thereby began another exercise in talking at cross purposes with rich London Greeks who did not seem to grasp the mores of academic life any more than I understood the mechanics of ship broking, and whose main concern appeared to be with *provoli*, promoting a favourable image of Greece in the outside world.

In an attempt to resolve the impending impasse, Campbell and I in the summer of 1994 met with George Lemos, the shipowning chairman of the Foundation and Vatikiotis. Also present was Professor Nick Bouras, an academic psychiatrist and a member of the Foundation with a useful understanding of the conventions of the academy in the United Kingdom. The tone of the meeting could best be described as 'frank and comradely', although it did afford an opportunity to clear up a number of misunderstandings. That there was no real meeting of minds was strikingly demonstrated when I said that I understood that the primary purpose of Professor Thanos Veremis' sojourn in Oxford during the 1993/4 academic year was to give him time to complete a book on Greece and the Balkans. Lemos' response was that Veremis' book would not be published for at least a year, whereas Greece was facing a crisis right now, a reference to the ongoing dispute over the Macedonian issue. Hence his wish that the visiting fellows should enjoy a much higher profile within the college. In what was intended as a conciliatory gesture, we proposed the establishment of a small committee to select future fellows. This would consist, besides Campbell and myself, of Tony Nicholls, the director of the European Studies Centre at the college, together with Vatikiotis and a further nominee of the Hellenic Foundation. But this proposal was not accepted.

What seems to have been the final straw for the London Hellenic Foundation and which led to the removal of the fellowship from St Antony's was a workshop which I organised at the college in 1994 on minorities in Greece. This had been supposedly a more or less non-existent subject, as Greece had long been considered the most ethnically homogeneous country in the Balkans, and the state has succeeded in hellenising, not always using kid gloves in the process, the various minorities that have been incorporated into the country as it has gradually expanded over almost 200 years. I had long been interested in the question ever since one of my early postgraduate students told me of an experience during his national service in the Greek army. At the time a committed *ethnikophron*, or nationalist, he had found himself in the 1960s in charge of a platoon posted on the Greek–Bulgarian frontier. Most of its members consisted of Turks, Pomaks (Slav-speaking Muslims) and Slav-Macedonians, drawn from Greece's small minority populations. The fact that non-ethnic Greeks were entrusted with guarding the sacred frontiers of Hellenism offended his *ethnikophrosyni*, or sense of national honour. On complaining to his commanding officer about this he was told that the reason was obvious: in the event of an invasion they would be the first in the firing line. And so, disconcertingly, would my student have been.

From the outset Orthodox Christianity and the Greek language have been the key determinants of Greek identity. Article three of the 1975 Constitution declares the dominant religion in Greece to be Orthodoxy. There is only one group that is officially recognised as having minority status, namely the 'Muslims' of Eastern Thrace, the great majority of whom now consider themselves to be Turks. Nonetheless, there are small communities, living in the Greek state and never totalling more than a small percentage of the total population, that have a different sense of identity. Given the furore that had arisen over the Macedonian issue more or less at the time that I arrived at St Antony's, it seemed appropriate to cast an academic eye on the question of ethnic and religious minorities, particularly as in the last decade of the twentieth century, Greece was moving from being a country that exported its citizens (between 1950 and 1980 some 12 per cent of the population had taken the path of emigration, either permanent or temporary, many of them as Gastarbeiter) to a country that attracted immigrants. The result was that that by the end of the 1990s some 10 per cent of the population consisted of migrants, mainly from Eastern Europe and particularly Albania. A significant number of these were ethnic Greeks, such as the Rosopontioi, Pontic Greeks from the former Soviet Union, and members of Albania's Greek minority. More recently, the Eurozone debt crisis of 2009, and Greece's near bankruptcy, has pushed an increasing number of young Greeks into once again taking the traditional path of emigration.

I therefore organised a workshop at the college to consider most of the significant ethnic and religious minorities in the country, the Muslims (Turks, Pomaks and Gypsies); Jews (once a very significant element in the population of Thessaloniki until the community's virtual destruction during the German occupation); Catholics (mainly to be found in certain of the Aegean islands); Protestants (for the most part the descendants of Greeks converted by American missionaries in Asia Minor); Armenians (many of them the descendants of refugees caught up in the Asia Minor disaster); Vlachs (speaking a form of

Romanian); Slav-Macedonians (speaking a form of Bulgarian), Sarakatsani (transhumant shepherds who have now been integrated into Greek society); and Old Calendarists. A regrettable omission was the Orthodox Christian but Albanian-speaking Arvanites.

The workshop was by no means an attempt to depict Greece as a mosaic of ethnic, religious and linguistic minorities, but rather to establish for the Greekless reader (and indeed for many Greeks) the nature and situation of minorities in the country. A particularly valuable contribution, for instance, by Bishop Kallistos Ware, focused on the Old Calendarists, the not negligible minority of Orthodox Greeks who are religiously conservative, and had refused to accept the adoption of the Gregorian calendar in the 1920s and who remain firmly attached to the Julian calendar. No one could consider this group as anything other than ethnically Greek, but their numbers and beliefs remained something of a mystery to many. The proceedings of the workshop were published in 2002 as *Minorities in Greece: Aspects of a Plural Society*.

One of the difficulties that arises in discussing the question of minorities in Greece is that, until recently, there was no unambiguous expression in Greek for 'ethnic minority', despite the fact that the adjective 'ethnic' in English is clearly of Greek derivation. The generally used expression *ethniki meionotita* used in connection with minorities is unsatisfactory, as the term 'national minority' has rather different connotations than the term 'ethnic minority'. It could be argued that neighbouring countries might be entitled to take a greater interest in a 'national' minority than in an 'ethnic' one, or, indeed, that a 'national minority' might have claims to secede or unite with another state and thus be perceived as a kind of Trojan horse. There is now an expression in Greek for 'ethnic minority', i.e. *ethnotiki meionotita*. But this usage is largely confined to academic discourse, and is not one that would be widely understood at a popular level. I had deliberately not invited to the conference two Greeks with expert knowledge of the situation of minorities in Greece. They could have made a valuable contribution to the conference but their presence might have led to publicity which I did not want. Nor did I advertise the workshop. But Thanos Veremis, then at the college as the Greek visiting fellow, had, without consulting me, tipped off a Greek journalist who wrote a needlessly offensive article about the workshop in *Oikonomikos Takhydromos*, a move that was distinctly unhelpful to my attempts to ensure that the workshop remained a low key and strictly academic affair. The very idea of looking into the question of minorities in Greece offended the nationalistically minded and it would appear that holding of such a workshop, combined with my efforts to instil some sense of order into the selection of the visiting fellows, contributed to the Hellenic Foundation removing the Greek fellowship to another college where it might be able to exercise more control.

The Foundation was deaf to our efforts to retain the fellowship at St Antony's and it was subsequently moved to Brasenose College, and more generously endowed than it had been at St Antony's. Brasenose was a less obvious location than St Antony's, which has a strong focus on contemporary history, politics and international relations. The reason for the choice of Brasenose appears to have been that one of its fellows, Tony Courakis, an economist, was a Greek. Brasenose cast its net widely and invited applications in any area of 'Hellenic studies' including 'economics, history (ancient, byzantine or modern), law, literature (ancient, byzantine or modern), philosophy, politics, sociology, theology and all other aspects of art and culture'. It was hoped that fellows would be able to visit for a year, but no election would be made for less than a term. Funds were provided to enable the visiting fellow to run a seminar. The committee to select the visiting fellow was to consist of Courakis; Vatikiotis, the Hellenic Foundation's academic adviser in London; a representative of the Foundation for Hellenic Culture; and a Brasenose classicist. Three out of the four electors would therefore be Greeks.

In the summer of 1996, it was announced that one of the visiting fellows for the next academic year would be Professor Nestor Courakis, a criminologist. When he arrived in Oxford, Nestor Courakis organised a seminar, in conjunction with Professor Roger Hood, of the Oxford Centre for Criminological Research, on 'The changing face of crime and criminal policy in Europe'. Professor Courakis spoke on the topic of 'Football violence: not only a British problem'. This was about football hooliganism in Greece but none of the other speakers spoke on a topic which had any bearing on 'Hellenic studies'. The remaining seminars in the series were about aspects of crime and penal policy in Europe: typically, one of the other subjects was 'Policing in France: the crisis of Europeanization'. At Oxford, those of us involved with modern Greek studies were in the habit of meeting once a term for lunch to discuss developments in our beleaguered field. None of us could see in what way the revamped visiting fellowship in Hellenic studies was promoting the study of modern Greece. We therefore we sent a somewhat pompous round-robin letter of protest to Brasenose.

This elicited a peevish reply from the acting principal of the college, Professor Leighton Reynolds. Our collective letter had, he said, caused considerable personal distress. Tony Courakis had, he assured us, worked tirelessly to set up the scheme for the benefit of both the college and the university and had conducted its affairs 'with the most scrupulous care and unstinted expenditure of his own time'. Some of the implications of our letter 'on any view' were offensive not only to the individuals concerned but also to the college. He concluded that the college that he had had the privilege of serving for the past 40 years had 'always acted, and will continue to act, according to the highest academic standards and in the interests of our whole academic community'. We copied this correspondence to the London Hellenic Foundation. Whether as a consequence of this or not, the visiting fellowship was soon afterwards transferred to St Cross College, and survived for a further four years. The saga of the Greek visiting fellowship proved to be yet another example of the expenditure of a considerable amount of Greek money with little visible result. The tale of the fate of the fellowship at Brasenose appeared in *Private Eye*.

In 2002 our daughter, Rachel, was awarded the Max Hayward Visiting Fellowship at St Antony's. This enabled her to continue work on Fazil Iskander, who was of partly Abkhazian descent. Iskander was one of the most prominent novelists writing in Russian and was considered in a review in the *New York Times* as being in the same league as Swift, Gogol and Mark Twain. Perhaps his best known work is *Sandro of Chegem*, a novel set in Abkhazia, which was first published in Russian in a heavily censored form. I was not remotely involved in Rachel's appointment or in her decision to apply, but was naturally pleased that she was able to spend time at the College where there is such a well-established tradition in Russian and East European studies.

Of more pressing concern for me personally than the fate of the Greek visiting fellowship was the need to find the modest financial support necessary to enable me to remain at St Antony's when my five-year sabbatical from King's came to an end in 1995. After 1995, my early retirement pension kicked in, so I was not going to starve, but there was still a need to cover the costs connected with the senior research fellowship, to which I had now been elected, giving me membership of the governing body. The college had a small sum given by the Latsis family for the promotion of modern Greek studies, and permission was given for this money to go to me. This could be justified by the fact that I was now supervising a reasonable number of graduate students and exercising a general oversight of Greek studies in the college. This would enable me to remain at St Antony's for a further five years.

There remained, however, the need to try to secure funding for a permanent senior research fellowship in Greek history, which would enable the tradition in the field, established by John Campbell and continued by me, to be maintained after I finally retired in 2005. It was rather embarrassing to go cap in hand to potential donors. Oxford University, despite its continual complaints of poverty in comparison with American universities, was hugely wealthy when compared with the Greek higher education system. When approaching potential Greek donors I was always aware that if they were prepared to dispense money for the promotion of Greek studies then their first priority should be to help Greek universities, which seldom proved to be the case. Another source of embarrassment was that, in recent years, very large numbers of Greek students have attended British universities. In some years these amounted to more than 25,000, enough to fill two entire universities. Surely with such a huge influx of Greek students, some of whom were getting modest value for their fees, British universities or the British government should be able to fund a small number of positions in Greek studies. There was no indication of such a willingness, however, and with the advice and encouragement of John Campbell, I set about trying to fundraise.

I rather naively thought that a trump card in our fundraising endeavours would be that the university had been involved in the establishment of an entire 'Greek' College in Oxford some 300 years previously. The story is one that had fascinated me ever since Eric Tappe, a colleague who taught Romanian at SSEES, had alerted me to his short but still fundamental study of this extraordinary educational experiment. Further light was thrown on the Greek College and its troubled history by a conference organised in 2001, to mark its 300th anniversary, by Peter Doll, the chaplain of Worcester College, which is built on the site of the short-lived enterprise.

In the seventeenth century, both the Church of England and the Ecumenical Patriarchate had felt themselves under threat from a common enemy, a Papacy re-invigorated by the Counter-Reformation. Relations between the two churches were particularly close during the late seventeenth and early eighteenth centuries. In the 1670s a Greek Orthodox Church, the first in the English-speaking world, was established in London, although the Bishop of London would not countenance wall paintings and icons, nor would he permit prayers to the saints. A trickle of Greeks made their way to England, of whom an even smaller number made their way to Oxford. One of these, Nathanail Konopios, after becoming chaplain of Christ Church, eventually became metropolitan of Smyrna. He is credited with introducing Oxford to the delights of coffee drinking.

Towards the end of the seventeenth century, an Anglican clergyman, the Reverend Benjamin Woodroffe, sought to institutionalise these somewhat haphazard contacts by creating a Greek college in Oxford, housed in the run-down Gloucester Hall, subsequently the site of Worcester College. This would enable a small number of young Greek clerics to study for several years at the university. The aim was not to convert the students to Anglicanism but rather to hope that, on their return to the Orthodox world, they might gradually rise to positions of influence within the hierarchy of the Orthodox Church. Then, so it was hoped, they might be in a position to do away with such 'Romish' practices as the veneration of the Virgin Mary and of icons and the invocation of the saints.

Woodroffe outlined the harsh regimen to which the students were to be subjected in a leaflet preserved in the Bodleian Library. While the students, who never numbered more than a handful, were to be provided with lodging, meat, drink, clothes, medicine, books and other necessities, they seem to have found English food unpalatable, and they took exception to what one of their predecessors had termed the 'nasty stinking beer' that, in the absence of good water, was widely drunk. The dank Oxford weather came as a shock to those used to a Mediterranean climate. At all times they were to be dressed in 'the gravest sort of Habit worn in their own Country'. They were to enjoy no vacations. Their daily 'solemn devotions' were to commence at 5.30 in the morning. They were required to converse for the first two years in ancient Greek, a language to which Woodroffe found them to be 'utter strangers'. Latin was to be their 'constant language' for a further one or two years, when they were to embark on the study of Hebrew. The study of Aristotle, Plato and 'the Greek Scholiasts' was to be combined with the study of the Greek Fathers, thus fitting them to become 'Learn'd and Able Preachers and Schoolmasters in their country'. Further, they were to be taught about 'the chiefest Controversies' between the Papists on the one hand and the Orthodox and the Protestant churches on the other.

The college during the six years of its short existence attracted at most 15 students. Not surprisingly, a number of them rebelled against such a gruelling regime and absconded. One of them was accused of molesting a young girl and was forced to flee to Holland. Another, Frangiskos Prossalendis, became a bitter critic of his would-be Oxonian mentor, Woodroffe. He denounced Woodroffe's heretical diatribes and what he termed his bogus college (*pseudophrontistirion*). Steven Runciman, in his study of the Orthodox Church under Ottoman rule, *The Great Church in Captivity* (1968), puzzlingly described Prossalendis' tract, *O airetikos didaskalos ypo tou Orthodoxou mathitou elegkhomenos* (The heretical teacher censured by the Orthodox pupil) (Amsterdam 1706) as a 'friendly little book describing Dr Woodroffe's quirks and foibles', when it is in fact, as its title suggests, a hostile polemic. Given the vicissitudes of the Greek college, it comes as no surprise that in 1705 the Ecumenical Patriarchate, adverting to 'the irregular life of some priests and laymen of the Greek Church living in London', placed a ban on Orthodox students going to Oxford and the college ceased to exist. Woodroffe himself was bankrupted by the episode and ended up for a time in the notorious Fleet prison for debtors, an unusual fate for a canon of Christ Church.

Given my interest in the Orthodox church in the eighteenth century I was intrigued to discover that, just a short walk from our home in Muswell Hill, there was to be found in the grounds of the Methodist centre in Pages Lane the tombstone of an Ecumenical Patriarch, Meletios II, who was briefly Patriarch in 1768-9 and who died in 1780. When I first set eyes on it, in the mid-1970s, the stone lay half-buried in the undergrowth of the garden of North Bank, the last of the great houses with enormous gardens that dominated the area before the building boom of the early twentieth century turned Muswell Hill into the largest Edwardian suburb in the country. North Bank has always reminded me of Charles Augustus Fortescue, the subject of one of Hilaire Belloc's cautionary tales. Obsequious and obnoxious in equal measure, ever anxious as a child to parse Latin words and for the greasiest morsel of mutton fat, he married well and ended up immensely rich and residing 'in affluence still' in a splendid mansion called The Cedars, Muswell Hill.

I first became aware of the stone in 1977. I could not make any sense of it and was disappointed to find that it was not, as I had originally hoped, an inscription in *karamanlidika*, or Turkish in Greek characters. It was in time deciphered by Julian Chrysostomides and Charalambos Dendrinos of Royal Holloway College, who expanded the various ligatures in the Greek which had baffled me. Meletios' reign as patriarch had lasted only a matter of months, such was the rapid turnover, the consequence of endemic corruption, of the office of patriarch in the eighteenth century. Indeed, an Armenian at the time made the gibe that the Greeks changed their patriarch more often than their shirts. The stone, which must be one of the oldest surviving memorials of a post-Byzantine patriarch, may have been gathered by one of the families living in North Bank while making a kind of Grand Tour in the Levant, but this is only speculation. After I had first set eyes on it, the stone, already broken into pieces, had been scattered throughout the grounds by vandals, but the pieces had been gathered together by the enterprising gardener of the Methodist centre. It was eventually repatriated to the Ecumenical Patriarchate in Istanbul, which was manifestly a more appropriate resting place for Meletios II's gravestone than a garage in Muswell Hill, where it had latterly been stored.

The Church of England has always harboured the delusion that it enjoys a special relationship with the Orthodox churches. A long-cherished aspiration of those Anglicans who have sought closer relations, and eventual union, with the Orthodox churches has been the recognition of the validity of Anglican orders, the issue which has long been a major bone of contention with the Roman Catholic Church, which flatly denies that they are valid. Such recognition was eventually vouchsafed in 1922 when the Ecumenical Patriarch, Meletios Metaxakis, and the Holy Synod in Constantinople, decreed that Anglican orders had the same validity as those of the Roman Catholic, Old Catholic and Armenian Churches. Prominent among the enthusiasts for

Anglican/Orthodox union was Canon J.A. Douglas of the Crusade for the Redemption of Saint Sophia, which sought the return of the Emperor Justinian's great church in Constantinople to Orthodox worship in the aftermath of the defeat of the Ottoman Empire in World War I, and who had been one of Arnold Toynbee's severest critics in the senate of the University of London during his time of troubles at King's College. He rejoiced that henceforth Anglicans and Orthodox would be 'bone of the same bone'. It was not beyond the realms of possibility, he optimistically imagined, that within a few years the Anglican and Orthodox Churches would together constitute 'not only numerically the largest but immeasurably the most potent force in world-wide Christianity'.

The Ecumenical Patriarchate's recognition was signalled at the end of July 1922 to the Archbishop of Canterbury, Randall Davidson. The patriarch's letter was written at a critical juncture when the Greeks, as R.W. Seton-Watson maintained, faced the greatest threat since the time of Xerxes. A month later saw the beginning of the rout of the Greek expeditionary force in Asia Minor at the hands of the Turkish nationalists, a disaster of enormous proportions, known in Greece simply as 'the catastrophe'. Patriarch Meletios had highly sensitive political antennae, and it is clear that there was a strong element of political calculation in his move, which was not in any case binding on the other Orthodox patriarchates. The Greeks, with their backs to the wall, were clutching at any straw in their desperation, and the Church of England at that time wielded a great deal more political clout than it does today. After all, Canon Douglas' Crusade for the Redemption of Saint Sophia numbered, in the early 1920s, two future foreign secretaries in its membership. While the Church of England, like the Pope, may not have deployed any divisions, it was nonetheless able to ensure that the Ecumenical Patriarchate remained in Istanbul and was not caught up in the exchange of populations between Greece and Turkey in the 1920s.

Would-be donors to the fund to establish a permanent post in modern Greek history at St Antony's seem not to have been impressed by the fate of the Greek College. I thought, however, that an opportune occasion to launch our fundraising campaign would be at the time a prominent Antonian, and a first-rate historian of modern Greece, Michael Llewellyn Smith, who was the British ambassador in Athens. To this end, a lecture was organised at the British School at Athens to mark John Campbell's 75th birthday in 1998. It was given by Yannis Koliopoulos, professor of history in the University of Thessaloniki. Koliopoulos had not actually been one of Campbell's many graduate students, but he was a great admirer of Campbell's work. A small fundraising committee was established, headed by Professor Yannis Stournaras, the

Chairman of the Council of Economic Advisers in Greece, but it never really functioned and nothing came of the initiative. The fundraising situation was complicated, moreover, by the arrival at St Antony's in 1999 of Kalypso Nicolaidis, who had previously been at Harvard, as lecturer in international relations. She was an adviser to George Papandreou, the son of Andreas, and at the time foreign minister in Costas Simitis' PASOK government, and had her own ideas as to the future of Greek studies at the college. She was more interested in policy making and 'action research' than in history, and there was some confusion between her fundraising activities and mine. Eventually, a large sum was forthcoming from the Greek foreign ministry to fund a programme in south-east European studies at St Antony's. Part of this enabled me to continue at the college until I reached the retirement age of 65 in 2005.

Kalypso Nicolaidis became chair of SEESOX (South-East European Studies at Oxford) and a director, Dr Othon Anastasakis, was appointed. I did not become a member of the steering committee because it appeared to me that SEESOX was not simply concerned to analyse current developments, particularly in the field of Greek–Turkish relations, but sought also to promote particular policies which were in effect those of the Greek government. These were essentially two: trying to persuade the Greek Cypriots to accept the Annan plan, or some variant of it, and thus bring about a settlement of the Cyprus problem, and seeking to promote the accession of Turkey to the European Union, which of course would be facilitated by a resolution of the long-running Cyprus dispute. These may or may not have been worthy objectives, but it did not seem to me that their promotion was the function of a university. In the course of the establishment of SEESOX, the original project of funding a permanent post in the modern history of Greece fell by the wayside. Thus the tradition of the advanced study of Greek history and society which had existed at St Antony's for some 50 years appears to have come to an end. The similar tradition at King's College, London also came to an end a few years later when the Cyprus Hellenic Foundation Lecturer in Modern Greek History, Philip Carabott, who was my successor, took early retirement and was not replaced. In 2014, there came better news about the future of the study of the modern history of Greece in British universities when a three-year lectureship was established at Royal Holloway, a constituent college of the University of London. Emphasis was given to the study of the Greek diaspora. In 2016 it was extended for a further three years thanks to the generosity of the Leventis Foundation but whether it will become a permanent position remains to be seen.

In the 1990s, with the breakup of Yugoslavia, Greece was gripped by furious controversy over the issue of Macedonia. This feeding frenzy was precipitated by the emergence of what had been the Yugoslav Federal Republic of Macedonia as an independent state. Ever since the creation of the Federal Republic by Tito after World War II there had been tension with Greece. This collective Greek neurosis was prompted in part by the flight of considerable numbers of Slav-Macedonians from Greece to Yugoslavia during the civil war in the late 1940s. This migration had increased following the defeat of the communist Democratic Army in 1949, for, towards the end of this savage conflict, as much as a half of the rebel forces consisted of Slav-Macedonians. Demands had emanated periodically from Skopje and Belgrade for the creation of an 'Aegean' Macedonia, which would have embraced a large area of northern Greece, including Thessaloniki, Greece's second city. While Tito was alive the lid was more or less kept on such aspirations, but with his death and the emergence of an independent Macedonia there were fears that its very name presaged territorial claims at the expense of Greece. The making of such demands inevitably created indignation in Greece, some of it voiced in exaggerated fashion. One of the crazier manifestations of Macedonian fever was the proposal by a group of rich Greek–Americans to fund the carving of a giant head of Alexander the Great, four times the size of the famous Mount Rushmore carvings of American presidents in South Dakota, on a mountainside in northern Greece. This is a scheme that, mercifully, ran into the sand.

Outside Greece, the Macedonian issue prompted a certain amount of posturing by 'philhellenicly' inclined academics. One such row arose out of Cambridge University Press' timorous refusal to publish Dr Anastasia Karakasidou's *Fields of Wheat, Hills of Blood: Passages to Nationhood in Greek Macedonia 1870–1990*, a revised version of her PhD thesis for which she had carried out the fieldwork in the early 1990s, a time when hysteria in Greece over the Macedonian issue was at its height. In her book, which appeared under the imprint of the University of Chicago Press in 1997, she demonstrated the way in which a sense of Greek identity had been instilled, at times harshly, in the ethnically diverse populations that had been incorporated into the Greek state in the course of its expansion and, in particular, at the time of the Balkan Wars of 1912-13. Her anthropological study of villages in Greek Macedonia ran counter to the official Greek line that, while there might be Slav-speakers in Greece, there is no Slav-Macedonian minority. Anastasia had been a participant in my workshop on minorities in Greece.

I had first met Anastasia at a conference of the US-based Modern Greek Studies Association held at the University of Florida in Gainesville in November 1991. We had participated in the same panel on minorities in Greece, which had been chaired by my old friend George Frangos. While Anastasia had come in for the lion's share of the flak, I had myself been denounced as a 'second Lord Elgin' (Anastasia was subsequently to be pilloried as a 'female Fallmerayer') for having the temerity to suggest that Greece should treat its minuscule minorities (at that time amounting to less than 5 per cent of the total population) with benign neglect, i.e. by leaving them alone, neither encouraging them nor discriminating against them. Frangos had barred local members of the Greek–American community from videoing our session for transmission on a local TV station, which led to accusations that our panel had been plotting the dismemberment of Greece. I remember being puzzled and rather alarmed by the advice given to Anastasia after our session at the conference by Michael Herzfeld, an anthropologist and leading light in the Modern Greek Studies Association, that she should find herself a lawyer. Our panel appears also to have disconcerted the Greek ambassador in Washington, Christos Zacharakis, who gave the keynote speech at the conference. Fears were expressed that Greek government and Greek embassy funding might not in future be forthcoming for Modern Greek Studies Association conferences.

A characteristic example of the fierce passions that had been aroused over the Macedonian issue in Greece, and more particularly in the Greek diaspora, which, in the way of such communities, tend to be more catholic than the Pope, was the arrest in 1992 of four students for protesting against the wave of nationalist hysteria that was sweeping the country by distributing a pamphlet with the anodyne slogan 'Our neighbours are not our enemies. No to nationalism, no to war.' On their conviction they were sentenced to 19 months in prison, whereupon 169 academics and others signed a petition protesting against the sentence and defending their right to free speech, only to provoke a counter-petition by 1,000 or so teachers and administrators at the University of Thessaloniki. This attacked the 169 for 'national betrayal'.

I was able to witness at firsthand some of the passions that had been aroused over Macedonia when, in May 1993, I attended the trial in Athens of five Trotskyists who had been arrested for publishing a pamphlet in Greek entitled *The Crisis in the Balkans: The Macedonian Question and the Working Class*. The defendants included Panos Garganas, the brother of Nikos Garganas, at that time deputy-governor of the Bank of Greece and someone whom I had known in London during the years of the Colonels' dictatorship. The five were charged, *inter alia*, with endangering the friendly relations of the Greek state with other states and of creating a climate of fear and dissension by claiming that there is a Slav-Macedonian minority in the country. The defendants faced maximum prison sentences of five years.

When approached by members of the UK-based Committee to Defend Greek Socialists (sponsored, *inter alia*, by Tony Benn), I was happy to go along with the request that I attend the trial as an observer. I held no very strong views on the Macedonian question but it seemed to me unsatisfactory, to say the least, that in a member state of the European Union people could be put on trial merely for expressing an opinion. I was in any case interested to observe a trial in a Greek court on a highly charged political issue. So I sat through much of the trial, taking extensive notes of proceedings whose informality contrasted favourably with the archaic and arcane stuffiness of British court proceedings. Such, indeed, was the informality that I appeared to be keeping a fuller record of the trial proceedings than the official court stenographer. The issues were debated at length and the defendants had every opportunity to expound their position. Much of the trial was devoted to consideration of whether there is indeed a Slav-Macedonian minority in Greece; whether it is oppressed; and whether it had been subject to forced 'Hellenisation' on the part of the Greek state. A point that was in particular contention was whether the parallel drawn in the pamphlet between the treatment of Kurds in Turkey and of Slav-Macedonians in Greece was a reasonable one. This led to consideration of whether the '*kratidio ton Skopion*' (the statelet of Skopje), as the newly independent state of Macedonia was derisively termed by Greek nationalists, harboured territorial designs on Greek Macedonia.

There were some genuinely humorous moments, some occasioned by the rather loquacious presiding judge, and none of the stilted attempts at wit on the part of pompous and bewigged judges so characteristic of British trials. All the defendants, defence witnesses and defence lawyers were given plenty of time to get their points across and, indeed, there were occasional interjections from the crowded courtroom. Although there were a number of heated moments and occasions when at least three people were speaking at once, I was struck by the generally good-natured way in which the proceedings were conducted. I was somewhat disconcerted when, at one stage, one of the defence lawyers read out a list of historians whose writings indicated that they accepted that there is a Slav-Macedonian minority in Greece. He not only included me in this company but said that I was actually present in the court. My initial rather selfish reaction was that bang would go the use of the Greek translation of my *A Short History of Modern Greece* as a prescribed text for students of history at the University of Athens. I never made much money from the substantial distribution of the book (copies of which were given free of charge to students), but, until royalties began to be paid, I did receive a useful number of books in lieu from the publisher, who doubled up, as is often the case in Greece, as a bookseller. Greece being Greece, there was in the event no agitation for my book no longer to be distributed on the ground that it was anti-national, and it continued to be used for many years subsequently.

All the accused were acquitted, a decision which took me aback almost as much as it did the defendants. I had been pretty certain that in the prevailing political climate they would be found guilty. Had the trial taken place in the preceding autumn, 1992, when passions over the Macedonian issue were at their height, then the outcome might have been different. The way in which the issue was no longer front page news was perhaps indicated by the paucity of newspaper reporting of the trial. *Kathimerini*, for instance, covered the result in a single short paragraph. In my view, the trial was a credit to the Greek judicial system, even if the charges levied against the five had been absurd and the trial should never have taken place.

If the Greek judicial system did the right thing in the case of the five Trotskyists, Anastasia Karakasidou's experiences were seriously alarming. She was subjected to violent verbal abuse, including threats of rape and death. In a menacing move, the ultra-right-wing (and very small circulation) newspaper *Stokhos* (Target) provocatively published details of her address in Greece and her car registration number. At one stage she was offered the right of asylum in the US consulate in Thessaloniki (her husband and children were US citizens) should the need have arisen, while she was given 'discreet' police protection by the Greek authorities.

The row over Cambridge University Press's refusal to publish Karakasidou's book was aired, *inter alia*, in an article by Leonard Doyle in the *Guardian*. This revealed that, in considering whether or not to go ahead with publication, the Press had sought 'a terrorist threat assessment' from the British embassy in Athens. While the assessment did not advise CUP not to publish, it did warn that protests could encompass 'public criticism, protests and demonstrations, or violence or threat of violence against the author or publishers', although it seems that no one from the embassy had actually read the manuscript. The advice of MI6, or the Secret Intelligence Service, was also sought. In an internal memorandum, an official of Cambridge University Press argued that it was impossible to discount the advice given by the embassy which had 'warned that publication might put at risk the lives of Press staff in Athens, and of Cambridge University personnel in Greece'.

The Press apparently believed that because of the threat of terrorist violence there was a 'moral imperative' not to go ahead with publication. No contract had been issued in respect of the book, but the two referees who had read it for the Press, the historian Mark Mazower and the anthropologist Charles Stewart, had strongly recommended publication. Doyle pointed out that in arriving at its decision no advice had been taken from Greeks or from British and American academics in the field. He suggested that the Press's decision may have been influenced by fears of a boycott of its lucrative market in Greece, particularly in the field of English language teaching textbooks, and of the loss of the very considerable revenue which Cambridge University derived from Cambridge Certificate of Proficiency in English examinations taken under its auspices. Doyle noted that two members of the editorial board of the Press's anthropological monograph series, Michael Herzfeld of Harvard and Stephen Gudeman of the University of Minnesota, had resigned in protest at the decision, while another member, Jack Goody of Cambridge, had signalled his decision to resign if it were not reversed.

I thought some of the polemics over the Karakasidou affair rather overblown and that the picture that had emerged in the press had been painted too much in black and white terms. I tried to put this view across in an article in the *Times Higher Education Supplement*. While I made it clear that I thought Cambridge University Press's decision not to offer Karakasidou a contract had been unnecessarily pusillanimous, and expressed a certain puzzlement that the Press had not seen fit to consult with me as someone with considerable experience of publishing in Greece (and as one of its authors), I pointed out that the Press's hesitations were not entirely groundless. If I had been consulted, I should have reminded CUP of an incident which appears to have slipped from its collective memory but which, from its own point of view, might have proved to be useful ammunition in the polemics over the Karakasidou affair. Some 20 years previously, following CUP's publication of Stanford Shaw's *History of the Ottoman Empire and Modern Turkey*, the Press had received threats from Armenians outraged by Shaw's denial that Turkey's mistreatment of the Armenians during World War I had constituted genocide.

I also argued that some of CUP's critics had been rather too cavalier in dismissing the possibility of violence. Professors Herzfeld and Gudeman had argued that CUP's decision had constituted not only a threat to academic freedom but a slur on the Greek people who were caricatured as being 'prone to violent, unreasoned responses'. Athens (at least until the eruption of violent protests towards the end of 2008) was one of the safest of European cities, but Greece, like many European countries, has experienced a fair degree of terrorism. There was a rocket attack against the US Embassy in Athens at much the same time news of that the Karakasidou affair had broken. What is more, violence in Greece had in the past been targeted at cultural institutions. Ten years previously, the deputy head of the British Council in Athens and a member of his staff were blown up by a car bomb, while scarcely a year previously the Council's German equivalent, the Goethe Institute, had been bombed. But to say this no more stereotypes the Greeks as a violent people than pointing to the undoubted fact of IRA violence characterises the Irish collectively as terrorists.

During the Macedonian frenzy, Greece received a very bad press in the UK and, indeed, in Europe. Much of this was caused by Greek government propagandists' insistence on basing Greek claims on events in antiquity. The English-speaking visitor was bombarded with not entirely felicitous slogans such as 'Macedonia is Greek 4000 years'. I once received a package from Greece stamped: 'Macedonia is and has been Greek for over 3000 years. This is an indisputable historical fact'. At much the same time (1994) letters from Greece were postmarked 'Macedonia Greece 4000 years of hellenic civilisation.' The average tourist must have been baffled by propaganda which made great play of Philip of Macedon and Alexander the Great, essentially seeking to answer the question of who got to Macedonia first, the Greeks or the Slavs. Particular objection was taken in Greece to the appropriation by the Yugoslav Macedonians (the *gyphtoskopianoi* or 'gypsy Skopians' as Greek nationalists derisively termed them) of the 16-pointed star of Vergina, found in the tomb of Philip of Macedon, for the national flag of the new Macedonian Republic. The seemingly exaggerated reaction of many Greeks over the issue of the name of the new state led to much criticism in the European press. One *Times* leader called on Greece to 'grow up'. Another claimed that Greece was the 'least pleasant' country in Europe in which to live – not a view that would be universally shared. The right-wing press in Britain traditionally has had a pro-Turkish bias. A notorious leader in *The Times* during the Cyprus crisis of the 1950s had hailed Turkey as our ally in two world wars. Even the *Guardian*, normally well disposed towards Greece, viewed the prospect of a Greek presidency of the European Union as absurd, and went on to argue that if Greece were not already a member, she would scarcely qualify for admission to the EU. Andreas Papandreou's imposition of a blockade of Macedonia was universally criticised. Bureaucrats in Brussels muttered in private that Greece should never have been admitted to a European Community which it looked on as little more than a milch cow.

For their part, the Greeks felt hurt and abandoned. Like the Serbs, for whom many Greeks had a strong sympathy in the Yugoslav wars of the 1990s, they felt themselves to be a 'brotherless' nation in a volatile and threatening world. During a visit to Belgrade, the Ecumenical Patriarch, Bartholomaios, had pronounced it the duty of all Orthodox Christians to rally to the defence of the embattled Serbs, a brave position to adopt given the strength of sentiment in Turkey in support of the Bosnian Muslims. When, in 1994, the Hellenic Centre, a splendid and long overdue venue for Greek-related cultural events, was opened in London, the ambassadors of the Orthodox countries alone were invited from the diplomatic corps to the opening reception. The organisers were apparently unaware that the Bulgarian ambassador at the time was, in fact, a Roman Catholic, the Papacy being the object of considerable suspicion on the part of Greek nationalists. At the same time there was a tendency on the part of some to believe that the west owed Greece a profound debt of obligation because Greece was the *fons et origo* of Western civilisation. This conceit was reinforced by Western politicians and their hyperbolic platitudes.

There seemed little understanding of the reasons for the seemingly irrational attitudes of many, although, of course, by no means all, Greeks on the Macedonian issue. I sought to offer an explanation for these attitudes in an article entitled 'Greek-bashing' which was published in *The London Review of Books* in 1994. The thrust of the piece was that official Greek propaganda was mistaken in focusing so heavily on Macedonia in antiquity and in saying so little about much more recent events, which went a long way towards explaining Greek attitudes.

Greek government pronouncements did not mention the fact that during World War II, a large chunk of northern Greece, including part of Greek Macedonia, had been in the grip of a vicious Bulgarian occupying force which engaged in brutal ethnic cleansing of the Greek population. This occupied territory was formally annexed by Bulgaria. Moreover, the bulk of the million or more refugees who had flooded into Greece early in the 1920s had been settled in Greek Macedonia. Some had come from Bulgaria. Some had fled from Bolshevik Russia. Most were Greeks from Asia Minor (many of them Turkish-speaking) caught up in the compulsory exchange of populations that followed Greece's catastrophic defeat in the 1919-22 conflict with the Turkish nationalists. Then, soon after the end of World War II, Greece was wracked by a ferocious civil war which in some sense can be seen as a struggle for Greek Macedonia. By the closing stages of the civil war in 1949, as we have seen, as many as half of the combatants in the communist Democratic Army were Slav-speakers from Greece's northern provinces. At a late stage in the conflict, the Communist Party of Greece had advocated self-determination for the Slav-Macedonians, which, in the event of a communist victory, would have meant detaching a large section of northern Greece that had been won from the Turks as recently as during the Balkan wars of 1912-13.

Many of the present inhabitants of the region are the descendants of populations forcibly uprooted and transplanted in the 1920s. They are disinclined to repeat the experiences of parents, grandparents and great-grandparents, and see their world, as had their forebears, turned upside down. I expressed the view that it was these bitter recent experiences, which had taken place within living memory, which played a far larger part in shaping the fears of Greeks over the Macedonian issue than arcane disputes over the history of the region in antiquity. I rather doubt, however, that my piece for *The London Review of Books* led, as was intended, to a more nuanced understanding of Greek fears and aspirations.

The furore over the Macedonian issue and the bad press that Greece was receiving as a consequence was presumably one of the factors that prompted the establishment by the Greek government in 1992 of the Foundation for Hellenic Culture. This was a kind of Greek equivalent of the British Council, intended both to promote Greek culture and to highlight the continuities between ancient and modern Greece. One of the earliest public events organised by the Foundation was described as the 'First Ecumenical Gathering of the Friends of Greek Culture'. This took the form of a somewhat chaotic evening, devoted to poetic and musical works inspired by Greek ideals, at the Herodus Atticus theatre at the foot of the Acropolis. This was followed by a short but delightful cruise in the Aegean in June 1993 to which a large number of those deemed to be philhellenes from various parts of the world were invited as guests by the Foundation. When I received my invitation I naturally accepted with alacrity, and telephoned a friend working for the Foundation, intending to ask whether the validity of my plane ticket to Greece could be extended so that I could carry out some research, naturally at my own expense. Before I had time even to make this modest request, my friend said, 'Of course you must bring Mary Jo.'

So the two of us departed on a magical trip, made marginally more entertaining for some of my colleagues by the sight of Roddy Beaton and me trying to avoid each other, with Mary Jo trying to bring us together, on what was not a very large ship. For me one of the highlights of the cruise was an hilarious incident when a short-sighted professor of classics at the University of Birmingham asked one of the participants, 'Haven't we met somewhere before?', to which the reply was 'Yes, I'm a member of your department.' Someone whom I was particularly glad to meet on board was Odysseus Dimitriadis, for many years a major figure on the Soviet musical scene. What was of particular interest to me was that he had been been in the 1930s the musical director, before Stalin decreed its closure, of the Greek theatre in Sukhum, Abkhazia, when the Abkhazian capital witnessed a remarkable efflorescence of Greek culture during the early years of Bolshevik rule.

In the second half of the 1990s, whether travelling on the London underground or sitting on a beach in Greece, or indeed elsewhere, it was difficult not to catch sight of someone reading Louis de Bernières' novel, *Captain Corelli's Mandolin*. At the end of the film comedy *Notting Hill*, Hugh Grant is seen reading the ubiquitous book. Set on Cephalonia during World War II, it tells the story of an Italian army captain who falls in love with the daughter of a doctor on the island, against the background of German massacres of Italian soldiers, who had switched sides following the Italian surrender in September 1943. I struggled to read the book right through, sharing the opinion of one reviewer who found it as 'overwritten to a bloodcurdling degree', while Jeremy Paxman's hailing of the book as 'absolutely brilliant' was scarcely an enticing recommendation. The poor film that was made of the book was written off by Alexander Walker in the *Evening Standard* as akin to a 'Mills and Boon novelette'.

Sorting through papers when writing this memoir I came across a letter of August 1992 from de Bernières saying that he had read my *A Concise History of Greece* with great interest and enjoyment and asking me if I would compile for him a reading list on Cephalonia during and after World War II as he was writing a novel set on the island. The bibliography appended to my *Concise History* was apparently not specific enough for what he described as his 'immediate requirements'. He wanted to know which units of the Italian army occupied the island; whether it had been caught up in the civil war; and what had happened during the earthquake of 1953 which had devastated the island. A postscript vouchsafed that he did not speak Greek. This was something of a tall order as I did not know much about the history of the Ionian islands during this period.

The deluge of publicity about the book and subsequent film passed me by. But when I learned that the book was to become an A level set text I did become rather concerned. For, quite apart from the issue of the literary merit or otherwise of the book, it presented a warped view of Greek history during the Italian, German and Bulgarian occupation and I was alarmed that for many thousands of British schoolchildren this would be the sole source of whatever knowledge they might have of Greece during World War II.

In an author's note de Bernières made his view of Greek communists unambiguously clear: 'when they were not totally useless, perfidious, and parasitic, they were unspeakably barbaric'. His loathing of Greek communists was made abundantly clear:

> in Cephalonia the Communists began to deport awkward characters to concentration camps; from a safe distance they had watched the Nazis for years, and were well-versed in all the arts of atrocity and oppression. Hitler would have been proud of such assiduous pupils.

And this from someone who, by his own admission, knew no Greek. His views on the role of the communists led to an unseemly exchange with the *Morning Star*. When the paper accused de Bernières of 'crude and brazen anti-communism', he intemperately replied, 'how long are you people going to sit in the dark in an air-pocket wanking each other off? Your ship has sunk, brothers. It was historically inevitable.' De Bernières' views on the Greek left, unsurprisingly, aroused controversy in Greece itself, so much so that, extraordinarily, he seemingly authorised his Greek translator and publisher to moderate some of his language and opinions. This cannot have happened to many translations of novels into Greek or, indeed, into any language.

What particularly exercised me was the way in which de Bernières caricatured real individuals who had formed part of the British military mission to the Greek resistance. He has the long-dead Tom Barnes, a New Zealander, say of the blowing up of a bridge, 'top-hole explosion [...] absolutely ripping. Cantilevers all over the shop. It'll keep the wops and jerries busy for weeks', although there are no grounds for believing him to be a real-life Biggles. Brigadier Eddie Myers, the first commander of the military mission, was still alive when *Captain Corelli's Mandolin* was published in 1994. He was irritated at the way he was portrayed, although he was not caricatured as were some of the other members of his mission. Myers died in 1997, at the age of 91. I had always assumed that his longevity was in some way connected with the months spent as a relatively young man tramping around the Greek mountains and living off a healthy diet of *horta* (wild greens) and yoghurt. I was somewhat taken aback, therefore, to see at his funeral two younger sisters who bore a striking resemblance to Eddie, while I subsequently learned that an *older* sister had not been well enough to attend. It would seem that genes, and not the diet of mountain Greece, were responsible for the longevity of the Myers family.

The most caricatured of the figures that appear in de Bernières' book is 'Bunny' Warren. He is depicted as going around in the traditional *fustanella*, or kilt, of the *evzones*, the presidential guard, and speaking ancient Greek. This de Bernières renders as Chaucerian English, in the process making him out to be an utter buffoon: 'Sire, of youre gentillesse, by the leve of yow wol I speke in pryvetee of certeyn thyng.' De Bernières writes that:

> it had been an awful burden to be speaking the finest public school Greek, and not be understood. He had been told that he was the nearest thing to a real Graecophone [*sic*] that could be found under the circumstances, and he knew perfectly well that modern Greek was not quite the same as the Greek of Eton, but he had had no idea that he would be found quite so incomprehensible. It was also very clear that someone in Intelligence had contrived a completely aberrant notion of what was worn in Cephalonia.

Like Barnes, he, too, is depicted as employing Biggles-speak: using expressions such as 'spiffing', 'simply ripping', 'absolutely ghastly' and 'frightfully grateful'. In the book, Lieutenant 'Bunny' Warren, shortly after the liberation of Greece in the autumn of 1944, is invited to a party by 'the Communists' and shot. The real-life Warren, as we shall see, met with quite a different fate.

De Bernières is, of course, perfectly free to create and caricature fictional Englishmen in wartime in any way he likes but it is tasteless, to say the least, to make idiots of people who really did exist and who risked, and, in a few cases lost, their lives in occupied Greece. The question arises as to how de Bernières lighted on the name 'Bunny' Warren for the most ludicrous of his characters. Eddie Myers, Tom Barnes, Patrick Leigh-Fermor and Billy Moss all figure in the book and all were in SOE. Some of them are given speaking parts. De Bernières maintains that he used the name Bunny Warren by chance: 'oddly enough, it turned out there really had been a SOE officer called Bunny Warren, which is also the name of one of my characters'. Yet a few years before the novel was written, there had been much mention of the real-life Bunny Warren, Captain D.A. La Touche Warren, in the controversy surrounding the former secretary-general of the United Nations Kurt Waldheim's convenient amnesia in his memoirs about his inglorious record of wartime service in the Balkans. The joke at the time was that doctors had discovered a new variant of Alzheimer's disease, namely Waldheimer's. This, in contrast to Alzheimer's, involves a selective rather than a total loss of memory.

The real Warren was no foppish and affected Etonian but an Australian educated at Geelong Grammar School. On the outbreak of the war he had enlisted in the British army, not the Australian, joining the Royal Northumberland Fusiliers and, subsequently, SOE. In March 1944, he had been charged with evacuating escaped prisoners of war from Greece. En route for Italy, his caique had broken down and was blown back to Cephalonia. He was captured, sent to Thessaloniki for interrogation, and, in May of that year, executed by the Sicherheitsdienst, the Nazi party security service, under the terms of Hitler's notorious *Kommando-Befehl* of October 1942. This edict had been issued after the ill-fated Dieppe raid, whereby 'sabotage troops' operating in German-occupied countries were to be executed, even if captured in uniform. The chronically forgetful Waldheim was not directly involved in Warren's interrogation, although he was responsible for handling the resulting interrogation reports. Far from falling victim to 'the communists', as de Bernières maintains, Warren was executed by the Nazis. There is only one case recorded of a British liaison officer being killed by communists in Greece. Lieutenant William Arthur Hubbard was shot by a member of ELAS, the communist-controlled resistance army, in October 1943. Churchill publicly claimed that Hubbard had been murdered, but it was subsequently established that his killing had been accidental. In retrospect, I am relieved that I did not equip de Bernières with the reading list he requested. I should not have relished having my help being in any way connected with such a one-sided, erroneous and pretentious reading of recent Greek history. De Bernières is of the opinion that 'literary truth lies not in the details, but in the flavour'. Quite so.

My relationship with some, but, given its diversity, by no means all members of the London Greek community, was not always the easiest. The rich ship owners who played a dominant role in the cultural life of the community had little idea of the conventions of British academic life. A case in point was the row that ensued following the award for the first time of the Hellenic Foundation Prize, which had been established by a section of the Greek community in London. In 1986, the academic adjudicators had recommended that the prize for the best PhD thesis in the field of modern Greek studies be shared between Dr Victoria Solomonidis, a student of mine, and Dr Dimitris Tziovas of the University of Birmingham. The Foundation, however, had rejected this adjudication and, without consulting the adjudicators, awarded the prize to Dr Solomonidis, who was employed by the Greek embassy. What was described as an 'extensive' and somewhat heated correspondence had then ensued between members of the Standing Committee on Modern Greek in the Universities (SCOMGIU), which brought together teachers in the field of 'modern' Greek studies, and the Hellenic Foundation, although the minutes of SCOMGIU subsequently reported that 'a measure of amicability' had now been restored.

I was not party to this particular row, although I did cross swords with the Foundation a year or two later. In the early years of the Hellenic Foundation Prize, the Foundation had required that university departments should nominate the 'best' thesis completed in the three fields in which it was offered: classics, Byzantine studies and 'modern' Greek studies. It was, in my view, quite inappropriate for a department to declare publicly that one completed PhD thesis was superior to another, least of all for a supervisor publicly to proclaim one of his/her students to be superior to the others. My particular difficulty had arisen when identical twins, whose supervision I had taken over from Douglas Dakin on his retirement, completed theses after labouring on them for a number of years. In the characteristic fashion of identical twins, both theses were finally completed within a few weeks of each other, and both were of excellent quality. My objection to proclaiming to all and sundry that one student was superior to another was even stronger when the two students were siblings and, in this particular case, was anyway simply not possible. Trying to explain these difficulties to the Foundation met with blank incomprehension and the impression that I was being awkward for the sake of it.

Some strange ideas existed among some of the London Greeks to the effect that I was more than a mere historian of Greece, and that my interest in the subject was motivated by more than intellectual curiosity. Indeed, there were some erroneous, if to a degree flattering, notions as to the degree of influence which I wielded over British foreign policy. An indication of just how far-fetched some of these perceptions were was illustrated in correspondence that appeared in 1992 in *Kathimerini*, the nearest thing that Greece has to a newspaper of record. A reader had written to the newspaper that he had heard over Cairo Radio, of all places, that the Greek ministry of culture was considering, or even had already decided upon, the abolition of the Bywater and Sotheby chair at Oxford. Characterising the chair as a veritable bastion of Greek culture and history, the letter writer described the decision as calamitous given that the Turks had launched a cunning programme of endowing chairs of Turcology and institutes of Turkish studies in Europe and the Middle East. He might also have mentioned the United States. He was concerned that the national interest could be so casually damaged. Why the writer of the letter should have thought that any decision to abolish the chair lay within the competence of the Greek ministry of culture rather than Oxford University is not obvious.

The letter prompted a response from Michael Moschos, a member of the Council of the Hellenic Foundation, which was essentially the cultural arm of the Greek shipping fraternity in London. He wrote that the future of this most distinguished chair had in fact been secured thanks to a generous benefaction made two years previously by the Greek government and other well-wishers at the prompting of the Hellenic Foundation and with the help of the Greek embassy in London. The chair had been held since 1968 by the well-known Byzantinist Cyril Mango. He was expected to retire in 1995 when his successor would be chosen by the authorities at Oxford University. He described Mango as frequently expressing '*sui generis* anti-Greek views on byzantine politics and art', although what an 'anti-Greek' view on Byzantine art might be is not immediately obvious.

Having made clear that the future of the Bywater and Sotheby Chair was secure, Moschos spoke of the imperative need to save what he termed the 'unofficial' chair of John Campbell at St Antony's. Campbell, according to Moschos, had for 30 years had been 'an eminent, unpaid [*amisthos*] and dedicated researcher' in the fields of Greek sociology [read anthropology] and history. In reality, Campbell had at one stage held a university lectureship in modern Balkan history, but he had given this up some 20 years previously, while retaining his fellowship at the college. Here, besides acting as sub-warden and senior tutor, he had supervised, until his retirement in 1990, a large number of DPhil theses in anthropology (his primary discipline) and history, most of them related to Greece. Campbell's place, Moschos continued, had in part and 'for the time being' (this was particularly irritating) been filled by the *gnostos* (well-known) Richard Clogg. I was described as an adviser on matters of Balkan policy to the Foreign Office 'among other bodies' (it would be interesting to know which he had in mind here). My historical interests, he said, encompassed 'the whole Balkans and focus principally on its flash points'. This fact, he puzzlingly continued, rendered 'Greek positions of secondary significance in the political briefing' of the Foreign Office. Moschos had already drawn attention to the need to do something about St Antony's in an earlier article in *Kathimerini*, and the Hellenic Foundation 'at the risk of exhausting its limited funds' (although much of the money in fact appears to have come from the Leventis Foundation) was subsidising two visiting fellowships at the college. The Hellenic Foundation meanwhile was trying to raise money for the 'national objective' of a permanent 'professorship' at the college.

Although this was probably the nearest that I ever came to being described in print as someone whose historical interests were secondary to political concerns, its author presumably thought he was being helpful in writing his letter, so much so that he sent me a copy of it. Ironically, I received this letter just as a Foreign Office-sponsored conference on the Balkans was being held at its Wilton Park conference centre. This had the title *Europe's troubled corner: how to overcome instability and tensions in the Balkans*, an optimistic one in the early 1990s. I had not been invited to this conference, a strange omission, one might have thought, of the person purportedly influencing Britain's Balkan policy. Not only was I not invited to this particular gathering by the Foreign Office, but I have never been invited to any of its conferences on Greek–Turkish relations, the Cyprus problem or other subjects on which I have some specialised knowledge. But I suppose some would hold that the fact that the Foreign Office kept me at arm's length in this way only goes to demonstrate how deep my cover was.

Although I was irritated by Moschos' remarks, I did not propose to answer them. It not being possible to prove a negative, how could I possibly demonstrate that I was not someone who was more or less single-handedly responsible for the neglect of Greece's concerns by the Foreign Office? John Campbell, however, was understandably exercised at his depiction as a solitary scholar, beavering away unpaid for three decades in his zeal to promote the Greek cause. So we duly penned a joint reply for publication in *Kathimerini*. This gist of this was that John was not an unpaid, unofficial researcher and that I was not an influential figure shaping the Balkan policies of the Foreign Office and other unnamed bodies. Shortly before its publication, we received a letter from George Lemos, the ship-owning treasurer of the Hellenic Foundation, emphasising that the views which Moschos had expressed were his alone and did not reflect the views of the Foundation. Costas Hadjipateras, another London-based shipowner, wrote to me that he had been in touch with Moschos to let him know my unhappiness over his letter. Moschos had apparently replied that he was amazed at the construction that I had put on it. He could not understand how I had arrived at such an impossible interpretation of what he had written. Moschos told Hadjipateras that he regarded me as a friend but when, some weeks after the exchange in *Kathimerini*, I came across him at some Anglo-Greek gathering in London and I said that I thought he owed me some kind of apology, he simply walked away.

Given that I seem to have acquired a reputation in some Greek quarters as someone with an animus against PASOK and as a mishellene, if not an out and out *praktoras*, I was surprised but gratified to be awarded a Greek honour, the Gold Cross of the Legion of Honour, by the PASOK government in 2002. I have never been an enthusiast for the British honours system, which appears to me to be an effective instrument in the hands of the establishment to inhibit those, such as vice-chancellors and other careerists, from rocking the boat. I particularly dislike the way that the recipients of some honours end up changing their names, which can be tiresome for the historian. However, in the case of my Greek award I did not have the opportunity of considering whether or not to accept it. The first I heard about it was when I was rung up at home in London by a student at the time in Athens on the day of the now traditional reception in Athens on 24 July to mark the restoration of democracy in 1974, and told that the presentation by President Stephanopoulos would take place that very evening.

My first reaction was one of panic, fearing it might appear that I had snubbed the Greek authorities by not being there. I considered calling the British ambassador to ask him to purvey my apologies. But when I called Paul Cartledge of the University of Cambridge, a fellow recipient of the award, I discovered that he likewise had no inkling of what was afoot. The other two British academics who were awarded this honour at the same time, Cartledge and Judith Herrin of King's College London, were both supporters of the 're-unification' of the Elgin or Parthenon marbles by their return to Greece. This is a cause about which I have no strong views, and I have never lent my name to the campaign for their return. But this clearly had not been held against me. The nearest I ever came to backing the restitution of the Parthenon marbles campaign was when Neil Kinnock, at the time leader of the Labour party, declared that they are as Greek as (the old) Wembley stadium is English, and that the Parthenon without the marbles is akin to a smile with a tooth missing.

In the summer of 1993, I paid my first visit to Cyprus. This was arranged by Sodos Georgallis, the Press and Information Officer at the Cyprus High

Commission in London, and I was shepherded round the southern part of the island by Rolandos Katsiaounis, a former student. Rolandos, who died too young in 2014, had a formidable knowledge of Cypriot history and supplied a most useful insight into Cypriot politics, where everyday matters seem, if anything, to be even more politicised than those of mainland Greece. The KEO beer to which I am rather partial is, I learned, a centrist beer, which I balanced by a liking for Haggipavlu brandy, whose politics were not merely of the right but of the far right. The *Laiko Kafekopteio*, or People's Coffee Grinder is, as its name suggests, in the left-wing camp, but nonetheless has a somewhat politically incorrect logo in the form of a black boy. Another insight into the politicisation of everyday life in the Greek world was afforded by the 1984 elections for control of the Association of Dentists of Attica. These were contested by no fewer than six political groupings: the ruling PASOK; the main opposition party, New Democracy; the mainstream Communist Party of Greece; the reformist Communist Party of the Interior; a left-wing offshoot of PASOK; and the Trotskyists. I took pleasure in recording this obscure fact in my *Parties and Elections in Greece* (1987).

During my 1993 visit to Cyprus, I was intrigued to discover that in Limassol there were still streets named after two of the philhellene protagonists in the Toynbee affair, Ronald Burrows, the principal of King's College, and William Pember Reeves, the director of the London School of Economics, although these have, sadly, now been changed. Apparently, in colonial times, the members of city councils on the island would attempt to annoy their colonial masters by naming streets after prominent British supporters of the *enosis* or union of the island with Greece. I have long been intrigued by the use of street names as political weapons. A classic instance of this was the renaming in 1956 of the section of Odos Loukianou outside the British ambassador's Athenian residence, the magnificent house originally built for Eleftherios Venizelos, after Michalis Karaolis and Andreas Dimitriou. These were the first EOKA militants to be hanged by the British authorities in Cyprus, an ill-advised move that provoked a huge demonstration in Athens which left four dead and over 150 wounded. It still retains the name although I doubt whether, after more than half a century, more than one in a thousand Britons, if that, would have any idea who the two were, while not all that many Greeks will be aware of the significance of the names either.

A more recent instance of the deployment of a street name with what I had, wrongly, assumed the intent to provoke was the naming of the street that separates the Megaro Mousikis, Athens' fine relatively new concert hall, from the American Embassy, as Odos Petrou Kokkali. Petros Kokkalis, a distinguished professor of surgery, had been the minister of health in the

Provisional Democratic Government established by the communists in the mountains during the 1946–9 civil war and, somewhat paradoxically, the father of Socrates Kokkalis, one of Greece's richest tycoons and reputedly one of the 500 richest men in the world. I assumed that this particular name was intended by the PASOK government to needle the Americans. I first noticed the name when, one day in the 1990s, I paid a visit to the US embassy. When I finally got into the building, after repeatedly setting off the metal detector for no apparent reason ('It must be your suspenders', the brusque woman overseeing the process finally, and correctly, deduced), I casually mentioned to the diplomat I was visiting that I was surprised by the name of the street outside. 'Why?', he asked. When I explained to him, he said in a somewhat pained tone, 'Richard, I wish you hadn't told me that. None of us in the embassy had the least idea who Petros Kokkalis was.' In fact, I subsequently learned that the name was not an attempt to provoke the embassy, but rather to recognise the very large donation that Socrates Kokkalis had contributed to the building of the Megaro Mousikis. My mistaken assumption about the naming was an example of a little knowledge being a dangerous thing. But it occurs to me that perhaps the naming of the street was intended to serve a dual purpose, namely recognition of Kokkalis junior's beneficence while at the same time annoying the Americans.

On one of our Cypriot excursions, Rolandos took me to the remote Stavrovouni monastery. He introduced me to the monks as a professor from the University of Oxford. I was indeed a professor and I was at the University of Oxford, but, for rather complicated reasons, I was not a University of Oxford professor. But this fine distinction was lost on the monks who shared to the full the excessive respect that exists throughout the Greek world for 'professors' and they had clearly heard of Oxford. I was therefore given a respectful and privileged welcome. My enjoyment of VIP status was, however, short-lived, for soon afterwards a Serbian bishop arrived. I do not recall his name, but apparently he was at the time the youngest bishop in the Serbian hierarchy. As may easily be imagined, the reception that he received made my own appear positively modest. Nonetheless, Rolandos and I were allowed to tag along and sit in on the homily that he gave to the assembled monks. This was delivered in excellent, if somewhat formal, Greek, for the bishop had studied in the theological faculty of the University of Athens. The war in Bosnia was then at its height and he gave a report, as it were, from the front line in the struggle, as he portrayed it, between Orthodoxy and Islam.

The basic gist of his homily was that the war was the outcome of an unholy alliance between Germany, the United States and the Vatican to destroy Orthodoxy. There was nothing startlingly original in this argument. Such talk was commonplace at a popular and also, sad to record, at a not so popular level. I once heard a very distinguished British commentator on Balkan affairs, himself of Croat origin, claim at a conference held at the School of Oriental and African Studies that Serbia's irredentist project had been hatched at Hilandari, the Serbian monastery on Mount Athos. Nonetheless, it was intriguing to hear such views emanate, as it were, from the horse's mouth, and it was fascinating to watch how the prelate's talk was received by the Cypriot monks. They hung on his every word with rapt attention and clearly found his analysis compelling. They were enthralled by the bishop's despatch in the struggle, as they saw it, between Orthodoxy, with its back to the wall, and an unholy Catholic/Muslim alliance.

The visit to Stravrovouni brought home in a vivid fashion the degree to which the often far-fetched rhetoric of Serbian nationalists struck a chord in the Greek psyche. Many Greeks share with the Serbs a belief that they are permanent underdogs, that they are, in effect, apart from each other, a brotherless people. I received an early indication of the way in which the sympathies of most Greeks would be engaged on the side of the Serbs at the time of the NATO bombing of Serbia in 1999, when I was in Melbourne for the 25 March Greek Independence Day celebrations. When the Australian prime minister, John Howard, an outspoken supporter of the NATO intervention, turned up for the Greek celebrations in Sydney he was roundly booed, and not only by the Greeks but also by the Macedonians, who more usually showed up only to heckle the Greeks.

One advantage of my time at St Antony's was that I was not tied to a rigid teaching timetable. This meant that, if an interesting conference were scheduled, even during the frenetic Oxford terms, which last for only eight weeks, then I was more or less free to take part. One such conference, perhaps the most interesting that I ever attended, focused on an aspect of the history of the Greek communist diaspora in Eastern Europe and the Soviet Union that emerged following the defeat of the Democratic Army in the 1946–9 civil war, a subject that awaits further research, although there have recently been a number of excellent recent publications on the topic. No dimension of this communist diaspora has aroused more controversy than the *paidomazoma*, the evacuation in 1948 of as many as 28,000 children from the areas of Greece controlled by the Democratic Army to the communist countries of Eastern Europe. The term *paidomazoma*, literally 'gathering of the children', is a loaded one, recalling as it does the janissary levy, the forcible recruitment and conversion to Islam in the early centuries of Ottoman rule of Christian children in the Balkans for subsequent service to the Sultan as elite soldiers or civil servants. This was indeed a harsh system, although Greek nationalists would no doubt be disconcerted to learn that there were instances of Christian parents seeking to enrol their offspring in the levy, for it afforded an avenue of social advancement that would otherwise not be available to their children. Janissaries, once they had risen to positions of power and influence, were sometimes able to dispense favours to their relatives and *patrides*, their birthplaces.

While anti-communists have denounced the 1948 evacuation as a second janissary levy, aimed at the de-Hellenisation of the children and their indoctrination as communist militants in the absence of their parents, those on the left, for their part, have emphasised that the evacuation was essentially inspired by humanitarian motives, and was a well-intentioned effort to remove the children from the hazards of the war zone and to offer them a better future than was in prospect in their war-ravaged and poverty-stricken villages. Not surprisingly, perhaps, there are elements of truth in the viewpoints both of critics and defenders of the *paidomazoma* or, to use a more neutral term, the evacuation. The bitter, and wholly predictable, passions aroused by the civil war in Greece have greatly subsided over the past quarter-century. Nonetheless, the issue of the evacuated children still remains a *kafto thema*, or burning topic.

When, in 2003 I received an invitation to attend a conference devoted to the fate of these evacuees, I accepted with alacrity. The conference was held in Hungary in a grand mansion that the communist government had expropriated after World War II from the Károlyi family, one of the country's old aristocratic families, and had been used to house, in the late 1940s and 1950s, as many as 600 of the Greek children. Once they had made the arduous and often hazardous trek over the borders, sometimes with older children carrying their younger siblings on their backs, the children were housed and educated in institutions known as *paidikoi stathmoi* or children's stations. There were four such children's stations in Albania, 17 in Bulgaria, nine in Romania and Czechoslovakia, three in Poland, one in East Germany, 15 in Yugoslavia, and ten in Hungary, of which Fehérvárcsurgó was one. The conditions in which the children were held were often good. Apart from any other consideration, the communist authorities in the various countries that hosted the children had a strong incentive to treat well those they portrayed as victims of Greek 'monarcho-fascism' and of Anglo-American 'imperialism'. Indeed, a number of propaganda films were made contrasting the purportedly idyllic life of the children in the communist bloc with the fate that would have awaited them in Greece. One such, filmed in Czechoslovakia, was shown in Britain at the time of the Greek civil war by the League for Democracy in Greece, a communist front organisation. It came to King's when I arranged for the housing of the archive of the League as it was being wound up. I showed this ponderous propagandistic effort at Fehérvárcsurgó where it aroused considerable interest.

In some cases, mansions such as Fehérvárcsurgó, confiscated from the old aristocratic families of Eastern Europe, were converted into boarding schools and the children had the run of their huge grounds. The evacuees had their first taste of luxuries such as chocolate, and many of them could scarcely believe their luck at being able to eat nourishing food five times a day. Apart from malnourishment, many of the children had health problems, such as lice, scabies and psoriasis, not to mention the psychological problems engendered by prolonged separation from their parents, and by their often harrowing experiences during the civil war. As few as 10 per cent of the children were completely healthy on their arrival behind the Iron Curtain. Standards of medical treatment were good, and, in many cases, better than they might have received in their home villages.

Above all, the children received for the most part a good education, again in many cases superior to that which they would have received had they remained in their *patrides*. The Greek children were beneficiaries of one of the strengths of the communist system, namely its emphasis on education, particularly technical education. Many of the children went on to become engineers, architects, doctors and teachers or to follow other professional careers. But it is important not to present too rosy a picture. If the children received a good education, it was an education that was always subject to tight control by the Greek Communist Party, which was unquestioningly loyal to Stalin and the Soviet Union. The children were being trained to act as leaders in a hoped-for communist Greece, for the exiled communist leadership continued to entertain the hope that the struggle might continue, even after the collapse of the insurgency in the summer of 1949. Moreover, when, following the 1949 defeat, many of the parents themselves took the road to exile in the communist bloc, and it was often many years before families were once again reunited behind the Iron Curtain. Correspondence was tightly censored and parents frequently experienced difficulty even in visiting their children. In Czechoslovakia, for instance, parents who had failed to achieve the stipulated work norm in the factories to which they had been assigned were denied the right to see their children. From time to time there were harrowing scenes when mothers tried to take their children away from the *paidikoi stathmoi* only for the police to intervene to ensure that the children remained in their allocated institution.

On graduating from the *paidikoi stathmoi* some of the children went on to various forms of higher education. Inevitably, many took local husbands and wives, despite anguished appeals from parents in Greece for their children not to marry non-Greeks. Many settled permanently with their new families in the countries of the Eastern Bloc, where some remain to this day. From the outset the International Red Cross was active in trying to bring together divided families, although the local Red Cross societies in the host countries were not always helpful. A major difficulty was that some of the children only knew their first names, and the babies among them not even that. Moreover, family reunification was complicated by the fact that each country had its own system of transliterating Greek with the result that names were often garbled. The number of families still in Greece who sought the help of the Red Cross in locating their children was relatively small, but this may be explained in part by the families fearing that their children might be penalised in some way by their parents seeking their return.

From the mid-1950s onwards some children were repatriated to Greece. It might be thought that these were the lucky ones, but the situation was more complicated than it appears at first sight. Not all the returning refugee children were enthralled by exchanging the relatively privileged existence that they had enjoyed in Eastern Europe for the impoverished life of Greek mountain villages that were yet to recover from the traumas of the wartime occupation and the post-liberation civil war. They did not relish the idea of arranged marriages with villagers of a markedly lower educational level. The young women and girls among them did not like having to wear headscarves, and resented being banned from wearing trousers and the (relatively) fashionable clothes to which they had become accustomed in the Eastern Bloc. By the 1980s, however, when a second wave of repatriations took place, the situation had been reversed. It was the prosperity, not the poverty, of their native villages that took the returnees by surprise. By then, partly thanks to Greece's membership of the European Union, rural Greece was far removed from the poverty and backwardness that the children had been taught was the reality in their capitalist homeland.

Many of those who were housed at Fehérvárcsurgó or Csurgó, as its alumni refer to it, have made their mark as engineers, doctors, teachers and in other walks of life. Georgios Vassiliou went on to make his fortune in Cyprus, and became president of the Republic in the late 1980s and early 1990s. Stergios Babanasis, another former pupil, became a distinguished academic economist. In a strange paradox, Georgios Georgalas, a former teacher at Fehérvárcsurgó, earned notoriety as one of the principal ideologists of the obsessively anti-communist junta that misruled Greece between 1967 and 1974.

One thing was clear at the conference: those of the evacuated children who had returned to Fehérvárcsurgó after half a century had strong feelings of gratitude to the Hungarian authorities and particularly to their teachers. It is a good thing that the *paidomazoma* is now the subject of academic study while many of the children, their teachers, and the devoted *manes* who acted as substitute mothers, are still alive to be interviewed about their extraordinary experiences. It is often alleged by nationalist critics of the *paidomazoma* that one of one of its objectives was the de-Hellenisation of the children, but it was interesting to learn of the experiences of a small group of those who had spent time at Fehérvárcsurgó and whom I encountered at the conference. They were part of a group evacuated in 1948 from a village near Konitsa. They had spoken Vlach (a form of Romanian) in their native village, but in Hungary they became Greek-speakers, a process that was, of course, quite the reverse of de-Hellenisation.

In the course of the conference we visited Beloiannisz, a village built to house communists who had fled Greece at the end of the civil war. It was named after Nikos Beloyannis, a communist cadre who had returned clandestinely to Greece in 1950, was subsequently arrested, charged with treason and executed in 1952, an act which caused an outcry in left-wing circles worldwide, and prompted a famous Picasso drawing of 'the man with the carnation'. In a further example of use of street names to score political points, the street outside the US embassy in Budapest was named after Beloyannis. By the early years of the twenty-first century Beloiannisz had acquired a church, which would never have happened in communist times, and had in effect become something of a tourist attraction.

On my return I wrote an article on the *paidomazoma* and the conference for *Odyssey*, the glossy magazine aimed at members of the world-wide Greek diaspora. This provoked an intemperate attack by Nicholas Gage, the author of the bestselling *Eleni* (1983), which was subsequently turned into a rather poor film. This was a work of 'faction' in which he recounted the circumstances which had led to his mother being tortured to death by communists during the civil war and his efforts to track down her persecutors. In some ways, it was a flawed book (although I had reviewed it favourably in *New Society*), not least in the way in which the book is replete with verbatim conversations, which always make a historian uncomfortable, although it would be unreasonable to expect Gage to write about the appalling circumstances of his mother's death with the sobriety of a PhD thesis. Gage denounced me for taking too charitable a view of the *paidomazoma*. From 'the warm comfort' of my study in Oxford, he complained, I had pronounced the *paidomazoma* to have been 'not cruel or even benign, but actually benevolent'. But, as well as pointing to the benefits of the *paidomazoma* for some of the children, I had certainly mentioned the negative consequences for those caught up in it.

Another reader criticised my use of 'gathering of the children' as a translation of *paidomazoma*. I argued, no doubt in vain, that this was a *literal* translation of the term and challenged critics to come up with a better *literal* usage. As far as I am aware, they were unable to. But the heated reaction of critics demonstrated what I had known from the outset, namely that the issue remained very sensitive, and difficult to discuss at the popular level in a journal such as *Odyssey*.

Another conference of particular interest was devoted to the 1990s Balkan crisis and organised by the British Council at Taormina in Sicily. Flying back to London when it ended, I was amused to read a report of our deliberations in the *Gazzetta del Sud*. These, according to the paper, were conducted 'secondo l'antica tradizione inglese della Chatham House Rules'. These it proceeded to break by naming the individuals who had advanced specific views. But for me the conference was overshadowed by the curious goings on at the University of Messina, where the opening session of our conference was held before we moved on to Taormina. This session was held in the Aula Magna of the university and was presided over by the *rettore magnifico*'s deputy. He looked a little jumpy and left early. The next morning it emerged that the *rettore*'s car had been stolen and he had received a note saying 'Come and collect it at the cemetery.' It transpired that the university had been infiltrated by the Sicilian mafia, and the Calabrian *'ndrangheta* (a word apparently derived from the Greek *andragathia* or valour), with whom the *rettore* was accused of having contacts. The stealing of his car was subsequently revealed to be an inside job carried out by a member of the *rettore*'s own family in an effort to put the police off the scent. A few weeks later, he resigned and was charged with aiding and abetting the mafia. Still later, 37 employees of the university were arrested as part of police investigations. Some were accused of selling exam passes, an alarming number of these being medical exams.

One research project in which I was particularly glad to be involved, albeit peripherally, was Martin Biddle's archaeological survey of the *kouvouklion* or *edicule*, the supposed tomb of Christ in the Church of the Holy Sepulchre in Jerusalem. The present edifice housing the tomb dates from 1810, following the destruction of the existing structure in a fire, which the Greeks claimed had been started by the Armenians, who have a long-standing dispute with the Greek Orthodox over control of parts of the Church, a quarrel which from time to time continues to erupt in low-level violence. The 1810 structure, propped up by a steel cradle erected in 1947, is built in an ornate Ottoman rococo style, which many have criticised but which I found in a curious way rather attractive. The reason why I was involved in the project was to work on the Greek inscriptions which are found on the outside of the *edicule*. These seem never to have been properly published and it was thought that some might be in *karamanlidika/karamanlıca*, or Turkish in Greek characters. In fact, while the donors of the 1810 building were Turkish-speaking Greeks from Anatolia, who had Turkish names, the inscriptions were all in Greek. Martin Biddle has published *The Tomb of Christ* (1999), a fascinating historical account of the edicule, in which he convincingly demonstrates that it was indeed likely to have been built over the place where the body of Christ was laid after the crucifixion. For the last 70 years the *kouvouklion* has been propped up by steel girders, but the religious communities with rights over the Church of the Holy Sepulchre have agreed to its restoration, which was completed in 2017.

I took advantage of being in Jerusalem, delivering a paper at a conference at the Hebrew University, to spend a few days with Mary Jo working on the inscriptions. We arranged to stay at a Catholic pilgrim hostel, the Casa Nova, in the Old City. This sounded rather spartan and I feared that we might even have to sleep in dormitories. In fact, the accommodation was very comfortable and included a private bathroom. The food was excellent. Our stay in 1990 took place during the first intifada and the Old City was ominously quiet at night. There was a considerable amount of tension in the air and occasional squads of heavily armed soldiers patrolling the narrow streets. Once when Mary Jo went exploring in the Muslim quarter a man watering some plants turned his hose on her. Respectfully covering her shoulders when entering the Church of the Holy Sepulchre she was taken aback one day to see Coptic monks counting up their takings on the altar which they control and which is attached to the sepulchre.

The Greek Orthodox enjoy the lion's share of control over the *kouvouklion*, and deeming that our research could only strengthen their claims, offered us every facility, even allowing us to use the hidden staircase which gives access to the roof of the *kouvouklion*. I teased Mary Jo that she should refuse to come down and lay claim to the (extremely dusty) roof for the Quakers, adding a further dimension to the complex squabbles of the Orthodox, Latins, Armenians, Copts, Ethiopians and Syriac Orthodox for control over parts of the church. After all, the Ethiopians have charge of a small monastery on the roof of the Church itself. The periodic brawls between Greek and Armenian monks over their rights under the Status Quo agreement established by the Ottomans and codified during the period of the British Mandate in Palestine gave rise, in Mark Twain's words, to 'unseemly impostures of every kind'. This helps to explain such Ottoman sayings as the one I quote at the beginning of Chapter 4: 'a Greek can no more be a brother to an Armenian than you can make a prayer mat out of the skin of a dog', a particularly repellent notion to Muslims.

One project with which I was involved while at St Antony's was the writing, in the mid-1990s, of a pamphlet on British–Greek relations for the British embassy in Athens during the ambassadorship of Oliver Miles. Produced by the Foreign Office, it was distributed in connection with various manifestations of British–Greek cultural ties, friendship and co-operation under the general heading of Britain in Greece. It was an enjoyable undertaking. The pamphlet was lavishly produced and heavily illustrated so, as when I was writing *A Concise History of Greece*, I had much fun in digging out some striking illustrations, and was able to include two or three photographs that I had taken myself. One of these was of the Radcliffe Observatory in Oxford (now part of Green College), a copy, built in 1794, of the Tower of the Winds in Athens and based on the drawings of James ('Athenian') Stuart and Nicholas Revett. To get a good shot involved my scaling the fire escape outside one of the maternity wards of the Radcliffe Infirmary. This I managed to do without getting myself arrested as a peeping tom.

There were other difficulties associated with the pamphlet, notably the choice of cover. The ghost of Byron loomed over the undertaking, and, characteristically, the pamphlet was introduced by one of the poet's descendants Robin Byron. This was not my idea, but was perhaps inevitable, although I was determined that, at the least, we should take an unclichéd view of the philhellene's philhellene. I therefore proposed that for the cover we use a striking illustration, a painting made in Kapsalis' house in Mesolonghi, shortly before the poet's death in 1824, of Byron pointing with a stick over his dog Lion, a rather fierce looking wolf hound. This suggestion, however, was blackballed by the embassy on the grounds that it could be construed as Byron trying to bring the Greeks to heel. Prolonged discussions failed to overturn the veto, and we had to fall back for the cover on the clichéd oil painting by Theodoros Vryzakis in the National Gallery of Greece, depicting Byron being welcomed on his arrival at Mesolonghi by Alexandros Mavrokordatos. The sketch of Byron with Lion did, however, appear in the body of the pamphlet (see Plate 21). In retrospect, I should perhaps have used the striking portrait of Maria Zambaco, born Cassavetti, who was Edward Burne-Jones' model and mistress, although I suppose that this might have been seen as too literal an interpretation of Anglo-Greek relations. Having failed in the matter of the cover, I did, however, win the battle over the Greek spelling of Britain, i.e. Vretania with only one n. Oddly, the earliest English spelling of Vrettania had two t's and one n. My pamphlet was probably the first time in an official British publication that Vretania had been spelled with one n, a small victory.

Although the pamphlet was intended to underline the ties of friendship uniting the two countries, there were a number of thorny issues which could not be ignored. One of these was the dynastic connection between the British and Greek royal families. The monarchy in Greece, an institution foisted on the country by the Great Powers, had been decisively rejected in the referendum of 1974, when anti-monarchical feelings ran high. Despite the vicissitudes of the monarchy in Greece, however, the Greek and British royal families remain very close. After all, the Duke of Edinburgh was a member of the Greek royal family and had been born in 1921 in Corfu, from where he had been hastily evacuated by a British destroyer with his mother after his father, Prince Andrew, at that time a general in the Greek army, had been sentenced to banishment for life for purportedly disobeying an order during Greece's ill-fated occupation of Asia Minor. I was able to surmount this particular hurdle by including a charming photograph from the 1920s showing King George II of Greece, then in exile, with his arms around the young Prince Philip and his cousin the young Prince (later King) Michael of Romania, both of whom were born in 1921. The most exotic of the illustrations (and the most expensive in terms of reproduction fees) was a miniature taken from a manuscript in Lambeth Palace library depicting the learned Byzantine emperor, Manuel II Palaiologos, being welcomed at Eltham Palace by King Henry IV in 1400, as the emperor toured Europe in an effort to drum up support in the face of the Ottoman threat to his capital, Constantinople.

I also included a photograph that I had taken myself in November 1992 on the fiftieth anniversary of the demolition of the Gorgopotamos viaduct bearing the railway line between Thessaloniki and Athens by a Special Operations Executive team, with the assistance of units of the resistance groups ELAS and EDES. The reunion was attended by six of the original 12 members of the party, code-named Harling. Two of these, Inder Gill, subsequently a high ranking officer in the Indian army, and Themi Marinos, a Greek army officer, had been photographed in Egypt in 1942 as young men with their arms around each other's shoulders just before they had been parachuted into Greece. I took a photograph of the pair in an identical pose 50 years later at the cave near Stromni where the party had laid up before the Gorgopotamos attack, and then juxtaposed the two photographs below the caption 'Comrades in arms.'

It is noteworthy that in November 1992 when the party of SOE veterans was in Athens before setting out for Gorgopotamos, John Major, the prime minister, was also paying a flying visit to the city but did not meet with the SOE team, all of whom were by then seriously elderly. Major would presumably have been informed of their presence, but as the first British prime minister with no recollection of World War II (he was born in 1943), their exploits probably had no particular resonance for him. The Greek prime minister, Constantine Mitsotakis, who had worked with SOE on Crete, did, however, meet with the British party, which gave them much pleasure. Sadly, political differences over the role of the wartime resistance in Greece could not be sunk even on the 50th anniversary of one its greatest achievements. Resistance veterans' organisations linked to the communist party and to Andreas Papandreou's PASOK held their commemorations on a different day from that of the ruling New Democracy party together with the veterans of Napoleon Zervas' EDES, the gathering that was attended by the British party.

Inevitably, in the text of my pamphlet for the British embassy I accentuated the positive in the relationship between Britain and Greece and rather skated over the negative, e.g. the pointless and destructive confrontation over Cyprus. I did not mention the paradoxical fact that British colonial rule, albeit unwittingly, had acted to preserve the far Left as a powerful player in the island's politics, whereas in Greece itself the communists were in effect destroyed as a political force during the civil war. I inevitably made much of the fact that, during the dark winter of 1940-1, Greece was Britain's only active ally in Europe against the might of the German-Italian Axis, when Greece's victories in Albania against the Italians had demonstrated that the Axis war machine was not invincible. It was the martial feats of the Greeks that had inspired the famous, although probably apocryphal, saying attributed to Churchill that henceforward we would no longer say that Greeks fought like heroes, but that heroes fought like Greeks. I was surprised, therefore, to read in a similar Foreign Office publication, *Britain and Poland: A Record of Friendship*, published at much the same time as *Vretania kai Ellada*, that it was Poland that had been Britain's only ally 'of any consequence' between the fall of France in June 1940 and Hitler's attack on the Soviet Union in June 1941. Honour might have been satisfied by mentioning that a Polish brigade formed part of the British expeditionary force sent to Greece in early 1941 as a German invasion became imminent. Shortly after becoming prime minister in 2010, David Cameron was criticised when, on a visit to the United States, he sought to ingratiate himself with the Americans by claiming that they had been fighting against the Nazis alongside the British in 1940. He subsequently corrected himself, but still seemed unaware of Greece's repulse of the attempted Italian invasion at the end of October of that year, a campaign that was one of the few bright spots during the grim winter of 1940-1 and one that occurred 15 months before the US entered the war.

When, at much the same time as writing the pamphlet, I was being interviewed for a programme on the History Channel about Prince Philip, I was told that the next port of call for the film crew would be former King Constantine who, at the time, lived, like me, in north London. I thought it might be a nice idea to give him a copy of *Vretania kai Ellada*. But this was not so simple a matter as it sounds. First of all, I did not know where exactly he lived. Secondly, there was the problem of how he should be addressed. Unless he is addressed as Constantine, King of the Hellenes, then anything sent to him apparently runs the risk of being binned. This form of address was not one that I was happy to use, but to send the pamphlet to ex-King Constantine or C. Glücksberg, as he is sometimes referred to in Greece, would have invited immediate consignment to the waste-paper basket. I therefore put a copy in the proverbial plain brown envelope, with no address, and gave it to the producer to hand to Constantine. This he duly did and I heard back from the programme makers that Constantine had found it 'interesting'. Honour was thus satisfied on both sides.

With the collapse of the Soviet Union in the early 1990s I became interested in the fate of the ethnic Greek population of southern Russia. This population was in large part descended from Greeks of Pontos, who had fled Ottoman rule in the nineteenth and early twentieth centuries in the aftermath of the numerous wars between the Russian and Ottoman Empire, and settled in Georgia and the regions of Russia bordering on the Black Sea and Sea of Azov. To these were added the Greek communists, who, following their defeat in 1949 in the civil war, fled to Eastern Europe and the Soviet Union, where many of them were settled in Tashkent, the capital of Uzbekistan.

One of the consequences of the period of *perestroika* and *glasnost* in the last years of the Soviet Union was the emergence of this hitherto submerged ethnic Greek population. In the early years of Soviet rule, Greeks in the region enjoyed a considerable degree of cultural autonomy, with their own schools, books and newspapers. These last were published in the Pontic Greek dialect for which a 20-letter alphabet was devised instead of the standard 24-letter alphabet. There was even a Greek-language theatre in Sukhum, the capital of the Abkhaz Autonomous Soviet Socialist Republic. These privileges were eventually abrogated and the Greeks of the region were in the late 1930s among the nationalities deemed by an increasingly paranoid Stalin to be 'disloyal'. In the late 1940s Greeks were among the ethnic groups who were deported to harsh exile in central Asia. It was only after the death of Stalin in 1953 that most of the deportees were permitted to return, but in many cases their properties were not restored. It is not easy to establish the current size of the Greek population of the former Soviet Union but a figure of some 350,000 seems plausible. Among these ethnic Greeks was the last commander of the Soviet Black Sea fleet, Admiral Mikhail Nikolayevich Khronopulo, whose command lasted from 1985 to 1991. In the early years after the collapse of the Soviet regime there was some talk of the possibility of establishing an autonomous Greek republic within the Russian Federation but nothing came of the idea.

This interest in the Greeks of the former Soviet Union led to my writing in 1994 an article on the Abkhazian/Georgian conflict in *The World Today*, the monthly magazine published by Chatham House. This was subsequently pirated in *Ogni Skani Nena* (the splendidly didactic title apparently translates as 'Learn your Language'), the first publication to appear partly written in Laz, a language spoken in the region near the Turkish border with Georgia. My article was published in Turkish and not Laz. I certainly had no objection to its pirating. *Ogni Skani Nena* was shut down after a few issues by the Turkish authorities, who have no wish to give encouragement to separate ethnic identities, and no doubt my pirated article earned me a place in the files of the Turkish secret police. At much the same time I wrote an article for *The Greek American* on the plight of the not insignificant Greek population of Abkhazia. Most of the Abkhazian Greeks were evacuated to Greece in 1992–3 in the midst of the conflict.

My interest in Caucasian matters extended beyond Abkhazia to the brutal conflict in Chechnya. A particular, and indeed peculiar, story reported in *The Times* in May 1995 caught my attention. This was a report by the paper's defence correspondent, Michael Evans, that 'Western intelligence sources' were claiming that 25 Russian soldiers had, according to the testimony of an unnamed refugee medical worker, been castrated 'with professional precision'. Evans wrote that these same intelligence sources were confident that the report was not part of a Russian black propaganda campaign. While it was certainly true that atrocities were committed by both sides in this savage conflict, it struck me that Evans' report was implausible on a number of counts. Why should the Chechens, whose medical facilities were stretched to the utmost, have diverted precious medical resources to the 'clinical' castration of as many as 25 Russian prisoners? Some years later, I attended a talk given by a Chechen doctor at the Regent's Park mosque in London. He had emphasised how scarce medical resources were on the Chechen side, so much so that urine was routinely used as an antiseptic and yoghurt and honey were used to treat burns. If the castration had indeed taken place then its purpose would presumably have been to terrorise and demoralise Russian troops, and so one might expect the victims of the atrocity to have been returned to the Russian lines so that their comrades would have been made aware of their possible fate were they to fall into Chechen hands. But would not such a practice have proved counter-productive, for it would presumably have encouraged Russian soldiers, few of whom had much stomach for the conflict, to fight to the bitter end rather than surrender? Why the figure of 25 castrati? Surely one, if sufficiently publicised, would have been enough to inspire the sought-after terror?

My doubts prompted me to write to Evans, expressing some of these doubts. He replied that he, too, had been worried that the story might have contained an element of black propaganda so he had carefully checked it out in so far as he had been able. Since his sources had been extremely authoritative he had felt justified in running it. His reply did little to still my doubts. The Russians had failed to produce a single one of these unfortunates, whose fate would have been a gift to their cack-handed propagandists. Moreover, organisations such as Amnesty International and Médecins sans Frontières had received no reports of the purported atrocity. As there had been no news in the press about the incident in the course of the following year, I wrote to the editor of *The Times*, Peter Stothard, asking whether the paper still stood by the original report and, if not, would it print a correction, since *The Times* prides itself on being a newspaper of record. I received a reply from the assistant managing editor, David Hopkinson. On checking the story, Evans had given him 'precise details about his sources'. Although he could not disclose who these were, they were 'senior people', and Evans' practice was only to utilise information from contacts whom he had known and trusted for a very long time. He remained convinced of the authenticity of the original report.

It not being possible to prove a negative, I, of course, could not state with absolute certainty that such an atrocity had not taken place, but the story left a number of unanswered questions, not least the identity of the Western intelligence agency that had apparently leaked/fabricated the initial report. In an article which I wrote on this deception for *Central Asia Survey* (1997) I did not point fingers, although I assumed that the report had emanated from the CIA. Now I am not so sure in the light of revelations about dirty tricks practised by the MI6. One such was the attempt by MI6 to pin responsibility for the notorious bombing in August 1995 of the marketplace in Sarajevo not on the Serbs but on Bosnian Muslims, seeking to attract sympathy, and hopefully help, from the outside world. Moreover, it became clear that Michael Evans had good contacts with MI6. Ten years or so later, in 2007, I attended a lecture given by Sir Richard Mottram, who had responsibility in the Cabinet Office for 'Intelligence, Security and Resilience'. A principal theme of his lecture was how to overcome the disaffection manifestly felt by many British Muslims. I subsequently wrote to him, enclosing a copy of my article, seeking to make the point that Muslim disaffection in the UK had long anteceded Blair's distastrous entanglement in the Iraq war, which many commentators had seen as the root of the problem, and that videos of the Chechen conflict had regularly been shown in British mosques long before the invasion of Iraq. I pointed out that the dissemination of bogus atrocity stories implicating Muslims by 'Western intelligence sources' was scarcely the best way of winning over hearts and minds. It would seem that the episode of the 25 castrati was an instance of 'fake news' of which there has been so much talk during the presidency of Donald J. Trump. It was disconcerting, however, that in this case the 'fake news' did not appear to originate with the enemies of the 'free world' but with its supposed defenders.

This curious incident begs the following question. What could have been the purpose of spreading false reports of such horrendous atrocities? A possible answer might have been that Western politicians were desperately anxious to ensure the re-election of Boris Yeltsin as president of the Russian Federation and to this end had demonstrated that they were quite prepared to turn a blind eye to Russian behaviour in Chechnya. Stories of the kind I have outlined would have gone far to justify Russian claims that they were fighting not against a people legitimately seeking its independence but against savage bandits, whose behaviour placed them quite beyond the pale. Probably the lowest point in the west's indulgence of Yeltsin occurred at the G7 Meeting in Moscow in April 1996. Here President Clinton had displayed a deplorable, if understandable, ignorance of Chechen history, and an equally deplorable, and much less excusable, ignorance of his own country's history when he compared the fighting in Chechnya to the American civil war. Such an analogy (with its implication that Yeltsin was a latter-day Lincoln) was manifestly absurd. The Chechens had never voluntarily submitted to the Tsarist Empire, any more than they had willingly adhered to the Soviet Union or the Russian Federation. Indeed, in the 1920s, a Chechen *imam* had declared that he was plaiting a rope with which to hang engineers, students and all those who write from left to right. If any analogy is to be drawn between the Chechen conflict and events in US history it is with the genocidal Indian wars that accompanied America's westward expansion during the nineteenth century. But Clinton would scarcely have admitted to such a parallel even if he were capable of seeing it. Even more crass was President George W. Bush's hailing of Vladimir Putin, during the yet more savage repression of the second Chechen war, as 'the kind of guy I like to have in a foxhole with me'. Given that Bush, thanks to his connections, served in the Texas Air National Guard during the Vietnam war, the likelihood of his ever coming within a country mile of a foxhole is remote.

I also crossed swords with *The Times* over the strange case of the purported Abkhazian stamps that the newspaper printed in early 1999. These depicted President Clinton in his underpants, clutching a glass of champagne, with his arms around Monica Lewinsky. These were demonstrable fakes published by fraudsters seeking to make a quick buck from the Lewinsky scandal at the expense of gullible stamp collectors. Among various irregularities, the only word in Abkhaz on the stamps was wrongly spelled, while their face value was absurdly high. Moreover, the de facto government of Abkhazia had been quick to deny that it had anything to do with their production. Getting *The Times* to publish a correction was another matter. The paper's initial response was that there was insufficient evidence to merit running a correction and that this view was shared by the *New York Times*, which had likewise published the stamps. After I had written to the *New York Times*, the paper, after making its own checks, quickly accepted that it had done so mistakenly and published a correction, saying that the stamps had been printed and sold by private stamp speculators and not by the government of Abkhazia. The London *Times* only got round to conceding that it had made an error at the end of May, whereas I had written to draw attention to the reasons why the 'stamps' could not conceivably be genuine at the end of January. So much for *The Times's* reputation as a newspaper of record. Had these purported stamps come to the notice of President Clinton or his advisers there might have been an understandable, if regrettable, urge to teach these upstarts a lesson.

In 2002 I was appointed visiting fellow at the British School at Athens. This required staying at the School for the months of January, February and March, which was scarcely a hardship. Just before leaving, however, we saw on the television news pictures of Athens under deep snow, so Mary Jo and I, mindful also of the perishing winter conditions in the School that had existed during our last prolonged stay in 1966-7, came with a full range of winter clothes. In fact, no sooner had we arrived in Athens than the weather dramatically improved and for the best part of a month we basked in the tranquil warmth of what were known, in antiquity, as the Halcyon days. A sunny winter day in Greece, particularly now that the *nephos*, or smog, has more or less been brought under control, is delightful. But the moment you step out of direct sunshine things can quickly get distinctly nippy. Could this be the reason why Diogenes of Sinope, the fourth century BC philosopher who lived in a barrel, famously, although perhaps apocryphally, replied 'stand out of my sunlight' when Alexander the Great, perhaps also apocryphally, asked if there was anything he could do for him? If this was indeed the case, then the thought is my sole contribution to classical scholarship. But perhaps it has already been made.

I felt that, living among a bevy (if that is the right collective noun) of archaeologists, I should make some kind of genuflection in the direction of the archaeological biases of the School. So I decided to look at what happened to archaeology in Greece during the two world wars and, in particular, at the activities of the foreign archaeological schools during these critical times. This was a subject that dovetailed with my long-delayed research on the role of the

Special Operations Executive in Greece, as a number of SOE's operatives in Greece during World War II had been Students at the School.

A classicist, R.G.C. Levens, a fellow of Merton College, had written in the *Oxford Magazine*, soon after Greece's rejection of Mussolini's humiliating ultimatum of 28 October 1940, that a classical education had overnight become a national asset: 'a year spent in the British School at Athens is worth three months in an O[fficer] C[adet] T[raining] U[nit]'. The classical atlas had become a war map. He noted that the Athens correspondent of the *Daily Telegraph* had compared the trapping of an Italian Alpine division in a valley of the Pindus range to the 'battle' of the Caudine Forks of 321 BC, in which the Romans had surrendered to a Samnite army. Now that Greece was at war with Rome, Levens rather puzzlingly wrote, 'British scholarship finds itself mercifully allied with the side on which its sympathies would naturally lie.'

A number of those associated in peacetime with the American School of Classical Studies in Athens (ASCSA) had served during the war in the Office of Strategic Services, the approximate American counterpart of SOE, where they were known, not altogether flatteringly, as the 'archaeological captains'. It turned out that all the major archaeological schools had good reason to keep quiet about their activities in time of war, and none had demonstrated much respect for the notion of Greek sovereignty at these critical junctures. So this particular piece of research represented yet another of those *kafta themata*, or troublesome topics, to which I have been irresistibly drawn throughout my academic career.

I spoke at a seminar held in the director's house at the British School on my preliminary findings. These had turned up some curious results. None was stranger than that, after the United States had entered World War II in December 1941, three American archaeologists had been permitted to stay on in Greece. There were, of course, cases of 'enemy aliens' in occupied Europe in the shape of the men over military age, wives, ex-governesses or, indeed, the Scottish doctors and nurses, again women, who had come out to Romania and Serbia in World War I under the aegis of Dr Elsie Inglis, and had married Serbian men and were to remain in Yugoslavia throughout the German and Italian occupation. There were certainly some American and British citizens who remained in Greece throughout the years of occupation. But there can have been few cases of men being permitted to caretake what after all was enemy property. The reasons for this privilege, for privilege it was, accorded to the Americans are not clear.

The American School had been caught up in the wave of patriotic euphoria prompted by Greece's heroic resistance to the would-be Italian invasion of the country on 28 October 1940. The School presented an ambulance, painted with crossed American and Greek flags, to the Greek Red Cross. This was driven, until he was seriously wounded on the Albanian front, by Rodney Young, the archaeologist and wartime OSS operative. Young, indeed, was recovering in the Evangelismos Hospital when the Germans arrived in Athens at the end of April 1941. In the US itself, an American School Committee for Aid to Greece was established, to which the royalties of a book of photographs by two members of the staff of the Agora excavation, Alison Frantz and Lucy Talcott, were donated. Over $20,000 was raised for medical supplies, clothing and mobile canteens at the front. Assistance and finance was also given to the Greek Archaeological Service to help in protecting antiquities from possible war damage.

When the British expeditionary force arrived in March 1941, lectures for the troops were given on the Acropolis on Sunday afternoons by members of the American School, while women attached to the School participated in the American Women's Bandage Circle. After the British had been driven from mainland Greece and subsequently from Crete, the American School had, while the United States remained neutral, looked after the interests of the British School. All in all, the American School did all that could reasonably be expected of it in contributing to the Greek war effort. Moreover, the School had behaved creditably in giving an academic home to Heinrich (Henry) Immerwahr (a postwar director of the School) as German refugee fellow between 1939–41. Yet, following the repatriation of US nationals living in Greece, the story becomes more mysterious and, potentially, more murky. Lucy Shoe Meritt in her *History of the American School of Classical Studies at Athens 1939–1980* (1984) says that, following the repatriation of the remaining Americans at the School, 'Mr. and Mrs. Stevens and the Vanderpool family elected to stay, and Mr. Hill did not consider leaving.' Gorham Stevens had been appointed acting director of the School in 1939 and remained as such throughout the war and immediate postwar period until 1947. When the US entered the war in December 1941, American and British interests (including the property of the American and British Schools) were placed under the protection of the Swiss Legation. (The magnificent residence of the British ambassador, which had originally been built for Eleftherios Venizelos, appears to have been unoccupied. Even the contents of the wine cellar seem to have remained intact throughout the occupation.)

Much of the American School was sealed, but Gorham Stevens and his wife Annette were allowed to remain in the main building. Here, *inter alia*, Stevens was occupied in creating a large plaster model of the Acropolis in the fourth century BC. He also had postcards made of some of his drawings, which the Acropolis custodians sold to Italian and German soldiers. Bert

Hodge Hill, after a brief period of detention, was released to live in his home in Athens, which, at one stage, he was sharing with four German officers. An indication of the ambiguities of Hodge Hill's situation is indicated in a draft letter among his papers addressed to the Italian responsible for the Department of Civil Affairs in the Peloponnese, requesting permission to live in the American dig house at Corinth to enable him to complete a book on ancient fountains. Hodge Hill wrote that:

> It is naturally understood that if this request is granted I shall be ready to conform both to the letter and to the spirit of whatever regulations apply to my case, and in any event I should consider myself bound in honor by the obligations of my position as a sort of guest of the army of occupation as I have been these many years a guest of Greece.

Curiously, preserved among Hodge Hill's papers at the American School of Classical Studies are Nazi insignia given to him by the German consul-general in Athens as the Germans withdrew from Greece in the autumn of 1944.

Meritt ascribes the 'special lenience' accorded to Hodge Hill during the occupation to the efforts of Otto Walter of the Austrian Institute. But the Austrian Institute no longer existed as such at this time for the Österreichisches Archäologisches Institut had been *gleichgeschaltet*, or 'melded', with the Archäologisches Institut des Deutschen Reiches following the 1938 *Anschluss* of Germany and Austria, and the German and Austrian Archaeological Institutes in Athens subsequently operated as a single unit. The director of the combined School was the archaeologist Walther Wrede, an unregenerate Nazi, who had doubled as the Landesgruppenleiter of the Nazi Party's Auslandsorganisation for German expatriates living in Greece, carrying out these duties long before the German occupation. The assistant director was Otto Walter, who, to hold the position he did, would either have been a paid-up Nazi or, at the very least, a committed fellow-traveller.

Lucy Shoe Meritt believes that the special treatment accorded to Hodge Hill was 'an expression of the international scholarly respect' enjoyed by the American School. But there may have been a more particular reason for Walter's 'special lenience' towards Hodge Hill. In December 1940, shortly after Greece was caught up in World War II, William Dinsmoor, the architectural historian, and at that time president of the Archaeological Institute of America, had publicly announced his resignation as a member of the German Archaeological Institute, although he had been a member for 26 years, a membership which it seems he had not relinquished even when the United States had entered World War I in 1917. The catalyst for his resignation had been a letter, signed by 36 archaeologists and classical scholars styling themselves 'former Austrians', protesting against criticism of the Nazi annexation of Austria. In announcing his resignation, Dinsmoor wrote that ancient Greece had not only created the notion of democracy and the idea of freedom but had inspired 'an intellectual development which has never been equalled'. The only surviving heirs to these ideals were, he maintained, the modern countries of Greece, Britain and America. As Dinsmoor wrote, 'one cannot but wonder if scholarship is worth serious consideration, when it can bend so easily and stultify its voice in the service of political aggression'. Dinsmoor's open letter provoked a ban by the German Archaeological Institute on its members and 'former Austrians' accepting invitations to attend lectures and functions held at the American School.

It also prompted a visit by Hodge Hill to the German Institute to apologise for Dinsmoor's behaviour and to explain that the American School was not a branch of the Archaeological Insitute of America. Hodge Hill urged that the existing relationship between the American and German schools be maintained. This was at a time when Germany's partner in the Axis, Italy, had unsuccessfully sought to invade Greece and was only a few months before the German invasion. The fact that Georg Karo, a scholar of Jewish descent, had been removed from the directorship of the German Institute in 1936 (and for a time given refuge at the British School) should have been enough to give Hodge Hill pause for thought. But if he can be criticised, he was no anti-Semite. Among his papers in the American School is a note in a shaky hand from Karo, written in 1958, thanking Hodge Hill for looking after two of his trunks seemingly for some 20 years, while Karo had been very grateful for Hodge Hill's help after he had been ousted from the German Archaeological Institute.

When a distinguished German archaeologist died in April 1940, the American School sent a message of sympathy, which was acknowledged. In the words of its historian, the School was seeking to 'continue its traditional principle of acting as a scholarly organization without political involvement of any kind'. Archaeologists often seem to have a kind of tunnel vision which leads them to turn a blind eye to nasty phenomena in whatever country in which they are working. The report of the Italian Archaeological School in Athens for 1940, for instance, makes reference to international events that had led to a sudden interruption of the School's activities, a curious euphemism for Italy's attempted invasion of Greece. The French School, subject to the Vichy regime, remained open in Athens throughout the occupation and carried on with some of its archaeological activities. Foreign archaeologists tended to turn a blind eye to such unpleasantnesses within Greece as the

Metaxas dictatorship, Nazis polluting the German Archaeological Institute and the Colonels' dictatorship. The American director of the Agora excavations referred, in his annual report, to the establishment of military dictatorship as 'the change in the Greek government in April of 1967'.

As Stephen Dyson has observed in *Ancient Marbles to American Shores* (1998), 'unfortunately' American classicists, and especially classical archaeologists, have been 'generally conservative', an observation that could equally apply to a number of their British counterparts. Stevens had been born in 1876 and Hodge Hill in 1874 and were thus well over 60, and therefore over military age, at which Germany permitted enemy aliens, P.G. Wodehouse among them, to live 'under supervision'. It was presumably this provision that was exploited to enable Stevens and Hodge Hill to remain in Athens. The case of Eugene Vanderpool, who was born in 1906, and thus only 35 when the US entered the war, was different and even more mysterious, as he was of military age. Vanderpool and his wife were not under restriction, and for the best part of a year he continued to bicycle to work in the Agora, while his wife ran a soup kitchen for starving Greek children in Marousi, as Greece was beset by one of Europe's worst famines in modern times. Not until almost a year after the United States entered the war was Vanderpool interned in Germany with other civilian internees. A member of the American School once told me that Vanderpool had been impressed by the entrepreneurial way in which Greek fellow internees had bred lice for sale to their German guards, for whom an infestation of lice was apparently one way to avoid being sent to the eastern front. Vanderpool was repatriated to the United States in early 1944. Only a classical archaeologist suffering from tunnel vision could have written of a fellow archaeologist that Vanderpool was the greatest American philhellene of the twentieth or any other century.

It would have been inconceivable that two or three British archaeologists would have been permitted to stay on at the British School during the German occupation, while archaeologists and classicists such as Nick Hammond and Monty Woodhouse were causing mayhem in the mountains. I have already said something of the way in which the British School, in flagrant disregard for Greek sovereignty, had been mobilised during World War I in furtherance of the British war effort as a centre of intelligence gathering despite the fact that, for much of the war, Greece was a neutral country.

In the run-up to the 1981 election which saw a massive victory for Andreas Papandreou's PASOK, the larger-than-life actress, Melina Mercouri, who subsequently became minister of culture, had called for closure of the foreign archaeological schools on the grounds that they were training schools for spies. She was wrong on this count, but it cannot be denied that once hostilities had broken out in both world wars alumni of the foreign schools, on account of their linguistic skills and knowledge of the terrain and culture of the country, were frequently made use of by the intelligence services and military authorities of their respective homelands. Incidentally, once Mercouri had become minister of culture, the American School bent over backwards to flatter her. In an issue of the School's newsletter that appeared soon after PASOK came to power there were no fewer than five pictures of Mercouri and three of Margaret Papandreou, Andreas Papandreou's American-born wife.

While at the School, as was customary for visiting fellows, I gave a public lecture. I chose as a theme 'Writing the history of Greece forty years on'. This reflected on some of my experiences in trying to write the history of Greece over the years. In the course of this I inadvertently committed an embarrassing gaffe. I spoke of the knitting circle established in the autumn of 1940, after the attempted Italian invasion but before Greece and Germany were at war. It met in the British minister's residence and was organised by Lady Palairet, the wife of the minister, Sir Michael Palairet, to knit comforts for the Greek troops fighting on the Albanian front. Lady Palairet seems to have been something of a battleaxe, prompting a Legation wag to dub the group 'The Four Horsewomen of the Acropolis'. I assumed that this was an episode safely in the past, and, as I had hoped, my mention of Lady Palairet's militant knitters (the German minister's wife was apparently engaged in a parallel endeavour) raised a mild laugh. But, to my astonishment, I learned after the lecture that the circle, known as the British Ladies' Sewing Group, continued to exist some 50 years later. For most of the postwar period it had carried on meeting at the embassy under the aegis of successive ambassadors' wives until, in the 1990s, one of them contrived to winkle them out of the embassy.

As retirement drew near I organised, in 2005, a small workshop as my swan song at St Antony's. This was entitled 'Bearing gifts to Greeks: humanitarian aid to Greece in the 1940s', and the papers given were subsequently published in 2008 in the St Antony's/Palgrave Macmillan series. This examined the appalling famine that afflicted Greece during the early part of the occupation; the international efforts that were made to alleviate its consequences (the initial steps being launched from Turkey); and at other initiatives to bring help to the beleaguered civilian population. This included a consideration of the role of *Ethniki Allilengyi* (National Solidarity), the welfare agency of EAM, the communist-controlled National Liberation Front; of the welfare activities of the Orthodox Church; and of the complex diplomacy that lay behind the decision of the British government partially to lift the economic blockade that had been imposed on Greece and on the rest of occupied Europe. This opened the way for the relief efforts mounted by the Swedish and Swiss Red Cross.

It was appropriate that such a workshop be held in Oxford, for in the autumn of 1942 the Oxford Committee for Famine Relief, which after the war was to metamorphose into Oxfam, was established with the specific objective of seeking to alleviate famine in Greece and Belgium. During the course of a 'Greek Week' held in the city in October 1943, the astonishing sum of £12,700 was collected, equivalent in today's prices to £250,000. Mary Jo contributed a paper on the relief efforts of Quakers in Greece in the 1940s. In this she was able to pay appropriate tribute to the efforts of the Quaker Edith Pye in laying the groundwork for the creation of the Oxford Committee for Famine Relief, a decisive role that had been played down in the official history of Oxfam. I lighted on the topic of humanitarian aid as a means of getting away from the endless debates about Britain's role in Greece during the occupation, and, in particular, its relations with the resistance organisations and Churchill's stubborn support for the unpopular cause of King George II. These were issues which in the 1970s and 1980s had aroused furious controversy, and much criticism of British policy, both in Greece and in Britain. But in considering the various humanitarian initiatives, in which Britain played an important role, British policy still came under fire. For it was only reluctantly, and as a result of a very effective lobbying campaign launched by the Greek–American community and mediated through President Roosevelt, that the British government had agreed to a partial lifting of the economic blockade of occupied Greece. But it should be remembered that this blockade, which applied to the Channel Islands, as well as the rest of occupied Europe, was one of the few weapons that Britain could deploy against the Axis in the early stages of the war. The workshop proved an interesting and worthwhile end to my academic career.

Epilogue

My career as a fully paid-up academic had lasted barely 20 years, from 1968, when I became a lecturer in history at Edinburgh University, to 1990, when I effectively became not a university teacher, but a *Privatgelehrter*, with few of the obligations of a 'working' academic. Having spent 20 years at universities in which the shots were increasingly being called by careerists, time-servers and gong-seekers, I was conscious of being fortunate to spend the last part of my career in an environment in which academics, rather than bureaucrats, were still more or less in charge. This was despite the efforts towards the end of my time at Oxford of John Hood, significantly the first outsider to be appointed Vice-Chancellor in the university's 800 year and more history, to subordinate the university to a board of unelected 'businessmen' trustees, and thus bring an end to a venerable system of self-government best described as 'byzantine democracy'. In his memoir, *Marginal Comment*, Kenneth Dover, recorded hearing, when he was president of Corpus Christi College, his bugbear Trevor Aston say that 'the great thing about being a Fellow is that you can tell the President to go to hell'. Dover conceded that this was true. Marrack Goulding, the Warden of St Antony's during part of my time at the college, seems not to have grasped this. I remember him telling Gary Hart, the former US senator and one-time front runner for the Democratic presidential nomination in 1987, when he was working towards a DPhil in politics at St Antony's, that running the college was akin to being in charge of a middle-ranking embassy. But those staffing embassies do not have the power to defenestrate the ambassador.

The more I learned of developments at the universities of London and Edinburgh, where I had previously taught, the more thankful I was to have found an intellectually stimulating and comfortable perch at St Antony's for a sizeable part of my academic career. The debt of gratitude that I owe to

St Antony's is without measure. I tried to give some indication of this in the valedictory speech that is customarily given by retiring Fellows at the Honorary Fellows dinner when I myself retired from the college in 2005. This I append as it was given:

> Last week, in the course of our mammoth deliberations to elect a new warden, I found myself recalling a novel which, at the time it was published, enjoyed a considerable éclat. This was C.P. Snow's *The Masters*, an account of the intrigue-ridden election of the master of a Cambridge college, written in a prose the leaden quality of which was matched only by the pomposity of its author. If you can remember the book you must, like me, be pretty long in the tooth, for it was published in 1951.
>
> But just a few years later came Kingsley Amis' *Lucky Jim*. Published almost exactly 50 years ago, in 1954, it has always struck me not only as the best thing that Amis ever wrote but as perhaps the best novel ever about British academic life, a book written in anything but leaden prose. The novel is clearly based on Amis' experiences as a lecturer at Swansea. Indeed, his head of department apparently tried to get him sacked for bringing into disrepute not only the University of Swansea but the entire academic profession.
>
> At this distance in time I cannot remember whether I read *Lucky Jim* at school or university, but when I did I immediately identified with the book's eponymous anti-hero, Jim Dixon, a young lecturer in history. Dixon had two great fears. The first was that he would be rumbled. The second was that he would be summoned to a musical evening by his professor and dragooned into singing madrigals.
>
> Today I can breathe a huge sigh of relief that I have made it to retirement without having been rumbled. At least I am not aware of having been rumbled, so I hope that none of you will spoil my retirement by letting on that I have been. I have also mercifully avoided the fate of warbling madrigals alongside the professor's wife, although, curiously, the nearest I came to such a grisly fate was here at St Antony's, not the first institution that comes to mind when one thinks of madrigals.
>
> When I came to the college 15 years ago there was a tradition, since abandoned, of college centres taking it in turns to organise an evening entertainment. Almost the first college event that I attended was one of these entertainments sponsored by the European Studies Centre, the centre of which I am a member. This was an evening of madrigals put on, in a touch worthy of Amis himself, by William Wallace's[1] *au pair*. She doubled as a music student and came up from London with a group of her music college chums. The ghastliness of the evening was increased by the fact that the madrigalists trilled and fa-la-la'ed their way around the ten (or was it 12?) members of the EU. We may even have been treated, I seem to recall, to a madrigal from Luxembourg. But, mercifully, we were not expected to join in.
>
> Another thing that puzzled me about the college when I arrived was its motto – *Plus est en vous* – a motto which, thanks to Antonin Besse, we share with Gordonstoun School, the school which educated, or failed to educate, according to your point of view, Prince Charles.

EPILOGUE

Gordonstoun offers an official translation of Besse's motto – '*There is more in you than you think*'. But a more demotic translation of *Plus est en vous* might be the phrase beloved of schoolmasters and schoolmistresses through the ages when compiling reports on their charges – '*Could try harder*'.

Besse died while on a visit to Gordonstoun, and Hilda Besse wrote a lengthy obituary for the *Gordonstoun Record*. She concluded this by noting that it had been Antonin's 'earnest hope' that boys educated at Gordonstoun might complete their education at St Antony's. It would be interesting to know whether there has been an alumnus, or more recently an alumna, of Gordonstoun at St Antony's in its 50-year history.

I must say that I find the college motto, however one chooses to translate it, a somewhat dispiriting one. I should myself have preferred the motto of the proud mercantile city of Ragusa, the present day Dubrovnik, in the part of the world which I study – *Non bene pro toto libertas venditur auro*. This could roughly be translated as 'Liberty is not to be traded for all the gold in the world'.

Under the new university regime our liberties, which date back the best part of a millennium, are manifestly under threat from a particularly crass form of managerialist dogma. The notion that Oxford would have reached its present eminence if its teachers had been under the threat of redundancy if they did not publish enough is simply bizarre. No less bizarre are the earnest calculations to determine how many citations result from each million dollars of research money.

I think that those, like me, who are relative newcomers to Oxford and come from academic cultures where managerialism took hold in the 1980s are particularly alive to the dangers implicit in the proposed changes, changes which I decline to dignify as 'reforms'. At my own undergraduate university, the University of Edinburgh, for instance, the University Librarian is now designated the Vice-Principal for Knowledge Management. How long will it be, I wonder, before we have a Bodley's Knowledge Manager instead of a Bodley's Librarian?

I am greatly honoured to have been made an Emeritus Fellow, not least because I arrived at the college in unusual circumstances, and for my first five years here I was actually on the payroll of the University of London. I must then have been very much an unknown quantity (perhaps I still am), but I am truly grateful to the college for granting me what can only be described as a form of academic asylum. I shall not bore you with the details that led to my involuntary departure from King's College, London. It is a complicated story, not unconnected with my writing a book about the young Arnold Toynbee's own involuntary departure from King's in the early 1920s, after a furious row with the Greek benefactors of his chair. I realised rather late in the day that writing frankly about a scandal in the history of the institution by which you are employed, and which involves benefactors, may not always be the path to academic preferment. Anyway, the gory details will form part of a memoir of my academic life on which I am now embarked.

Fortunately, my time of troubles at King's College coincided with John Campbell's retirement in 1990 from St Antony's, and thanks to the good offices of John and of the college I was able to continue his pioneering work, if not in anthropology, then in the modern history of Greece. I have thus been able to contribute to the maintenance of a worthy tradition at the college, dating back almost 50 years, in this somewhat recondite field. When I last counted, there were at Oxford 23 historians of the ancient world and one of modern Greece, myself. And, unlike the serried ranks of the classicists, I have not held a university post, nor did John for a good part of his academic career.

Sadly, the tradition of the study of modern history of Greece looks like coming to an end at the college and hence in the university. This is not for want of trying on my part. Ever since coming to the college I have tried to secure permanent funding for my Senior Research Fellowship. Last autumn I thought success was at last in reach following a meeting with a hugely rich Greek–American property developer in Sacramento, California. Characteristically, but nonetheless sadly, when a member of the family approached Oxford University last Christmas he was told that there was no call for a post in the modern history of Greece. Instead the foundation in question was asked to consider endowing a chair in byzantine studies. The foundation lost interest and the money is now, I understand, going to Stanford.

It occurs to me, however, that we still might possibly be able to attract an endowment. The Greek–American in question is proposing to erect a replica of the Parthenon on top of a 29-storey office block he is building in Sacramento at a cost of over $100 million.[2] I haven't measured up the Besse Building precisely but at a glance it looks roughly the size of the Parthenon. And whatever you might think of its architecture, the Besse building is certainly of robust construction and could probably stand the weight of a replica of the Parthenon, complete with casts of the Elgin Marbles. This would also nicely complement the Tower of the Winds at Green College. Were we to go ahead with such a plan then our chances of securing funding for an endowment in modern Greek history would, I believe, be much enhanced.

I shall certainly miss the college and hope to remain in touch. Some things, however, I shall not miss, in particular what I call my 'birds and bees' talk to those of my supervisees whose DPhil theses are nearing completion. On such occasions I have the delicate task of urging some circumspection in dedicating the thesis to current boy or girl friends. I try to hint that the only person to whom you can safely dedicate your thesis in the most fulsome terms without the possibility of future embarrassment is your mother, because, at the moment at least, you can have only one of these.

So I wish the college every success in the future. I shall watch your progress with interest and sympathy. Above all, my overriding feeling towards the college is one of gratitude for providing me with a stimulating and, above all enjoyable, intellectual home for the last 15 years.

The Tsakopoulos-Kounalakis Professorship in honour of Constantine Mitsotakis was duly established at Stanford a few months later. Its declared purpose is support for 'the study of Greek ideas in contemporary society'. Needless to

EPILOGUE

say, this is not what I had in mind at St Antony's. Professor Richard Martin, the chairman of the Department of Classics at Stanford, declared that the university would now be able to offer intensive courses giving students 'a thorough grounding in the Greek roots of politics, economics, philosophy, the arts, medicine, the law and much more'. He even expected the endowment to inspire 'nothing less than a renaissance of interest in the classics'. This might seem a peculiarly American example of crass pandering to the sensibilities of donors. But it was far exceeded by the University of Cambridge when, with a flourish of progonoplectic hyperbole similarly aimed at benefactors, it declared, on the establishment in 2008 of the A.G. Leventis Professorship of Greek Culture, that:

> the culture of the ancient Greeks is the fountainhead of western civilization. Their political thought, philosophy, scientific inquiry, historiography and visual art have inspired Rome, Renaissance humanism, the European enlightenment and the Classical revival in art and architecture, as well as opera, ballet, poetry, and theatre from Shakespeare and Monteverdi, through Handel and Stravinsky to Harrison Birtwistle, Tony Harrison, and Balanchine.

Bombast of this sort reminds me irresistibly of Gus, the Greek–American father of Toula Portokalos, the heroine of the highly amusing film *My Big Fat Greek Wedding* (1992), apparently the highest-grossing romantic comedy of all time. He saw Greek roots for everything, famously claiming that *kimono* derives from *kheimonas*, the Greek for winter.

In the years since I had left King's, the college developed a close relationship with the Ministry of Defence. It assumed 'full responsibility for academic support for military training' at the Joint Services Command and Staff College at Shrivenham and the Royal Air Force College at Cranwell and 'deployed' staff, with 'experience in working with the military' an advantage, to Shrivenham. An advertisement for a chair of Strategic Studies called for a 'demonstrated ability to operate effectively in a military environment'. Some advertisements for posts in the Department of War Studies stipulated that successful candidates would have to obtain security clearance before they could be confirmed. Such a requirement, in effect, yields ultimate sovereignty over an appointment to the Ministry of Defence rather than the college.

Another instance of military influence in the college was the announcement in 2006 of the creation of a 'specialist strategy consultancy' by various panjandrums in war and defence studies at the college. The consultancy's methodology, so it claimed, had been developed by the War Studies Group and deployed the principles of war-gaming used by the military to test 'business systems to destruction in a way that allows lessons to be safely learned'. The newly created consultancy promised to utilise 'the British military's approach to strategy that has proved its worth over generations', an odd commitment in view of the recent fiascos of British military involvement in Afghanistan, Iraq, and Libya. This King's College enterprise brought to mind posters that I had seen in Jerusalem holding out the possibility of studying the Torah and Talmud using the techniques of Mossad. But no doubt such arrangements with the military were financially profitable to the college, just as the Centre for Hellenic Studies had been crafted so as to appeal to Greek benefactors.

One of the most effective and biting satires of university life in the Thatcher era was Andrew Davies' *A Very Peculiar Practice*. This followed the hilarious doings of the worst medical practice in the UK, the student health service in a post-Robbins university. Davies had taught at the University of Warwick. In the last instalment of the splendid television adaptation of the novel, the vice-chancellor triumphantly engineers the merger of the university with the nearby police training college. No doubt Davies would have considered a similar deal with the Ministry of Defence as altogether too far-fetched a scenario. Although I do not know if this is the case at King's, at Birmingham University representatives of the Ministry of Defence actually sit on appointment boards for lectureships established by the ministry. No one at the university seems to find this at all out of the ordinary.

The spirit of the age was epitomised in the establishment in 1998, while she was still living, of a Margaret Thatcher Professorship of Enterprise Studies at Cambridge, a university presumably chosen as her own university, Oxford, had refused her the customary honorary degree because of her destructive policies towards the British university system. Equally dispiriting was the establishment of the Nestlé lectureship in the politics of development at Birkbeck College, London, and the Coca-Cola lectureship at the University of Edinburgh, worthy companions to the Robert Maxwell fellowship in politics at Balliol College, Oxford. Even more depressing was the setting up at the University of Bath of a chair in death studies, in conjunction with the National Association of Funeral Directors.

By the early years of the new millennium, it was becoming commonplace for vice-chancellors to talk of their aspiration to create the 'Manchester United' of the British academic league and for Labour ministers to claim that top-up fees would enable universities to attract the academic counterparts of such soccer superstars as Ronaldo and Beckham to their campuses. Professor Alan Smithers of the University of Buckingham compared University College, King's College and Imperial College to the Arsenals, Chelseas and Tottenhams of the Premier League.

EPILOGUE

Perhaps the most dispiriting instance of such mindless and populist philistinism of which I had direct knowledge occurred at my own *alma mater*, the University of Edinburgh. In 2003, a retiring professor, David Wright, an ecclesiastical historian, was, as is customary, charged with delivering a speech at one of the ceremonies for new graduates. In this, he poked gentle fun at such developments as the university's decision to re-brand the university librarian as Vice Principal for Knowledge Management; at the establishment of a School of Health and Well-being; and at the Minister of Education, Charles Clarke's, dismissal of degrees in medieval studies as 'ornamental'. But Professor Wright had been required to submit the text in advance to the powers that be. This led the principal of the university, Professor Timothy O'Shea, to ban his speech, although Wright's name was already on the programme. The university's new motto, incidentally, is 'Enlightenment for the 21st Century'. I recall from dim recollections of my undergraduate years that one of the things the Enlightenment had stood for was opposition to censorship.

The text of Professor Wright's mildly satirical, but basically good-natured homily was subsequently printed in the newsletter of the Edinburgh History Graduates Association. On reading that the text had been banned, my first reaction was that this was some kind of rather feeble joke. But it proved to be all too true. A few elderly alumni who remembered better days protested in vain at the gagging. For my part, I decided to ask Tam Dalyell, the Rector of the University, elected in the Scottish manner by the students, the Labour 'father' of the House of Commons, and the champion of a myriad radical causes (while being imaginative in his use of the MPs' expenses allowance), to raise the issue with the principal, confident that he would be as appalled as the rest of us old fogeys at O'Shea's intervention. Far from it. A few days later, Dalyell telephoned me to say that he had been in the 'robing room' on the day when the speech was due to be given and that the principal had been 'entirely justified' in banning the speech. When I asked Dalyell precisely what it was in the speech to which he had taken exception, he replied that he was unable to remember and this despite the fact that I had sent him a copy of Wright's text. I was irresistibly reminded of Churchill's, possibly apocryphal, reported words in the War Cabinet in early 1945 when informing his colleagues that the British had sacked George Papandreou as prime minister of Greece and replaced him by General Nicholas Plastiras: 'I hear the Greeks have a new prime minister. He's called Plaster-arse. Let's hope he doesn't have feet of clay'. Alas, Dalyell, that icon of radicalism, did prove to have feet of clay. When people such as he take the side of a university establishment unable to accept a little gentle ribbing, then the time had indeed come to take my leave of the academy, which I did two years later, in 2005.

Notes

Introduction
1 Now in a second edition (2009), revised and extended by Roger Bartlett to cover the period until 2005.

1 *Industria*. First steps in Greece: Edinburgh, Athens, London
1 A rare instance is the case of A.J. Church, Professor of Latin at University College, London in the late nineteenth century who, with no known relevant ailments, is reported to have fallen asleep while his students were construing Latin texts. Who can blame him?
2 This process can also be traced in Peter Calvocoressi's autobiography, *Threading My Way* (1994). Both Pallis and Calvocoressi had been brought up in Liverpool and both had been educated at Eton.
3 Opponents of the regime made quite a good joke, as the anti-junta activist, Rodis Roufos, noted, by juxtaposing two of the regime's fatuous slogans. The first was 'On 20 April 1967 Greece stood poised on the edge of an abyss.' The second was 'On 21 April 1967 Greece took a giant step forward.'

2 The Colonels and the stage army
1 *To Imerologio tou Londinou: simeioseis apo tin epokhi tis Diktatorias* (London Diary: notes from the time of the dictatorship) (2007).
2 Margaret Papandreou's book, *Nightmare in Athens* (1970), is a revealing source for the Greece of the Colonels. Even more revealing about the personality of her husband is the book by Papandreou's first wife, Christina Rassia, a Greek–American psychiatrist. The book, *10 khronia syzygos tou Andrea Papandreou* (Ten years as the wife of Andreas Papandreou) (1992) is a rarity. According to Ms Rassia, she was paid $90,000 by Andreas Papandreou to withdraw the book. Another version has it that all the copies were bought up on Papandreou's behalf by George Koskotas, who was at the centre of the Bank of Crete scandal in the late 1980s.
3 That is to say, at the time that the *Sunday Times* revealed that Fraser was employing an MP as a lobbyist.

NOTES

3 *Sancte et sapienter*. King's College and the School of Slavonic and East European Studies

1 This shop, as was only to be expected, continued to exist throughout the period of communist rule and Russian books that were difficult to find in the Soviet Union could sometimes be found there. I myself in the late 1980s bought a superbly printed two volume edition of Victor Lazarev's monumental history of Byzantine art for a ridiculously low price. Published in Moscow by Iskusstvo in 1986, it initially struck me as an indication that at last communist regimes had mastered the art of fine printing until I discovered that it had actually been printed in Vienna. At the same time I bought a two volume edition of Anna Karenina as a present for my daughter Rachel who was learning Russian at school. After a few minutes she came downstairs and said 'Da, this is in a funny kind of Russian'. It was, to my eternal shame, a Bulgarian translation of Tolstoy's work.

4 Knitting a sock for my head: on washing dirty academic linen in public

1 The passage, in Greek, with which Toynbee had wished to conclude his letter of 3 January 1924 to *The Times* in which he made public his resignation from the Koraes chair. A longer version of this chapter is contained in my *Miscellanea Graecoturcica: Essays on Greek and Turkish History* (Istanbul 2015).
2 I owe this reference to Professor Peter Mackridge.
3 Characteristic is the attitude of Kenneth Dover, the highly distinguished classicist and sometime president of the British Academy, to the 'modern' Greeks as evidenced in his fascinating, if rather peculiar, memoir, *Marginal Comment* (1994): 'although the scenery and the sites [of Greece] move me profoundly, I can't help having mixed feelings about the culture of the country. Their vitality is enchanting, but I am put off by melodramatic chauvinism, whether it is British or Greek.' Ingram Bywater, the Regius Professor of Greek at Oxford University between 1893 and 1908, never set foot in Greece, while Werner Jaeger, the German classicist and for many years a professor at Harvard, visited Greece only once in old age to receive an honorary degree.

5 The sock knitted

1 Ms Dimitra Liani, the youngish air hostess, universally known as Mimi, with whom Andreas Papandreou took up in his dotage, famously declared that historians in the future would come to look upon her as Aspasia, Pericles' partner, to Papandreou's Pericles.

6 Greeks bearing chairs: chairs bearing Greeks

1 In Canada, chairs of ethnic studies have been established in a number of universities with subventions from the Federal Government as part of its policy of multiculturalism. As of the early 1990s, some 23 such chairs were in existence.

Epilogue

1 William Wallace was at the time a senior research fellow of the college.
2 I confused our potential donor with his cousin. It was the cousin who was planning to build the replica Parthenon. In the event, alas, the project did not receive planning permission.

Index

Abdul the Damned 114
Abkhazia 30, 293, 306, 327-30
academic freedom 177, 180, 197-201, 208, 220-1, 265, 285, 305
academic politics 3-5, 174, 217, 267
age limits for serving on university bodies 261-2, 265
Agnew, Spiro 92, 94
Albania 111-13, 126, 136
Alexander, George 274-5
Alexander the Great 304, 330
Alexandris, Alexis 49
American School of Classical Studies in Athens (ASCSA) 331-6
Amery, Julian 136, 155
Amis, Kingsley 152, 340
Amnesty International 65
Anargyreios School, Spetses 182
Anastasakis, Othon 298
Anderson, Matthew 217
Andrews, William Wayte 32
Andrikopoulos, Yannis 58, 92-4
Angelis, Odysseus 63

Anglican orders, validity of 296
Anglo-Hellenic League 88, 182-3, 220-1, 236
The Annual Register 129-30
anonymous reviewing 62
Anthimos, Patriarch of Jerusalem 107
Antonescu, Ion 123-4
Apostolou, Lefteris 148
archaeology 22-7 *passim*, 330-2
Argenti, Philip 253-4
Armenian community in the US 221-2
Armenian genocide 283, 303
'Armenian visits' 161
Arnaoutis, Makis 93
Ascham House, Gosforth 12
Ascherson, Neil 145
Ashcroft, Peggy 57
Aston, Trevor 6, 339
Atatürk, Mustafa Kemal 24, 26, 32, 38, 128, 191, 195
Atchley, S.C. 41
Athanasios of Smyrna 35
Athénée Palace hotel, Bucharest 110

INDEX

Athens Review of Books 171
Athens University 169
Athinagoras, Patriarch 38, 167–8, Plate 22
Athos, Mount 17, 54–6
atrocities 195–9, 327–9
Auden, W.H. 255
Augustine, Mary Jo *see* Clogg, Mary Jo (wife of author)
Australia, Greeks in 285
authorised histories of academic institutions 7–9, 135–9, 180–3, 219
Auty, Phyllis 130, 134–5
Ayvalik 39–40

Babanasis, Stergios 319
Bachtin, Nicholas 253, 255
Baerentzen, Lars 171, 246
Bagier, Gordon 74, 83–5
Bailey, S.W. ('Bill') 131
Baldwin, Stanley 267
Baldwin Brown, Gerald 20
Balfour, David 90–1, 133
Balliol College, Oxford 70–1, 140, 188, 210–11, 214, 344
Barber, E.A. 253
Barker, Elisabeth 131, 275
Barker, Ernest 197–204, 219, 224
Barnes, Tom 308–9
Barry, John 71–2, 76
Bartholomaios, Patriarch 25, 304
Bath University 344
Baynes, Norman 253, 255
Beaton, Roderick 233, 241–6, 259, 270, 306
Beazley, J.D. 47–8
Beazley, Lady 48

Belloc, Hilaire 296
Beloff, Nora 150–3
Beloyannis, Nikos 71, 320
Benn, Tony 300
Bennett, E.N. 203
Bennett, Jeremy 127
Berkowitz, Peter 7
Berlin, Irving 222
Berlin, Isaiah 267
Bernières, Louis de 306–10
Berza, Mihai 110
Besse, Antonin 288, 340–1
Besse, Hilda 341
Best, Geoffrey 103–6
Bible House, London 33
Biddle, Martin 321–2
Birkbeck College 344
Birmingham University 66, 265, 344
Birnberg, Benedict 96, Plate 7
Birt, John 153
Blair, Tony 15, 153, 266, 328
Blinkhorn, Martin 270–1
Blunt, Anthony 118
Boardman, John 164
Bodosakis-Athanasiadis, Prodromos 272–5
Bogarde, Dirk 12
Boileau, Sir John 32
Bolsover, George 114–15, 120
Boulter, Veronica 178
Bouras, Nick 289
Bousbourellis, Charalambos 161
Bowra, Maurice 267
Boxshall, Eddie 134
boycotts, academic 66
Boyle, Sir Edward 254
Brademas, John 218–9, 280

350

INDEX

Brailsford, H.N. 181
Brandram, Lady Katherine 183
Brandt, Willi 80
Brasenose College 292–3
Brezhnev, Leonid 114
brigandage 226
British Academy 232–4, 238–1
British Broadcasting Corporation, Greek Service (BBC) 52–3, 57, 61, 76, 81, 87, 99-100, 125-9, 140–1, 147–52
  director-generalship of 143, 151-4
British Council 65, 149
British and Foreign Bible Society 33
British Museum 34-5, 75-6, 166-7
British National Byzantine Committee (BNBC) 230
British School [of Archaeology], Athens 41-2, 45-52, 211, 213, 288, 330–2, 335
Brown, Julian 249
Browning, Robert 65, 177–8, 263
Bryce, Lord 193–4
Bryer, Anthony 230, 238–241
Buchan, John 196
Bucharest 110-11, 118
Bucharest University Library 159
Buck, Anthony 81-2
Buckingham University 344
Buhayer, Constantine 216
Burgess, Thomas 35
Burke, Edmund 129
Burlin, Terence 158-9
Burne-Jones, Edward 323
Burrows, Ronald 8, 106-7, 180–92, 201, 207-10, 215, 218-19, 314
Burrows, Una 179, 202–3

Burrows Library, King's College 65, 98, 121, 192, 217
Bush, George H.W. 156
Bush, George W. 239
Byron, Lord 170, 323, Plate 21
Byron, Robin 323
Bywater, Charlotte 256-8
Bywater, Ingram 256-7
Byzantine civilisation 21, 27, 187, 225-6
'byzantine' machinations 6, 229-3, 257-8
Byzantine studies 230-1, 235, 251, 257-8, 264, 342
Byzantinism 226-7

Caclamanos, Dimitrios 224, 254
Çakmak, Cem 217
Caldwell, Malcolm 7-8
Calvocoressi, Peter 63, 154, 177
Cambridge University 275, 343–4
Cambridge University Press 66, 163, 245, 299, 302-3
Cameron, Averil 225, 230-44, 247, 251, 259, 264-6
Cameron, David 325
Cameron, Neil 117, 124, 138
Camp Bucca 67
Campbell, John 225, 239, 246-7, 275, 288-9, 293-4, 297, 311-12, 341-2
Captain Corelli's Mandolin (book and film) 306–10
Carabott, Philip 172, 298
Carnegie Trust for the Universities of Scotland 29, 56, 103
Carr, Raymond 5
Carter, Frank 120

Cartledge, Paul 313
Cass, Frank 217, 220
Cassavetti, D.J. 182
Castle Howard 177-8
Cavafy, Constantine 188, 225
Cavanagh, Nick 31
Ceauşescu, Elena 69-70, 155-8, 240
Ceauşescu, Nicolae 69, 85, 110-11, 154-9
Ceauşescu family 158-9
Çelebi, Evliya 30
Çelik Palas hotel, Bursa 37-8
censorship 62, 150
Central Intelligence Agency (CIA) 94, 143, 150, 162-3, 288, 328
Centre for Hellenic Studies (King's College) 235-7, 243-7, 344
Center for Hellenic Studies (New York University) 279-84
Cevdet, Muallim 209
Chadwick, Owen 31-2
Chalmers-Wright, Fergus 137-8
Chamberlain, Neville 144
Channel Four television 141-2, 147-52
Chapman, Ann 91-4
Chapman, Edward 92, 94
Charanis, Peter 31
Charles, Prince of Wales 55, 109, 159, 166-7, 340
Chastelain, John de 14-15
Chatham House (Royal Institute of International Affairs) 64, 327
Chechnya 327-9
Checkland, Michael 153
Christodoulos, Archbishop of Athens 173
Chrysostomides, Julian 296

Chrysostomos, Archbishop of Smyrna 174
Church of the Holy Sepulchre, Jerusalem 321-2
Churchill, Clementine and Mary 9
Churchill, Winston 9-10, 127, 132, 136, 142, 146, 150, 272-6, 309, 325, 337, 345-6
Churchill College, Cambridge 16, 272-6
Clarke, Charles 345
Clinton, Bill 329-30
Clissold, Stephen 131
Clive, Nigel 89-90, 161
Clogg, Derek 61
Clogg, John (brother of the author) 12, 94
Clogg, Mary Jo (wife of author) 8, 12, 26-33, 39-42, 46-50, 56-7, 59, 63-4, 71, 88, 94-5, 100-5, 116, 132, 136, 138, 160-1, 216, 223, 248, 278-9, 282, 306, 322, 330, 337, Plates 11 and 18
Clogg, Nathan (son of the author) 30-1, 95, Plates 8 and 12
Clogg, Rachel (daughter of the author) 30, 64, 71, 95, 105-6, 111, 293, Plates 11, 12 and 19
Clogg, Richard
  family backgroud 12
  school education 11-14, 159
  as an undergraduate 18-19
  interest in and first visit to Greece 11, 16-17, 26-7
  work on the Hagia Sophia wall paintings, Trebizond 18-25
  other early work experience 31-3, 36-8

INDEX

work at the British School, Athens 41–2, 45–52
travels in Europe 29, 109–10
opposition to Greek junta 57–9, 103, 108, 139
broadcasting career 57, 65, 100, 125
offered a job at the BBC 125
publications 3–4, 65–6, 98, 107, 111, 117, 122, 129, 134, 140, 160, 165–6, 169–74, 175–7, 179, 217, 236, 245–6, 301, 323, 336
work on the history of SOE in Greece 140, 330–1

Academic career:
research fellowships 56, 103, 293, 342
lectureships at London and Edinburgh Universities 76, 84, 86, 93, 104, 106–8, 116, 176, 339
readership in modern Greek history at King's College 124, 233
personal chair in Modern Balkan history 242–3, 247
departure from King's College 220, 246–8, 341

At St Antony's College, Oxford:
Senior Research Fellow later Emeritus Fellow 293, 341–2
fundraising activities 294, 297–298, 342
end of academic career 337, 340–2, 348

In Greece:
awarded the Gold Cross of the Legion of Honour 313

appointed Visiting Fellow at the British School, Athens 330
coenobitic system of monastic governance 55–6
Columbia University 71
Colville, John 9–10
Constantine I and II, Kings of Greece 46, 49, 92–3, 183, 325–6
Cook, J.M. 44
Corfu 37, 100–1
Cornford, F.M. 4
Corpus Christi College, Oxford 6
Cottrell, Richard 94
Courakis, Nestor 292
Courakis, Tony 292
Cox, Barry 141
Crampton, Richard 116, 159, 248; Plates 9 and 10
Crawley, C.W. 71
Crichton-Miller, Donald 13
Crook, Arthur 60, 62
Crosland, Tony 109
Cruickshank, Charles 136, 139
Cumberland Lodge conference on Balkan resistance (1972) 90, 130, 134–6, 139
Cumming, Mansfield 162
Cyprus 11, 18, 95, 98, 100, 127, 163, 184, 200, 203, 226, 268, 298, 313–14, 325

Dahrendorf, Ralf 3, 219, 246
Dakin, Douglas 93, 108, 239, 273, 310
Dalyell, Tam (and Dalyell family history) 19, 345
Damaskinos, Archbishop of Athens 142
Dasgupta, Biplab 7

Davenport, Mike 19
Davidson, Basil 131, 136
Davidson, Randall 297
Davies, Andrew 344
Davis Hanson, Victor 6
Dawkins, R.M. 188, 251-4
Deakin, F.W.D. ('Bill') 131, 137
death studies 344
Deletant, Dennis 159; Plate 9
Delilbaşi, Melek 100
Deliyannis, Theodoros 227
Demophantos 98
Dendrinos, Charalambos 296
Denning, Lord 78-9
Der Spiegel 3, 136
Dershowitz, Alan 5
Desai, Meghnad 266
Dimaras, Alexis 63, 76
Dimitriadis, Odysseus 306, Plate 13
Dimitriou, Andreas 314
Dinsmoor, William 333-4
Diogenes of Sinope 330
Dixon, Pierson 10, 41
Djilas, Aleksa 122
Dodds, E.R. 267
Doll, Peter 294
Douglas, J.A. 24, 205, 296-7
Douglas-Home, Sir Alec 87
Dover, Kenneth 6, 10, 241, 339
Doyle, Leonard 302-3
Dragoumis, Mark 58
Droppers, Garrett 44
Duțu, Alexandru 110
Dyson, Stephen 335

East Anglia University 103
Eden, Anthony 9-10, 15-16

Edinburgh, Duke of 323-4
Edinburgh University 18-19, 26, 28, 32, 76, 84, 104-6, 248-9, 339, 341, 344-5
Eftim, Papa 38-9
Egon, Nicholas 223, 240
Elgin Marbles 35, 166-7, 170, 313
Eliot, T.S. 47, 195
Elizabeth II, Queen 155-6
Elliot, Sir Francis 212
Elliot, Sir Henry 226
Elytis, Odysseus 165
Encounter 143, 151-2
Engel, Arthur 219, 223
Erdoğan, Recep Tayyip 49
Ergenekon affair 39
'ethnic chairs' 3, 267, 269
Eugenides, Eugene 47
Eumorfopoulos, Nicholas 185, 189, 190-200
European Union 173, 298, 304, 319
Evans, Harold 75-7
Evans, Michael 327-8
Evans, Richard 103
Evening Standard 68, 153, 307
Evensen, Jens 99
Ezekiel, Bishop of Melbourne 168

Fallmerayer, Jakob Philipp 198, 225-6, 236
Farrow, Mia 57
Featherstone, Kevin 272
Federal Bureau of Investigation (FBI) 122, 222
Fehérvársurgó 317-20
Ferguson, Alan 121-2
Fettes College 11-16, 28, 132
Fine, John 29

INDEX

Finkelstein, Norman 5
Finlay, George 21, 24, 51, 225
Fisher, H.A.L. 267
Fisher, 'Jacky' 132
Flashtig, Alan 18-20, 22
Fleming, Sir Alexander 62, 234-5
Fleming, Lady Amalia 43, 62, 71, 234-5, Plate 7
Fleming, Katherine 218
Fletcher, Robin 255-6
Flowers, Lord 240, 246-7
Foot, Hugh 67
Foot, M.R.D. 9, 12, 68, 137-9
Foot, Michael 68
Foot, Paul 67-9
Ford, Sheila 246
Foreign Office 57, 59, 69, 87-8, 90, 123, 127, 133-7 *passim*, 157-8, 190, 205, 272, 274, 312, 323, 325
Forrest, George 96
Foundation for Hellenic Culture 306
Frangos, George 51-3, 299-300, Plate 3
Frankel, Peter 125
Frankland, Noble 4
Frantz, Alison 332
Fraser, Hugh 136
Fraser, Maurice 60, 72-86
Freedom of Information Act 234, 241-2
French, Lisa 42

Gabriel, Jane 141-3, 146
Gage, Nicholas 320
Gaitskell, Hugh 15-16
Galbraith, J.K. 58, 97
Galton, Dorothy 122-3
Ganasoulis, Photios 67-8
Garganas, Nikos 269

Garganas, Panos 300
Gaselee, Stephen 253-5
de Gaulle, Charles 87-9
Gazzetta del Sud 321
Gennadeios Library, Athens 178
Gennadius, Joannes 178, 184, 186, 189-191, 198-5
Georgakopoulos, Theodoros 271
Georgalas, Georgios 319
Georgallis, Sodos 313-14
George I and II, Kings of Greece 127, 226, 272, 324, 337
Geraldine, Queen of Albania 126
Germanos, Bishop of Old Patras 173
Gertler, Mark 255
Gibb, Hamilton 5
Gibbon, Edward 36, 51, 228
Giddens, Anthony 266-7, 269-1
Gill, Inder 324
Gilmour, Ian 237
Giscard d'Estaing, Valéry 237
Gizikis, Phaedon 66
Gladstone, W.E. 256
Glasgow, George 201-4
Glen, Sandy 13, 131-2
Glenconner, Lord 100-1
Glezos, Manolis 144, 148, Plate 6
Godley, A.D. 287-8
Goldbloom, Maurice 63-4
Golden Dawn party 171, 173
González, Maria Jesus 5
Gordon, G.S. 254
Gordonstoun School 288, 340-1
Gorgopotamos viaduct 134, 324
Gorky, Maksim 123
Goulding, Marrack 219, 288, 339
Gounaris, Elias 261

INDEX

Grabar, André 29
Grande Bretagne hotel, Athens 100-1
Grant, Hugh 306
Greece - The Hidden War (television documentary) 142-9, 153
Greek College, Oxford 294-7
Greek Colonels' coup (1967) 49-54
Greek community in Britain 3-4, 175-90, 198-210, 222-3, 227, 231, 234-5, 240, 245, 252, 268, 285, 310-11
Greek Constitution 40-1, 292
Greek diaspora studies 280, 298
Greek economy 17, 130
Greek exceptionalism 270
Greek language 12
 dialects of 252, 254
 katharevousa and *dimotiki* forms of 187
Greek minorities 289-91, 300
Greek monarchy 323
Greek Observer (magazine) 58
Greek students at British universities 293-4
Green, Peter 60, 72
Greene, Sir Hugh 96-7, Plate 7
Grivas, George 127
Guardian 77
Gubbins, Sir Colin 131
Gudeman, Steven 303
Guétary, Georges 11-12
Guild, R.A. 28-9
Guilford, Fifth Earl of 34-5
The Guns of Navarone (film) 170
Gyzis, Nikolaos 172-3

Hackett, John 109, 124, 225
Hadjipateras, Costas 313

Hagia Sophia wall paintings, Trebizond 18-25, Plates 1 and 2
Hale, Bill 22
Hallett, Judith 6
Hambro, Charles 131
Hamid Bey 194
Hammond, N.G.L. ('Nick') 131-3, 137, 335
Hardie, Margaret 42
Harrison, Jane 242
Harrison, Richard 217
Hart, Gary 339
Hartley, Frank 158, 240
Harvard University 6-7, 22, 221, 266, 282
Hasluck, F.W. 42, 187-8
Hatzivasiliou, Giorgos 285
Haugland, Jens 99
Hawke, Bob 168, Plate 25
Hawthorne, William 273-5
Hay, Denys 104
Hayter Report (1961) 106
Hearnshaw, F.J.C. 8, 180
Heath, John 6
Hellenic continuity 235-6, 244
Hellenic Observatory 164, 267-8
Hellenic Review 65, 75, 91
Hellenism 227-8, 268
Henniker-Major, John 131
Herodotus 214
Herrin, Judith 313
Herringham, Wilmot 205
Herzfeld, Michael 300, 303
Hippocrene Books 166
historians 2, 4, 9, 95, 97, 149–50
Hitler, Adolf 309, 325

Hobsbawm, Eric 266
Hochhuth, Rolf 136
Hodge, Margaret 72
Hodge Hill, Bert 332-5
Hodgkin, Dorothy 157-8
Hodgson, Patricia 152
Hoffa, Jimmy 30
Holton, David 61-2, 65, 276
honorary degrees 157, 344
Hood, John 264-5, 339
Hood, Roger 292
Hooper, Robin 86-90, 273
Hopkinson, David 328
Horn, D.B. 104
Horne, Alistair 72-3
Hornsby-Smith, Patricia 131
Howard, John 169, 316
Howard-Johnston, James 259
Hoxha (Hodja), Enver 112-13, 126, 136
Hubbard, William Arthur 309
Hudson, D.T. ('Bill') 134-5
Huelin, Gordon 8, 180
Hurst, Christopher 129
Hussein, Saddam 16, 67
Hussey, Joan 51, 71
Hussey, Marmaduke 151-3

Iatrides, John 280-1
idiorrythmic system of monastic governance 55-6
If... (film) 15
Ill Met by Moonlight (film) 12, 170
Immerwahr, Heinrich 332
Imvros 48-9
Independent Broadcasting Authority (IBA) 143, 149, 152
Independent Television Authority 83

Inglis, Elsie 105, 331
Institute for Turkish Studies, Washington DC 283-4
Institute of Public Relations 82, 85
International Monetary Fund 130
Ionian Academy, Corfu 34
Iremonger, Tom 79
Isaacs, Jeremy 141, 143, 150-3
Iskander, Fazil 30, 295
Isigonis, Alec 54-5

janissaries 316-17
Jannaris, Antonios 182
Jeffreys, Elizabeth 262, 264
Jellicoe, George 124, 154
Jenkins, Romilly 225-8, 236, 253, 255, 276
Jenkins, Roy 65, 159-60
Joachim, Joachim 178
Johnson, John 252-4
Johnson, Lyndon 58
Johnston, Reginald 8
Johnston, Russell 74
Johnstone, Kenneth 131
Joll, James 117-19, 274-5
Jupp, James 168-9
Justinian, Emperor 23-4

Kaczynski, Theodore 6
Kakoulidis, Alexandros 26
Kallistos, Bishop of Diokleia 259
Kaloumenos, Dimitris 167
Kandemir, Nuzhet 283-4
Karadžić, Radovan 118
Karakasidou, Anastasia 299-3
karamanlides and *karamanlidika* 32-4

INDEX

Karamanlis, Konstantinos 60, 66-7, 75-6, 89-90, 100, 120, 148-9
Karaolis, Michalis 314
Karapanayiotis, Byron 272
Karavia, Maria 58, 98
Karidis, Viron 88
Kark, Austen 61, 125
Karo, Georg 334
Károlyi family 317
Kathimerini (newspaper) 75, 302, 311-13
Katsiaounis, Rolandos 313-15
Kazantzakis, Nikos 255
Keble, C.M. ('Bolo') 132
Kedourie, Elie 5, 179-80, 223
Kee, Robert 151-2
Keeley, Edmund ('Mike') 239
Kemal, Yusuf 209
Kenny, Anthony 258-2, 264
Kenyon Jones, Christine 8, 181
Khatzis, Thanasis 148-9
Khronopulo, M.N. 326
King, Francis 17
King George II hotel, Athens 97
King's College London 2-4, 7-9, 106-9, 117-25, 150, 172, 175-6, 179-2, 196-201, 216, 219-20, 225, 230-49, 298, 343-4
  Library 75, 194
  see also Burrows Library; Koraes professorship
Kinnock, Neil 313
Kissinger, Henry 4
Kitromilides, Paschalis 271
Kitsikis, Dimitri 179
Kokkalis, Petros 314-15
Kokkalis, Socrates 314-15

Kokkinakis, Athinagoras 96
Koliopoulos, John 225, 229
Kondis, Ioannis 51
Konopios, Nathanail 294
Koraes professorship at King's College 3-4, 8, 108-9, 119, 121, 124, 158, 174, 176-81, 186-7, 191-2, 197-210, 215-20, 223-34, 237-45, 251-2, 267, 285
Korais, Adamantios 35-6, 186-7
Koumoundouros, Alexandros 227
Koutsoyannopoulos, Captain 146
Kreipe, Karl 12-13
Krekić, Bariša 222

Ladas, Ioannis 63
Lake, Christopher 58-9
Lakeview and Lake County, Oregon 30, 132, 278-9
Lambrias, Takis 60, 100
Lambrou, Vasilis 63
Lancaster, Osbert 252
Lansing, Robert 44
Laskaridou, Aikaterini 36
Lasky, Mel 143
Latsis family 293
Laurantus, Nicholas 285
Lausanne, Treaty of (1923) 26
Lauxtermann, Marc 265
le Carré, John 288, Plate 14
League for Democracy in Greece 162
Leeper, Rex 90, 133-4
Lefkowitz, Mary 5
Leifer, Michael 130
Leigh Fermor, Patrick 12-13, 309
Leka, Mbret 126-7

INDEX

Lemos, George 289, 312
Levens, R.G.C. 331
Leventis, A.G. 343
Leventis Foundation 276-7, 288, 298, 312
Leverhulme Trust 247
Levi, Peter 46-7, 220-1, 256
Lewis, Victor 82
Lex Hornby and Partners 78
Liakos, Antonis 228
Lifton, Robert Jay 283-4
Lindsay, Franklin 132
Lingua Franca (magazine) 2
Livingstone, Ken 72
Llewellyn Smith, Michael 107, 297
Lloyd, Selwyn 15
Lloyd-Jones, Hugh 67
Loch, Joyce 17
London Hellenic Foundation 288-93, 310-13
London Review of Books 15-16, 305-6
London School of Economics 5, 32, 124, 164-5, 186, 219, 266-71, 275
London University 1-2, 178-9, 218, 237, 248, 339
  Senate House 1, 178-9
Loules, Dimitris 162-3
Louros, Nikolaos 91
Lowry, Heath 283-4
Luke, Harry 45
Lynch, H.F.B. 20-2

Macadam, Ivison 181
Macaulay, Rose 20
Maccas, Leon 188

Macedonia 34, 120, 168-9, 289-1, 298-6
MacGregor, John 124
MacGregor, Neil 166
Machiavelli, Nicolò 265
Mackenzie, Compton 42-5, 75, 162
Mackenzie, W.J.M. 135
Mackridge, Peter 109, 205-6, 245-6, 255-64 *passim*
Maclean, Fitzroy 131-3, 151
Macmillan (publishers) 134
Macmillan, George 189
Macmillan, Harold 136, 265
McNeill, William H. 178, 210, 216
McQuillen, Kenneth 273, 275
Magdalino, Paul 260-2
Major, John 324
Makarios, Archbishop 95-6, 100
Malalas, John 262
managerialism 341
Manchester Guardian 192-5, 199, 202
Mangakis, Georgios-Alexandros 86-7
Mango, Andrew 125-7, 220-1
Mango, Cyril 36, 108, 225-9, 232-4, 236, 238 *passim*, 256, 311
Mann, Colin 85
Manning, Olivia 117-18
Manuel II Palaiologos, Emperor 324
Marcellas, Anna 168
Mare, Albinia de la 249
Marett, R.R. 254-5
Marinatos, Spyridon 51
Marinos, Themi 324
Markezinis, Basil 275
Markezinis, Spyros 93, 273-5
Markov, Georgi 70

359

Marr, James 12
Marreco, Anthony 53, 59, 61, 96, 98, Plate 7
Marshall, F.H. 224-5, 255
Marshall, Peter 240
Martin, Anthony 5
Martin, Richard 343
Martindale, John 232
Martis, Nikolaos 168-9
Marx Memorial Library 115
Masaryk, Tomáš Garrigue 106
Matthews, Kenneth 182
Maudling, Reginald 86
Maurice, Frederick Denison 180-1
Mavrogordatos, George 252-5, 271
Mavrogordato, John 188, 195-6, 206-8, 224-5
Mavrokordatos, Alexandros 323
Maxwell, Robert 5, 69-70, 157, 344
Mayhew, Lady 124
Mazower, Mark 302
Megaro Mousikis concert hall, Athens 314
Megaw, A.H.S. 45
Meiggs, Russell 48
Melas, G. 198
Melbourne 168-9
Meletios II, Patriarch 296
Meletios Metaxakis, Patriarch 296-7
Menderes, Adnan 23
Mercouri, Melina 35, 59-60, 91, 166-7, 170, 231, 236, 335-6, Plate 7
Meritt, Lucy Shoe 332-3
Merton College, Oxford 276-7
Messina University 321
Metaxas, General 144

Meteora 17
MI6 42-5, 94, 153, 161-3, 277, 302, 328
Michael, Prince (later King) of Romania 324
Michaelides, Chris 35
Middle Eastern Studies (journal) 179-80, 217, 223
Mihailović, Draža 134, 152
Mikes, George 17
Miles, Oliver 323
Miller, William 184-7, 219
Millet, Gabriel 19-20
Ministry of Defence 343-4
mishellenism
  of Arnold Toynbee 210-16
  King's College accused of 284
Mitsakis, Karolos 255
Mitsis, Phillip 281
Mitsotakis, Konstantinos 58, 145, 324-5, 342-3
'modern' Greece, use of the term 163-4
modern Greek studies 248, 251, 284, 342
Modiano, Mario 128
Montgomery Watt, William 28
Moran, Lord 9-10, 146, 274
Morgan, John 53, 83
Morgan Grenfell (merchant bank) 131
Morning Star 307-8
Moschos, Michael 311-13
Moss, Billy 12-13, 309
Mottram, Richard 328
Mouskondis, Nicholas 168
Mouzelis, Nikos 271
MPs' outside interests 79, 82-6

INDEX

Murray, Gilbert 181, 188-9, 194, 199-201, 204-5, 267
Mussolini, Benito 144, 203
Muswell Hill 72, 129, 295-6, Plate 20
My Big Fat Greek Wedding (film) 343
Myers, E.C.W. ('Eddie') 90, 131-4, 137, 308-9
Mytilini 39

Nathanail, Paul 125, Plate 6
National Society Ellas 165
nationalism 196, 220
Navarino, battle of (1827) 122
Nelson, Frank 131
neo-martyrs 35
Nesson, Charles 6-7
New Scientist 156–7, 159
New Statesman 16
New York Times 330
New York University (NYU) 218-19, 235, 243, 251, 277-81
Newton, A.P. 206
Nicol, Donald 109, 117, 119, 153–4, 160, 222-3, 225, 228-4, 240, 245
Nicolaidis, Kalypso 298
Nind, Philip 154, 243, 246
Noble, Peter 109, 177, 229
Noble Report (1971) 119
Noel-Baker, Barbro 52
Noel-Baker, Francis 52-3, 73, 81
Nolan, Lord 86
Norman, Richard 158
North, Lord Francis 34-5
North, Frederick *see* Guilford, Fifth Earl of
North, Peter 262

Nuffield Foundation 131

Obolensky, Dimitri 238-1
Observer 77, 162, 170-1, 203, 224
Odyssey (magazine) 277, 281, 320-1
Oeconomos, Lysimachos 188, 205
Oikonomides, Nikos 49-50, 53, 65, 71
Oikonomides, Veta 53, 71
Old Calendarists 291
Olympic Airways 97
Onassis, Aristotle 280
Onassis Foundation 218-1, 235-6, 277, 280-4
Oregon 30-1, 278-9
Orwell, George 1
Orwell, Sonia 58
O'Shea, Timothy 345
Ottoman rule in Greece 172-3
Owen, David 155
Oxfam 337
Oxford University 160, 287, 341-4
Oxford University Gazette 262, 264, 267

Packard, Martin 92-4
Page, Bruce 100
Page, Denys 67
paidomazoma, the (1948) 316-21
Palairet, Lady 336
Pallis, A.A. 40-1
Palme, Olaf 82
Panagoulis, Alekos 91
Papacostea-Danielopolu, Cornelia 110
Papadiamantis, Alexandros 229
Papadimitriou, Stelios 236, 281

INDEX

Papadopoulos, George 64–5, 72–7, 80, 86–91, 273
Papadopoulos Vretos, Andreas 34
papal elections 265
Papandreou, Andreas 50, 58–9, 82, 97–9, 128, 144, 166, 270, 304, Plate 3
Papandreou, George 49, 268, 298, 345
Papandreou, Margaret 60, 336
Papanikolas, George 34–5
Papanikolas, Helen 168
Papanoutsos, E.P. 227–8
Papastavrou, Stavros 183, 276
Papathemelis, Stelios 168–9
Pappas, Zapheiris 79–80
Pares, Bernard 122, 204
Park, Daphne 153
Parker, J.S.F. 219–20
Pascoe, Marion 51, 161; *see also* Sarafis, Marion
PASOK party 144–5, 153–4, 266–9, 313, 335
Patrikios, Titos 172
Pattakos, Brigadier 53
Pavlowitch, France: Plate 10
Pavlowitch, Stevan 159, 248, Plate 9
Pawson, David and Pamela 131
Paxman, Jeremy 307
Pearson, J.D. 8, 104
Pembroke College 70–1, 86
Pera Palace hotel, Istanbul 38
Perry, Cooper 186, 201, 205, 217
Pesmazoglou, Miranda 95
Pesmazoglou, Yanko 63, 71, 95
Petropoulos, Elias 128
Petropulos, John 239–40
Philip of Macedon 304

Philips, Cyril 7
Pirie, Ian 140
Pirie-Gordon, Harry 198
Plastiras, Nicholas 345
Plunket Green, Richard 19
Polish Library, London 114
Politis, N.G. 187
Polybius 175, 203
Polytechnic of Central London 157–8
Popham, Mervyn 46
Porson, Richard 36
positive vetting 138
postmodernism 2
'Potemkin' professorships 263–4
Potts, Captain 43
Powell, Dilys 127
Pravda 76
Preece, Howard 83
Prentice, Ronald 137
Price, Clair 39
Pritchard, Stephen 171–2
Private Eye 60, 67–9, 150, 153, 261–2, 293
prosopography 232–4, 238–2
Prossalendis, Frangiskos 295
Psarros, Dimitrios 146
public relations on behalf of the Greek junta 72–4, 78–82, 85–6
Putin, Vladimir 329
Puttkamer, Jesco von 80
Pye, Edith 337
Pym, Diana 96, 162
Pyromaglou, Komninos 148, Plate 6

Quataert, Donald 284
Queen Mary College (QMC) 119–20

362

INDEX

Rabnett, Jane 45-6
Radcliffe Observatory and Radcliffe Infirmary, Oxford 323
Ranke, Leopold von 4, 9
Rawlings, Baroness 124
Reeves, William Pember 182, 189, 199, 219, 314
referees, academic 238-9
Reid Thomas, David 18
Religious Tract Society 54
Repousi, Maria 172-3
Research Assessment Exercise (RAE) 164
Research Excellence Framework (REF) 164
Revett, Nicholas 323
Reynolds, Leighton 292-3
Rice, Duncan 218, 277-8
Richard, Ivor 77-9
Richardson, Tom 22
Richmond, Leigh 54
Riley, Chris 150
Rinsler, Norma 237, 240
Robeck, Sir John de 24, 184
Robert College, Constantinople 209
Roberts, Bob 16
Roberts, I.W. 8, 115, 123
Robinson, Christopher 259
Romania 154-5, 201
Roosevelt, Franklin D. 337
Rosenthal, Tom 62-3
Ross, Jonathan 119
Rothstein, Andrew 8, 115, 122
Roufos, Rodis 63-5
Roussel, Thierry 277
Routledge, Paul 16
Royal Holloway College 280, 298

Royal Institute of International Affairs *see* Chatham House
Royal Institute/Society of Chemistry 157-9, 240
Royal Society 157
Runciman, David 15-16
Runciman, Steven (and Runciman Prize) 154, 220, 231, 236, 263, 295
Russell, Ralph 8
Russell Trust 18-19, 23
Russia, Greeks in 326-7
Rutgers University 31
Ryan, Alan 265

Said, Wafic 260
Sainsbury, Lord 64-5
Sainsbury's supermarkets 234
St Andrew's University 182
St Antony's College, Oxford 3, 5, 68-9, 72, 123, 140, 154, 219-20, 246-7, 287, 289, 293, 298, 311-12, 316, 336, 339-3
St Clair, William: Plate 15
St Cross College 293
St Peter's College 70
Sanjian, Avedis 221
Santas, Apostolos: Plate 6
Santoro, Antonio 25
Sarafis, Marion 148-50, 161-3
Sarafis, Stephanos 51, 145-6, 161
Sargent, Orme 90
Scargill, Arthur 111
Schenck, Baron 44
Schilizzi, Helena 185
School of Oriental and African Studies (SOAS) 7, 22, 27, 119, 121

363

INDEX

School of Slavonic and East European Studies (SSEES) 7-8, 106-10, 114-24, 131, 184
Scobie, Ronald 142
Scottish nationalism 14, 105-6
'secret school' legend 172-3
Seferis, George 46-7, 256, 266
Selborne, Lord 131
Serapheim, Archbishop 66
Service, Robert 116
Seton-Watson, Hugh 117-19, 131, 137, 179
Seton-Watson, R.W. 106, 117, 123-4, 175, 177, 179, 184, 201-5, 297
Ševčenko, Ihor 259-60
Sèvres, Treaty of 191
Shakespeare, Nicholas 47
Shaw, Stanford 221-2, 282, 303
Sherrard, Philip 55, 108-9, 205, 227, 245
Shevardnadze, Eduard 156
Sikorski, Wladyslaw 136
Simitis, Costas 268, 298
Slaughter and May (law firm) 132
Smith, Agnes and Margaret 276
Smith, Alasdair 270
Smith, Helena 171
Smith, Reggie 117-19
Smithers, Alan 344
Snow, C.P. 340
Society for the Promotion of Byzantine Studies 240, 257
Sokal, Alan 2
Solomonidis, Victoria 223, 310
Somerset House 243
Sorokos, Ioannis 183
Sotheby, Hans 256
Soumela monastery 24-5
South-East European Studies at Oxford (SEESOX) 298
Sparrow, Gerald 59
Special Operations Executive (SOE) 9, 12-13, 20, 44, 52, 68, 99-101, 117-18, 130-40, 146, 150, 309, 324, 330-1
Speros Basil Vryonis Center for the Study of Hellenism, Sacramento 281-2
Spitzberg, Irving 218
Stalin, Joseph 122-3, 306, 326
Stamatopoulos, Viron 91
Stanford University 342-3
Stavrou, Theophanis 218
Stavrovouni monastery 315
Steel, David 84-5, 155-6
Steinberg, Saul 278
Stephanopoulos, Konstantinos President of Greece 313
Stevens, Annette 332
Stevens, Gorham 332, 335
Stevens, John 131, 133
Stevenson, Robert Louis 11, 13
Stewart, Charles 302
Stone, Tom 166
Stothard, Peter 328
Stournaras, Yannis 297-8
street names 314-15
Stuart, James ('Athenian') 323
Sturdza, Mihail 123-4
Suez crisis (1956) 15
Sunday Telegraph 77-81
Sunday Times 61, 71, 76-9, 82-3, 100
Sussex University 106
Sutherland, Stewart 225, 231-44, 247-9

INDEX

Sviatopolk-Mirsky, Prince Dimitri Petrovich 123
Svoronos, Nikos 172
Swansea University 340
Sweet-Escott, Bickham 12-13, 131-2, 135-6, 140
Syntagma Square shooting (1944) 170-2

Tachtsis, Costas 87
Talbot Rice, David 19-21, 27, 29
Talbot Rice, Tamara 26
Talcott, Lucy 332
Tappe, Eric 106, 294
Taylor, George 131
Taylor, William 179
television documentaries 141-50
tenure, loss of 242-3, 246-7
Thanos, Constantine 71
Thatcher, Margaret 1, 99, 140, 151, 220, 223, 229, 242, 344, Plate 15
Theodorakis, Mikis 172
Thompson, Peter 96, Plate 7
Thomson, Lord 80-1
Thomson, George 266
Thomson, Robert 22
Thorpe, Richard 16
Thubron, Colin 220-1
Time magazine 3
The Times 77, 119, 202-4, 304, 327-30
Times Higher Education Supplement 303
Times Literary Supplement 60, 62, 136, 161, 198, 216
Tippett, Michael 14
Tito, Marshal 122, 132, 134, 151, 299

Tomalin, Claire 220-1
Tomkys, Roger 86
tourism 17, 37, 112
Toynbee, Arnold 3-4, 7-8, 124, 174, 175-81, 188-216, 219-25, 228, 242, 251, 254, 284-5, 297, 341
Toynbee, Rosalind 193-5, 214
Trapezuntine Empire 21-2
Trapp, J.B. 233, 238-41
Trebizond 18-27
Treholt, Arne 63-4, 98-9
Trevor-Roper, Hugh 60
Triandaphyllidis, Manolis 187-8
Trump, Donald J. 6, 279
Trypanis, Constantine 255
Tsakopoulos, Angelo 282
Tsatsos, Konstantinos 266
Tsirkas, Christos: Plate 17
Tsoukalis, Loukas 269-2
Tuckerman, Charles 236
Turkey 17-18, 23-4
Turkish studies 283, 311
Tziovas, Dimitris 310

University of California, Los Angeles (UCLA) 221
University College, London 41, 56, 104, 119-21, 124, 344
University Grants Committee (UGC) 230, 232
university places for sale 70-1

Vafiadis, Markos 144
Vanderpool, Eugene 335
Vasilikos, Vasilis 144
Vassiliou, Georgios 319
Vatikiotis, P.J. 225, 288-9, 292
Vatopedi 54-5

Venizelos, Eleftherios 182–6, 190–2, 332
Venizelos, Evangelos 166–7
Veremis, Thanos 289, 291
vice-chancellors 1, 313, 339, 344
Villoison, D'Ansse de 35
Vincent, Alfred 285
Vivian, Valentine 44
Vlachou, Eleni 58–9, 63, 65, 72, 75, 77, 91, 98, 156
Voulgaris, Aristides 79
Vryonis, Speros 221–2, 226, 277, 281–5
Vryzakis, Theodoros 173, 323
Vulliamy, Ed 171–2

Wace, A.J.B. 42, 187–8, 213, 223–4
Waldegrave, William: Plate 9
Walden, Brian 84
Waldheim, Kurt 309
Walker, Alexander 307
Wallace, David 45
Waller, Ian 84–5
Wallington, Jeremy 141
Walsh, John 27–8
Walter, Otto 333
war studies 343–4
Warburg Institute 238–9
Ward, Michael 135
Ware, Kallistos 291
Warren, D.A. La Touche ('Bunny') 308–9
Waterhouse, Helen 47
Waterlow, Sydney 45, 255
Waugh, Evelyn 19
Way, Richard 124
Weale, A.P. 258

Webster, Charles 4
Weidenfeld, Lord 260
Weinberger, Caspar 156
Wellesley College 5
West, M.L. 236, 248
White-Gaze, Nan 183
Whitlam, Gough: Plate 17
Whittle, Charles 15–16
Wilde, Oscar 229
Wilford, Hugh 288
Wilkinson, Peter 137
William of Ockham 234
Williams, Michael 125
Willis, Kirk 217
Wilson, Harold 82, 85, 119
Wilson, General Henry Maitland 'Jumbo' 132
Winfield, David 22–6, Plate 1
Wings Air Tours 37, 39, 170
Wittek, Paul 27
Wodehouse, P.G. 335
Woodhouse, C.M. ('Monty') 52, 57, 63–4, 87–9, 96, 131, 133–4, 137, 146–8, 152–4, 246–7, 275, 335; Plates 6 and 7
Woodroffe, Benjamin 294–5
The World Today (magazine) 327
Worrall, Philip 137
Wrede, Walther 333
Wright, David 345

Xydis, Alekos 63, 66

Yannoulopoulos, Yannis 64
Yannopoulos, George 58–9, 63–4, 67, 93, 98–9
Yapp, Malcolm 218, 221
Yeltsin, Boris 329

INDEX

Yorkshire Post 203
Young, Kenneth 60-1, 72
Young, Rodney 332
Yudkin, John 181

Zacharakis, Christos 300
Zachariadou, Elisavet 49-50
Zaharoff, Basil 185-6

Zaharopoulos, George 63
Zambaco, Maria 323
Zervas, Napoleon 145-9, 325
Zhivkov, Todor 68-9
Zhivkova, Lyudmila 5, 68-70
Zog, King 114, 126
Zolotas, Xenophon 71